Eyes *Right!*

Eyes *Right!*

Challenging the Right Wing Backlash

Edited by Chip Berlet

South End Press
Boston, Massachusetts

A Political Research Associates Book

Cover Design by David Gerratt
Cover Art by Michael Duffy
Book Design and Production by File Ferrets

Political Research Associates
120 Beacon Street, 3rd Floor
Somerville, MA 02143-4304

Support for the research and networking required to edit this book was provided by the Funding Exchange, List Foundation, HKH Foundation, New World Foundation, Unitarian–Universalist Veatch Program at Shelter Rock, Public Welfare Foundation, and the Nathan Cummings Foundation.

Manufactured in the USA

Library of Congress Cataloging in Publication Data:

Eyes right! : challenging the right wing backlash / edited by Chip Berlet.

  p. cm.

"A Political Research Associates book."

Includes bibliographical references and index.

ISBN 0–89608–523–6. —ISBN 0–89608–524–4

1. Conservatism—United States. 2. Liberalism—United States.

3. Politics, Practical—United States. I. Berlet, Chip.

JC573. 2. U6E93   1995

320.5'2'0973—dc20   95–25597

                                      CIP

South End Press, 116 Saint Botolph Street, Boston, MA 02115

01 00 99 98 97 96 95 1 2 3 4 5 6 7 8 9

Acknowledgments

The core of this collection is articles originally appearing in *The Public Eye* newsletter, under the editorship of Jean Hardisty, Margaret Quigley, and Judith Glaubman.

Thanks to the current staff of Political Research Associates (PRA), who pitched in to read endless galleys: Judith Glaubman, Francine Almash, Surina Khan, Peter Snoad, Vanessa Mohr, and intern Aaron Katz. Kudos to the last–minute volunteers, Tim Plenk and Maria Torre.

For the past 15 years I have worked under the tutelage of the director of PRA, Jean Hardisty. Her vision for the organization has guided my research in many valuable and insightful ways. I can never hope to adequately repay her for her assistance through thick and thin.

Credit goes to all the editors and staff of the various publications from which articles in this collection were extracted—they mined the nuggets, I merely polished them; and an extra tip of the hat to Matthew Rothschild of *The Progressive* for his special assistance.

Appreciation is due to Holly Sklar and Tarso Ramos who completely rewrote their chapters to make them more detailed and timely. This book would never have gone to press without the persistent prodding of my editor at South End Press, Loie Hayes.

It would have been impossible to even consider this project without the support of my family, Karen and Bobby, who have not only been generous in allowing me extra time, but also, over the years, have had to withstand public vilification, harassment, lawsuits, and death threats. They deserve better, and have my gratitude and love.

The original Public Eye network was organized in the 1970s by Eda Gordon, Sheila O'Donnell, Harvey Kahn, Russ Bellant, Tim Butz, Mark Ryter, William Steiner, and other researchers, journalists, activists, and paralegal investigators studying the relationship between reactionary political movements and government repression.

The Public Eye newsletter, now published by Political Research Associates, follows in their footsteps.

Thanks also to Suzanne Pharr, Dennis King, Dan Junas, Loretta Ross, Leonard Zeskind, and Daniel Levitas for their tireless work against neofascism; and to Peggy Shinner, PRA staff person during the organization's first six years in Chicago.

The path that led me to this book began in the 1960s in New Jersey church–basement coffee houses with high school friends in the civil rights movement, including Curt Koehler, Susan Kaiser, Mary Eich, "GM", and Maggie and Terre Roche—all of whom have remained committed to the principles of peace and social justice.

Between then and now, I have benefited from the kind and patient assistance of many friends and colleagues, and this book is a reflection of that spirit of cooperation and collective effort.

+ + +

Some words about style. The current transitional period regarding language and identity makes consistency more than a hobgoblin; it creates small mines for the grammatically–aware. There is no agreement as to whether Black or White should be capitalized, or one but not the other, or neither. Similarly, anti–Semitism and antisemitism both refer to bigotry against Jews. The capitalization scheme throughout this book reflects individual preferences and editing decisions rather than an arbitrary attempt to impose consistency. For the same reasons, the terms hard right, religious right, theocratic right, etc. are preferred by different authors and left alone.

To the memory of
Margaret Quigley
1958—1993

Margaret brought great energy and joy
to her work with us at Political Research Associates.
When Margaret and her partner of many years,
Susie Chancey–O'Quinn, died in a collision with a car
driven by a drunk driver, it was a personal tragedy for
all of us at PRA, as well as a loss to the movement for
democracy and diversity. Our best tribute is to carry
on their work for human rights and human dignity as
they did: with mettle tempered with mischievousness;
for bread. . .but roses, too.

Table of Contents

Divisions

Strategies

Resources

Index

Preface

In the 1970s, it appeared that the political right in the United States was isolated and irrelevant. Barry Goldwater's 1964 presidential candidacy had resulted in a decisive defeat. Major legislative initiatives coming from Congress promoted political reform and liberal social programs, giving the impression that liberalism was a potent and long–lasting force. And the Democratic Party and its multi–racial, multi–class coalition seemed to represent the majority of American voters.

Today, the right has a virtual lock on US politics. It has the momentum, the money, the new ideas, and the votes to dominate the political scene. Worse still, this is not a "New Right," as its architects would have us believe, but the old right in new clothing. That old segregationist army of vengeful reactionaries is now a slick, media–savvy, professional marching troop, bent on the same agenda of retribution against liberalism and deliverance from reform. They are directing a populist revolt against taxes, government, and secularism under the banner of family values and a narrow, rigid brand of Christianity.

Chip Berlet has assembled an anthology designed to inform and motivate the average reader to move to a deeper understanding of the current resurgence of the right. This deeper understanding is not an intellectual exercise, but a political necessity. The right's agenda—the complete defeat of liberalism and the left, the silencing of progressive opinions, the restoration of Christian hegemony, and the re-marginalization of all cultures other than that of European Americans—cannot be fought without a thorough understanding of it.

We must know the answers to some basic questions about the right's history and the strategies and tactics that have led to its current success: What are the ideological roots of the right's agenda? What economic and social conditions have allowed the right to thrive? How has race been transformed from a blunt instrument of repression to a trick card to be played with subtlety and finesse for cynical political gain? How has the average voter been won over to the right's agenda? What are the ingredients of that agenda that the public finds so appealing? What are the cleavages within the right that threaten its current success? What is the role of scapegoating in right–wing movements?

These are just some of the questions addressed by the articles collected in *Eyes Right!* The questions are approached from a progressive political perspective; that is, they are the work of researchers who aim to expose the motives and goals of the right. In this respect, the book is a classic example of opposition research. Nevertheless, the collection is markedly free of rhetoric, oversimplification, or demonization.

Eyes Right! does not attempt to cover the entire scope of the US right. Instead, Chip Berlet—informed by his 25-year history of research and analysis in this field—has chosen articles that he feels reflect the complexity of the right.

The authors selected understand that the right's central themes of theocracy, racism, patriarchy, homophobia, and the defense of corporate power extend from the margins of society to the mainstream. Further, Berlet has used the book's major sections as a way to organize the presentation of the right's key themes. In this way, the book's internal organization itself becomes a guide to an informed overview of the right.

As a result, *Eyes Right!* is a useful and usable primer that will help the average person both understand the right and become more effective in defending the democratic reforms of the past 50 years. It is not an organizer's handbook, but rather presents a number of strategies for involvement and self–education intended to present realistic options for those who are alarmed by the right's resurgence.

Eight of the book's lengthier articles are drawn from *The Public Eye*, the quarterly newsletter of Political Research Associates, where Berlet is the senior analyst. They stand the test of time very well, and appear here with minor updates primarily relating to dates. Other articles in the collection are reprinted from the publications of fight–the–right organizations such as the Center for Democratic Renewal, Fairness and Accuracy in Reporting, the Western States Center, the Women's Project, the Coalition for Freedom of Expression, the National Gay and Lesbian Task Force, the University Conversion Project, the Lambda Legal Defense and Education Fund, and others.

Still other articles are the work of investigative journalists who understand that the right is not a monolith, but instead a series of interlinked movements that rest on a variety of ideologies. As these chapters demonstrate, most right–wing movements are reactionary, some are narrowly focused on a specific grievance or goal, some are simply vengeful; all promote intolerance.

Eyes Right! is an anthology for the 1990s and beyond. It is both a response to and a reflection of the careful movement building that the right has done for the last 20 years. That movement building has been a major factor in the sea change that has occurred in American politics. It is not possible to say now whether the next 10 years will lead the country farther down the path to the end of democracy as we know it. The readers of this primer could make an important contribution to preventing that outcome.

Jean Hardisty
Executive Director
Political Research Associates
Somerville, MA

Theocracy & White Supremacy

Behind the Culture War to Restore Traditional Values

We are America, they are not America.
GOP Party Chief Rich Bond

Chip Berlet & Margaret Quigley

As the United States slides toward the twenty–first century, the major mass movements challenging the bipartisan status quo are not found on the left of the political spectrum, but on the right. The resurgent right contains several strands woven together around common themes and goals. There is the electoral activism of the religious fundamentalist movements; the militant anti-government populism of the armed militia movement; and the murderous terrorism of the neonazi underground—from which those suspected of bombing the Alfred P. Murrah Federal Building in Oklahoma City appear to have crept.*

---

* Berlet wishes to acknowledge the input of pro–democracy researchers and activists who met at the Blue Mountain Conference Center in upstate New York (including Suzanne Pharr, Loretta Ross, Russ Bellant, Skipp Porteous, Frederick Clarkson, Robert Bray, Tarso Ramos, Scot Nakagawa, Marghe Covino, and others); discussions at Lumiere Productions (with Frances Fitzgerald, Leo Ribuffo, John C. Green, and George Marsden); and the staff of Political Research Asso-

It is easy to see the dangers to democracy posed by far right forces such as armed militias, neonazis, and racist skinheads. However, hard right forces such as dogmatic religious movements, regressive populism, and White racial nationalism also are attacking democratic values in our country.

The best known sector of the hard right—dogmatic religious movements—is often called the "Religious Right." It substantially dominates the Republican Party in at least 10 (and perhaps as many as 30) of the 50 states. As part of an aggressive grassroots campaign, these groups have targeted electoral races from school boards to state legislatures to campaigns for the US Senate and House of Representatives. They helped elect dozens of hardline ultraconservatives to the House of Representatives in 1994. This successful social movement politically mobilizes a traditionalist mass base from a growing pious constituency of evangelical, fundamentalist, charismatic, pentacostal, and orthodox churchgoers.

The goal of many leaders of this ultraconservative religious movement is imposing a narrow theological agenda on secular society. The predominantly Christian leadership envisions a religiously–based authoritarian society; therefore we prefer to describe this movement as the "theocratic right." A theocrat is someone who supports a form of government where the actions of leaders are seen as sanctioned by God—where the leaders claim they are carrying out God's will. The central threat to democracy posed by the theocratic right is not that its leaders are religious, or fundamentalist, or right wing—but that they justify their political, legislative, and regulatory agenda as fulfilling God's plan.

Along with the theocratic right, two other hard right political movements pose a grave threat to democracy: regressive populism, typified by diverse groups ranging from members of the John Birch Society out to members of the patriot and armed militia movements; and White racial nationalism, promoted by Pat Buchanan and his shadow, David Duke of Louisiana.

The theocratic right, regressive populism, and White racial nationalism make up a hard right political sector that is distinct from and sometimes in opposition to mainstream Republicanism and the internationalist wing of corporate conservatism.

Finally, there is the militant, overtly racist far right that includes the open White supremacists, Ku Klux Klan members, Christian Patriots, racist skinheads, neonazis, and right–wing revolutionaries. Although numerically smaller, the far right is a serious political factor in some rural areas, and its propaganda promoting violence reaches into major metropolitan centers where

ciates (especially with Jean Hardisty), as well as private conversations with Sara Diamond, Holly Sklar, and Matthew N. Lyons.

it encourages alienated young people to commit hate crimes against people of color, Jews, and gays and lesbians, among other targets. The electoral efforts of Buchanan and Duke serve as a bridge between the ultraconservative hard right and these far right movements. The armed milita movement is a confluence of regressive populism, White racial nationalism, and the racist and antisemitic far right.

All four of these hard right activist movements are antidemocratic in nature, promoting in various combinations and to varying degrees authoritarianism, xenophobia, conspiracy theories, nativism, racism, sexism, homophobia, antisemitism, demagoguery, and scapegoating. Each wing of the antidemocratic right has a slightly different vision of the ideal nation.

The theocratic right's ideal is an authoritarian society where Christian men interpret God's will as law. Women are helpmates, and children are the property of their parents. Earth must submit to the dominion of those to whom God has granted power. People are basically sinful, and must be restrained by harsh punitive laws. Social problems are caused by Satanic conspiracies aided and abetted by liberals, homosexuals, feminists, and secular humanists. These forces must be exposed and neutralized.

Newspaper columnist Cal Thomas, a long–standing activist in the theocratic right, recently suggested that churches and synagogues take over the welfare system "because these institutions would also deal with the hearts and souls of men and women." The churches "could reach root causes of poverty"—a lack of personal responsibility, Thomas wrote, expressing a hardline Calvinist theology. "If government is always there to bail out people who have children out of wedlock, if there is no disincentive (like hunger) for doing for one's self, then large numbers of people will feel no need to get themselves together and behave responsibly."

For regressive populism, the ideal is America First ultra–patriotism and xenophobia wedded to economic Darwinism, with no regulations restraining entrepreneurial capitalism. The collapsing society calls for a strong man in leadership, perhaps even a benevolent despot who rules by organically expressing the will of the people to stop lawlessness and immorality. Social problems are caused by corrupt and lazy government officials who are bleeding the common people dry in a conspiracy fostered by secret elites, which must be exposed and neutralized.

Linda Thompson, a latter–day Joan of Arc for the patriot movement, represents the most militant wing of regressive populism. She appointed herself "Acting Adjutant General" of the armed militias that have formed cells across the United States. Operating out of the American Justice Federation of Indianapolis,

Thompson's group warns of secret plots by "corrupt leaders" involving "Concentration Camps, Implantable Bio Chips, Mind Control, Laser Weapons," and "neuro–linguistic programming" on behalf of bankers who "control the economy" and created the illegal income tax.

The racial nationalists' ideal oscillates between brutish authoritarianism and vulgar fascism in service of White male supremacy. Unilateral militarism abroad and repression at home are utilized to force compliance. Social problems are caused by uncivilized people of color, lower–class foreigners, and dual–loyalist Jews, who must all be exposed and neutralized.

Samuel Francis, the prototypical racial nationalist, writes columns warning against attempts to "wipe out traditional White, American, Christian, and Western Culture," which he blames on multiculturalism. Francis's solutions: "Americans who want to conserve their civilization need to get rid of elites who want to wreck it, but they also need to kick out the vagrant savages who have wandered across the border, now claim our country as their own, and impose their cultures upon us. If there are any Americans left in San Jose, they might start taking back their country by taking back their own city. . . .You don't find statues to Quetzalcoatl in Vermont."

For the far right, the ideal is White revolution to overthrow the corrupt regime and restore an idealized natural biological order. Social problems are caused by crafty Jews manipulating inferior people of color. They must be exposed and neutralized.

The Truth at Last is a racist far right tabloid that features such headlines as "Jews Demand Black Leaders Ostracize Farrakhan," "Clinton Continues Massive Appointments of Minorities," and "Adopting Blacks into White Families Does Not Raise Their IQ," which concluded that "only the preservation of the White race can save civilization. . . .Racial intermarriage produces a breed of lower–IQ mongrel people."

There are constant differences and debates within the right, as well as considerable overlap along the edges. The relationships are complex: the Birchers feud with Perot on trade issues, even though their other basic themes are similar, and the theocratic right has much in common with regressive populism, though the demographics of their respective voting blocs appear to be remarkably distinct. These antidemocratic sectors of the hard right are also distinct from traditional conservatism and political libertarianism, although they share some common roots and branches.

All of these antidemocratic tendencies are trying to build grassroots mass movements to support their agendas which vary in degrees of militancy and zealousness of ideology, yet all of which (consciously or unconsciously) promote varieties of White privilege and Christian dominion. These are activist movements that seek a mass base. Across the full spectrum of the right one hears calls for a new populist revolt.

Many people presume that all populist movements are naturally progressive and want to move society to the left, but history teaches us otherwise. In his book *The Populist Persuasion*, Michael Kazin explains how populism is a style of organizing. Populism can move to the left or right. It can be tolerant or intolerant. In her book *Populism*, Margaret Canovan defined two main branches of Populism: agrarian and political.

Agrarian populism worldwide has three categories: movements of commodity farmers, movements of subsistence peasants, and movements of intellectuals who wistfully romanticize the hard–working farmers and peasants. Political populism includes not only populist democracy, championed by progressives from the LaFollettes of Wisconsin to Jesse Jackson, but also politicians' populism, reactionary populism, and populist dictatorship. The latter three antidemocratic forms of populism characterize the movements of Ross Perot, Pat Robertson, and Pat Buchanan, three straight White Christian men trying to ride the same horse.

Of the hundreds of hard right groups, the most influential is the Christian Coalition led by televangelist and corporate mogul Pat Robertson. Because of Robertson's smooth style and easy access to power, most mainstream journalists routinely ignore his authoritarianism, bigotry, and paranoid dabbling in conspiracy theories.

Robertson's gallery of conspirators parallels the roster of the John Birch Society, including the Freemasons, the Bavarian Illuminati, the Council on Foreign Relations, and the Trilateral Commission. In Robertson's book *The New World Order*, he trumps the Birchers (their founder called Dwight Eisenhower a communist agent) by alluding to an anti–Christian conspiracy that supposedly began in ancient Babylon—a theory that evokes historic anti–Jewish bigotry and resembles the notions of the fascist demagogue Lyndon LaRouche, who is routinely dismissed by the corporate media as a crackpot. Robertson's homophobia is profound. He is also a religious bigot who has repeatedly said that Hindus and Muslims are not morally qualified to hold government posts. "If anybody understood what Hindus really believe," says Robertson, "there would be no doubt that they have no business administering government policies in a country that favors freedom and equality."

Robertson's embrace of authoritarian theocracy is equally robust:

There will never be world peace until God's house and God's people are given their rightful place of leadership at the top of the world. How can there be peace when drunkards, drug dealers, communists, atheists, New Age worshipers of Satan, secular humanists, oppressive dictators, greedy money changers, revolutionary assassins, adulterers, and homosexuals are on top?

Mainstream pundits are uncertain about the magnitude of the threat posed by the theocratic right and the other hard right sectors. Sidney Blumenthal warned recently in *The New Yorker* that "Republican politics nationally, and particularly in Virginia, have advanced so swiftly toward the right in the past two years that [Oliver] North's nomination [for the US Senate] was almost inevitable." But just a few years ago, after George Bush was elected President, Blumenthal dismissed the idea that the theocratic right was a continuing factor in national politics.

"Journalists like Blumenthal are centrists who believe that America always fixes itself by returning to the center. They have the hardest time appreciating the danger the right represents because they see it as just another swing of the political pendulum," says Jean Hardisty, a political scientist who has monitored the right for more than 20 years. "As the McCarthy period showed, however, if you let a right–wing movement go long enough without serious challenge, it can become a real threat and cause real damage. Centrists missed the significance of the right–wing drive of the past fourteen years as it headed for success."

The defeat of George Bush in 1992 did not deter the hard rightists as they increasingly turned toward state and local forums, where small numbers can transform communities. They learned from the humiliating defeat of Barry Goldwater in 1964 that to construct a conservative America would take strategic planning that spanned decades.

Now, after decades of organizing, the right has managed to shift the spectrum of political debate, making conservative politics look mainstream when compared with overt bigotry, and numbing the public to the racism and injustice in mainstream politics. When, for example, Vice President Dan Quayle was asked by ABC what he thought of David Duke, Quayle sanitized Duke's thorough racism and said: "The message of David Duke is . . .anti–big–government, get out of my pocketbook, cut taxes, put welfare people back to work. That's a very popular message. The problem is the messenger. David Duke, neonazi, ex–Klansman, basically a bad person."

The pull of the antidemocratic hard right and its reliance on scapegoating, especially of people of color, is a major factor in the increased support among centrist politicians for draconian crime bills, restrictive immigration laws, and punitive welfare regulations. The Republican Party's use of the race card, from Richard Nixon's southern strategy to the Willie Horton ads of George Bush's 1988 campaign, is made more acceptable by the overt racism of the far right. Racist stereotypes are used opportunistically to reach an angry White constituency of middle– and working–class people who have legitimate grievances caused by the failure of the bipartisan status quo to resolve issues of economic and social justice.

Scapegoating evokes a misdirected response to genuine unresolved grievances. The right has mobilized a mass base by focusing the legitimate anger of parents over inadequate resources for the public schools on the scapegoat of gay and lesbian curriculum, sex education, and AIDS–awareness programs; by focusing confusion over changing sex roles and the unfinished equalization of power between men and women on the scapegoats of the feminist movement and abortion rights; by focusing the desperation of unemployment and underemployment on the scapegoat of affirmative–action programs and other attempts to rectify racial injustice; by focusing resentment about taxes and the economy on the scapegoat of dark–skinned immigrants; by focusing anger over thoughtless and intrusive government policies on environmental activists; and by focusing anxiety about a failing criminal justice system on the scapegoat of early release, probation, and parole programs for prisoners who are disproportionately people of color.

Such scapegoating has been applied intensively in rural areas which see emerging social movements of "new patriots" and "armed militias" who are grafting together the conspiracy theories of the hard right John Birch Society with the ardor and armor of the paramilitary far right.

These hard right and far right forces are beginning to influence state and local politics, especially in the Pacific Northwest and Rocky Mountain states, through amorphous patriot and armed militia groups, sovereignty campaigns, and county autonomy movements as well as some portions of the anti–environmentalist "Wise Use" movement. The same regions have seen contests within the Republican Party on the state level between mainstream Republicans and the theocratic right. Some Republican candidates pander to the patriot and militia movements as a source of constituent votes. The political spectrum in some states now ranges from repressive corporate liberalism in the "center" through authoritarian theocracy to nascent fascism.

The Road to Backlash Politics

How did we get here? Despite the many differences, one goal has united the various sectors of the antidemocratic right in a series of amorphous coalitions since the 1960s: to roll back the limited gains achieved in the United States by a variety of social justice movements, including the civil rights, student rights, antiwar, feminist, ecology, gay and lesbian rights, disability rights, and anti–militarist movements.

Hard right nativists formed the core of Joseph McCarthy's constituency after World War II. After McCarthy's fall, they retreated until the late 1950s and early 1960s, when a network of anti–communists spread the gospel of the communist and secularist threats through such books as Dr. Fred Schwartz's 1960 *You Can Trust the Communists (to be Communists)*. At the 1964 Republican convention, the growth of hard right forces became apparent. Goldwater's candidacy represented a reaction to the values of modernity. Unlike traditional conservative politics, which sought to preserve the status quo from the encroachments of the modern world, Goldwater's politics sought to turn back the political clock. This reactionary stance remains a key component of the US hard right today. In 1961, Goldwater said, "My aim is not to pass laws but to repeal them." Twenty years later, Paul Weyrich, chief architect of the New Right, said, "I believe in rollback."

Hard right activists such as Phyllis Schlafly and John Stormer had helped engineer Goldwater's nomination. Schlafly was a convention delegate in 1964, and went on to found the Eagle Forum, which fought the Equal Rights Amendment. Stormer wrote a book called *None Dare Call It Treason*. Their aggressive anti–communist militarism worried many conventional voters, and their conspiracy theories of secret collusion between corporate Republican leaders and the communists—Schlafly called them the "secret kingmakers" in her pro–Goldwater book *A Choice Not an Echo*—brought the hard right and far right out of the woodwork as Goldwater supporters, which cost votes when they began expounding on their byzantine conspiracy theories to the national news media.

Most influential Goldwater supporters were not marginal far right activists, as many liberal academics postulated at the time, but had been Republican Party regulars for years, representing a vocal reactionary wing far to the right of many persons who usually voted Republican. This hard right reactionary wing of the Republican Party had an image problem, which was amply demonstrated by the devastating defeat of Goldwater in the general election. The current right–wing avalanche began when a group of conservative strategists decided to brush off the flakes who had burdened the unsuccessful 1964 Goldwater presidential campaign. They decided it was time to build a "New Right" coalition that differentiated itself from the old, nativist right in two key ways: it embraced the idea of an expansionist government to enforce the hard right's social policy goals, and it eschewed the old right's explicitly racist rhetoric. Overt White supremacists and segregationists had to go, as did obvious anti–Jewish bigots. The wild–eyed conspiratorial rhetoric of the John Birch Society was unacceptable, even to William F. Buckley, Jr., whose *National Review* was the authoritative journal of the right.

While the old right's image was being modernized, emerging technologies and techniques using computers, direct mail, and television were brought into play to build the New Right. After Goldwater's defeat, Richard Viguerie painstakingly hand–copied information on Goldwater donors at the Library of Congress and used the results to launch his direct–mail fundraising empire, which led to the formation of the New Right coalition. And to reach the grassroots activists and voters, right–wing strategists openly adopted the successful organizing, research, and training methods that had been pioneered by the labor and civil rights movements.

When Richard Nixon was elected president in 1968, his campaign payoff to the emerging New Right included appointing such right–wing activists as Howard Phillips to government posts. Phillips was sent to the Office of Economic Opportunity with a mandate to dismantle social programs allegedly dominated by liberals and radicals. Conservatives and reactionaries joined in a "Defund the Left" campaign. As conservatives in Congress sought to gut social–welfare programs, corporate funders were urged to switch their charitable donations to build a network of conservative think tanks and other institutions to challenge what was seen as the intellectual dominance of Congress and society held by such liberal think tanks as the Brookings Institution.

Since the 1960s, the secular, corporate, and religious branches of the right have spent hundreds of millions of dollars to build a solid national right–wing infrastructure that provides training, conducts research, publishes studies, produces educational resources, engages in networking and coalition building, promotes a sense of solidarity and possible victory, shapes issues, provides legal advice, suggests tactics, and tests and defines specific rhetoric and slogans. Today, the vast majority of "experts" featured on television and radio talk shows, and many syndicated print columnists, have been groomed by the right–wing infrastructure, and some of these figures were first recruited and trained while they were still in college.

Refining rhetoric is key for the right because many of its ideas are based on narrow and nasty Biblical interpretations or are of benefit to only the wealthiest sector of society. The theocratic right seeks to breach the wall of separation between church and state by constructing persuasive secular arguments for enacting legislation and enforcing policies that take rights away from individuals perceived as sinful. Matters of money are interpreted to persuade the sinking middle class to cheer when the rich get richer and the poor get poorer. Toward these ends, questionable statistics, pseudo–scientific studies, and biased reports flood the national debate through the sluice gates of the right–wing think tanks.

Thus, the right has persuaded many voters that condoms don't work but trickle–down theories do. The success of the right in capturing the national debate over such issues as taxes, government spending, abortion, sexuality, child–rearing, welfare, immigration, and crime is due, in part, to its national infrastructure, which refines and tests rhetoric by conducting marketing studies, including those based on financial response to direct–mail letters and televangelist pitches.

Corporate millionaires and zealous right–wing activists, however, can't deliver votes without a grassroots constituency that responds to the rhetoric. Conveniently, the New Right's need for foot soldiers arrived just as one branch of Christianity, Protestant evangelicalism, marched onward toward a renewed interest in the political process. Earlier in the century, Protestant evangelicals fought the teaching of evolution and launched a temperance campaign that led to Prohibition. But in the decades preceding the 1950s, most Protestant evangelicals avoided the secular arena. Their return was facilitated by the Reverend Billy Graham, perhaps the best known proponent of the idea that all Protestants should participate in the secular sphere to fight the influence of Godless communism at home and abroad, and others ranging from the international Moral Re–Armament movement to local pastors who helped craft theological arguments urging all Christians to become active in politics in the 1950s and 1960s.

A more aggressive form of Protestant evangelicalism emerged in the 1970s, when such right–wing activists as Francis A. Schaeffer, founder of the *L'Abri* Fellowship in Switzerland and author of *How Should We Then Live?*, challenged Christians to take control of a sinful secular society. Schaeffer (and his son Franky) influenced many of today's theocratic right activists, including Jerry Falwell, Tim LaHaye, and John W. Whitehead, who have gone off in several theological and political directions, but all adhere to the notion that the Scriptures have given dominion over the Earth to Christians, who thus owe it to God to seize the reins of secular society.

The most extreme interpretation of this "dominionism" is a movement called Reconstructionism, led by right–wing Presbyterians who argue that secular law is always secondary to Biblical law. While the Reconstructionists represent only a small minority within Protestant theological circles, they have had tremendous influence on the theocratic right (a situation not unlike the influence of Students for a Democratic Society or the Black Panthers on the New Left in the 1960s). Reconstructionism is a factor behind the increased violence in the anti–abortion movement, the nastiest of attacks on gays and lesbians, and the new wave of battles over alleged secular humanist influence in the public schools. Some militant Reconstructionists even support the death penalty for adulterers, homosexuals, and recalcitrant children.

One key theocratic group, the Coalition on Revival, has helped bring dominionism into the hard right political movement. Militant antiabortion activist Randall Terry writes for their magazine, *Crosswinds*, and has signed their Manifesto for the Christian Church, which proclaims that America should "function as a Christian nation" and that the "world will not know how to live or which direction to go without the Church's Biblical influence on its theories, laws, actions, and institutions," including opposition to such "social moral evils" as "abortion on demand, fornication, homosexuality, sexual entertainment, state usurpation of parental rights and God–given liberties, statist–collectivist theft from citizens through devaluation of their money and redistribution of their wealth, and evolutionism taught as a monopoly viewpoint in the public schools." Taken as a whole, the manifesto is a call for clerical fascism in defense of wealth and patriarchy.

While dominionism spread, the number of persons identifying themselves as born–again Christians was growing, and by the mid–1970s, rightists were making a concerted effort to link Christian evangelicals to conservative ideology. Sara Diamond, author of *Spiritual Warfare*, assigns a seminal role to Bill Bright of the Campus Crusade for Christ, but traces the paternity of the New Right to 1979, when Robert Billings of the National Christian Action Council invited rising televangelist Jerry Falwell to a meeting with right–wing strategists Paul Weyrich, Howard Phillips, Richard Viguerie, and Ed McAteer. According to Diamond, "Weyrich proposed that if the Republican Party could be persuaded to take a firm stance against abortion, that would split the strong Catholic voting bloc within the Democratic Party." Weyrich suggested building an organization with a name involving the idea of a "moral majority."

While Falwell's Moral Majority began hammering on the issue of abortion, the core founding partners of the New Right were joined in a broad coalition by the growing neoconservative movement of former liberals concerned over what they perceived as a growing communist threat and shrinking moral leadership. Reluctantly, the remnants of the old right hitched a ride on the only electoral wagon moving to the right. The New Right coalition was built around shared support for anti–communist militarism, moral orthodoxy, and economic conservatism, the themes adopted by 1980 presidential candidate Ronald Reagan.

The ardor and activism of the paranoid nativist and Americanist wing of the New Right made many mainstream Republicans nervous. Even Goldwater divorced himself from the more extreme New Right partisans, saying, "These people are not conservatives. They are revolutionaries."

The Reagan Administration was masterful at buying the loyalty of the paranoid nativist wing of the New Right. While Reagan gave mainstream Republicans a green light for the lucrative trade with such communist countries as the Soviet Union and the People's Republic of China, he gave the meager markets in Central America, Africa, and Afghanistan to the hard right as a testing ground for their plans to fight communism and terrorism through covert action. While he negotiated with the Soviet Union, he continued to celebrate Captive Nations Day.

Under Reagan, the nativist–Americanist rightists received appointments to executive agencies, where they served as watchdogs against secular humanism and subversion. For example, a Phyllis Schlafly *protégé* in the Department of Education succeeded in blocking for several years all federal funds for the Boston–area Facing History and Ourselves project, which produces a curriculum on the Holocaust, genocide, and racism; the staffer denounced the program as secular humanist psychological manipulation.

The first attempt to build a broad theocratic right movement failed in part because Jerry Falwell's Moral Majority, with its Baptist roots and pragmatic fundamentalist Protestant aura, had only a limited constituency; it failed to mobilize either the more ethereal charismatic and Pentecostal wings of Christianity or the more moderate branches of denominational Protestantism. Apart from the abortion issue, its appeal to conservative Catholics was microscopic.

But as early as 1981, Falwell, Weyrich, and Robertson were working together to build a broader and more durable alliance of the theocratic right through such vehicles as the annual Family Forum national conferences, where members of the Reagan Administration could rub shoulders with leaders of dozens of Christian right groups and share ideas with rank–and–file activists. This coalition–building continued through the Reagan years.

Most Christian evangelical voters who had previously voted Democratic did not actually switch to Reagan in 1980, although other sectors of the New Right were certainly influential in mobilizing support for Reagan the candidate, and new Christian evangelical voters supported Republicans in significant numbers. But by 1984, the theocratic right had persuaded many traditionally Democratic but socially conservative Christians that support for prayer in the schools and opposition to abortion, sex education, and pornography could be delivered by the Republicans through the smiling visage of the Great Communicator. Reagan did try to push these issues in Congress, but many mainstream Republicans refused to go along.

Despite its successes, the hard right felt that Reagan lacked a true commitment to their ideology. In 1988, during Reagan's second term, some key New Right leaders, including Weyrich, Viguerie, and Phillips, began denouncing Reagan as a "useful idiot" and dupe of the KGB, and even a traitor over his arms control negotiations with the Soviet Union.

Under the Bush Administration, this branch of the right wing had less influence. It was this perceived loss of influence within the Republican Party, among other factors, that led to the highly publicized schism in the late 1980s between the two factions of the New Right that came to be called the *paleoconservatives* and the *neoconservatives.*

Patrick Buchanan, who says proudly, "We are Old Right and Old Church," emerged from this fracas as the leader of the paleoconservatives. (The term neoconservatives, once restricted to a small group of intellectuals centered around *Commentary* magazine, came within this context to refer to all conservatives to the left of the paleoconservatives, despite substantial differences among them. For example, traditional neoconservatives like Midge Decter were concerned with a perceived deterioration of US culture, while the conventional conservatives at the Heritage Foundation were concerned almost exclusively with the economy.)

The paleoconservatives' America First policy supports isolationism or unilateralism in foreign affairs, coupled with a less reverent attitude toward an unregulated free market and support for an aggressive domestic policy to implement New Right social policies, such as the criminalization of sodomy and abortion.

The paleoconservatives are also more explicitly racialist and anti-democratic than the neoconservatives, who continue to support immigration, civil rights, and limited government.

The strongest glue that bound together the various sectors of the New Right's pro–Reagan coalition was anti–communist militarism. Jewish neoconservatives were even willing to overlook the long–standing tolerance of racist and antisemitic sentiments among some paleoconservatives. This led to some strange silences, such as the failure to protest the well–documented presence of a network of *émigré* reactionaries and anti–Jewish bigots in the 1988 Bush campaign. The neocons could not be budged to action even when investigative writer Russ Bellant revealed that one aging Republican organizer proudly displayed photos of himself in his original Waffen SS uniform, and that Laszlo Pasztor, who had built the Republican *émigré* network, was a convicted Nazi collaborator who had belonged to the Hungarian Arrow Cross, which aided in the liquidation of Hungary's Jews. (Pasztor is still a key adviser to Paul Weyrich.)

The hard right saw Bush as an Eastern elite intellectual, and even his selection of Dan Quayle as his running mate to pacify the theocratic right was not enough to offset what they perceived as Bush's betrayal over social issues.

When the scandals of Jimmy Swaggart and Jim Bakker rocked televangelism and Pat Robertson failed in his 1988 presidential bid, some predicted the demise of the theocratic right. But they overlooked the huge grassroots constituency that remained connected through a Christian right infrastructure of conferences, publications, radio and television programs, and audiotapes. Robertson lost no time in taking the key contacts from his 1988 presidential campaign and training them as the core of the Christian Coalition, now the most influential grassroots movement controlled by the theocratic right.

Still, the theocratic right kept its ties to the Bush White House through chief of staff John H. Sununu, who worked closely with the Free Congress Foundation and even sent a letter on White House stationery in July 1989 thanking Weyrich for his help and adding, "If you have any observations regarding the priorities and initiatives of the first six months or for the Fall, I would like to hear them." The Bush White House also staffed an outreach office to maintain liaison with evangelicals.

After the election of Clinton, the New Right alliance eventually collapsed. That became clear during the Gulf War, when Buchanan's bigotry was suddenly discovered by his former allies in the neoconservative movement. Neoconservatives who championed the anti–Sandinista Nicaraguan contras were offered posts in the Clinton Administration. And Barry Goldwater, toast of the reactionaries in 1964, lambasted the narrow–minded bigotry of the theocratic right, which owes its birth to his failed presidential bid.

The 1992 Republican Party convention represented the ascendancy of hard right forces, primarily the theocratic right. The platform was the most conservative ever, and speakers called repeatedly for a cultural war against secular humanism.

The similarities between Goldwater's 1964 campaign and the 1992 Republican convention were marked. Phyllis Schlafly was present at both, arguing that liberals were trying to destroy the American way of life. In 1964, Goldwater had targeted the deterioration of the family and moral values; in 1992, the Republicans targeted traditional values.

The genius of the long–term strategy implemented by Weyrich and Robertson was their method of expanding the base. First, they created a broader Protestant Christian right that cut across all evangelical and fundamentalist boundaries and issued a challenge to more moderate Protestants. Second, they created a true Christian right by reaching out to conservative and reactionary Catholics. Third, they created a theocratic right by recruiting and promoting their few reactionary allies in the Jewish and Muslim communities.

This base–broadening effort continued through the mid–1990s, with Ralph Reed of the Christian Coalition writing in the Heritage Foundation's *Policy Review* about the need for the right to move from such controversial topics as abortion and homosexuality toward bread–and–butter issues—a tactical move that did not reflect any change in the basic belief structure. Sex education, abortion, objections to lesbian and gay rights, resistance to pluralism and diversity, demonization of feminism and working mothers continued to be core values of the coalition being built by the theocratic right.

John C. Green is a political scientist and director of the Ray C. Bliss Institute at the University of Akron in Ohio. With a small group of colleagues, Green has studied the influence of Christian evangelicals on recent elections, and has found that, contrary to popular opinion, the nasty and divisive rhetoric of Pat Buchanan, Pat Robertson, and Marilyn Quayle at the 1992 Republican Convention was not as significant a factor in the defeat of Bush as were unemployment and the general state of the economy. On balance, he believes, the Republicans gained more votes than they lost in 1992 by embracing the theocratic right. "Christian evangelicals played a significant role in mobilizing voters and casting votes for the Bush–Quayle ticket," says Green.

Green and his colleagues, James L. Guth and Kevin Hill, wrote a study entitled *Faith and Election: The Christian Right in Congressional Campaigns 1978–1988.* They found that the theocratic right was most active—and apparently successful—when three factors converged:

• The demand for Christian Right activism by discontented constituencies.

- Religious organizations that supplied resources for such activism.
- Appropriate choices in the deployment of such resources by movement leaders.

The authors see the Christian Right's recent emphasis on grassroots organizing as a strategic choice, and conclude that "the conjunction of motivations, resources, and opportunities reveals the political character of the Christian right: much of its activity was a calculated response to real grievances by increasingly self–conscious and empowered traditionalists."

The Roots of the Culture War

Spanning the breadth of the antidemocratic hard right is the banner of the Culture War. The idea of the Culture War was promoted by strategist Paul Weyrich of the Free Congress Foundation. In 1987, Weyrich commissioned a study, *Cultural Conservatism: Toward a New National Agenda*, which argued that cultural issues provided antiliberalism with a more unifying concept than economic conservatism. *Cultural Conservatism: Theory and Practice* followed in 1991.

Earlier, Weyrich had sponsored the 1982 book *The Homosexual Agenda* and the 1987 *Gays, AIDS, and You*, which helped spawn successive and successful waves of homophobia. The Free Congress Foundation, founded and funded with money from the Coors Beer family fortune, is the key strategic think tank backing Robertson's Christian Coalition, which has built an effective grassroots movement to wage the Culture War. For Robertson, the Culture War opposes sinister forces wittingly or unwittingly doing the bidding of Satan. This struggle for the soul of America takes on metaphysical dimensions combining historic elements of the Crusades and the Inquisition. The Christian Coalition could conceivably evolve into a more mainstream conservative political movement, or—especially if the economy deteriorates—it could build a mass base for fascism similar to the clerical fascist movements of mid–century Europe.

For decades anti–communism was the glue that bound together the various tendencies on the right. Ironically, the collapse of communism in Europe allowed the US political right to shift its primary focus from an extreme and hyperbolic anti–communism, militarism, and aggressive foreign policy to domestic issues of culture and national identity. Multiculturalism, political correctness, and traditional values became the focus of this new struggle over culture. An early and influential jeremiad in the Culture War was Allan Bloom's 1987 book *The Closing of the American Mind*. But neither the collapse of communism in the former Soviet Union, nor the publication of Bloom's book accounts for the success of this Culture War in capturing the high ground in popular discourse. Instead, it resulted from the victory of hard–right forces within the New Right (which helped lead to its demise as a coalition), and the concomitant embrace by hard right activists of a nativist, theocratic ideology that challenged the very notion of a secular, pluralistic democracy.

At the heart of this Culture War, or *kulturkampf*, as Patrick Buchanan calls it, is a paranoid conspiratorial view of leftist secular humanism, dating to the turn of the century and dependent upon powerful but rarely stated presumptions of racial nationalism based on Eurocentric White supremacy, Christian theocracy, and subversive liberal treachery.

The nativist right at the turn of the century first popularized the idea that there was a secular humanist conspiracy trying to steer the US from a God–centered society to a socialist, atheistic society. The idea was linked from its beginnings to an extreme fear of communism, conceptualized as a "red menace." The conspiracy became institutionalized in the American political scene and took on a metaphysical nature, according to analyst Frank Donner:

> The root anti–subversive impulse was fed by the [Communist] Menace. Its power strengthened with the passage of time, by the late twenties its influence had become more pervasive and folkish. . . .A slightly secularized version, widely shared in rural and small–town America, postulated a doomsday conflict between decent upright folk and radicalism—alien, satanic, immorality incarnate.

This conspiratorial world view continued to animate the hard right. According to contemporary conspiratorial myth, liberal treachery in service of Godless secular humanism has been "dumbing down" schoolchildren with the help of the National Education Association to prepare the country for totalitarian rule under a "One World Government" and "New World Order." This became the source of an underlying theme of the armed militia movement.

This nativist–Americanist branch of the hard right (or the pseudo–conservative, paranoid right, as Richard Hofstadter termed it in his classic essay, "The Paranoid Style in American Politics") came to dominate the right wing of the Republican Party, and included Patrick Buchanan, Phyllis Schlafly's Eagle Forum, Pat Robertson's Christian Coalition, the Rockford Institute, David Noebel's Summit Ministries, and Paul Weyrich's Free Congress Foundation and Institute for Cultural Conservatism. Of more historical importance are the John Birch Society, the Christian Anti–Communism Crusade, and Billy James Hargis' Christian Crusade, although the John Birch Society's membership doubled or tripled since the Gulf War in 1991 to over 40,000 members. Despite some overlap at the edges, reactionary hard right electoral activists should be distinguished from the extra–electoral right–wing survivalists, militia members, and armed White racists on their right, and from the Eastern establishment conservative branch of the right wing represented by George Bush on their left.

Secular humanism has been called the bogey–man of right–wing fundamentalism; it is a term of art, shorthand for all that is evil and opposed to God. While historically there has been an organized humanist movement in the United States since the mid–1800s, secular humanism as a large religious movement exists more in the right's conspiracy theories than in actual fact. Secular humanism is a non–theistic philosophy with roots in the rationalist philosophies of the Enlightenment that bases its commitment to ethical behavior on the innate goodness of human beings, rather than on the commands of a deity.

The conspiracy that the right wing believes has resulted in secular humanism's hegemony is both sweeping and specific. It is said to have begun in 1805, when the liberal Unitarians, who believed that evil was largely the result of such environmental factors as poverty and lack of education, wrested control of Harvard University from the conservative Calvinists, who knew that men were evil by nature. The Unitarian drive for free public schools was part of a conscious plan to convert the United States from capitalism to the newly postulated socialism of Robert Owen.

Later, according to the conspiracy theorists, John Dewey, a professor at Columbia University and head of the progressive education movement (seen as "the Lenin of the American socialist revolution"), helped to establish a secular, state–run (and thus socialized) educational system in Massachusetts. To facilitate the communist takeover, Dewey promoted the look–say reading method, knowing it would lead to widespread illiteracy. As Samuel Blumenfeld argued in 1984, "[T]he goal was to produce inferior readers with inferior intelligence dependent on a socialist education elite for guidance, wisdom and control. Dewey knew it. . . ."

For the hard right, it is entirely reasonable to claim both that John Dewey conspired to destroy the minds of American school-children and that contemporary liberals carry on the conspiracy. As Rosemary Thompson, a respected pro–family activist, wrote in her 1981 book, *Withstanding Humanism's Challenge to Families* (with a foreword by Phyllis Schlafly), "[H]umanism leads to feminism. Perhaps John Dewey will someday be recognized in the annals of history as the 'father of women's lib.'"

To these rightists, all of the evils of modern society can be traced to John Dewey and the secular humanists. A typical author argued:

> Most US citizens are not aware that hard–core pornography, humanistic sex education, the 'gay' rights movement, feminism, the Equal Rights Amendment, sensitivity training in schools and in industry, the promotion of drug abuse, the God–Is–Dead movement, free abortion on demand, euthanasia as a national promotion. . .to mention a few, highly publicized movements. . .have been sparked by humanism.

According to the right, by rejecting all notions of absolute authority and values, secular humanists deliberately attack traditional values in religion, the state, and the home.

The link between liberalism and treachery is key to the secular humanist conspiracy. In 1968, a typical book, endorsed by Billy James Hargis of the Christian Crusade, claimed, "The liberal, for reasons of his own, would dissolve the American Republic and crush the American dream so that our nation and our people might become another faceless number in an internationalist state."

Twenty–five years later, Allan Bloom, generally put forth as a moderate conservative, argued that all schoolteachers who inculcated moral relativism in school children "had either no interest in or were actively hostile to the Declaration of Independence and the Constitution."

The Culture War & Theocracy

Most analysts have looked at the Culture War and its foot soldiers in the traditional family values movement as displaying a constellation of discrete and topical beliefs. These include support for traditional, hierarchical sex roles and opposition to feminism, employed mothers, contraception, abortion, divorce, sex education, school–based health clinics, extramarital sex, and gay and lesbian sex, among other issues.

Traditional values also include an antipathy toward secular humanism, communism, liberalism, utopianism, modernism, globalism, multiculturalism, and other systems believed to undermine US nationalism. Beliefs in individualism, hard work, self–sufficiency, thrift, and social mobility form a uniquely American component of the movement. Some traditional values seem derived more immediately from Christianity: opposition to Satanism, witchcraft, the New Age, and the occult (including meditation and Halloween depictions of witches). Less often discussed but no less integral to the movement are a disdain for the values of egalitarianism and democracy (derived from the movement's anti–modernist orientation), and support for Western European culture, private property, and *laissez–faire* capitalism.

This orthodox view of the traditional values movement as an aggregate of many discrete values, however, is misleading, for it makes it appear that Judeo–Christian theism is simply one value among many. Rather, Judeo–Christian theism, and in particular Christianity, is the *core* value of the traditional values movement and the basis for the Crusades–like tone of those in the hard right calling for the Culture War.

Traditional values start from a recognition of the absolute, unchanging, hierarchical authority of God (as one commentator noted, "The Ten Commandments are not the Ten Suggestions") and move from there to a belief in hierarchical arrangements in the home and state.

As Pat Robertson said at the Republican convention, "Since I have come to Houston, I have been asked repeatedly to define traditional values. I say very simply, to me and to most Republicans, traditional values start with faith in Almighty God." Robertson has also said, "When President Jimmy Carter called for a 'Conference on Families,' many of us raised strenuous objections. To us, there was only one family, that ordained by the Bible, with husband, wife, and children."

In part, the moral absolutism implicit in the Culture War derives from the heavy proportion of fundamentalist Christians in the traditional family values movement. Their belief in the literal existence of Satan leads to an apocalyptic tone: "The bottom line is that if you are not working for Jesus Christ, then you are working for someone else whose name is Satan. It is one or the other. There is no middle of the road."

The hard right activist, as Richard Hofstadter noted, believes that all battles take place between forces of absolute good and absolute evil, and looks not to compromise but to crush the opposition.

A comment by Pat Robertson was typical:

> What is happening in America is not a debate, it is not a friendly disagreement between enlightened people. It is a vicious one–sided attack on our most cherished institutions. Suddenly the confrontation is growing hotter and it just may become all out civil war. It is a war against the family and against conservative and Christian values.

Paul Weyrich sees the struggle today between those "who worship in churches and those who desecrate them."

The root desire behind the Culture War is the imposition of a Christian theocracy in the United States. Some theocratic right activists have been quite open about this goal. Tim LaHaye, for example, argued in his book *The Battle for the Mind* that "we must remove all humanists from public office and replace them with pro–moral political leaders."

Similarly, in Pat Robertson's *The New World Order: It Will Change the Way You Live* (which argues that the conspiracy against Christians, dating back to Babylon, has included such traditional conspirators as John Dewey, the Illuminati, the Free Masons, the Council on Foreign Relations, and the Trilateral Commission), the question of who is fit to govern is discussed at length:

> When I said during my presidential bid that I would only bring Christians and Jews into the government. . .the media challenged me, "How dare you maintain that those who believe the Judeo–Christian values are better qualified to govern America than Hindus and Muslims?"
>
> My simple answer is, "Yes, they are." If anybody understood what Hindus really believe, there would be no doubt that they have no business administering government policies in a country that favors freedom and equality. . . .There will never be world peace until God's house and God's people are given their rightful place of leadership at the top of the world.
>
> How can there be peace when drunkards, drug dealers, communists, atheists, New Age worshipers of Satan, secular humanists, oppressive dictators, greedy moneychangers, revolutionary assassins, adulterers, and homosexuals are on top?

The most extreme position in the Culture War is held by Christian Reconstructionists who seek the imposition of Biblical law throughout the United States. Other hard right activists, while less open or draconian, share an implicitly theocratic goal. While it denies any desire to impose a theocracy, the Center for Cultural Conservatism, which defines cultural conservatism as the "necessary, unbreakable, and causal relationship between traditional Western, Judeo–Christian values. . .and the secular success of Western societies," breaks with conservative tradition to call upon government to play an active role in upholding the traditional culture which they see as rooted in specific theological values.

The Culture War & White Supremacy

The theory of widespread secular subversion spread by proponents of the Culture War was from the beginning a deeply racialized issue that supported the supremacy of White Anglo–Saxon Protestants. To the nativist right, in the 1920s as well as now, the synthesis of traditional values constituted "Americanism," and opponents of this particular constellation of views represented dangerous, un–American forces.

As John Higham argued in *Strangers in the Land: Patterns of American Nativism 1860–1925*, subversion has always been identified with foreigners and anti–Americanism in the United States, and particularly with Jews and people of color. In the 1920s, subversion was linked to Jews, and the immigration of people of color was opposed in part because they were seen as easy targets for manipulation by Jews.

While antisemitism was never the primary ingredient in anti–radical nativism, the radical Jew was nevertheless a powerful stereotype in the "communist menace" movement. For example, some members of the coercive immigrant "Americanization" movement adopted the startling slogan, "Christianization and Americanization are one and the same thing."

Virtually any movement to advance racial justice in the US was branded by the reactionary right as a manifestation of the secular humanist conspiracy. The National Education Association's bibliography of "Negro authors," foundation support for "Black revolutionaries," and the enlistment of Gunnar Myrdal as an expert on the "American Negro" were all framed in this way. Similarly, the African American civil rights movement was from its beginning identified by the right wing as part of the secular humanist plot to impose communism on the United States.

In 1966, David Noebel (then of Billy James Hargis' Christian Crusade, now head of the influential Summit Ministries) argued, "Anyone who will dig into the facts of the Communist involvement in the 'civil rights' strife will come to the conclusion that these forces have no stopping point short of complete destruction of the American way of life." (In the preface, Noebel thanks Dr. R. P. Oliver, who is now perhaps best known as a director of the Institute for Historical Review, which denies that the Holocaust took place.)

In 1992, the civil rights movement is still seen in this light, as the rightist Catholic magazine *Fidelity* makes clear:

> It is no coincidence that the civil rights movement in the United States preceded the largest push for sexual liberation this country had seen since its inception . . . . The Negro was the catalyst for the overturning of European values, which is to say, the most effective enculturation of Christianity.
>
> The civil rights movement was nothing more than the culmination of an attempt to transform the Negro into a paradigm of sexual liberation that had been the pet project of the cultural revolutionaries since the 1920s.

The identification of sexual licentiousness and "primitive" music with subversion and people of color is an essential part of the secular humanist conspiracy theory, and one that has been remarkably consistent over time. The current attacks on rap music take place within this context.

In 1966, David Noebel argued that the communist conspiracy ("the most cunning, diabolical conspiracy in the annals of human history") was using rock music, with its savage, tribal, orgiastic beat, to destroy "our youths' ability to relax, reflect, study and meditate" and to prepare them "for riot, civil disobedience and revolution." Twenty years later, these views were repeated practically verbatim by Allan Bloom, who wrote that rock music, with its "barbaric appeal to sexual desire," "ruins the imagination of young people and makes it very difficult for them to have a passionate relationship to the arts and thought that are the substance of liberal education."

The hard right's attack on multiculturalism derives its strength from the right's absolutism, as well as from its White racial nationalism. Samuel Blumenfeld was among the first to attack multiculturalism as a new form of secular humanism's values relativism, writing in 1986 that multiculturalism legitimized different lifestyles and values systems, thereby legitimizing a moral diversity that "directly contradicts the Biblical concept of moral absolutes on which this nation was founded."

Patrick Buchanan bases his opposition to multiculturalism on White racial nationalism. In one article, "Immigration Reform or Racial Purity?," Buchanan himself was quite clear:

> The burning issue here has almost nothing to do with economics, almost everything to do with race and ethnicity. If British subjects, fleeing a depression, were pouring into this country through Canada, there would be few alarms.

> The central objection to the present flood of illegals is they are not English–speaking white people from Western Europe; they are Spanish–speaking brown and black people from Mexico, Latin America and the Caribbean.

Buchanan explicitly links the issue of non–White immigration with multiculturalism, quoting with approval the xenophobic and racist American Immigration Control Foundation, which said, "The combined forces of open immigration and multi–culturalism constitute a mortal threat to American civilization. The US is receiving a never–ending mass immigration of non–Western peoples, leading inexorably to white–minority status in the coming decades [while] a race–based cultural–diversity is attacking, with almost effortless success, the legitimacy of our Western culture." The Free Congress Foundation's Center for Cultural Conservatism disavows any racial nationalist intent while bluntly arguing that all non–White cultures are inferior to traditional Western cultures.

Race & Culture

The major split inside the right–wing crusaders for the Culture War is based on whether or not race and culture are inextricably linked. Buchanan and the authors of the *Bell Curve* argue for biological determinism and White supremacy, while Weyrich and Robertson argue that people of all races can embrace Americanism by adopting northern European, Christian, patriarchal, values—or, in their shorthand: traditional family values.

It's important to state clearly that neoconservatives, for the most part, share Buchanan's distaste for multiculturalism. *The American Spectator*, for example, has argued, "The preservation of the existing ethnocultural character of the United States is not in itself an illegitimate goal. Shorn of Buchanan's more unhygenic rhetoric, and with the emphasis on culture rather than ethnicity, it's a goal many conservatives share. If anything, a concern that the ethnocultural character of the United States is being changed in unwholesome ways is the quality that distinguishes the conservatism of *Commentary* and the *Public Interest* from the more economically minded conservatism that pervades the Washington think tanks."

In part, it is legitimate to argue that the distinction between the old and new conservatives on the issue of race is slim. At the same time, however, the distinction between the approaches the old and new conservatives take on race is the distinction between White racism and White racial nationalism. While systemic racism enforced by a hostile, repressive state is dangerous, the massed power of racial nationalism, as expressed in the activities of the racial nationalist, clerical fascist regimes in Eastern Europe during World War II, is vastly more dangerous.

The embrace of White racial nationalism by the paleo–conservatives has been extensive. *Chronicles* magazine wrote in July 1990:

> What will it be like in the next century when, as *Time* magazine so cheerfully predicts, white people will be in the minority. Our survival depends on our willingness to look reality in the face. There are limits to elasticity, and these limits are defined in part by our historical connections with the rest of Europe and in part by the rate of immigrations. High rates of non–European immigration, even if the immigrants come with the best of intentions in the world, will swamp us. Not all, I hasten to add, do come with the best intentions.

In his distaste for democracy, Buchanan has explicitly embraced racial nationalism. In one column, titled "Worship Democracy? A Dissent," Buchanan argued, "The world hails democracy in principle; in practice, most men believe there are things higher in the order of value—among them, tribe and nation, family and faith." In April 1990, he made a similar statement: "It is not economics that sends men to the barricades; tribe and race, language and faith, history and culture, are more important than a nation's GNP."

Buchanan has also stated:

> The question we Americans need to address, before it is answered for us, is: Does this First World nation wish to become a Third World country? Because that is our destiny if we do not build a sea wall against the waves of immigration rolling over our shores. . . .Who speaks for the Euro–Americans, who founded the USA? . . .Is it not time to take America back?

The basic thesis of White racial nationalism is expressed by David Duke, who won 55 percent of the White vote in Louisiana while arguing:

> I think the basic culture of this country is European and Christian and I think that if we lose that, we lose America. . . .I don't think we should suppress other races, but I think if we lose that White—what's the word for it—that White dominance in America, with it we lose America.

It is difficult not to see the fascist undercurrents in these ideas.

The Hard Right's Disdain for Democracy & Modernity

In the 1920s, at a time, not unlike today, of isolationism, anti–immigrant activism, and White racial nationalism, democracy was seriously challenged. With its anti–elitist, egalitarian assumptions, democracy did not appeal to the reactionary rightists of the 1920s, who insisted that the US was not a democracy but a representative republic. Today, Patrick Buchanan, Paul Weyrich, and the John Birch Society also insist on this distinction, which can more easily accommodate the anti–egalitarian notion of governmental leadership by an elite aristocracy. As Hofstadter pointed out, the pseudo–conservatives' conspiratorial view of liberals leads them to impugn the patriotism of their opponents in the two–party system, a position that undermines the political system itself.

While hard rightists claim to defend traditional US values, they exhibit a deep disdain for democracy. Dismissive references to "participatory democracy, a humanist goal," are common; Patrick Buchanan titled one article, "Worship Democracy? A Dissent." Like many hard rightists, Allan Bloom mixes distaste for humanism and democratic values with elitism when he argues:

Humanism and cultural relativism are a means to avoid testing our own prejudices and asking, for example, whether men are really equal or whether that opinion is merely a democratic prejudice.

More specific rejections of democracy are common currency on the hard right these days. Paul Weyrich, for example, called for the abolition of constitutional safeguards for people arrested in the drug war. Murray Rothbard called for more vigilante beatings by police of those in their custody. Patrick Buchanan has supported the use of death squads, writing, for example:

Faced with rising urban terror in 1976, the Argentine military seized power and waged a war of counter–terror. With military and police and free lance operators, between 6,000 and 150,000 leftists disappeared. Brutal, yes; also successful. Today, peace reigns in Argentina; security has been restored.

Perhaps the most disturbing manifestation of antidemocratic sentiment among the reactionary rightists has been their apparently deliberate embrace of a theory of racial nationalism that imbues much of the protofascist posturings of the European New Right's Third Position politics. Third Position politics rejects both communism and democratic capitalism in favor of a third position that seems to be rooted historically in a Strasserite interpretation of National Socialism, although it claims to have also gone beyond Nazism.

Third Position politics blends a virulent racial nationalism (manifested in an isolationist, anti–immigrant stance) with a purported support for environmentalism, trade unionism, and the dignity of labor. Buchanan has endorsed the idea of antidemocratic racial nationalism in a number of very specific ways, arguing for instance, "Multi–ethnic states, of which we are one, are an endangered species" because "most men believe there are things higher in the order of value [than democracy]—among them, tribe and nation." In support of this view, Buchanan even cites Tomislav Sunic, an academic who has allied himself with European Third Position politics.

Over the past several years, Third Position views have gained currency on the hard right. The Rockford Institute's magazine *Chronicles* recently praised Jorg Haider's racial nationalist Austrian Freedom Party, as well as the fascist Italian Lombardy League. In a sympathetic commentator's description, the Third Position politics of *Chronicles* emerge with a distinctly *volkish* air:

Chronicles is somewhat critical of free markets and spreading democracy. It looks back to agrarian society, small towns, religious values. It sees modern times as too secular, too democratic. There's a distrust of cities and of cultural pluralism, which they find partly responsible for social decay in American life.

Similarly, Paul Weyrich's Center for Cultural Conservatism has praised corporatism as a social model and voiced a new concern for environmentalism and the dignity of labor.

In the wake of the schism within the right wing, the formation of coalitions is just beginning. Whether the US is indeed endangered because it is multicultural may depend on whether mainstream conservatives embrace a paranoid, conspiratorial world view that wants a White supremacist theocracy modeled on the volatile mix of racial nationalism and corporatism that escorted fascism to Europe in the mid–century.

Defending Democracy & Diversity

If the left of the current political spectrum is liberal corporatism and the right is neofascism, then the center is likely to be conservative authoritarianism. The value of the Culture War as the new principle of unity on the right is that, like anti–communism, it actively involves a grassroots constituency that perceives itself as fighting to defend home and family against a sinister threatening force.

Most Democratic Party strategists misunderstand the political power of the various antidemocratic right–wing social movements, and some go so far as to cheer the theocratic right's disruptive assault on the Republican Party. Democrats and their liberal allies rely on short–sighted campaign rhetoric that promotes a centrist analysis demonizing the "Radical Right" as "extremists" without addressing the legitimate anger, fear, and alienation of people who have been mobilized by the right because they see no other options for change.

That there is no organized left to offer an alternative vision to regimented soulless liberal corporatism is one of the tragic ironies of our time. The largest social movements with at least some core allegiance to a progressive agenda remain the environmental and feminist movements, with other pockets of resistance among persons uniting to fight racism, homophobia, and other social ills.

Organized labor, once the mass base for many progressive movements, continues to dwindle in significance as a national force. It was unable to block the North American Free Trade Agreement, and it has been unwilling to muster a respectable campaign to support nationalized health care. None of these progressive forces, even when combined, amount to a fraction of the size of the forces being mobilized on the right.

"It's a struggle between virtual democracy and virulent demagoguery," says author Holly Sklar, whose books on Trilateralism document the triumphant elitist corporate ideology implemented in the United States, Europe, and Japan. Trilateralist belt–tightening policies have caused material hardships and created angry backlash constituencies.

The right has directed these constituencies at convenient scapegoats rather than fostering a progressive systemic or economic analysis. Ironically, among the right–wing's scapegoats is a conspiratorial caricature of the Trilateralists as a secret elite rather than the dominant wing of corporate capitalism that currently occupies the center and defends the status quo.

Suzanne Pharr, an organizer from Arkansas who moved to Oregon to help fight the homophobic initiative Measure Nine, is especially concerned that even in states where the theocratic right has lost battles over school curricula or homophobic initiatives, it leaves behind durable right–wing coalitions poised to launch another round of attacks. Pharr says:

> Progressives need to develop long–term strategies that move beyond short–term electoral victories. We have to develop an analysis that builds bridges to diverse communities and unites us all when the antidemocratic right attacks one of us.

Obviously, individuals involved with the antidemocratic right have absolute constitutional rights to seek redress of their grievances through the political process and to speak their minds without government interference, so long as no laws are violated. At the same time, progressives must oppose attempts by any group to pass laws that take rights away from individuals on the basis of prejudice, myth, irrational belief, inaccurate information, and outright falsehood.

Unless progressives unite to fight the rightward drift, we will be stuck with a choice between the nonparticipatory system crafted by the corporate elites who dominate the Republican and Democratic parties and the stampeding social movements of the right, motivated by cynical leaders willing to blame the real problems in our society on such scapegoats as welfare mothers, immigrants, gays and lesbians, and people of color.

The only way to stop the antidemocratic right is to contest every inch of terrain. Politics is not a pendulum that automatically swings back and forth, left and right. The "center" is determined by various vectors of forces in an endless multidimensional tug of war involving ropes leading out in many directions. Whether or not our country moves toward democracy, equality, social justice, and freedom depends on how many hands grab those ropes and pull together.

Chip Berlet is senior analyst at Political Research Associates in Cambridge, MA. Margaret Quigley was an analyst at PRA from 1987 until her untimely death in 1993. She and Berlet had been working on this manuscript, which Berlet completed. Portions of this chapter previously appeared in the December 1992 issue of *The Public Eye* and the October 1994 issue of *The Progressive*. © 1995, Chip Berlet and the Estate of Margaret Quigley.

The Christian Right Seeks Dominion

On the Road to Political Power & Theocracy

Sara Diamond

The past two decades have seen a growing symbiosis between the mass movement of evangelical Christians and the Republican Party. Since the 1968 presidential election, when nearly 10 million Americans voted for segregationist Alabama Governor George Wallace, the Republicans have worked to broaden the class base of their party downward. That has meant following Wallace's lead in using issues of race, crime, and "morality" to attract white middle and lower middle class voters.

In the mid–1970s and 1980s, Gallup poll surveys showed that one–quarter to one–third of the US population identified itself as "born–again" evangelicals. Most of them have become politically active only since about 1980. Certainly not all are right–wing, but their numbers are large and numbers win elections. In June 1994, a *New York Times* poll revealed that about 9 percent of a national sample identified themselves as part of the Christian Right.

The handwriting was on the wall for anyone who cared to read. Since 1975, leaders of the Christian Right have built one organization after another, with the avowed purpose of winning state power, i.e. the power to influence, if not dictate, public policy. Leaders of the Christian Right worked hand–in–glove with the Reagan and Bush administrations to wage murderous wars on civilians in Central America and southern Africa. Meanwhile, the North American left cackled along with the rest of the country at the ridiculous TV preacher scandals, which diverted people's attention from the really important players in the Christian Right. While everyone else was laughing, the Christian Right grew into the most formidable mass movement on the political scene today. We will enter the new millennium with the Christian Right in positions of state power.

Exit poll data indicate that about 25 percent of the people who voted in November 1994 were white evangelical Christians. Among these, about two–thirds voted Republican. There was nothing "stealth" about it. The stated agenda of the Christian Right in 1994 was to help deliver the Senate and Congress to the Republicans—and to credibly claim credit for doing just that. Each time around, the Christian Right is doing a better job of getting its people to the polls. In the 1992 presidential election, about 18 percent of the voters were self–identified white evangelicals. The figure for the 1990 midterm election was 15 percent.

The trend began in the late 1970s when the Christian Right registered several million new voters to vote for Ronald Reagan. In 1980, when Reagan won with only 26 percent of the eligible electorate, white evangelical voters accounted for two–thirds of Reagan's ten–point lead over Jimmy Carter. Then in 1984, the Christian Right pulled out all the stops to re–elect Reagan. In 1992, despite Bush's defeat, exit poll data showed that there were only two constituencies consistently loyal to the Republican Party: people with incomes over $200,000 a year, who are few in number, and the Christian Right.

The single most important, though by no means the only, movement organization is the Christian Coalition. The Coalition's Annual Road to Victory conferences draw thousands of hard–core activists for two days of strategizing in Washington, DC. The Coalition claims more than a million members, which is probably a mailing list figure. More importantly, the Coalition, since its founding in 1989, has built 1,700 local chapters in all 50 states. Some chapters hold regular meetings with a couple hundred people. Many of the chapters are headed by women, as are some of the Coalition's state branches. Each chapter includes members of multiple charismatic and Baptist churches, meaning that the outreach capability of the Coalition goes well beyond its own numerical strength, which is phenomenal.

The Coalition's chapters are responsible for distributing voter guides by identifying sympathetic churches and by finding "pro–family" voters on a one–by–one basis. In the 1994 Congressional election, the Coalition sent voter registration packets to 250,000 churches. Christian Coalition executive director Ralph Reed explained that the voter guides allow candidates and campaigners to bypass "expensive and biased media." On one piece of paper, the Coalition makes a chart showing pictures of the Democratic and Republican candidates for Senate, Governor, and Congressional seats. The chart lists four to six issues phrased as the right sees them—in 1994 they included abortion on demand, homosexuals in the military, banning ownership of legal firearms, voluntary prayer in schools, parental choice in education—along with the words "supports" or "opposes" under each candidate's picture.

Finally, people on the left are talking about emulating the grassroots organizing tactics of the right. This idea is sensible, but one does not create a citizen lobbying apparatus overnight. For years, people in the Christian Right have learned to make their activism a regular habit. Not a week goes by that the movement's TV, radio stations, and scores of organizational newsletters aren't mobilizing people to call and write their elected officials. Here are people who believe in the efficacy of their own small but persistent actions. They believe their individual postcards and phone calls make a difference, and they do. After Clinton proposed allowing openly gay military personnel, Christian Right activists shut down the Congressional switchboard and deluged their representatives with mail. It worked, and it worked again in early 1994 when an amendment that would have required certification of home school teachers was attached to a federal education bill. Within a week, home schooling leader Mike Farris went on two nationally syndicated Christian radio talk shows and revved up the phone trees of his 37,000–member Home School Legal Defense Association. Eight hundred thousand phone calls later, only one member of Congress was willing to vote for the amendment.

Is this the kind of activity the left could or would emulate? Probably not, because these dramatic incidents do not occur in a vacuum. They are made possible by the day-in-and-day-out organizing the Christian Right does, and they are made possible by the network of institutions the movement has built over several decades. These institutions include a $2.5 billion per year religious broadcasting industry, a slew of independent book publishing companies, dozens of independent regional monthly newspapers, several dozen state–based think tanks that do legislative lobbying, and an array of legal firms devoted exclusively to Christian Right causes.

During the mid–1990s, some left media watchers focused on Rush Limbaugh, an important, though easy target. Limbaugh has millions of listeners and he has played an influential role in the Clinton–bashing of the early 1990s. Limbaugh attracts the left's attention because he allegedly lies with some regularity and because he's a loud–mouthed boor. He fits the image leftists have of people on the right. But to credit the Johnny–come–lately Rush Limbaugh with the mobilization of the right would be like claiming that the demagogic 1930s radio priest Father Charles Coughlin was responsible for the hundreds of pro–fascist organizations that flourished in the United States during the 1930s and 1940s. Most of what goes on in right–wing broadcasting is not like the Limbaugh show. Limbaugh is a recent phenomenon, and long after his stardom passes, the Christian Right will continue to produce much subtler and effective programming.

It is the coherence of the Christian Right's cultural institutions and ideological message that makes millions of people want to participate. This is a political movement built on the foundation of some very tightly held religious views. We need to understand the religious sentiments of our fellow citizens. For evangelical Christians, one of the most politically relevant tenets is the idea that they are being persecuted by secular society. Sacrifice and martyrdom are essential themes of the Christian faith. Translated into right–wing politics, the theme enables people to claim that queers and other minorities are somehow attacking the dominant culture when they demand equality. We have the most powerful political movement in the country continually claiming to be persecuted by "the left," which the right defines as the Clinton Administration and centrist lobbies like People for the American Way. It is illogical, but the religious persecution theme keeps activists mobilized and enables them to feel comfortable about trying to deprive other people of their civil rights.

Average people active in the Christian Right genuinely feel that the country is going to hell in a hand basket, which is true. The problem is that through a long process of ideological formation most have arrived at a distorted view of their own best interests. They look at the stagnant economy and see "illegal aliens," not runaway capitalism, which they generally support. They look at teenage delinquency and then blame teachers' unions instead of the consumer culture that trains young people to shop and not think.

What people in the Christian Right want is pretty basic. They want laws to outlaw abortion, which they consider a form of infanticide. They want to change the tax code to encourage married mothers to stay home and raise good kids. They want queers to get back in the closet and pretend not to exist. They want high quality schools; they think the public schools are failing not for lack of resources but because kids can't pray or read Genesis in biology class.

The Christian Right wants these and related things so badly that they organized to win the political power necessary to change the direction of public policy. Early on, the Republican Party realized that it could become the majority party by hitching its sails to the evangelical mass movement. For two decades, the Democrats stood idly by, unwilling and unable to respond because Democrats will challenge neither the prerogatives of big business nor the ideological premises that keep people from challenging class, racial, and gender inequality. As the Christian Right continues to march steadily, though less noisily, toward assuming political power, movement leaders are now debating their future as unyielding moral crusaders, as rank–and–file Republicans, or as some combination of both. Opponents of the Christian Right stand to lose if they do not recognize that, while the movement indeed has some wild policy goals, the agenda is supported by millions of people as common as the neighbors next door.

Unfortunately, the real left, battered down by external repression and its own internal foibles, has not responded either. The left has been unidimensionally focused on the atrocities waged at the highest levels of state power, and has been unwilling to recognize that significant numbers of our fellow citizens are decidedly reactionary. In places where fascism has taken hold, it has been through a convergence of state and corporate power with a mass base of reaction. We saw this vividly in Chile in the 1970s. I am not suggesting that our country will face a military coup. In the era of "democracy," from Nicaragua to the former Soviet republics, elections are the primary means through which the right takes power.

While the Christian Right stands to mature in the process of charting its own course, liberal centrist critics of the movement seem to be wearing blinders; they continue to depict politically active evangelicals as "extremists" somehow outside of or not belonging to "mainstream" culture, let alone everyday party politics. Liberal centrists delight in labeling the Christian Right the "radical right," a misnomer if there ever was one. Liberal centrists have an interest in policing the margins of political dissent and analysis so that rotten apples—right and left—can be exposed, while the rules of the system escape scrutiny.

The idea of a radical right full of extremists was first popularized during the 1950s and 1960s when prominent political scientists, in dutiful service to the liberal wing of the Cold War establishment, labeled Senator Joseph McCarthy and his admirers as paranoid "radicals," alien to the American body politic. In reality, McCarthy drew his support from the same Republican faithfuls who had elected President Dwight Eisenhower. Popular right–wing groups like the John Birch Society emerged only in the late 1950s, well after political elites had turned the pursuit of "communist subversion" into a national religion. By then, polite society was keen to depict wild–eyed Birchers as "extremists," even as they played by democratic rules and helped win the Republican nomination for Barry Goldwater. Academia's warnings about "radical right extremism" held influence when the massive Christian right mobilized in the late 1970s. Throughout the 1980s and continuing now, centrist outfits like People for the American Way have promoted a view of dangerous "radical right" Christians as something separate from the US political and economic system itself.

But there is nothing particularly "radical" about most politically active evangelical Christians. To be "radical" is to seize the roots of a problem and to advocate and work for profound social change. The Christian Right, on the contrary, supports existing conditions that effectively maintain inequality between rich and poor, white and black, men and women. The Christian Right supports capitalism in all its forms and effects and seeks to uphold traditional hierarchies between the genders and, less overtly, between races. What is "radical" about a movement that, throughout the 1980s, worked hand-in-glove with the Reagan–Bush White House to wage war on revolutionaries and civilian populations from one end of the globe to the next? Through its close ties with political and economic elites, the Christian Right flourished and, now, has turned its attention against the least powerful in our own country.

Like other political forces before it—such as the civil rights, women's, and environmental movements—the Christian Right is evolving an organizational style geared for success. At the same time, the Christian Coalition's hundreds of thousands of grassroots activists are the same people who harass women's health clinics and spread lies about homosexuality. The right's elite–oriented and mass–based contingents are autonomous but mutually dependent on each other. To call them names like "radicals" or "fascists" will not stop them. To understand them and organize against them just might.

Sara Diamond holds a doctorate in sociology, and teaches that subject and journalism at several California colleges. She is the author of *Spiritual Warfare: The Politics of the Christian Right* (South End Press, 1989), and *Roads to Dominion: Right–Wing Movements and Political Power in the United States* (Guilford, 1995). Portions of this chapter previously appeared in different form in her columns in *Z Magazine* and *The Humanist*. © 1995, Sara Diamond.

Pious Moralism

Theocratic Goals Backed by Misrepresentation and Lies

Liz Galst

Newton, Massachusetts, hardly seems a likely target for a campaign by ultraconservatives and religious fundamentalists: it's liberal, it's rich, it's got a large Jewish population. But likely or not, the Garden City has been the focus of intense political activity since the winter of 1992, when the city's school department released recommendations for a revamped sexuality–education program.

The Newton program was designed to be even–handed and objection–proof. It talked about abstinence as the only sure way to avoid sexual transmission of HIV. It talked about the benefits of marriage. It addressed condom–failure rates. There was even a clause that allowed parents to keep their children out of the program if they found it objectionable.

None of that impressed Newton Citizens for Public Education (NCPE), a group opposed to comprehensive sexuality education in the public schools. They wanted a curriculum that would teach young people that abstinence and subsequent monogamous, heterosexual marriage were the only paths to follow.

Despite rhetoric that echoes that of ultraconservative Christian groups, members of NCPE consistently denied any connection to groups such as Focus on the Family or Pat Robertson's Christian Coalition, groups with the goal of imposing a fundamentalist theocracy on the US.

Around the state and across the country, the theocratic right has been gaining prominence, and its strategy—often starting with the sensitive issue of sex education—has become a familiar one. In 1992, the theocratic right's candidates won 40 percent of the local and statewide races they ran in, sometimes employing a tactic called "stealth campaigning," revealing their true aims only to a select group of voters.

Aside from waging battles over sex education and AIDS curricula, members of the theocratic right have called for an end to school breakfast programs and bilingual education, and sought to deny women access to abortion. They've pushed referenda that would deny lesbians, gays, and bisexuals civil rights protections.

Though NCPE denies any connection to the theocratic right, or any larger political aims, a forum it held in March 1993 featured nationally renowned right–wingers: *Boston Herald* columnist Don Feder (who's Jewish and gets a lot of play in Religious Right circles because of it), American Family Association bigwig Judith Reisman, and William Kirkpatrick, author of *Why Johnny Can't Tell Right From Wrong: Moral Illiteracy and the Case for Character Education.* One Newton resident who attended the forum said it was "one of the most hate–filled events I've ever witnessed. They characterized sexuality education as an apocalyptic failure, and called sexuality educators 'pedophiles.' It was incredibly homophobic."

In March 1993, NCPE released a lengthy position paper titled "Sex Education: Values in a Decade of Decision" which, rather than exposing what the group saw as the problems with the proposed curriculum, buttressed the commonly–held belief in Newton that the organization was in the pocket of the theocratic right.

If it can happen in liberal Newton, it can happen anywhere.

Because fundamentalist Christian teachings assert that God intended sex only for procreation, sex education is a natural focal point for Religious Right activities, says Skipp Porteous of the Institute for First Amendment Studies in Great Barrington, Massachusetts. A self–described "recovering fundamentalist minister," he has become a watchdog of the theocratic right.

The theocratic right "has a lot of problems dealing with sex," Porteous says." They're not supposed to think about it a lot. And when they do, they feel guilty, so they fight it."

That fight often attracts individuals who wouldn't necessarily sign on to the rest of the theocratic right's program—if they knew about it. "Some people's concerns are that they know AIDS is out there, but they don't know how to protect their kids," says Ellen Brodsky, coordinator of Planned Parenthood's Heart to Heart Project, which teaches parents to talk to their children about sexuality and AIDS. "Parents are afraid that if they start talking about sex, it's only going to make their kids more interested in it."

Indeed, that's one of the assertions made by members of the theocratic right when they oppose curricula that discuss subjects like risk reduction, condom usage, and "outercourse."

But the claim is unfounded, says Douglas Kirby, Ph.D., a Santa Cruz, California, sociologist who evaluates sex education and AIDS education curricula.

"The evidence is really quite clear from probably about 10 different studies that sex education programs do not hasten the initiation of intercourse," Kirby says. "And some specific programs that cover both postponing sexual involvement and contraception have been clearly demonstrated to delay the onset of intercourse and to increase the use of contraception."

But battles over sex education, AIDS curricula, and the discussion of homosexuality in the schools are more than simple conflicts over what and how kids will learn about sex. The theocratic right uses these controversies as stepping stones to local political power, Porteous says. "Their agenda extends far beyond sex education, but they use sex education as a hot button. It's an issue that evokes a lot of fear, especially when they talk about AIDS. It hits close to home, and they can use it to raise a lot of money."

That money is channeled into efforts to build political organizations whose express purpose is the establishment of a fundamentalist theocracy in the United States.

"Look at Focus on the Family," Porteous says of the Colorado Springs–based media empire that, in 1992, operated on an annual budget of $78 million and broadcasted on over 1,550 radio stations worldwide. "They send out millions of pieces of literature a year. They're really slick. And when they teach something they call their 'Community Impact Seminars,' they say the separation of church and state is a myth."

There's evidence of that attitude closer to home: in a 1993 recruiting letter, for instance, the Massachusetts coordinator for the Christian Coalition, Pat Hoffman, told Worcester County clerics that "'separation of church and state' is a bogus phrase. Our country was founded on Biblical principles and we need to turn back to God and His precepts."

Further proof of the theocratic ends of ultraconservative fundamentalists comes from quotes like this one from *Pat Robertson Perspective,* the newsletter published by the leading light of the 1.7 million–member Christian Coalition:

I believe that during the next couple of years there will be a fierce struggle between the militant leftists, secular humanists, and atheists who have dominated the power centers of American culture since the 1940's and the Evangelical Christians, pro–family Roman Catholics, and their conservative allies. The radical left will lose its hold, and by the end of the decade control of the major institutions of Society will be firmly in the hands of those who share [a] pro–family, religious, traditional values perspective.

Porteous's colleague Frederick Clarkson, an investigative journalist, confirms that Robertson's objectives are as religious as they are political. "I snuck into the first Christian Coalition National Strategy Conference, in the fall of 1991," Clarkson says. "Robertson said that what we need to understand is that we're not just up against human beings in these elections, we're engaged in spiritual warfare. What he means is that there's a supernatural struggle between the forces of God and the forces of Satan. And the contest involves building the kingdom of God on earth, the theocracy."

Robertson even prophesies a bloody conflict between good and evil: "We will be living through one of the most tumultuous periods of human history," he wrote in a 1992 newsletter. "When it is over, I am convinced that God's people will emerge victorious. But no victory ever comes without a battle. . . . I don't want to see it go that way, but violence is inevitable."

Most of the time, however, Robertson advocates electoral politics. As recently as the summer of 1992, he and other theocratic right luminaries had hoped to play out this apocalyptic battle at the national level by influencing policy through their connections to the Republican Party. In fact, the Christian Coalition claimed to have the largest faction at the 1992 Republican National Convention—300 of the 2,000 delegates. (The proportion of delegates who identified themselves as "Christian evangelicals" was 40 percent.)

The theocratic right can be effective because its agenda of tight control and strict morality is a salve to an increasingly frightened and dislocated public. And it can win locally in areas where the message has limited appeal, because it knows how to manipulate the political system.

That manipulation is called "the 15 percent solution" by Christian Coalition strategists because statistics indicate that 15 percent of the electorate is all that's needed to win an election, especially a local one.

According to Guy Rodgers, one of the organization's strategists, only 60 percent of eligible voters are registered. Of those, only half vote (30 percent). Therefore, elections are decided by a mere 15 percent of the electorate. In local elections, where turnout is often significantly smaller and name recognition significantly lower, the percentage of voters needed to win, say, a school board seat, may be as low as six percent or seven percent.

It's those six or seven percent that Religious Right candidates try to appeal to. Often, Religious Right candidates take to the stump at fundamentalist religious congregations, and use underhanded campaign polling techniques to appeal to uninformed voters.

In Virginia Beach, Virginia, where the Christian Coalition headquarters is located, the group used phone polling to target undecided voters in state legislative races.

According to Clarkson, Christian Coalition pollsters asked voters if they had voted for Bush or Dukakis and what their party affiliation was. If the voters answered "Dukakis" and "Democrat," the polling ended. But if the voter answered either question "correctly," the interview continued. Voters were asked their position on abortion and what they felt was the most pressing issue in their community. Using that information, the Christian Coalition sent out computer–generated letters tailored to the issues mentioned by a particular voter. And if the voter was pro–choice, the letters didn't mention the candidate's stand against abortion.

That strategy was used with equal efficacy in San Diego County, California, in 1990, says Matthew Freeman, director of research at People for the American Way, a Washington, DC–based "nonpartisan constitutional liberties organization" with 300,000 members nationwide. "In 1990," says Freeman, "a coalition of local chapters of national Religious Right organizations including the Christian Coalition and Citizens for Excellence in Education, along with some unaffiliated Religious Right activists, cobbled together a slate of 90 candidates for a number of different positions."

In San Diego, as in most of the rest of California, the ballot is extremely long and the electorate votes on a number of positions that in other states and municipalities are often filled by appointment. "So they put together this slate," Freeman says, "and they worked to elect them by campaigning fast and furious in their own religious community."

How these candidates didn't campaign is as significant as how they did, says Freeman. "They didn't do debates. They didn't do public appearances. They declined interviews with the mainstream media."

"And the consequence," says Freeman, "was that by the time election day rolled around, a fairly significant number of voters who hadn't kept track of who was running for what office were confronted with names they knew nothing about."

"One other factor comes into play in San Diego," Freeman says. "San Diego County has 43 separate school districts, which means that a vote count of 1,000 people can win an election. So, if you have a concentration of folks from one or two church groups, you can win." In fact, two–thirds of the candidates on the theocratic right slate were elected.

This strategy of "stealth" campaigning was originally endorsed by Christian Coalition executive director Ralph Reed, who told the *LA Times*, "It's like guerrilla warfare. If you reveal your location, all it does is allow your opponent to improve his artillery bearings. It's better to move quietly, with stealth, under cover of night. It comes down to whether you want to be the British army in the Revolutionary War or the Viet Cong. History tells us which tactic is more effective." (Such gory metaphors, however, have sometimes backfired on the Christian Coalition. To address this problem, the group hired a public relations firm, which told them to lay off the war metaphors and to start using sports analogies instead.)

Because the San Diego elections received so much press, and because local groups in San Diego County have subsequently worked hard to expose such stealth candidacies, Reed has backed away from his position.

"I don't really think this [stealth] is a national strategy," Reed told Boston's *Phoenix* newsweekly in 1993. "Most of this talk comes from radical–left organizations like People for the American Way. They're the ones who've accused us of running 'stealth' candidates." Reed cites the Christian Coalition's open participation in the 1993 New York City school board election as proof positive that it has no intention of stealthily turning the nation into a theocracy, no matter what his boss Pat Robertson might say.

"I think our motivation is primarily a parental–rights agenda," says Reed. "We're not interested in creationism, or prayer in school. I think People for the American Way has tried to cloud the issue by mentioning creationism. This isn't about creationism, this is about parental rights."

The actions of one school board that had a theocratic right majority, however, contradict Reed's statement. In San Diego County, the Vista school board considered a creationist text called *Of Pandas and People* for the school curriculum in 1993. (One of the board members was an employee of the Institute for Creation Research.) And the board began its meetings not with a moment of silence, but with a prayer to Jesus.

The theocratic right's misrepresentation of political motives is a marked departure from the sort of lying that's commonplace in mainstream American politics, Clarkson says, as are attempts by candidates to keep their Religious Right affiliation secret. "This type of lying tends to have more in common with the secret–cell group structure of underground political movements, because the degree of radical change they espouse requires a covert strategy."

Moreover, Clarkson says, "The lies are interesting because these people are supposed to be professing Christians and are supposed to be bringing a higher level of integrity and truth–telling to public policy." After all, he says, "they're bound by the Ten Commandments."

Reed contends that parents on the theocratic right don't have a creationist agenda, but he doesn't think there's anything wrong with introducing creationism in public schools. "We think that you should not censure alternative views in the classroom," says Reed. "We believe local school boards, in consultations with local parents, should be allowed to present more than one view."

More than one view may be all well and good when the views relate to the origin of the species. But alternative views of the family and of sexuality are anathema to the Christian Coalition's executive director.

"We are opposed to students being taught about human sexuality apart from parental input," Reed says.

In many cases, though, "parental input" seems to be a code for parental input by opponents of sex education and gay–tolerant curricula. At the Newton School Committee meeting in May 1993, for instance, a huge number of parents spoke in favor of the sex–ed curriculum, which includes discussion of homosexuality. Yet, even after that meeting, the Newton Citizens for Public Education continued to assert that the school committee was riding rough-shod over Newton parents.

"Parents were shocked and outraged when the school committee unanimously approved this curriculum," NCPE wrote in its published document titled "Confronting the New Sexuality Agenda in the Newton Public Schools. Why We Need Your Help."

"[Parents] feel this is not only grossly inappropriate for 14–year–old children, but totally out of place for the public school setting," the tract says. "Nevertheless, the School Committee believes strongly in the importance of implementing it."

Such misrepresentation is not unique to Newton. In New York City, the Protestant theocratic right formed a historic coalition with the Catholic hierarchy and some Orthodox Jewish groups to marshal forces against the Children of the Rainbow multicultural curriculum by calling it "The Gay and Lesbian Curriculum."

"The First–grade curriculum came out and the Religious Right suddenly got very organized," says Frances Kunreuther, executive director of the Hetrick–Martin Institute, a program for gay, lesbian, and bisexual youth in New York City. "They called it 'a conspiracy to teach sodomy to first–graders.'" In fact, there was no mention of gay or lesbian sexuality in the 450–page curriculum guide, only six or seven references to families with gay or lesbian parents. The books *Heather Has Two Mommies* and *Daddy's Roommate* were included in a list of storybooks teachers might read with their classes.

Kunreuther says that the Religious Right succeeded in completely misrepresenting the curriculum. "A lot of people didn't even know it was a multicultural curriculum at all, and that lesbians and gays were just a small part of it." And when supporters of the curriculum challenged the theocratic right and the archdiocese to substantiate their assertions, the opponents of Children of the Rainbow pointed to things like the curriculum guide's purple cover. "They said purple was just a code for homosexuality," Kunreuther says.

Eventually, the controversy led to the ouster of New York City Schools Chancellor Joseph Fernandez and the rejection of the curriculum by some local school districts within New York City. But, just as important, the fight cemented the union of the largely Protestant theocratic right and the archdiocese, an alliance that will no doubt have significant bearing on New York City electoral politics for years to come.

Kunreuther says the Catholic/theocratic right coalition used parents' legitimate anger at the failing New York City schools to push a social agenda that has very little to do with education. "The people who opposed the Children of the Rainbow curriculum were also opposed to the free breakfast program for low–income kids, and favored putting prayer in schools. Basically, they used the issue of homosexuality to push their agenda."

What gets lost in this political power struggle is the young people's need for accurate information about sexuality and sexually transmitted diseases, information that could literally save their lives. Most health professionals believe the information is most effective when delivered in comprehensive, age–appropriate programs taught in the context of comprehensive health education.

Comprehensive sexuality education has four primary goals. It seeks to provide young people with accurate information about sex and sexuality; to help them explore their attitudes and values as they relate to sex; to develop interpersonal skills, including communication, assertiveness, and the ability to fend off peer pressure; and to help them exercise responsibility in sexual relationships.

AIDS education programs based on this model provide young people with the available information about the surest ways to prevent HIV infection (abstinence, "outercourse," and risk reduction), cite rates of condom failure, and, perhaps most important, teach young people to assess this information in keeping with their values. It is this process of evaluation that parents opposing comprehensive sexuality education object to.

The theocratic right "wants children to learn what to think, and not how to think," says Porteous. "They want people to be under subjection to the Bible. They feel if everybody's off thinking their own thoughts, they might rebel against God."

Proponents of "Just Say No" curricula (which teach young people to postpone sex until marriage, but don't teach about risk reduction, condom usage, or "outercourse") continually harp on statistics of dubious scientific merit. For instance, many point out that latex condoms contain small holes five microns in size, and that HIV is 0.1 micron in size. The conclusion drawn is that HIV can therefore slip through the holes in a condom.

"The statistics they use are not embraced by the medical community," says Betsy Wacker, director of public policy for the Sex Information and Education Council of the US, a nonprofit clearinghouse for information on sexuality and sex education and an advocate of comprehensive sexuality education. "The citations they use are from studies that are not peer–reviewed. So they're skating on pretty thin ice."

Also dubious are reports that the Sex Respect curriculum, which attempts to encourage abstinence until marriage through the use of slogans like "Pet your dog, not your date" or "Don't be a louse, wait for your spouse," has made a significant impact on the students who've participated in the program. "So far, there is no good research which indicates that curricula like Sex Respect and Teen–Aid have an impact on behavior," says sociologist Douglas Kirby.

Kirby says equally false are claims that the Sex Respect program has resulted in significantly decreased rates of teen pregnancy. "I'm familiar with two different programs they cite. One is the San Marcus, California, study. They claim that the number of teen pregnancies in the school dropped from about 140 one year to 20 the next. In that case, the principal of the school is on record saying '[supporters of Sex Respect] simply made that figure up.'"

Liz Galst is a freelance journalist who is currently pursuing graduate studies in writing at Columbia University. This chapter is adapted from a longer article that first appeared in the Boston *Phoenix* on July 30, 1993.
© 1993, the Boston *Phoenix*.

Christian Reconstructionism

Theocratic Dominionism Gains Influence

Frederick Clarkson

The Christian Right has shown impressive resilience and has rebounded dramatically after a series of embarrassing televangelist scandals of the late 1980s, the collapse of Jerry Falwell's Moral Majority, and the failed presidential bid of Pat Robertson. In the 1990s, Christian Right organizing went to the grassroots and exerted wide influence in American politics across the country.

There is no doubt that Pat Robertson's Christian Coalition gets much of the credit for this successful *strategic* shift to the local level. But another largely overlooked reason for the persistent success of the Christian Right is a *theological* shift since the 1960s. The catalyst for the shift is Christian Reconstructionism—arguably the driving ideology of the Christian Right in the 1990s.

The significance of the Reconstructionist movement is not its numbers, but the power of its ideas and their surprisingly rapid acceptance. Many on the Christian Right are unaware that they hold Reconstructionist ideas. Because as a theology it is controversial, even among evangelicals, many who are consciously influenced by it avoid the label. This furtiveness is not, however, as significant as the potency of the ideology itself.

Generally, Reconstructionism seeks to replace democracy with a theocratic elite that would govern by imposing their interpretation of "Biblical Law." Reconstructionism would eliminate not only democracy but many of its manifestations, such as labor unions, civil rights laws, and public schools. Women would be generally relegated to hearth and home. Insufficiently Christian men would be denied citizenship, perhaps executed. So severe is this theocracy that it would extend capital punishment beyond such crimes as kidnapping, rape, and murder to include, among other things, blasphemy, heresy, adultery, and homosexuality.

Reconstructionism has expanded from the works of a small group of scholars to inform a wide swath of conservative Christian thought and action. While many Reconstructionist political positions are commonly held conservative views, what is significant is that Reconstructionists have created a comprehensive program, with Biblical justifications for far right political policies. Many post–World War II conservative, anti–communist activists were also, if secondarily, conservative Christians. However, the Reconstructionist movement calls on conservatives to be Christians first, and to build a church–based political movement from there.

For much of Reconstructionism's short history it has been an ideology in search of a constituency. But its influence has grown far beyond the founders' expectations. As Reconstructionist author Gary North observes, "We once were shepherds without sheep. No longer."

What is Reconstructionism?

Reconstructionism is a theology that arose out of conservative Presbyterianism (Reformed and Orthodox), which proposes that contemporary application of the laws of Old Testament Israel, or "Biblical Law," is the basis for reconstructing society toward the Kingdom of God on earth.

Reconstructionism argues that the Bible is to be the governing text for all areas of life—such as government, education, law, and the arts, not merely "social" or "moral" issues like pornography, homosexuality, and abortion. Reconstructionists have formulated a "Biblical world view" and "Biblical principles" by which to examine contemporary matters.

Reconstructionist theologian David Chilton succinctly describes this view: "The Christian goal for the world is the universal development of Biblical theocratic republics, in which every area of life is redeemed and placed under the Lordship of Jesus Christ and the rule of God's law."

More broadly, Reconstructionists believe that there are three main areas of governance: family government, church government, and civil government. Under God's covenant, the nuclear family is the basic unit. The husband is the head of the family, and wife and children are "in submission" to him. In turn, the husband "submits" to Jesus and to God's laws as detailed in the Old Testament. The church has its own ecclesiastical structure and governance. Civil government exists to implement God's laws. All three institutions are under Biblical Law, the implementation of which is called "theonomy."

The Origin of Reconstructionism

The original and defining text of Reconstructionism is *Institutes of Biblical Law*, published in 1973 by Rousas John Rushdoony—an 800-page explanation of the Ten Commandments, the Biblical "case law" that derives from them, and their application today. "The only true order," writes Rushdoony, "is founded on Biblical Law. All law is religious in nature, and every non–Biblical law–order represents an anti–Christian religion." In brief, he continues, "Every law–order is a state of war against the enemies of that order, and all law is a form of warfare."

Gary North, Rushdoony's son–in–law, wrote an appendix to *Institutes* on the subject of "Christian economics." It is a polemic which serves as a model for the application of "Biblical Principles."

Rushdoony and a younger theologian, Rev. Greg Bahnsen, were both students of Cornelius Van Til, a Princeton University theologian. Although Van Til himself never became a Reconstructionist, Reconstructionists claim him as the father of their movement. According to Gary North, Van Til argued that "There is no philosophical strategy that has ever worked, except this one; to challenge the lost in terms of the revelation of God in His Bible. . .by what standard can man know anything truly? By the Bible, and *only* by the Bible." This idea that the correct and only way to view reality is through the lens of a Biblical world view is known as presuppositionalism.

According to Gary North, Van Til stopped short of proposing what a Biblical society might look like or how to get there. That is where Reconstructionism begins. While Van Til states that man is not autonomous and that all rationality is inseparable from faith in God and the Bible, the Reconstructionists go further and set a course of world conquest or "dominion," claiming a Biblically prophesied "inevitable victory."

Reconstructionists also believe that "the Christians" are the "new chosen people of God," commanded to do what "Adam in Eden and Israel in Canaan failed to do. . .create the society that God requires." Further, Jews, once the "chosen people," failed to live up to God's covenant and therefore are no longer God's chosen. Christians, of the correct sort, now are.

Rushdoony's *Institutes of Biblical Law* consciously echoes a major work of the Protestant Reformation, John Calvin's *Institutes of the Christian Religion*. In fact, Reconstructionists see themselves as the theological and political heirs of Calvin. The theocracy Calvin created in Geneva, Switzerland in the 1500s is one of the political models Reconstructionists look to, along with Old Testament Israel and the Calvinist Puritans of the Massachusetts Bay Colony.

Capital Punishment

Epitomizing the Reconstructionist idea of Biblical "warfare" is the centrality of capital punishment under Biblical Law. Doctrinal leaders (notably Rushdoony, North, and Bahnsen) call for the death penalty for a wide range of crimes in addition to such contemporary capital crimes as rape, kidnapping, and murder. Death is also the punishment for apostasy (abandonment of the faith), heresy, blasphemy, witchcraft, astrology, adultery, "sodomy or homosexuality," incest, striking a parent, incorrigible juvenile delinquency, and, in the case of women, "unchastity before marriage."

According to Gary North, women who have abortions should be publicly executed, "along with those who advised them to abort their children." Rushdoony concludes: "God's government prevails, and His alternatives are clear–cut: either men and nations obey His laws, or God invokes the death penalty against them."

Reconstructionists insist that "the death penalty is the maximum, not necessarily the mandatory penalty." However, such judgments may depend less on Biblical Principles than on which faction gains power in the theocratic republic. The potential for bloodthirsty episodes on the order of the Salem witchcraft trials or the Spanish Inquisition is inadvertently revealed by Reconstructionist theologian Rev. Ray Sutton, who claims that the Reconstructed Biblical theocracies would be "happy" places, to which people would flock because "capital punishment is one of the best evangelistic tools of a society."

The Biblically approved methods of execution include burning (at the stake for example), stoning, hanging, and "the sword." Gary North, the self–described economist of Reconstructionism, prefers stoning because, among other things, stones are cheap, plentiful, and convenient. Punishments for non–capital crimes generally involve whipping, restitution in the form of indentured servitude, or slavery. Prisons would likely be only temporary holding tanks, prior to imposition of the actual sentence.

People who sympathize with Reconstructionism often flee the label because of the severe and unpopular nature of such views. Even those who feel it appropriate that they would be the governors of God's theocracy often waffle on the particulars, like capital punishment for sinners and nonbelievers. Unflinching advocates, however, insist upon consistency. Rev. Greg Bahnsen, in his book *By This Standard*, writes: "We. . .endorse the justice of God's penal code, if the Bible is to be the foundation of our Christian political ethic."

Reconstructionism has adopted "covenantalism," the theological doctrine that Biblical "covenants" exist between God and man, God and nations, God and families, and that they make up the binding, incorporating doctrine that makes sense of everything. Specifically, there is a series of covenant "structures" that make up a Biblical blueprint for society's institutions. Reconstructionists believe that God "judges" a whole society according to how it keeps these covenantal laws, and provides signs of that judgment. This belief can be seen, for example, in the claim that AIDS is a "sign of God's judgment."

Reconstructionist Rev. Ray Sutton writes that "there is no such thing as a natural disaster. Nature is not neutral. Nothing takes place in nature by chance. . .Although we may not know the exact sin being judged," Sutton declares, "what occurs results from God."

Christian Historical Revisionism

Part of the Reconstructionist world view is a revisionist view of history called "Christian history," which holds that history is predestined from "creation" until the inevitable arrival of the Kingdom of God. Christian history is written by means of retroactively discerning "God's providence."

Most Reconstructionists, for example, argue that the United States is a "Christian Nation" and that they are the champions and heirs of the "original intentions of the Founding Fathers." This dual justification for their views, one religious, the other somehow constitutional, is the result of a form of historical revisionism that Rushdoony frankly calls "Christian revisionism."

Christian revisionism is important in understanding the Christian Right's approach to politics and public policy. If one's political righteousness and sense of historical continuity are articles of faith, what appear as facts to everyone else fall before the compelling evidence of faith. Whatever does not fit neatly into a "Biblical world view" becomes problematic, perhaps a delusion sent by Satan.

The invocations of the Bible and the Founding Fathers are powerful ingredients for good religious–nationalist demagoguery. However, among the stark flaws of Reconstructionist history is the way Christian revisionism distorts historical fact.

For example, by interpreting the framing of the Constitution as if it were a document inspired by and adhering to a Reconstructionist version of Biblical Christianity, Reconstructionists make a claim that denies the existence of Article VI of the Constitution. Most historians agree that Article VI, which states that public officials shall be "bound by oath or affirmation to support this Constitution; but no religious test shall ever be required as a qualification to any office or public trust under the United States," was a move toward disestablishment of churches as official power brokers and the establishment of the principles of religious pluralism and separation of church and state.

R. J. Rushdoony, in his influential 1963 book, *The Nature of the American System,* claims that "The Constitution was designed to perpetuate a Christian order," then asks rhetorically: "Why then is there, in the main, an absence of any reference to Christianity in the Constitution?" He argues that the purpose was to protect religion from the federal government and to preserve "states' rights."

Once again, however, such a view requires ignoring Article VI. Before 1787, most of the colonies and early states had required pledges of allegiance to Christianity and that one be a Christian of the correct sect to hold office. Part of the struggle toward democracy at the time was the disestablishment of the state churches—the power structures of the local colonial theocracies. Thus the "religious test" was a significant philosophical matter. There was little debate over Article VI, which passed unanimously at the Constitutional Convention. Most of the states soon followed the federal lead in conforming to it.

Reconstructionist author Gary DeMar, in his 1993 book *America's Christian History: The Untold Story,* also trips over Article VI. He quotes from colonial and state constitutions to prove they were "Christian" states. And, of course, they generally were, until the framers of the Constitution set disestablishment irrevocably in motion. Yet DeMar tries to explain this away, claiming that Article VI merely banned "government mandated religious tests"—as if there were any other kind at issue. He later asserts that Article VI was a "mistake" on the part of the framers, implying that they did not intend disestablishment.

By contrast, mainstream historian Garry Wills sees no mistake. In his book *Under God: Religion and American Politics,* he concludes that the framers stitched together ideas from "constitutional monarchies, ancient republics, and modern leagues. . . .but we [the US] invented nothing, except disestablishment. . . . No other government in the history of the world had launched itself without the help of officially recognized gods and their state connected ministers." Disestablishment was the clear and unambiguous choice of the framers of the Constitution, most of whom were also serious Christians.

Even Gary North (who holds a Ph.D. in History) sees the connection between Article VI and disestablishment and attacks Rushdoony's version of the "Christian" Constitution. North writes that "In his desire to make the case for Christian America, he [Rushdoony] closed his eyes to the judicial break from Christian America: the ratification of the Constitution." North says Rushdoony "pretends" that Article VI "does not say what it says, and it does not mean what it has always meant: a legal barrier to Christian theocracy," leading "directly to the rise of religious pluralism."

North's views are the exception on the Christian Right. The falsely nostalgic view of a Christian Constitution, somehow subverted by modernism and the Supreme Court, generally holds sway. Christian historical revisionism is the premise of much Christian Right political and historical literature and is being widely taught and accepted in Christian schools and home schools. It informs the political understanding of the broader Christian Right. The popularization of this perspective is a dangerously polarizing factor in contemporary politics.

A Movement of Ideas

As a movement primarily of ideas, Reconstructionism has no single denominational or institutional home. Nor is it totally defined by a single charismatic leader, nor even a single text. Rather, it is defined by a small group of scholars who are identified with Reformed or Orthodox Presbyterianism. The movement networks primarily through magazines, conferences, publishing houses, think tanks, and bookstores. As a matter of strategy, it is a self–consciously decentralized and publicity–shy movement.

Reconstructionist leaders seem to have two consistent characteristics: a background in conservative Presbyterianism, and connections to the John Birch Society (JBS).

In 1973, R. J. Rushdoony compared the structure of the JBS to the "early church." He wrote in *Institutes*: "The key to the John Birch Society's effectiveness has been a plan of operation which has a strong resemblance to the early church; have meetings, local 'lay' leaders, area supervisors or 'bishops.'"

The JBS connection does not stop there. Most leading Reconstructionists have either been JBS members or have close ties to the organization. Reconstructionist literature can be found in JBS–affiliated American Opinion bookstores.

Indeed, the conspiracist views of Reconstructionist writers (focusing on the United Nations and the Council on Foreign Relations, among others) are consistent with those of the John Birch Society. A classic statement of the JBS world view, *Call It Conspiracy* by Larry Abraham, features a prologue and an epilogue by Reconstructionist Gary North. In fact, former JBS chairman Larry McDonald may himself have been a Reconstructionist. Joseph Morecraft has written that "Larry [McDonald] understood that when the authors of the US Constitution spoke of law, they meant the law of God as revealed in the Bible. I have heard him say many times that we must refute humanistic, relativistic law with Biblical Law."

As opposed to JBS beliefs, however, Reconstructionists emphasize the primacy of Christianity over politics. Gary North, for example, insists that it is the institution of the Church itself to which loyalty and energy are owed, before any other arena of life. Christians are called to Christianity first and foremost, and Christianization should extend to all areas of life. This emphasis on Christianity has political implications because, in the 1990s, it is likely that the JBS world view is persuasive to more people when packaged as a *Biblical* world view.

A Generation of Reconstructionists

Reconstructionism's decentralist ideas have led to the creation of a network of churches, across a number of denominations, all building for the Kingdom. One Reconstructionist pastor writes that the leadership of the movement is passing to hundreds of small local churches that are "starting to grow, both numerically and theologically. Their people are being trained in the Reconstruction army. And at least in Presbyterian circles. . .we're Baptizing and catechizing a whole generation of Gary Norths, R. J. Rushdoonys and David Chiltons."

North writes that this percolation of ideas, actions, and institutions is largely untraceable. "No historian," he says, "will ever be able to go back and identify in terms of the primary source documents, [what happened] because *we* can't possibly do it."

Part of the reason for this is that Reconstructionism cloaks its identity, as well as its activities, understanding the degree of opposition it provokes. For example, Gary North was caught donating Reconstructionist books (mostly his own) to university libraries under the pretense of being an anonymous alumnus. What might seem a small matter of shameless self–promotion—getting one's books into libraries to influence American intellectual life by hook or by crook—is actually part of the larger strategy of covert influence and legitimation.

Similarly, while claiming to be reformers, not revolutionaries, Reconstructionists recognize that the harsh theocracy they advocate is revolutionary indeed. Gary North warns against a "premature revolutionary situation," saying that the public must begin to accept "the judicially binding case laws of the Old Testament before we attempt to tear down judicial institutions that still rely on natural law or public virtue. (I have in mind the US Constitution.)" Thus, radical ideas must be gently and often indirectly infused into their target constituencies and society at large. The vague claim that God and Jesus want Christians to govern society is certainly more appealing than the bloodthirsty notion of justice as "vengeance" advocated by some of the Reconstructionists.

The claim that they do not seek to impose a theocracy from the top down—waiting for a time when a majority will have converted and thus want to live under Biblical Law—is consistent with Reconstructionists' decentralist and anti–state populism, which they often pass off as a form of libertarianism. Even so, there is an inevitable point when the "majority" would impose its will. North bluntly says that one of his first actions would be to "remove legal access to the franchise and to civil offices from those who refuse to become communicant members of Trinitarian churches." Quick to condemn democracy as the idea that the law is whatever the majority says it is, North *et al.* would be quick to cynically utilize a similar "majority" for a permanent theocratic solution.

The Timing of the Kingdom

One of the variations within Reconstructionism is the matter of the timing of the Kingdom, as defined by when Christians take power. For example, Rev. Everette Sileven of Louisville, Nebraska thinks the Kingdom is overdue. (Rev. Sileven is best known for his battle with the state in the mid–1980s, when he refused to certify the teachers in his private Christian school as required by state law.) In 1987, Sileven predicted the crumbling of the economy, democracy, the judicial system, and the IRS before 1992. From this crisis, he believed, the Kingdom would emerge.

Rev. David Chilton has a longer–term vision. He believes the Kingdom may not begin for 36,000 years. Most Reconstructionists, however, would argue for the Kingdom breaking out within a few generations, possibly even the next.

A general outline of what the reconstructed "Kingdom," or confederation of Biblical theocracies, would look like emerges from the large body of Reconstructionist literature. This society would feature a minimal national government, whose main function would be defense by the armed forces. No social services would be provided outside the church, which would be responsible for "health, education, and welfare." A radically unfettered capitalism (except in so far as it clashed with Biblical Law) would prevail. Society would return to the gold or silver standard or abolish paper money altogether. The public schools would be abolished. Government functions, including taxes, would be primarily at the county level.

Women would be relegated primarily to the home and home schools, and would be banned from government. Indeed, Joseph Morecraft states that the existence of women civil magistrates "is a sign of God's judgment on a culture." Those qualified to vote or hold office would be limited to males from Biblically correct churches.

Democratic values would be replaced by intolerance of many things. R. J. Rushdoony, Reconstructionism's leading proponent,

writes that: "In the name of toleration [in contemporary society] the
believer is asked to associate on a common level of total acceptance
with the atheist, the pervert, the criminal, and the adherents of other
religions." He also advocates various forms of discrimination in the
service of anti–unionism: "an employer has a property right to prefer
whom he will in terms of color, creed, race, or national origin."

The Significance of Reconstructionism

The leaders of Reconstructionism see themselves as playing a
critical role in the history of the church (and of the world). They
envision   themselves   salvaging   Christianity   from   modern
fundamentalism as well as theological liberalism. Because they are
both conservative movement activists and conservative Christians
seeking to pick up where the Puritans left off, they have constructed
a theology that would provide the ideological direction and
underpinning for a new kind of conservatism. It is, as well, a
formidable theology designed to take on all comers. In order to wage a
battle for God's dominion over all aspects of society, they needed a
comprehensive analysis, game plan, and justification. This is what
Reconstructionism provides to a wide range of evangelical and other
would–be conservative Christians. New Right activist Howard
Phillips believes that Reconstructionism, as expressed by Rushdoony
and North, has "provided [evangelical Christian] leaders with the
intellectual self–confidence" to become politically active, whereas
many previously were not. Many conservatives apparently felt that
they had no positive program and had been left in the role of
reactionaries,   just   saying   no   to   modernism   and   liberalism.
Reconstructionism offers a platform that encompasses the religious
and the political.

Many Christian Right thinkers and activists have been
profoundly influenced by Reconstructionism. Among others: the late
Francis Schaeffer, whose book *A Christian Manifesto* was an
influential call to evangelical political action that sold two million
copies, and John Whitehead, President of the Rutherford Institute (a
Christian Right legal action group).

Francis Schaeffer is widely credited with providing the impetus
for Protestant evangelical political action against abortion. For
example, Randall Terry, the founder of Operation Rescue, says: "You
have to read Schaeffer's *Christian Manifesto* if you want to
understand Operation Rescue." Schaeffer, a longtime leader in Rev.
Carl McIntire's splinter denomination, the Bible Presbyterian
Church, was a reader of Reconstructionist literature but has been
reluctant to acknowledge its influence. Indeed, Schaeffer and his
followers specifically rejected the modern application of Old
Testament law.

The Rutherford Institute's John Whitehead was a student of both Schaeffer and Rushdoony, and credits them as the two major influences on his thought. The Rutherford Institute is an influential conservative legal advocacy group which has gained considerable legitimacy. Given this legitimacy, it is not surprising that Whitehead goes to great lengths to deny that he is a Reconstructionist. However, perhaps he doth protest too much. Rushdoony, introducing Whitehead at a Reconstructionist conference, called him a man "chosen by God." Consequently, he said, "There is something very important. . .at work in the ministry of John Whitehead." Rushdoony then spoke of "*our* plans, through Rutherford, to fight the battle against statism and the freedom of Christ's Kingdom."

The Rutherford Institute was founded as a legal project of R. J. Rushdoony's Chalcedon Foundation, with Rushdoony and fellow Chalcedon director Howard Ahmanson on its original board of directors. Whitehead credits Rushdoony with providing the outline for his first book, which he researched in Rushdoony's library.

Coalition on Revival

Whether it is acknowledged or not, Reconstructionism has profoundly influenced the Christian Right. Perhaps its most important role within the Christian Right can be traced to the formation in 1982 of the Coalition on Revival (COR), an umbrella organization which has brokered a series of theological compromises among differing, competing conservative evangelical leaders. These compromises have had a Reconstructionist orientation, thus increasing the reach and influence of Reconstructionism.

Founded and headed by Dr. Jay Grimstead, COR has sought in this way to create a transdenominational theology—a process that has involved hundreds of evangelical scholars, pastors, and activists, and the creation of a series of theological statements epitomized by the "Manifesto of the Christian Church."

The COR leadership has significantly overlapped with the Christian Right, and has included: John Whitehead, Don Wildmon of the American Family Association, televangelists Tim LaHaye and D. James Kennedy, Randall Terry of Operation Rescue, Houston GOP activist Steven Hotze, Rev. Glen Cole of Sacramento, CA, 1993 Virginia GOP Lt. Governor candidate Michael Farris, lobbyist Robert Dugan of the National Association of Evangelicals, former US Congressmen Bill Dannemeyer (R–CA) and Mark Siljander (R–MI), as well as such leading Reconstructionists as R. J. Rushdoony, Gary North, Joseph Morecraft, David Chilton, Gary DeMar of American Vision, and Rus Walton of the Plymouth Rock Foundation.

A major focus of COR has been to reconcile the two main evangelical eschatologies (end–times theologies). Most evangelicals in this century have been pre–millennialists—that is, Christians who generally believe that it is not possible to reform this world until Jesus returns (the Second Coming), which will be followed by a 1,000–year rule of Jesus and the Christians. The other–worldly orientation of pre–millennialism has tended to keep the majority of evangelicals on the political sidelines.

A minority of evangelicals are post–millennialists, believing that it is necessary to build the Kingdom of God in the here and now, before the return of Jesus is possible. Thus, for post–millennialists, Jesus will return when the world has become perfectly Christian, the return crowning 1,000 years of Christian rule. This eschatology urges political involvement and action by evangelicals, who must play a critical role in establishing Christian rule.

COR has sought to establish a "non–quarreling policy" on matters of eschatology, and has emphasized building the Kingdom of God *in so far as it is possible* until Jesus returns. This neatly urges political involvement and action, without anyone having to say how much can actually be accomplished. It reconciles the difference over eschatology that has divided evangelicals, and opens the door to political involvement and action without requiring either of the two sides to abandon its eschatology.

While COR is not an overtly Reconstructionist organization, much of COR doctrine is clearly Reconstructionist in orientation. Among other things, COR calls for exercising Christian dominion over 17 "spheres" of life—including government, education, and economics. COR chief Jay Grimstead has been hard–pressed, in the face of controversy, to explain the role of Reconstructionism in COR, but in a letter to COR members he gave it his best shot: "COR's goals, leadership and documents overlap so much with those of Christian Reconstruction that in the eyes of our enemies we. . .are a monolithic Reconstructionist movement. The fine technical distinctions we make between ourselves," he explains, "are meaningless to these enemies of Christ. To them, anyone who wants to rebuild our society upon Biblical Principles. . .is a Reconstructionist. So we must simply live with the Reconstructionist label, and be grateful to be in the company of brilliant scholars like. . .Gary North, and R. J. Rushdoony."

Grimstead can't help acknowledging the significance of Reconstructionism to the Christian Right: "These men were rethinking the church's mission to the world and how to apply a Christian worldview to every area of life and thought 10 to 20 years before most of the rest of us had yet awakened from our slumbers. We owe them a debt of gratitude for pioneering the way into Biblical world changing, even if we can't accept everything they teach."

Grimstead's fig leafs notwithstanding, a number of COR Steering Committee members have had to drop out because even mere association with Reconstructionism was too hotly controversial.

One evangelical critic observes, however, that those who signed the COR documents or "covenants" had to be "willing to die in the attempt to establish a theonomic political state. This statement makes the COR Manifesto Covenant more than just a covenant; it is a blood covenant, sworn on the life of the signers."

A key, if not exclusively Reconstructionist, doctrine uniting many evangelicals is the "dominion mandate," also called the "cultural mandate." This concept derives from the Book of Genesis and God's direction to "subdue" the earth and exercise "dominion" over it. While much of Reconstructionism, as one observer put it, "dies the death of a thousand qualifications," the commitment to dominion is the theological principle that serves as the uniting force of Christian Right extremism, while people debate the particulars.

Christian Reconstructionism is a stealth theology, spreading its influence throughout the Religious Right. Its analysis of America as a Christian nation and the security of complete control implied in the concept of dominion is understandably appealing to many conservative Christians. Its apocalyptic vision of rule by Biblical Law is a mandate for political involvement. Organizations such as COR and the Rutherford Institute provide political guidance and act as vehicles for growing political aspirations.

No Longer Without Sheep

Reconstructionism had been of interest to few outside the evangelical community until the early 1990s, when its political significance began to emerge. At the same time that the Coalition on Revival provided a catalyst (and a cover) for the discussion, dissemination, and acceptance of Reconstructionist doctrine, these ideas have percolated up through a wide swath of American Protestantism. Nowhere, however, is Reconstructionism (sometimes known as dominionism) having a more dramatic impact than in Pentecostal and charismatic churches.

Pentecostalists, best known for speaking in tongues and practicing faith healing and prophesy—known as "gifts of the spirit"—include televangelists Jimmy Swaggart and Oral Roberts. Among well–known charismatics are Pat Robertson and Supreme Court Justice Clarence Thomas. Historically, Pentecostals have been apolitical for the most part. However, since 1980 much of Pentecostalism has begun to adopt aspects of Reconstructionist or dominion theology. This is not an accident.

Reconstructionists have sought to graft their theology onto the experientially oriented, and often theologically amorphous, Pentecostal and charismatic religious traditions. Following a 1987 Reconstructionist/ Pentecostal theological meeting, Joseph Morecraft exclaimed: "God is blending Presbyterian theology with charismatic zeal into a force that cannot be stopped!"

Gary North claims that "the ideas of the Reconstructionists have penetrated into Protestant circles that for the most part are unaware of the original source of the theological ideas that are beginning to transform them." North describes the "three major legs of the Reconstructionist movement" as "the Presbyterian oriented educators, the Baptist school headmasters and pastors, and the charismatic telecommunications system."

What this means is that hundreds of thousands of Pentecostals and charismatic Christians, as well as many fundamentalist Baptists, have moved out of the apolitical camp. Many have thrown themselves into political work—not merely as voters, but as ideologically driven activists, bringing a reconstructed "Biblical world view" to bear on their area of activism.

This is probably the lasting contribution of Reconstructionism. Whether it is Operation Rescue activists called to anti–abortion work because of Francis Schaeffer's books, or Pentecostals who responded to the politicizing ministry and electoral ambitions of Pat Robertson during the 1970s and 1980s, the politicization of Pentecostalism is one of the major stories of modern American politics.

Indeed, Robertson has been pivotal in this process, mobilizing Pentecostals and charismatics into politics through his books, TV programs, Regent University, the 1988 presidential campaign, and his political organizations—first the Freedom Council in the 1980s and then the Christian Coalition.

Gary North and others see opportunities for Reconstructionism to build its influence through an activist response to crises in established institutions, from the public schools to democracy itself. This "decentralist" activism is not necessarily independent or "grassroots." Political brushfires are "a fundamental tool of resistance" observes North, "but it takes a combination of centralized strategy, and local mobilization and execution." This is precisely what we are beginning to see clearly in the contemporary politics of the Christian Right. From the lawsuits brought by the Rutherford Institute and the American Center for Law and Justice to stealth takeovers of school boards, the effort is to subvert the normal functioning of society in order to make room for the growth of theocratic evangelicalism.

North sees a special role for the Christian Broadcasting Network (CBN) TV satellite, as the epitome of the political effectiveness of televangelists. He appreciates CBN's ability to magnify local battles, and communicate them to a national audience. "Without a means of publicizing a crisis," writes North, "few pastors would take a stand." Thus, North sees CBN as a key component in increasing the impact of decentralized "brushfire wars" in which the battles over abortion, pornography, zoning for Christian schools, etc., happen in many places at once to strain the system.

Reconstructionism & the Christian Right

Reconstructionism has played an important role in shaping the contemporary Christian Right, as indicated by the number of Christian Right leaders involved in COR. Reconstructionism's influence is also pronounced in another major hub of the Christian Right: the multifaceted organization of Pat Robertson. Although it denies a Reconstructionist orientation, the Robertson organization is doing exactly what Gary North describes. Robertson's Christian Coalition, for instance, follows a clearly decentralist political plan, directed and encouraged by highly centralized media, educational, and political units.

The Christian Coalition, forged from Robertson's mailing lists and his 1988 presidential campaign, has become the largest and most politically significant formation within the Religious Right. Its comprehensive, locally focused efforts to take over the Republican Party "from the bottom up" and to run "stealth candidates" for local offices have been widely reported and discussed.

Robertson himself seems to lack the long–term vision of Reconstructionist thinkers, but he is clearly driven by a short–term militant "dominion" mandate—the mandate that Christians "Christianize" the country's social and political institutions. He offers a fevered vision of power and "spiritual warfare," perhaps even physical conflict with the forces of Satan in the near future. "The world is going to be ours," he once confided, "but not without a battle, [not] without bloodshed." At a 1994 Christian Coalition national strategy conference, Robertson railed against "Satanic forces," declaring: "We are not coming up against just human beings to beat them in elections. We're going to be coming up against spiritual warfare. And if we're not aware of what we're fighting, we will lose." No longer the exclusive revolutionary vision of Christian Reconstructionist extremists, dominionism has achieved virtual hegemony over many forms of Christian fundamentalism. Historian Garry Wills sees dominionist doctrine not only in those "thorough and consistent dominionists, the followers of Rousas John Rushdoony, who are called Christian Reconstructionists," but also clearly present in Pat Robertson's book *The Secret Kingdom*.

Robertson works not only dominionism, but Old Testament Biblical law into his books. In *The New World Order*, Robertson writes that "there is no way that government can operate successfully unless led by godly men and women operating under the laws of the God of Jacob." Impatient with Robertson's public equivocations,

Reconstructionist author Gary DeMar describes Robertson as an "operational Reconstructionist."

Reconstructionist influences are also evident at Robertson's Regent University. For example, the long–time Dean of the Law School, Herb Titus, though not himself a Reconstructionist, has used Rushdoony's book in his introductory Law course. Texts by North and Rushdoony have been used for years in the School of Public Policy, where Reconstructionist Joseph Kickasola teaches. The library has extensive holdings of Reconstructionist literature and tapes.

Regent University board chair Dee Jepson is a longtime COR Steering Committee member. She was an active advocate for the school's change of name from Christian Broadcast Network University to Regent University, arguing that "Regent" better reflected its mission. Robertson explained that a "regent" is one who governs in the absence of a sovereign and that Regent U. trains students to rule, until Jesus, the absent sovereign, returns. Robertson says Regent U. is "a kingdom institution" for grooming "God's representatives on the face of the earth."

Dee Jepson, in addition to her membership on the COR Steering Committee, is married to former Senator Roger Jepson (R–Iowa), who signed a fundraising letter for Rushdoony's Chalcedon Foundation in 1982.

The Conspiracy Factor

One aspect of Reconstructionism's appeal to the Christian Right is that it provides a unifying framework for conspiracy theories. Gary North explains that: "There is one conspiracy, Satan's, and ultimately it must fail. Satan's supernatural conspiracy is *the* conspiracy; all other visible conspiracies are merely outworkings of this supernatural conspiracy." Pat Robertson makes a similar argument in his book *The New World Order*, which all new members of Robertson's Christian Coalition receive.

R. J. Rushdoony states that "The view of history as conspiracy...is a basic aspect of the perspective of orthodox Christianity." A conspiratorial view of history is a consistent ingredient of Christian Right ideology in the United States, and is often used to explain the failure of conservative Christian denominations with millennial ambitions to achieve or sustain political power. The blame for this is most often assigned to the Masons, particularly an 18th–century Masonic group called the Illuminati, and, ultimately, to Satan.

Panicked Congregationalist clergy, faced with disestablishment of state churches (and thus their political power) in the 18th and 19th centuries, fanned the flames of anti–Masonic hatred with conspiracy theories. Pat Robertson claims Masonic conspiracies are out to destroy Christianity and thwart Christian rule. Throughout *The New World Order* Robertson refers to freemasonry as a Satanic conspiracy, along with the New Age movement. The distortion of reality that can follow from such views is well represented by Robertson's assertion that former Presidents Woodrow Wilson, Jimmy Carter, and George Bush are unwitting agents of Satan because they supported international groups of nations such as the United Nations.

Another example of Christian Right conspiracy theory is the writing of Dr. Stanley Monteith, a California activist who is a member of the Christian Coalition and the Coalition on Revival. He is a leading anti–gay spokesperson for the Christian Right. In his book, *AIDS, The Unnecessary Epidemic: America Under Siege*, Monteith argues that AIDS is the result of a conspiracy of gays, humanists, and other "sinister forces which work behind the scenes attempting to destroy our society."

Monteith's book is published by a self–described Reconstructionist, Dalmar D. Dennis (who is also a member of the National Council of the John Birch Society). Monteith's actions underscore his words. At a conference of the anti–abortion group Human Life International, Dr. Monteith, who insists he is not anti-Semitic, shared a literature table with a purveyor of crude anti–Semitic books, as well as books claiming to expose the Masonic conspiracy.

The Wrath of Morecraft

If the Christian Right ever came to power, it's anyone's guess what would actually occur. But it may be instructive to examine what has happened as theocratically informed factions advance locally. In Cobb County, Georgia, for example, where the powerful County Commission is controlled by the Christian Right, homosexuality has been banned, arts funding cut off, and abortion services through the county public employee health plan banned. These actions by the Cobb County Commission made national news in 1993.

Rev. Joseph Morecraft, whose very energetic and politically active Reconstructionist Chalcedon Presbyterian Church draws most members from Marietta, Georgia, the Cobb County seat, provided a clear Reconstructionist view of these events. Asked at the time where he saw Biblical law advancing, he cited "the county where I live," where "they passed a law...that homosexuals are not welcome in that county, because homosexuality was against the community standards. The next week," he continued, "they voted on whether or not they should use tax money of the county to support art—immoral, pornographic art, so they make the announcement, not only are we not going to use tax monies in this county to sponsor pornograph⁻

art, we're not going to use tax money to sponsor any art, because that's not the role of civil government. And last week," he concluded, "[they voted] that no tax money in Cobb County will be spent on abortions."

Such views pale before Morecraft's deeper views of life and government. In his book, and especially when speaking at the 1993 Biblical World View and Christian Education Conference, Morecraft discussed with relish the police power of the state. His belief in the persecution of nonbelievers and those who are insufficiently orthodox is crystal clear.

Morecraft described democracy as "mob rule," and stated that the purpose of "civil government" is to "terrorize evil doers. . . to be an avenger!" he shouted, "To bring down the wrath of God to bear on all those who practice evil!"

"And how do you terrorize an evil doer?" he asked. "You enforce Biblical law!" The purpose of government, he said, is "to protect the church of Jesus Christ," and, "Nobody has the right to worship on this planet any other God than Jehovah. And therefore the state does not have the responsibility to defend anybody's pseudo–right to worship an idol!"

"There ain't no such thing" as religious pluralism, he declared. Further, "There has never been such a condition in the history of mankind. There is no such place now. There never will be."

Transcendent Acts

Meanwhile, perhaps the most significant accomplishment of the Reconstructionist movement has been the forging of an ideological pole (and an accompanying political strategy) in American politics, a pole by which the Christian Right will continue to measure itself. Some embrace it completely; others reject it. As recently as the early 1990s, most evangelicals viewed Reconstructionists as a band of theological misfits without a following. All that has changed, along with the numbers and character of the Christian Right. The world of evangelicalism and, arguably, American politics generally will not be the same.

Among those Reconstructionists who have already moved into positions of significant power and influence are two directors of R. J. Rushdoony's Chalcedon Foundation; philanthropist Howard Ahmanson and political consultant Wayne C. Johnson epitomize the political strategy of the new Christian Right.

Heir to a large fortune, Howard Ahmanson is an important California power broker who has said, "My purpose is total integration of Biblical law into our lives." He bankrolls Christian Right groups and political campaigns, largely through an unincorporated entity called the Fieldstead Company, which has, for example, been a major contributor to Paul Weyrich's Free Congress Foundation. Fieldstead has also co–published, with Crossway Books, a series of Reconstructionist–oriented books called *Turning Point: Christian Worldview Series*, which is widely available in Christian bookstores.

Ahmanson and his wife have spent hundreds of thousands of dollars supporting California political candidates, as well as supporting the 1993 California school voucher initiative and the 1992 voucher initiative in Colorado. He has also teamed up with a small group of conservative businessmen, notably Rob Hurtt of Container Supply Corporation, to form a series of political action committees. The direct donations from these PACs and the personal contributions of Ahmanson and Hurtt, coupled with those of other PACs to which the group substantially contributed, amounted to nearly $3 million to 19 right–wing candidates for the California State Senate and various other conservative causes in 1992. A dozen candidates backed by the Christian Right won. Ahmanson himself is a member of the GOP state central committee, along with many other Christian Rightists, who have gained power by systematically taking over California GOP county committees.

A political operative named Wayne Johnson, who had been an architect of California's 1990 term limits initiative, managed the campaigns of several Ahmanson–backed candidates in 1992. The practical impact of term limits is to remove the advantage of incumbency (both Democratic and Republican) which the extreme Christian Right is prepared to exploit, having created a disciplined voting bloc and the resources to finance candidates.

At a Reconstructionist conference in 1983, Johnson outlined an early version of the strategy we see operating in California today. According to Johnson, the principal factor in determining victory in California state legislative races is incumbency, by a factor of 35 to 1. The legislature at the time was dominated by Democrats (and Republicans unacceptable to conservatives). The key for the Christian Right was to be able to: 1) remove or minimize the advantage of incumbency, and 2) create a disciplined voting bloc from which to run candidates in Republican primaries, where voter turn out was low and scarce resources could be put to maximum effect. Since the early 1990s, Christian Rightists have been able to do both. Thanks to Ahmanson, Hurtt, and others, they also now have the financing to be competitive.

Since the mid–1970s, the extreme Christian Right, under the tutelage of then–State Senator H. L Richardson, targeted open seats and would finance only challengers, not incumbents. By 1983, they were able to increase the number of what Johnson called "reasonably decent guys" in the legislature from four to 27. At the Third Annual Northwest Conference for Reconstruction in 1983, Johnson stated that he believed they may achieve "political hegemony. . .in this generation." In 1994, they were not far from that goal. Rob Hurtt won a 1993 open seat by–election for State Senate. In 1994, State Senator Hurtt was also the chairman of the Republican campaign committee for the State Legislature, an important power brokering role for a freshman State Senator. The GOP, led by conservative Christians, was only four seats away from majority control in 1994.

A Whole Generation of Gary Norths

Still, it is in the next generation that most Reconstructionists hope to seize the future. "All long–term social change," declares Gary North, "comes from the successful efforts of one or another struggling organizations to capture the minds of a hard core of future leaders, as well as the respect of a wider population." The key to this, they believe, lies with the Christian school and the home schooling movement, both deeply influenced by Reconstructionism.

Unsurprisingly, Reconstructionists seek to abolish public schools, which they see as a critical component in the promotion of a secular world view. It is this secular world view with which they declare themselves to be at war. "Until the vast majority of Christians pull their children out of the public schools," writes Gary North, "there will be no possibility of creating a theocratic republic."

Among the top Reconstructionists in education politics is Robert Thoburn of Fairfax Christian School in Fairfax, Virginia. Thoburn advocates that Christians run for school board, while keeping their own children out of public schools. "Your goal" (once on the board), he declares, "must be to sink the ship." While not every conservative Christian who runs for school board shares this goal, those who do will, as Thoburn advises, probably keep it to themselves. Thoburn's book, *The Children Trap*, is a widely used sourcebook for Christian Right attacks on public education.

Joseph Morecraft, who also runs a school, said in 1987: "I believe the children in the Christian schools of America are the Army that is going to take the future. Right now. . .the Christian Reconstruction movement is made up of a few preachers, teachers, writers, scholars, publishing houses, editors of magazines, and it's growing quickly. But I expect a massive acceleration of this movement in about 25 or 30 years, when those kids that are now in Christian schools have graduated and taken their places in American society, and moved into places of influence and power."

Similarly, the Christian "home schooling" movement is part of the long–term revolutionary strategy of Reconstructionism. One of the principal home schooling curricula is provided by Reconstructionist Paul Lindstrom of Christian Liberty Academy (CLA) in Arlington Heights, Illinois. CLA claims that it serves about

20,000 families. Its 1994 curriculum included a book on "Biblical Economics" by Gary North. Home schooling advocate Christopher Klicka, who has been deeply influenced by R. J. Rushdoony, writes: "Sending our children to the public school violates nearly every Biblical principle. . . .It is tantamount to sending our children to be trained by the enemy." He claims that the public schools are Satan's choice. Klicka also advocates religious self–segregation and advises Christians not to affiliate with non–Christian home schoolers in any way. "The differences I am talking about," declares Klicka, "have resulted in wars and martyrdom in the not too distant past." According to Klicka, who is an attorney with the Home School Legal Defense Association, "as an organization, and as individuals, we are committed to promote the cause of Christ and His Kingdom."

Estimates of the number of home schooling families vary enormously. Conservatively, there are certainly over 100,000. Klicka estimates that 85–90 percent of home schoolers are doing so "based on their religious convictions." "In effect," he concludes, "these families are operating religious schools in their homes." A fringe movement no longer, Christian home schoolers are being actively recruited by the arch–conservative Hillsdale College.

A Covert Kingdom

Much has been made of the "stealth tactics" practiced by the Christian Right. Whereas the Moral Majority, led by Jerry Falwell, was overt about its Christian agenda, many contemporary Christian Rightists have lowered their religious profile or gone under cover. In fact, these tactics have been refined for years by the Reconstructionist movement, as Robert Thoburn's education strategy suggests. Gary North proposed stealth tactics more than a decade ago in *The Journal of Christian Reconstruction* (1981), urging "infiltration" of government to help "smooth the transition to Christian political leadership. . . .Christians must begin to organize politically within the present party structure, and they must begin to infiltrate the existing institutional order."

Similar stealth tactics have epitomized the resurgence of the Christian Right, as groups like Citizens for Excellence in Education and the Christian Coalition have quietly backed candidates who generally avoided running as overtly "Christian" candidates. The Christian Coalition actually proposed something similar to Gary North's notion of "infiltration" when its 1992 "County Action Plan" for Pennsylvania advised that "You should never mention the name Christian Coalition in Republican circles." The goal, apparently, is to facilitate becoming "directly involved in the local Republican Central Committee so that you are an insider. This way," continues the manual, "you can get a copy of the local committee rules and a feel for who is in the current Republican Committee." The next step is to recruit conservative Christians to occupy vacant party posts or to run against moderates who "put the Republican Party ahead of principle."

Antonio Rivera, a New York Christian Coalition political advisor, suggested similar ideas at a 1992 Christian Coalition meeting. While urging that Coalition members seek to place themselves in influential positions, he advised that "You keep your personal views to yourself until the Christian community is ready to rise up, and then wow! They're gonna be devastated!" Some leaders have now publicly renounced "stealth" tactics.

Central to the Christian Right's strategy is to exploit the national pattern of low voter participation by turning out their constituents in a strategically disciplined fashion and in greater proportion than the rest of the population. An important vehicle for achieving this goal is the ideology of Christian Reconstructionism or its stripped–down root, dominionism, which at once deepens the political motivation of their constituency and widens that constituency by systematically mobilizing a network of churches, many of which were politically uninvolved until the early 1990s.

Much has been written about the success of Pat Robertson's Christian Coalition in accomplishing these goals. But it could be argued that the Christian Coalition would not have been possible without Reconstructionism, and that Operation Rescue would not have been possible without the Reconstructionist–influenced philosoper Francis Schaeffer. In the 1970s, Pat Robertson was an apolitical charismatic televangelist, and Randall Terry a would–be rock n' roll star.

Conclusion

Christian Reconstructionism's ultimate moment may or may not arrive; however it has had tremendous influence as a catalyst for an historic shift in American religion and politics. Christian colleges and bookstores are full of Reconstructionist material. The proliferation of this material and influence is likely to continue. Christian Reconstructionism is largely an underground, underestimated movement of ideas, the rippling surface of which is the political movement known as the Christian Right.

Frederick Clarkson is an author and lecturer who has written extensively on right–wing religious groups from the Christian Coalition to the Unification Church. He is co–author of *Challenging the Christian Right: The Activist's Handbook*, (Institute for First Amendment Studies, 1992), and is writing a new book titled *Eternal Hostility: The Struggle Between Democracy and Theocracy in the United States*, (Common Courage Press, 1996). This article originally appeared in the March and June 1994 issues of *The Public Eye*. © 1995, Frederick Clarkson.

Promise Keepers
Christian Soldiers for Theocracy

<u>Russ Bellant</u>

Promise Keepers is a rapidly growing Christian men's movement that in 1994 rallied about 300,000 men, filling six football stadia in colorful displays of male "spiritual renewal." The group's plan to double the number of participants and stadium events in 1995 seems realistic. Promise Keepers events in Detroit and Los Angeles in the early part of 1995 drew over 72,000 each. While projecting an image of spirituality, leaders of Promise Keepers seem to be bent on gaining social and political power. In the world of Promise Keepers, men are to submit to a cell group that in turn is closely controlled by a national hierarchy. Most important, women are to submit absolutely to their husbands or fathers.

Promise Keepers may be the strongest, most organized effort to capitalize on male backlash in the country during the 1990s. Conceived by University of Colorado football coach Bill McCartney in 1990, Promise Keepers says men should "reclaim" authority from their wives—to whom they have supposedly ceded too much. Bill McCartney's goal in 1990 was to fill a sports stadium with Christian men to exhort them into his philosophy. The following year, he attracted 4,200 men to a basketball arena; 22,000 men came to Boulder's Folsom Stadium in 1992, followed by 50,000 men in 1993. Promoted by powerful elements of the Religious Right, Promise Keepers filled six stadia in 1994; the largest event was in the Hoosier Dome in Indianapolis, which drew 62,000 men. The only women present were custodians and concession stand workers.

Don't Ask, Take

The manifesto of the movement is *Seven Promises of a Promise Keeper*, a book published for the group by James Dobson's organization, Focus on the Family. Evangelist Tony Brown, in his contributing essay, explains how to deal with women.

"I can hear you saying, 'I want to be a spiritually pure man. Where do I start?' The first thing you do," Brown explains, "is sit down with your wife and say something like this: 'Honey, I've made a terrible mistake. I've given you my role. I gave up leading this family, and I forced you to take my place. Now I must reclaim that role.' Don't misunderstand what I'm saying here. I'm not suggesting that you ask for your role back, I'm urging you to *take it back.*" [Emphasis in the original.]

While insisting to male readers that there is to be "no compromise" on authority, he suggests that women readers submit for the "survival of our culture."

Total Submission

While serving as an assistant football coach at the University of Michigan in Ann Arbor, Bill McCartney encountered and was deeply influenced by the Word of God (WOG) community. McCartney has said that WOG leader Jim Berlucci is one of the two men who most influenced his life. WOG, a select and insular group of about 1,600 adults, practiced "shepherding/discipleship," which required total submission to a person called the "head." Members were required to submit their schedules in advance and account for every hour of every day. Marriage partner, movie choices, jobs, and other decisions also had to be approved by this leader.

Members who questioned authority, or women who questioned their extreme submission to men, were subject to often traumatic "exorcisms." WOG members were trained to see the world with suspicion and contempt—as an enemy. They believed that they were specially chosen by God to fight the Antichrist.

When McCartney was hired by the University of Colorado, WOG introduced him to the WOG–linked "Vineyard" church, which has a parish in Boulder. Vineyard churches emphasize "signs and wonders" and "prophecy." Vineyard leader John Wimber calls their work "power evangelism" and describes his followers as "self–conscious members of God's army, sent to do battle against the forces of the kingdom of darkness." "One is either in God's Kingdom," Wimber insists, "or Satan's."

The Purpose of War

McCartney's pastor at the Boulder Valley Vineyard, Rev. James Ryle, whom McCartney says is the other major influence in his life, conducts a "prophetic" ministry and participates in conferences with men who claim to be prophets in the first-century sense of the term. Ryle believes Promise Keepers, of which he is a board member, is the fulfillment of the Biblically prophesied end-time army described in the Book of Joel—a terrifying army from which there is no escape. "Never have 300,000 men come together throughout human history," he declared, "except for the purpose of war." He says he has a vision of Promise Keepers purging America of secularism, which he considers "an abortion" of godliness.

Ryle spoke in 1994 at a secret Colorado conclave to plan anti-gay/lesbian electoral strategies. He said, "America is in the midst of a cultural revolution, which has poised our nation precariously on the brink of moral chaos, which is caused by what I am referring to as the crisis of homosexuality."

While Promise Keepers is not a political force in its own right in 1995, McCartney leads by example. He has repeatedly attacked reproductive rights, and he campaigned for the 1992 anti-gay Amendment 2 ballot initiative as a member of the board of Colorado for Family Values, the sponsor of the initiative.

His rally addresses have been uncompromising. "Take the nation for Jesus Christ," he directed in 1992. The following year he said, "What you are about to hear is God's word to the men of this nation. We are going to war as of tonight. We have divine power; that is our weapon. We will not compromise. Wherever truth is at risk, in the schools or legislature, we are going to contend for it. We will win."

No less militant is Promise Keepers co-founder Dave Wardell, who told *The Denver Post*, "We want our nation to return to God. We're drawing a line in the sand here. . . . There has already been controversy about abortion and homosexuality. I hope there won't be any physical confrontations. . . . "

Something Like Punching Your Lights Out

Promise Keepers' national staff has grown rapidly from a handful in 1990 to 150, with a $22 million budget in 1995. But its significance is primarily at the local and church levels.

Promise Keepers urges men to form "accountability" groups of no more than five members, within which they are expected to submit all aspects of their lives to review and rebuke. Each mem-

ber must answer any probes concerning his marriage, family, fi-
nances, sexuality, or business activity.

Such cells, usually operating within a church or para-church
group, are led by a "Point Man" who answers to an "Ambassador"
who reports to headquarters in Boulder. Decisions about local or
state activity are ultimately made in Boulder.

"All of our success here is contingent upon men taking part
in small groups when they return home," Promise Keepers
spokesman Steve Chavis told *Christianity Today*. Less elegantly,
Dave Wardell, the national coordinator for local leaders, explains,
"I can go home and maybe still be the same guy after a conference. But if I have another guy calling up, holding me accountable, asking, 'How are you treating your wife? Are you still
cheating on your income taxes? Are you looking at your secretar-
ies with lust?' it makes a difference. I don't think a woman would
get in my face, go toe to toe with a guy, whereas a guy could tell
me, 'I don't like it. And if you don't listen to me, I'll punch your
lights out.' Something like that."

These principles and structure, which are similar to the
shepherding/discipleship model of the Word of God, would take
years to implement and introduce a highly disciplined group.

Most men drawn to Promise Keepers have probably never
heard of shepherding/discipleship (which, in 1995, was still not
widely known even within the evangelical community) and may
be deeply offended if they experience the degree of manipulation
and control (to which they may be "submitting" themselves and
their families) that has occurred in many shepherding/disciple
situations.

Trojan Horses?

Top Christian Right leaders in 1994 joined Dobson in promoting Promise Keepers. These have notably included Pat Robertson
of the Christian Coalition and 700 Club, D. James Kennedy of
Coral Ridge Ministries, and Bill Bright of Campus Crusade for
Christ.

Dobson, who along with Robertson, Kennedy, and Bright, is a
member of the secretive, reactionary–right Council for National
Policy, is a central figure in Promise Keepers. Not only is he the
publisher of the main text of the movement, he is a featured
speaker at Promise Keeper events, which in turn sell tapes of his
speeches.

Focus on the Family's network of political action groups,
called Community Impact Committees, function much like Promise Keepers' cell groups within conservative churches. Largely
invisible to individuals outside these churches, these committees

are organized at the state and regional levels and controlled from Colorado.

Both Dobson's Community Impact Committees and the Promise Keepers cells are potential Trojan horses within churches and denominations, creating conflicting loyalties and lines of authority.

Leaders of Promise Keepers, in particular, come out of a movement that sees denominations as inhibiting evangelism and revivalism. Indicative of this is its use of Strang Communications to publish *New Man* magazine. Strang's *Charisma* magazine is contemptuous of traditional denominations. The senior editor of Strang's *New Ministries* magazine, Jack Hayford, is also on the board of Promise Keepers.

Promise Keepers scheduled more than a dozen rallies for purity, fidelity, and possibly social and political dominion in 1995. Promise Keepers had planned for over a year to draw one million men to a march in Washington, DC, just prior to the November 1996 elections.

Though postponed, the plans were evidently modeled after the Christian Right rallies called Washington for Jesus, which had similar backing and were held during the presidential elections in 1980 and 1988.

Considering the high–level backing by the leadership of the Christian Right, and the anti–democratic views of Promise Keepers' leaders, this movement ought not be underestimated.

Russ Bellant is a Detroit–based author whose books include *Old Nazis, the New Right, and the Republican Party: Domestic Fascist Networks and Their Effect on US Cold War Politics* (South End Press, 1991) and *The Coors Connection: How Coors Family Philanthropy Undermines Democratic Pluralism* (South End Press, 1991). He was a founding member of the *Public Eye* network. This article first appeared in *Front Lines Research*, Vol. 1, Number 5, May 1995 issue. Footnotes appeared in the original and can be ordered through Political Research Associates. © 1995, Russ Bellant.

Constructing Homophobia
Colorado's Right–Wing Attack on Homosexuals

> *History, despite its wrenching pain,*
> *Cannot be unlived, but if faced*
> *With courage, need not be lived again.*
> "On the Pulse of Morning,"
> Maya Angelou

Jean Hardisty

An eerie unease hangs in the air in Colorado. For lesbians, gay men, and bisexuals, nagging questions pervade everyday life: did the kindly person who just gave me her parking place vote for Amendment 2? Did my landlord vote for the amendment, knowing that I am gay? Will gay rights be pushed back to the days before Stonewall? Who or what is behind this hate?

Amendment 2 is a ballot initiative that seeks to amend the Colorado Constitution. The amendment was passed by a majority of Colorado voters in November 1992, and was to take effect on January 15, 1993. The American Civil Liberties Union, Lambda Legal Defense Fund, the cities of Boulder, Aspen, and Denver, and individual plaintiffs joined forces under the leadership of attorney Jean Dubofsky, a former Colorado Supreme Judicial Court judge, and filed a motion in Denver District Court seeking to enjoin the governor and state of Colorado from enforcing Amendment 2. On January 15, 1993, Judge Jeffrey Bayless granted a preliminary injunction, giving the plaintiffs the first victory in a legal struggle over the constitutionality of Amendment 2. That injunction was later made permanent, but was then appealed to the US Supreme Court.

Amendment 2 reads as follows:

> Neither the State of Colorado, through any of its branches or departments, nor any of its agencies, political subdivisions, municipalities or school districts, shall enact, adopt or enforce any statute, regulation, ordinance or policy whereby homosexual, lesbian, or bisexual orientation, conduct, practices or relationships shall constitute or otherwise be the basis of, or entitle any person or class of persons to have or claim any minority status, quota preferences, protected status or claim of discrimination. This Section of the [Colorado] Constitution shall be self–executing.

Historical Background to Colorado's Amendment 2

The gay rights movement in the US is often traced to June 27, 1969, in New York City, when police raided a Greenwich Village bar, the Stonewall Inn, and bar patrons rebelled in protest. Seven years later, in 1976, in Dade County, Florida, Anita Bryant led the first religious campaign against gay rights. Bryant's campaign (run by Bryant, her husband Bob Green, and a political operative named Ed Rowe, who went on to head the Church League of America briefly and later Christian Mandate) was in opposition to a vote by the Dade County commissioners to prohibit discrimination against gay men and lesbians in housing, public accommodation, and employment. Bryant promoted a successful referendum to repeal the commissioners' vote, and her campaign gained strength and notoriety.

In 1977, Anita Bryant inspired a similar campaign in California, where State Senator John Briggs, who had worked with Bryant in Miami, sponsored the "California Defend Our Children Initiative," a binding initiative on the general election ballot in November 1978. The initiative provided for charges against school teachers and others advocating, encouraging, or publicly and "indiscreetly" engaging in homosexuality. It prohibited the hiring and required the firing of homosexuals if the school board deemed them unfit. This was in reaction to a 1975 California law preventing local school boards from firing teachers for homosexuality. California Defend Our Children, the organizing group supporting the initiative, was chaired by State Senator John Briggs. Rev. Louis Sheldon, now head of the Anaheim–based organization Traditional Values, was executive director. The initiative failed, but Rev. Louis Sheldon would remain extremely active in anti–homosexual organizing. That same year, David A. Noebel, later to head Summit Ministries of Colorado, published *The Homosexual Revolution*, which he dedicated to Anita Bryant.

Bryant's anti–homosexual campaign ended in 1979 with the collapse of her two organizations, Anita Bryant Ministries and Protect America's Children, which were hampered by a lack of political sophistication. Contemporary techniques in influencing the political system—direct mail, computer technology, religious television ministries—were not available to Bryant. Although US history is dotted with right–wing movements led by preachers (such as Father Charles Coughlin, who used radio to enormous effect), at that time few religious fundamentalists and evangelicals were interested in the political sphere. Bryant herself was plagued by personal problems, such as divorce, and her organizations were unable to respond effectively to a boycott mounted against Florida's orange industry, for which Bryant was a major spokesperson. Her organizations collapsed because they were unable to expand their base through direct mail and fundraising, to use the media to build that base, or to use the political system for their own religious ends. With the creation of the New Right at the end of the 1970s, a political movement was born that incorporated conservative fundamentalists and evangelicals as full partners. Now there were tremendous political resources available to the Religious Right, and the success and influence of religious fundamentalists in the spheres of public policy and popular opinion improved dramatically.

Under the benign influence of the Reagan Administration, the New Right and its Religious Right component flourished. Several major leaders emerged, their individual fortunes rising and falling, but their collective political clout reaching into new spheres of influence, especially the political sphere. A focus of attention that emerged with the advent of the New Right was a rollback of gains made by the gay rights movement.

The Second Right–Wing Anti–Homosexual Campaign

The "second" anti–homosexual campaign, born within the New Right in the early 1980s, has been a far more sophisticated one. It has been planned at the national level, carried out by at least 15 large national organizations using the most refined computer technology, showing an understanding of the political system, and therefore exerting influence only dreamed of by the first movement.

The effects of this new sophistication are:

• to make local anti–homosexual campaigns appear to be exclusively grassroots efforts, when they are guided by major national organizations;

• to increase the effect of each New Right organization's efforts by building networks and coalitions among the organizations and by coordinating political campaigns;

• to camouflage the religious content of the organizing and create the more secular theme of "defense of the family";

• to pursue the anti–homosexual campaign under the slogan "no special rights," despite that slogan's inaccuracy.

The Anti–Homosexual Campaign of the Early 1980s

The opening of the second anti–homosexual campaign can be traced to three events:

• the 1982 publication of Enrique T. Rueda's massive *The Homosexual Network* (Old Greenwich, CT: Devin Adair Co.);

• the onset of the AIDS epidemic, which in its earliest days in the US, was almost exclusively confined to the gay male community. (For an account of the earliest days of the AIDS epidemic, see Randy Shilts, *And The Band Played On* (New York: St. Martin's Press, 1987.);

• the work of anti–gay activist Dr. Paul Cameron, director in the early 1980s of the Institute for the Scientific Investigation of Sexuality in Lincoln, Nebraska, and now chairperson of the Family Research Institute in Washington, DC. Paul Weyrich's Free Congress Foundation would prove an early supporter of Dr. Cameron: FCF distributed copies of Cameron's "Model Sexuality Statute" in 1983.

Enrique Rueda's massive book, *The Homosexual Network*, is a thorough examination of the organizations, activities, and ideology of the gay rights movement. The book does not discuss AIDS, and much of its critique of homosexual organizations is directed at their liberalism. Rueda, a native of Cuba and a Catholic theologian, is also interested in the moral dimension of homosexuality and its offense against the church.

In 1987, the Free Congress Foundation, which had sponsored Rueda's book, developed a new condensation that updated the critique of homosexuality to include the AIDS crisis. This book, *Gays, AIDS and You*, by Michael Schwartz and Enrique Rueda, stands as a seminal work in the right's analysis of homosexuality in the context of the AIDS crisis. A quote from the introduction illustrates the significance of this book to an understanding of Colorado's Amendment 2:

> For the homosexual movement is nothing less than an attack on our traditional, pro–family values. And now this movement is using the AIDS crisis to pursue its political agenda. This in turn, threatens not only our values but our lives. . . .
>
> They are loved by God as much as anyone else. This we believe while affirming the disordered nature of their sexual condition and the evil nature of the acts this condition leads to, and while fully committed to the proposition that homosexuals should *not* be entitled to special treatment under the law. That would be tantamount to rewarding evil.

It is significant that Rueda wrote his two important critiques of the gay rights movement at the suggestion of, and under the sponsorship of, Paul Weyrich and the Free Congress Foundation, which Weyrich directs. FCF's early and important work on the issue of homosexuality foreshadowed a national campaign to highlight homosexuality as a threat to the well–being of Americans.

Paul Weyrich is a founder and central leader of the New Right. He was more astute than many in the New Right in his early appreciation of the potential of anti–gay themes in building the success of the New Right. But he was not alone in understanding the appeal of this issue in right–wing organizing. As early as 1978, Tim LaHaye, "family counselor," husband of Beverly LaHaye (head of Concerned Women for America), and prominent leader in both the pro–family and Religious Right components of the New Right, wrote *The Unhappy Gays* (Wheaton, IL: Tyndale House Publishers, 1978).

In 1983, Jerry Falwell's Moral Majority sent out at least three mailings that highlighted the threats of homosexuality and AIDS.

In a similar vein, Robert G. Grant's organization, Christian Voice, used the threat of homosexuality as a major theme in a fundraising letter that began, "I am rushing you this urgent letter because the children in your neighborhood are in danger."

Phyllis Schlafly, head of Eagle Forum and grande dame of the pro–family movement, made heavy use of the accusation of lesbianism in her early 1980s attacks on Equal Rights Amendment organizers. She argued that the ERA would promote gay rights, leading, for example, to the legitimization of same–sex marriages, the protection of gay and lesbian rights in the military, the protection of the rights of persons with AIDS, and the voiding of sodomy laws.

Dr. Paul Cameron is a tireless anti–gay activist who has played an important roll in encouraging punitive measures against people with AIDS. In 1983, the American Psychological Association dropped Cameron from its membership rolls "for a violation of the Preamble to the *Ethical Principles of Psychologists*." Despite being discredited by reputable social scientists, Cameron has served as an "expert" on homosexuality at numerous right–wing and Religious Right conferences, and was hired as a consultant on AIDS by California Assemblyman William Dannemeyer.

As the 1980s unfolded and the New Right achieved substantial gains on economic, military, and foreign policy issues, its Religious Right and pro–family sectors devoted their most passionate organizing to the anti–abortion crusade, where there were significant successes. The campaign against homosexuality was not a major focus in the mid–1980s, though it was never repudiated as a goal of right–wing organizing. A shared alarm and loathing over the gains of the gay rights movement was understood within the New Right.

The Current Anti–Homosexual Campaign

In the late 1980s, three issues reinvigorated the New Right's anti–homosexual activism and focused added attention at the national level. The first issue was the promotion of school curriculum reform to reflect a greater acceptance of gay men and lesbians (e.g., Project 10 in southern California). The second was the religious and political right's objection to public funding for homoerotic art. The third issue was the passage of gay rights ordinances, bills, and initiatives in the local sphere and in state legislatures. According to People for the American Way, 19 states and more than 100 cities and counties now have laws or executive orders protecting gay and lesbian rights.

It is commonly thought that the local responses to each of these three gay rights issues are grassroots efforts, mounted by outraged citizens stirred to action by local manifestations of "gay power." In fact, while local anti-homosexual groups did and do exist, their power and effectiveness is enormously enhanced by the technical assistance provided by *national* New Right organizations.

Colorado provides a case study of the effective involvement of national right–wing groups at the local level. Colorado for Family Values (CFV), the local group that sponsored Amendment 2, was founded by Coloradans Kevin Tebedo and Tony Marco, and is headed by Colorado Springs car dealer Will Perkins. It promotes itself as a grassroots group, but its tactics, success, and power are largely the result of support from a national anti–homosexual campaign mounted by the New Right. Five of the national organizations active in this campaign are represented on the executive and advisory boards of CFV: Focus on the Family, Summit Ministries, Concerned Women for America, Eagle Forum, and Traditional Values. Pat Robertson's Christian Coalition is not officially represented on the board of CFV, but has a strong presence in Colorado and is ubiquitous in anti–homosexual organizing nationally. Many other New Right and "old right" organizations are climbing on the anti–homosexual bandwagon as the issue becomes more prominent.

Colorado for Family Values has maintained adamantly that its strategy was not coordinated by national religious or political groups. However, according to People for the American Way, a Washington, DC, organization that monitors the right wing, "the Religious Right's anti–gay vendetta is not, as its leaders often claim, a spontaneous outpouring of concern about gay issues. Theirs is a carefully orchestrated political effort, with a unified set of messages and tactics, that is deliberately designed to foster division and intolerance." A review of the national organizations involved with Colorado's Amendment 2 will support this analysis.

Key Homophobic Groups Active in Colorado

Rev. Louis Sheldon's Traditional Values

Traditional Values (often called the Traditional Values Coalition) is headed by Rev. Louis Sheldon and is based in Anaheim, California. Rev. Sheldon and his organization have taken leadership within the Religious Right's anti–homosexual campaign. In October 1989, Rev. Sheldon led the "West Coast Symposium on Homosexuality and Public Policy Implications" in Orange County, California. Two of the featured speakers were Roger Magnuson, Esq., author of *Are Gay Rights Right?*, and Congressman William Dannemeyer, author of *Shadow in the Land: Homosexuality in America*.

Building on the success of the west coast symposium, Rev. Sheldon convened a January 1990 conference in Washington, DC, that was billed as a "national summit meeting on homosexuality." One of the two dominant themes of the conference was that homosexuals have, since the 1960s, been seeking "special protection over and above the equal rights already given to all Americans." This theme would later appear in Colorado as the central theme of the Colorado for Family Values' promotion of Amendment 2.

Rev. Louis Sheldon was an aide to Pat Robertson in 1987, and he shares much of Robertson's interest in the legal codification of moral issues. In 1988, Sheldon led the opposition to Project 10, a counseling program for gay adolescents in the Los Angeles school system. In 1986 and 1988, his zeal against homosexuals led him to endorse the California anti–homosexual initiatives sponsored by far right extremist Lyndon LaRouche. The initiatives sought, in effect, to require quarantine for people with AIDS. Sheldon himself has advocated establishing "cities of refuge" for people with the HIV infection. In 1991, Sheldon submitted to the California attorney general a constitutional amendment that would bar civil rights laws from protecting homosexuals, unless approved by a two–thirds vote of the California voters. Sheldon has recently announced his intention to pursue in California an initiative modeled on Colorado's Amendment 2.

Barbara Sheldon, chairwoman of the Traditional Values Coalition of Colorado, is on the executive board of Colorado for Family Values. She is not related to Rev. Sheldon.

Focus on the Family

It is widely agreed that the 1991 arrival in Colorado Springs of Dr. James Dobson and his organization, Focus on the Family, was an important catalyst for Colorado Springs' local anti–homosexual organization, Colorado for Family Values. CFV had already led a successful campaign against a local gay rights ordinance. Focus on the Family, however, brought to Colorado Springs a tremendous influx of resources and sophisticated political experience: it arrived with 750 employees (and has since added another 300) and an annual budget of nearly $70 million, including a $4 million grant from the El Pomar Foundation to buy 50 acres in Colorado Springs. Focus on the Family is indeed a national organization. While it has no official ties to CFV, it has offered "advice" to CFV, and several Focus on the Family employees, such as public policy representative Randy Hicks, sit on CFV advisory boards. Focus on the Family has given an in–kind donation worth $8,000 to Colorado for Family Values.

Dr. Dobson's background is in pediatrics and he is best known as an advocate of traditional discipline and corporal punishment for children. However, his organization has also been heavily involved in anti–homosexual organizing. In 1988, Focus on the Family merged with the Washington, DC–based Family Research Council, headed by Gary L. Bauer. The Family Research Council distributed a "homosexual packet," available through Focus on the Family, which contained the lengthy document, *The Homosexual Agenda: Changing Your Community and Nation.* This detailed guide includes a section titled "Starting An Initiative." In October 1992, the Family Research Council separated from Focus on the Family after warnings from the Internal Revenue Service that the Council's lobbying activities were endangering Focus on the Family's tax–exempt status.

In keeping with the Family Research Council's anti–gay organizing, Focus on the Family's newsletters have shown an increase in anti–gay articles over the last several years. For instance, in the May 1990 *Focus on the Family* newsletter, Dr. Dobson himself began a column with the statement, "I am familiar with the widespread effort to redefine the family. It is motivated by homosexual activists and others who see the traditional family as a barrier to the social engineering they hope to accomplish." A March 1991 article in the newsletter uses this argument against treating gays equally: "There are people in our society who find sexual satisfaction from engaging in intercourse with animals. . . .Would anyone suggest that these groups deserve special protection?"

Summit Ministries

Summit Ministries of Manitou Springs, Colorado, is a little–known Religious Right organization whose work is national in scope. It is a 30–year–old Christian organization specializing in educational materials and summer youth retreats. Its president is Rev. David A. Noebel, formerly a prominent preacher in Rev. Billy James Hargis's Christian Crusade. As early as 1977, Noebel authored *The Homosexual Revolution*, in which he claims that "homosexuality rapidly is becoming one of America's most serious social problems." He has also written several books claiming that rock'n'roll and soul music are communist plots to corrupt US youth. Summit Ministries later published *AIDS: Acquired Immune Deficiency Syndrome: A Special Report*, co–authored by David Noebel, Wayne C. Lutton, and Paul Cameron. For the last several years, virtually every issue of *The Journal*, Summit Ministries' monthly newsletter, has contained several anti–homosexual entries. Summit Ministries has just published Noebel's new book, *Understanding the Times: The Story of the Biblical Christian, Marxist/Leninist and Secular Humanist Worldviews*.

Noebel's background with Rev. Billy James Hargis's Christian Crusade helps to explain the historical friendly relationship between Summit Ministries and the John Birch Society (JBS). Both the Christian Crusade and the John Birch Society represent a political sector known in political science literature as the "old right." Born out of the conviction that communism was rampant in the United States, both organizations believed that the civil rights movement was manipulated by communists, that the National Council of Churches promoted communism, and that the United Nations was controlled by communists. In 1962, Rev. Billy James Hargis purchased an old resort hotel in Manitou Springs, which was renamed The Summit. The Summit became a retreat and anti–communism summer college.

Summit's relationship with the John Birch Society is deeper than mere ideological affinity. In fact, in 1983, a donor responding to a John Birch Society fundraising letter sent a check to Robert Welch of JBS, and received a thank–you letter from Welch. The check, however, was made out to Summit Ministries.

Rev. David Noebel was a member of the John Birch Society until at least 1987, and for many years Summit Ministries took out full–page advertisements for its summer youth retreats in *Review of the News* and *American Opinion*, two John Birch Society publications.

Summit Ministries is also politically close to Dr. James Dobson and Focus on the Family. Dr. Dobson, especially since moving to Colorado, leads seminars at Summit Ministries, and his endorsement of Summit's work was prominent in Summit's material promoting its 30th anniversary. David Noebel is on the advisory board of Colorado for Family Values.

Beverly LaHaye's Concerned Women for America

Touting itself as the largest women's organization in America, Concerned Women for America claims a membership of 500,000, a number disputed by many. CWA was founded in 1979 as "the Christian women's answer to the National Organization for Women." It is based in Washington, DC, and organizes its member chapters through prayer circles and LaHaye's monthly newsletter. CWA distributes a pamphlet titled *The Hidden Homosexual Agenda* that condemns the homosexual agenda for seeking "to take away the right of those who believe that homosexuality is wrong and immoral to voice that opinion."

CWA's most recent anti–homosexual pamphlet is *The Homosexual Deception: Making Sin A Civil Right*. It is a reprint of a treatise by Tony Marco, co–founder of Colorado for Family Values, that CFV filed with the state of Colorado as evidence supporting the correctness of Amendment 2. Here, to give a local activist his due, we see the local group creating material that is then used by a national group—a reversal of the usual pattern. Concerned Women for America is represented on the CFV advisory board by the president of its Colorado chapter, Bert Nelson.

Phyllis Schlafly's Eagle Forum

Phyllis Schlafly's Eagle Forum, based in Alton, Illinois, is another national organization whose local affiliate is represented on the advisory board of Colorado for Family Values. Phyllis Schlafly is perhaps best known for her successful campaign against the Equal Rights Amendment. During that campaign, she used the threat of homosexual and lesbian privileges as a central argument to support her opposition to the ERA. Eagle Forum continues to oppose gay and lesbian rights.

Other National Groups Prominent in the Anti–Homosexual Campaign

Pat Robertson's Christian Coalition

Rev. Pat Robertson, longtime host of the cable television program "The 700 Club," and prominent leader of the Religious Right, ran unsuccessfully in the Republican presidential primary in 1988. In October 1989, Robertson used the 1.9 million names he had collected from his 1988 campaign to identify 175,000 key activists and donors, and launch the Christian Coalition. The new Coalition's stated goal was "to build the most powerful political force in American politics."

The 175,000 activists were contacted and urged to establish chapters of the Christian Coalition in their precincts. Five goals were identified:

• build a grassroots network using professional field organizers and training schools;

• construct a lobbying organization to work at the national and state levels in every state and in Washington, DC;

• create a mass media outreach program;

• build a legal arm to defend the gains made in state legislatures from challenge by the American Civil Liberties Union;

• build a prayer network to unite all evangelical and pro–family voters.

Paul Weyrich of the Free Congress Foundation was an early endorser of the Christian Coalition.

The Christian Coalition's training tapes teach activists to fight those forces pursuing "an agenda of chaos." An early videotape distributed by the Christian Coalition used homosexual scenes to illustrate the moral decline of America; opposition to homosexuality has always been a commitment of the Christian Coalition. However, it was the 1990 political battle over a gay rights initiative in Broward County, Florida, that moved the anti–homosexual agenda to prominence within the organization. In its literature, the Christian Coalition took credit for "spearheading" the defeat. It claims to have "led the charge and won a major political victory." Robertson calls on Christian Coalition members to "duplicate this success in your city and state and throughout the nation."

By 1992, the organization had grown dramatically. Ralph Reed, its executive director, claimed 250,000 members in 49 states and $13 million in the bank. The Christian Coalition launched an election year get–out–the–vote effort which included "in–pew" registration at churches, the distribution of up to 40 million "voter guides," and the use of computer–assisted telephone banks to help elect favored candidates in key races.

Reed's tactics are self–confessedly surreptitious. "I want to be invisible," he told one reporter. "I do guerrilla warfare. I paint my face and travel at night. You don't know it's over until you're in a body bag. You don't know until election night." Despite this statement, Reed later publicly distanced himself from the "stealth" strategy.

According to the *Wall Street Journal*, the Christian Coalition overwhelmingly has targeted local Republican Party precinct and county organizations for takeover. It works closely with Paul Weyrich's Free Congress Foundation, which was founded in 1974 with money from the Coors family and its foundation. County Christian Coalition chapters have been directed to subscribe to Weyrich's National Empowerment Television (NET) satellite program. Ralph Reed is on the NET board.

Colorado for Family Values is not an affiliate of, nor is it funded by, the Christian Coalition (unlike the group that led the anti–homosexual initiative campaign in Oregon, the Oregon Citizens Alliance); the link between the Christian Coalition and Colorado's Amendment 2 is an indirect one. The National Legal Foundation of Chesapeake, Virginia (a conservative Christian legal organization founded by Pat Robertson and funded by Robertson's Christian Broadcasting Network, but no longer affiliated with Robertson), gave advice to Colorado for Family Values as early as 1991, long before Amendment 2 was on the ballot. The consultation was intended to help CFV formulate ballot language that would survive legal and political challenges. By the end of 1992, the National Legal Foundation had taken over much of the legal work of CFV.

The Berean League

The Berean League, based in St. Paul, Minnesota, has published Roger J. Magnuson's much–cited book *Are Gay Rights Right?* This discredited work was used by Tony Marco in the treatise he wrote for Colorado for Family Values. In addition to publishing Magnuson's book, the Berean League developed a successful campaign to oppose a local civil rights ordinance for gay men and lesbians. On the basis of that success, it began to conduct workshops at national conferences on "Strategies for Defeating Homosexual Privilege Proposals."

A Christian organization, the Berean League states in its promotional literature that "the League's authority is Scripture." Recently, it has issued a "Back–grounder" report titled *Some Things You May Not Know About Homosexuality*. An inflammatory three–page document, it was circulated in Oregon as a tool to organize support for Oregon's 1992 anti–homosexual Measure 9, the Abnormal Behavior Initiative.

The American Family Association

Headed by Rev. Donald Wildmon and based in Tupelo, Mississippi, the American Family Association has an annual budget of $5 million, and focuses primarily on profanity, adultery, homosexuality, and other forms of anti–Christian behavior and language on television. An earlier Wildmon organization was called CLeaR–TV (Christian Leaders for Responsible Television) and was based in Wheaton, Illinois. Wildmon has specialized in boycotting the corporate sponsors of shows which he dislikes. He called for a boycott of American Express because it sponsored the television program "L. A. Law," which ran an episode featuring a bisexual woman kissing another woman. Wildmon opposes even the depiction of homosexuality. One of his "top goals" for 1989 was to force off the air three TV shows ("Heartbeat," "Hooperman," and "thirtysomething") that, he said, "promote the homosexual lifestyle and portray practicing homosexuals in a positive light." Wildmon was accused of anti–Semitism for inflammatory comments he made during his campaign against the film *The Last Temptation of Christ*.

The Rutherford Institute

The Rutherford Institute, based in Manassas, Virginia, and founded and headed by John W. Whitehead, is a non–profit, legal defense organization associated with the far–right fringe of the Religious Right. Speakers listed in its Speakers Bureau include R. J. Rushdoony, a prominent Christian Reconstructionist. Reconstructionists believe that the text of the Bible provides the only legitimate basis for civil law. The most zealous wing of Reconstructionism has called for the death penalty for homosexuals, adulterers, and recalcitrant children. In 1992, the Rutherford Institute spearheaded a suit in Hawaii to block implementation of that state's new gay rights law.

The John Birch Society

The John Birch Society is another national organization with a prominent anti–homosexual agenda. JBS is not properly categorized as a New Right organization, but is best seen as "old right." Historically, the John Birch Society has existed as an isolationist, anti–communist organization. It was founded near the end of the McCarthy era, and expanded on Senator Joseph McCarthy's conspiracy theory of communist penetration of the United States. Since the death of its founder, Robert Welch, the JBS has moved from Belmont, Massachusetts, to Appleton, Wisconsin. Its recent concerns have been family issues, AIDS, US internationalist foreign policy, opposition to government regulations, and the right to bear arms. High on its list of concerns within family issues is homosexuality. The September and October 1992 issues of its publication, *New American* (published immediately before the November votes on anti–gay initiatives in Colorado and Oregon), carried anti–homosexual stories. The October story was a two–page article supporting Oregon's Abnormal Behavior Initiative.

Lyndon LaRouche: A Special Case

Lyndon LaRouche is a far–right political extremist who is now serving a 15–year sentence in federal prison for mail fraud and tax evasion. LaRouche runs a vast empire of organizations with ideological positions that exactly mimic his bizarre conspiracy theories. His followers are seen in airports and on street corners, often campaigning to free LaRouche from jail or attacking the organization's mortal enemy—Henry Kissinger. LaRouche's many organizations have always incorporated sexual themes into their analysis, and have been obsessed with AIDS since the pandemic began. LaRouche has conducted a long–running and fanatical campaign against homosexuality. Most recently, LaRouche spearheaded Proposition 64 in California, which would have established restrictive public health policies regarding AIDS. Proposition 64 was opposed by virtually all public health officials and elected officials (one exception was legislator William Dannemeyer). A public health specialist for the California Medical Association described Proposition 64 as "absolute hysteria and calculated deception." LaRouche organizers continue to peddle hysteria over AIDS and homosexuality. Their embrace of anti–Jewish and other scapegoating conspiracy theories and use of demagoguery add a firm base to the claim that the LaRouchians are a neo–fascist movement. Many New Right groups avoid any official alliance with the LaRouchians.

Analyzing the Anti–Homosexual Campaign's Coordination & Networking

Since its earliest days in the late 1970s, the New Right has been a political and religious movement that has self–consciously networked among its members. The Religious Roundtable, the

Free Congress Foundation, the Heritage Foundation, Christian Voice, the Conservative Caucus, the Moral Majority, Eagle Forum, and Concerned Women for America, among others, have held frequent conferences, published in each other's journals and newsletters, and promoted legislation within the context of a sympathetic Republican administration.

The anti–homosexual campaign nests within a sector of the New Right known as the pro–family movement. The major national gathering for the pro–family movement is the Family Forum conference, held annually since 1981. The conference has usually been sponsored by Paul Weyrich's Free Congress Foundation and Jerry Falwell's Moral Majority. These conferences are symptomatic of the coordination and networking among the New Right leadership. The issues of concern to the pro–family movement are aptly described in a 1984 promotional letter for Family Forum III. They are "important moral issues such as: the economic survival of the family, parents' rights in education, the homosexual movement, personal charity, child pornography, and abortion."

Reflecting the New Right leadership's shared opposition to homosexuality, the Family Forum conferences nearly always feature an anti–homosexual speaker. With the arrival of the AIDS epidemic, and the publication of *Gays, AIDS and You*, sponsored by the Free Congress Foundation, the anti–homosexual profile became much higher. We see the fruits of a decade of organizing by the pro–family movement of the New Right in the many challenges to gay rights bills and initiatives, and most recently in the anti–gay initiatives in Colorado and Oregon.

The analysis underlying the pro–family movement's morality is a fervent distrust and irrational hatred of "secular humanism," which is used as a shorthand for all that is evil and opposed to God. This distrust of secular humanism can be traced to the US nativist right at the turn of the century, which believed secular humanists were engaged in a conspiracy to undermine the United States. The purported conspiracy was linked, from its beginning, to an extreme fear of communism and its undermining effect on Christianity and the Christian family. Today, a major focus of the New Right, and particularly of the pro–family movement, is unrelenting opposition to the perceived secular humanist conspiracy. As Paul Weyrich describes it, "Well, first of all, from our point of view, this is really the most significant battle of the age–old conflict between good and evil, between the forces of God and the forces against God, that we have seen in our country."

For a better understanding of how fear of secular humanism serves as the theoretical basis for right–wing organizing, see the chapter on Theocracy and Racism.

Camouflage of the Christian Agenda

In the discussion above, three of the four national New Right organizations playing the highest profile role in organizing support for Colorado's Amendment 2 are explicitly Christian organizations. However, the association of anti–homosexual organizing with religious (specifically Christian) principles is highlighted only when activists are targeting fellow Christians in order to recruit or educate them. When organizing in the wider political arena, anti–homosexual organizing is cast in the secular terms of "family values" and "defense of the family."

This is an important aspect of the Religious Right's organizing style. Since the mid–1980s, when the heavy–handed style of Jerry Falwell's Moral Majority lost popularity, the Christian Right has cast its campaigns in terms not so obviously linked to the Bible. Ralph Reed of the Christian Coalition refers to the soft–peddling of the religious message in his own organization's work as conducting a "stealth campaign."

In the case of the anti–homosexual campaign, the Religious Right has dwelt on calumnious depictions of predatory behavior by homosexuals. Various anti–gay campaigns have accused homosexuals of eating feces, molesting children, and destroying the family. Many of these characterizations are "documented" by the work of Dr. Paul Cameron and Roger J. Magnuson. Oregon's 1992 anti–gay initiative (which was rejected by the voters) equates homosexuality with "pedophilia, sadism or masochism." While it is only in explicitly religious attacks on homosexuals that homosexuality is equated with Satan, that connection is uncontroversial among many involved in organizing against homosexuals.

Though the religious basis of this anti–homosexual fervor often is not mentioned, occasionally this bias becomes clear. On February 10, 1992, Bill McCartney, head football coach at the University of Colorado at Boulder, said at a press conference that homosexuality is a "sin" that is "an abomination of almighty God." McCartney is a member of the advisory board of Colorado for Family Values. Former US Representative William Armstrong, who describes himself as having had a "life–changing experience" when he became born again, is chairman of the advisory board of CFV.

But the clearest revelation of the religious basis for the work of CFV is a talk given by Kevin Tebedo, CFV executive director, at the First Congregational Church in Colorado Springs on August 23, 1992. In this setting, Tebedo states that Amendment 2 "is about authority."

He goes on to say, "It's about whose authority takes precedence in the society in which we live. . . [I]s it the authority of

God? The authority of the supreme King of Kings and Lord of Lords? You see, we say we should have the separation of church and state, but you see, Jesus Christ is the King of Kings and the Lord of Lords. That is politics; that is rule; that is authority."

In spite of the obvious preeminence of Christian principles in the values of its national organizational supporters and some of its advisory board members, the literature of Colorado for Family Values does not refer to Christianity, Biblical admonitions regarding homosexuality, or religious principles. A large CFV packet of information dated January 9, 1992, does not mention a religious basis for CFV's work. Finally, there is no mention of religion in the CFV Mission Statement.

The History of "No Special Rights"

Another area of deception in the public face of the anti–homosexual campaign is its assertion that lesbians and gay men are seeking "special rights" or "special protections." This was the guiding premise behind Anita Bryant's campaign, was raised again by Enrique Rueda in *The Homosexual Network* and *Gays, AIDS and You*, and eventually emerged as the slogan of the national anti–homosexual campaign. In the case of Colorado's Amendment 2, the slogan was the dominant theme of CFV's advertising and promotion.

The use of "no special rights" is purposefully misleading. Gay rights initiatives do not provide "special rights," but a guarantee of equal rights for lesbians and gay men. Amendment 2 would deny equal protection against discrimination only to this group. CFV's decision to use "no special rights" only in its public materials and not in the legal language of the amendment itself was made on the advice of the National Legal Foundation.

A June 1991 letter from Brian McCormick of NLF advises CFV to stay away from the "no special rights" language in its legal formulations, but to use it as the centerpiece of its public campaign. Coloradans were bombarded with advertisements and flyers all drumming home the message that Amendment 2 did nothing but reverse the unfair granting of "special rights" through gay rights initiatives. Future anti–gay initiatives will undoubtedly continue the use of the "no special rights" slogan because the cohesiveness of the right's anti–homosexual campaign virtually guarantees that local initiatives will follow the lead of national organizations.

Legal Issues Raised by Amendment 2

After the voters in Colorado approved Amendment 2 by majority vote, a preliminary injunction was successfully sought by a group of plaintiffs that included individuals, gay rights organizations, and the three Colorado cities—Denver, Aspen, and Boulder—that had existing gay rights ordinances. The injunction was requested on the grounds that Amendment 2 would deprive gay men, lesbians, and bisexuals of any legal remedy for acts of discrimination against them, and deprive the state and all local governments from enacting any statutes, ordinances, or policies that prevent discrimination on the basis of sexual orientation. Discrimination may occur in such areas as insurance, employment, housing, and accommodation.

The plaintiffs faced the difficult burden of overcoming the "presumption of constitutionality" granted to any successful amendment. They also needed to prove that there was a reasonable likelihood that they would prevail on the merits of their case. The plaintiffs argued that the amendment denied fundamental constitutional rights and also violated the constitutional guarantee of equal protection because there was no rational relationship between its provisions and the accomplishment of a legitimate public goal. To prevail, the plaintiffs needed to establish that such a denial of rights would create real, immediate, and irreparable harm to lesbians, gay men, and bisexuals.

Colorado District Court Judge Jeffrey Bayless determined that there was a reasonable probability that the amendment denied the plaintiffs a fundamental right—the right to participate in the governmental process—and that the amendment could be upheld only if the defendants could show that it furthered a compelling governmental purpose.

Judge Bayless concluded that lesbians, gay men, and bisexuals are an identifiable group that deserves protection. Acknowledging that the Constitution cannot control private prejudices, he ruled that legislation must not indirectly "give them effect." Judge Bayless then granted the temporary injunction blocking Amendment 2. A later permanent injunction was then appealed to the US Supreme Court.

Conclusion

Homophobia is a bedrock value in our society, one that crosses lines of class, race, and even gender. Our Calvinist attitudes toward sex, based in religious teaching that sex is only for procreation, and a patriarchal culture that is discomforted by any breaking down of rigid sex roles, combine to create a culture that can deal with homosexuality, if at all, only in the artistic and commercial spheres. The lesbian and gay civil rights movement has pushed homosexuality out of the artistic and commercial world and into the political and social sphere. This is almost guaranteed to create a backlash while society absorbs and adjusts to new values.

While that backlash may be inevitable, it can be tamped down or fanned by political forces. This review of the right wing's organizing to promote a backlash against the gay rights movement is a study in *reaction*. Deprived of its old enemies and needing a new issue to promote, the right's anti–homosexual organizing is rank opportunism. The anti–gay backlash is in large part a creation of the right. It is generating funds, keeping right–wing organizations that were in danger of complete eclipse alive with an infusion of new support, and generating the all–important evidence of political power—media attention.

The threat this backlash represents is very real. Violence is its most blatant manifestation, but the litany of pain and waste caused by homophobia includes subtle attacks on gay men and lesbians as well. Furthermore, confronting the backlash distracts time, energy, and money from the work necessary to bring about equal rights for lesbians and gay men.

In the case of Colorado's Amendment 2, it would be comforting to think that the people who voted for the amendment were simply misled, and believed they were opposing special rights for homosexuals. While that deception was promoted by Colorado for Family Values, the vote also reflects the deep–seated persistence of homophobia in our society. The skillful manipulation of homophobia by the right wing creates anti–gay sentiment and actions that bolster and promote intolerance.

In the United States, we must decide what role the church and religious tenets are going to play, especially when those tenets are in conflict with the Constitution and the Bill of Rights. It is not an attack on Christianity or religion to question the propriety of imposing Biblical law on a secular society. If ours is a society in which church and state are separate, then the prohibitions of church dogma cannot overrule the protections provided by the Constitution. And the Constitution, to paraphrase Mr. Justice McKenna in the 1910 case of *Weems v. U.S.*, is *progressive*—it is not fastened to the obsolete, but may acquire new meaning as public opinion becomes enlightened by a humane justice.

Jean Hardisty, who holds a doctorate in political science, is Director of Political Research Associates. She is working on a book on the resurgent right. This article appeared in *The Public Eye*, March 1993. © 1995, Jean Hardisty.

Hate on Tape

The Video Strategy of the Fundamentalist Right

<u>Laura Flanders</u>

It was the military and the media that made *The Gay Agenda* popular, says Bill Horn, once a CBS sportscaster, now video maker for the Springs of Life charismatic Christian church that produced the tape.

"Since *The Gay Agenda* was featured on Larry King Live and ABC World News Tonight, calls have poured in on the 1–800 sales number requesting a copy," boast the producers. After appearing on Pat Robertson's "700 Club" with clips, Horn says he gets 500 requests a day.

The Gay Agenda poses as a teaching tape, revealing what Horn calls the "hidden" side of gay life. Using amateur footage from gay parades and demonstrations, the tape stars doctors and scholars and "recovered" homosexuals who recite lists of unsourced statistics on what they say are the unhealthy practices of gay men.

Ten thousand copies were distributed to voters in Colorado and Oregon in the fall of 1992, in time to influence voting on anti-gay initiatives that were on the ballots in those states. According to Horn, exit polls in Oregon showed that 70 percent of "yes" voters said they were influenced by the tape.

Then in December 1993, Marine Commandant General Carl E. Mundy received a copy. "After viewing it, I reproduced copies for each of my fellow service chiefs, the chairman and the vice chairman of the Joint Chiefs of Staff," he told Representative Pat

Schroeder in a letter. "It appears to be extreme, but its message is vivid and, I believe, warrants a factual assessment."

Eventually, each senator and representative in Washington has received a copy, and Rev. Donald Wildmon of the American Family Association distributed tapes to every legislator in the states of Washington, Maine, New Mexico, and Montana, where voters faced anti–gay initiatives.

Dueling Videos

Yet Bill Horn is right when he says that *The Gay Agenda* received little or no media attention until the gay and lesbian community launched its response.

Though writers for the gay and lesbian press had reported on the use of *The Gay Agenda* in the campaigns of 1992, and footage documenting the mass distribution of the tape was available from the award–winning filmmaking collective Testing the Limits, mainstream editors did not consider the Religious Right's anti–gay video a national story.

Only in February 1993, when the Gay and Lesbian Emergency Media Coalition (GLEMC) launched its own video response, *Hate, Lies and Videotape*, did the mainstream media react. *Hate, Lies and Videotape* compares the Religious Right's anti–gay effort to crude KKK films attacking African–Americans and Nazi propaganda vilifying Jews. With its release, the media had what *USA Today* dubbed "A Videotape Duel" and, *ipso facto*, a story.

"The dueling videos amount to a direct trade of volleys between the religious right and the gay rights movement, each now aggressively staking out its ground," reported the *Washington Post*. Quoting John C. Green, a monitor of grassroots movements, the *Post* suggested that the far right's tactics were reactive: "The gay–rights movement has become very organized and seems to be making strides, so they are a good target" for the Religious Right.

"Both sides in the [gays in the military] debate have been working hard trying to influence public opinion, using a variety of techniques," announced Diane Sawyer on ABC "World News Tonight." "A battle of dueling videotapes," CNN declared that same day.

The fact that the video war, rather than the human war, attracted mainstream attention exposes much of what is chronically wrong with the media's response to the anti–gay, anti–civil rights movement. *The Gay Agenda* is not a "volley" traded between equivalent players (as CNN put it, "Gay Rights vs. Religious Right"). This kind of "balance" equates vicious lies about gay and lesbian people (e.g., "92 percent of homosexuals engage in rimming. . . .You couldn't do it without some ingestion of feces") with the response to those lies.

Grassroots Camouflage

Presenting the tape as a new, grassroots response to an advancing gay movement is misleading and inaccurate. "To make local anti–homosexual campaigns appear to be exclusively grassroots efforts when they are guided by major national organizations" has been one of the New Right's primary objectives, according to Jean Hardisty, director of Political Research Associates. So, too, has the camouflaging of the religious content behind the secular "defend the family" theme.

While magazines such as *Vanity Fair* are writing about "the Gay Nineties" and "an influx of openly gay people in the corridors of power," the media's focus on gay gains obscures the assault organized by the right and veils its sources.

The far right has been using video for decades. Don Black, a former Imperial Wizard of the KKK, appears in the GLEMC tape lecturing on the prospects for VCRs and the need for Klan supporters to build "our own private network."

At the GLEMC press conference, Loretta Ross of the Center for Democratic Renewal, which researches hate groups, pointed out connections between the Religious Right and other far right groups. For example, Billy McCormick, a founder of Pat Robertson's Christian Coalition, which is selling *The Gay Agenda* over a 900–number telephone line, is also a key supporter of David Duke.

The far right routinely capitalizes on public fears generated by AIDS, Ross said, as when a Georgia–based Klan leader claimed that "interracial couples are an open door to infecting white people."

Documenting the political and historical connections of the Religious Right's attacks would be valuable work for the mainstream media. Instead, even when "Larry King Live" showed parts of *The Gay Agenda*, the GLEMC video, *Hate, Lies and Videotape*, was not excerpted. Instead, stand–in host Frank Sesno played on the discomfort that exists around gay and lesbian images and behavior. After screening clips from *The Gay Agenda*, Sesno turned to Rachael Williams of GLEMC and asked, "Do you condone that kind of behavior? It seems a fair question."

Our Own "700 Club"

Jessea Greenman, co–chair of the San Francisco Bay Area chapter of GLAAD (Gay & Lesbian Alliance Against Defamation), helped to organize a community forum to discuss *The Gay*

Agenda. "We have to learn a sense of entitlement," she says. "Whenever we get an article printed or a documentary produced, it is seen as advocacy and [conservatives] call up and complain."

Tongues Untied, a documentary on black gay male culture produced by Marlon Riggs and aired on PBS after much controversy, was seen as pornographic, Greenman points out. "No one's saying *The Gay Agenda* is porn." On the other hand, it's not very sexy to say that gay and lesbian lives are normal, and for that the gay community pays a price in the sex–obsessed media.

DeeDee Halleck of Deep Dish Television, an independent satellite distribution network, says that progressives need their own media. "Until we have our own '700 Club,' we'll continue to be the victims in the public theater of this society." GLEMC's new tape was distributed on the Deep Dish satellite in early May 1995.

Meanwhile, *The Gay Agenda* has its clones. In New York City, home of the world's largest gay and lesbian community, a Christian Right group is circulating its own video, a 30–minute tape called *Why Parents Should Object to the Children of the Rainbow.* According to the *New York Observer,* the tape was shown at P. T. A. meetings and in private homes, in some cases with the approval of school principals, to mobilize parental opposition to Schools Chancellor Joseph Fernandez, who supported a pro–tolerance curriculum. Fueled by their success in ejecting Fernandez from office, the tape's makers, Concerned Parents for Educational Accountability, used the tape in similar meetings around the New York City school board elections. Since then, Horn has made sequels to *The Gay Agenda,* and there are dozens of similar videos being circulated by the right.

"We have to begin to control the message," says Ann Northrop, once a producer for CBS TV, and now the executive director of GLEMC. "They're way ahead."

Laura Flanders is on the staff of Fairness and Accuracy in Reporting (FAIR). This article first appeared in the June 1993 issue of FAIR's newsletter *Extra!* © 1995, Laura Flanders.

Civil Rights, Special Rights & Our Rights

Suzanne B. Goldberg

Don't be fooled by the "special rights" rhetoric of the Religious Right. There is something legally wrong with initiatives seeking to limit civil rights protections to exclude sexual orientation–based discrimination or create a situation in which gay and lesbian citizens have lesser rights compared with other citizens.

The Religious Right's campaign of misinformation has very effectively manipulated public understanding of civil rights and anti–discrimination law. Right–wing initiatives and referenda are both an attack against civil rights and attempts to further manipulate public understanding of civil rights. This makes a thorough knowledge of the constitutional issues raised by anti–gay initiatives especially important. Knowledge about civil rights is a key tool for building successful organizing and educational campaigns to defeat right–wing attacks.

Although right–wing initiatives are often promoted through vicious anti–lesbian and gay rhetoric, the ballot question presented to voters on election day doesn't ask whether voters like gays and lesbians. Rather, the question is: do you want to amend your constitution or city charter and restructure the legal foundation of government and its promise of civil rights for all people? In organizing anti–initiative campaigns and in responding to right–wing rhetoric, it is critical to keep focused on this point. Remember, this is not a lesbian and gay popularity contest—it is a vote on restructuring the government.

As we organize our campaigns against right–wing ballot initiatives and formulate responses to their rhetoric, it is critical that we review the basic issues at the root of the debate. For our purposes, civil rights are the rights guaranteed by law. These rights are guaranteed to US citizens and in many cases also cover non–citizens who live or work in the US. What is often referred to as the Civil Rights Movement actually focused on one aspect of civil rights—protection against race–based discrimination.

Different governmental bodies provide varying degrees of protection from discrimination on the basis of sexual orientation.

The US Constitution guarantees "fundamental" rights to all. These include, for example, freedom of speech, association, and religion, as well as a guarantee of the separation between church and state. The First Amendment to the US Constitution sets these guidelines:

> Congress shall make no law respecting an establishment of religion, or prohibiting the free exercise thereof, or abridging the freedom of speech, or of the press; or the right of the people peaceably to assemble, and to petition the Government for a redress of grievances.

A state constitution guarantees fundamental rights for the citizens and residents of each state. State constitutions are generally similar to the US Constitution. Sometimes they provide more protection for citizens. They cannot provide less protection or violate the US Constitution.

Federal civil rights laws provide specific protections against discrimination in a wide range of areas, including employment, housing, and public accommodations. These laws prohibit discrimination based on race, gender, national origin, ethnicity, age, disability, and some other characteristics. A federal civil rights law that prohibited discrimination based on sexual orientation would stop most of these initiatives in their tracks—our collective attention and effort to push for passage of this legislation is critical. There is such a bill that in the past has been introduced in Congress to prohibit discrimination based on sexual orientation, but it has never passed.

State civil rights laws are similar to federal civil rights laws and often protect against other forms of discrimination as well (e.g., marital status). Eight states and Washington, DC, have laws that prohibit sexual orientation discrimination in a variety of areas, including housing, employment, and public accommodations. Several other state legislatures were considering similar legislation in 1993.

Local civil rights ordinances (sometimes called human rights ordinances) are similar to state and federal civil rights laws and often protect against an even wider range of discrimination (e.g., political beliefs, etc.).

With all this information in hand, it is also important to know what civil rights are not about. You do not have a right to have a job or housing. You do have the right not to be discriminated against for an illegal reason (a reason prohibited by law or the Constitution).

So what are "special rights"? Actually, no such "rights" exist. In its initiatives, the Religious Right defines special rights to include: minority status, affirmative action, quotas, and special class status. However, these terms do not have a legal meaning in the way the Religious Right uses them.

Minority status and special class status are not legal rights. Affirmative action (sometimes misdescribed as "quotas" for hiring people who fit certain demographic categories) is a remedy, not a right. Affirmative action is a remedy for a historical pattern of discrimination. Where an affirmative action plan is in place, it is not supposed to be permanent; the goal is to remove the vestiges of discrimination, not to give some sort of "special right" to certain people.

If "special rights" don't really exist, what then is wrong with the initiatives that seek to prohibit states from banning discrimination based on sexual orientation? The US Constitution guarantees all people equal protection under the law. This means that a state cannot single out one group of people and treat them differently without a compelling reason for doing so.

The anti-gay initiatives would require a state or local government not to respond to the complaints of lesbians, gay men, and bisexuals about discrimination against them because of their sexual orientation. Any other group could bring its complaints to the government and try to obtain protection. Because the initiative would bar the government from responding to lesbians, gay men, and bisexuals only, the initiative changes the entire political process and burdens the political participation of lesbians, gay men, and bisexuals. It requires the government to treat gay and lesbian people differently from all other people.

Even if an initiative prohibited a state from protecting anyone from sexual orientation–based discrimination (including heterosexuals), the burden of that prohibition would fall on the people with a minority sexual orientation (lesbians, gay men, and bisexuals) and would therefore violate the Constitution's guarantee of equal protection.

Finally, it is important to remember that these initiatives target identity, not conduct. Even when an initiative focuses on lesbian and gay conduct or behavior, its effect is to prohibit protection against discrimination. When someone is fired for being lesbian or evicted for being gay, the firing or eviction is almost never tied directly to that person's conduct. Rather, we are targeted for discrimination and sometimes violence because of who we are—lesbian, gay, or bisexual—and what others assume we will do on that basis.

Suzanne B. Goldberg is Staff Attorney with Lambda Legal Defense. This article is an edited version of a speech given at a Fight the Right Regional Conference organized by the National Gay and Lesbian Task Force Policy Institute in conjunction with the Lambda Legal Defense and Education Fund, Equality Colorado, and Ground Zero in Denver, Colorado in March 1993. It previously appeared in the NGLTF publication, *Fight the Right Action Kit.* © 1995, Suzanne B. Goldberg.

The Dying American Dream

And the Snake Oil of Scapegoating

Holly Sklar

The American Dream—always an impossible dream for many—is dying a slow death. As the systemic causes go untreated, a host of local and national leaders are peddling the snake oil of scapegoating. Many people are swallowing it, in anger and desperation.

One out of four children is born into poverty in this, the world's wealthiest nation. That's according to the government's own undercounting measure. Wealth is not trickling down. It is flooding upward. The richest one percent of American families have nearly as much wealth as the entire bottom 95 percent. Such obscene inequality befits an oligarchy, not a democracy. Manhattan's income gap is worse than Guatemala's.

We have the highest economic inequality since 1929. For more and more Americans, the future is an endless Depression—minus the New Deal.

The politically weakest New Deal "entitlement," Aid to Families with Dependent Children (AFDC), is the first to go. The assault was camouflaged with Big Lies about "welfare queens" and "illegitimate" children. Social Security and Medicare are being undone, beginning with the more vulnerable SSI (Supplemental Security Income) and Medicaid.

The United States grows increasingly disunited. Once—thriving communities are in decline. Instead of full employment, the United States has full prisons. The military budget continues consuming resources at Cold War levels, while programs to invest in people, infrastructure, and the environment are sacrificed on the altar of deficit reduction. People who should be working together to transform the economic policies that are hurting them are instead turning hatefully on each other.

Breakdown of the Paycheck

The scapegoating stereotype of deadbeat poor people masks the growing reality of dead–end jobs and disposable workers. Living standards are falling for younger generations despite the fact that many households have two wage earners, have fewer children, and are better educated than their parents.

Forty percent of all children in families headed by someone younger than 30 were *officially* living in poverty in 1990, including one out of four children in White young families and one out of five children in young married–couple families. If not for the increased work hours of women, married–couple families would be significantly poorer.

Real wages for average workers are plummeting—despite rising productivity. Workers' average inflation–adjusted weekly earnings crashed 16 percent between 1973 and 1993—falling below 1967 levels. A college degree is increasingly necessary, but not necessarily sufficient to earn a decent income. Since 1990, college graduates "have been losing ground at the same rate as workers with less education," reports the Economic Policy Institute's *The State of Working America 1994–95*. The 1993 real wages of college–educated workers were 7.5 percent below their 1973 level.

In 1967, a full–time, year–round worker paid minimum wage earned above the official poverty line for a family of three. Today, these workers (mostly women) are way below the poverty line for a family of two.

For corporate executives, meanwhile, compensation has skyrocketed. The average CEO of a major corporation "earned" as much as 41 factory workers in 1960, and 149 factory workers in 1993.

Rising productivity in the 1990s, says *Fortune*, demonstrates that the "productivity payoff" from information technology and corporate reengineering has arrived. Profits are booming, but there has been no wage payoff for workers. Fortune 500 profits shot up 54 percent in 1994—on a sales gain of just 8 percent. How did profits rise so much faster than sales? *Business Week* explained in an article on third quarter 1994 profits titled "Hot Damn! They Did It Again": "By slashing payrolls, investing in technology, or simply overhauling assembly lines, companies are making more efficient use of fewer workers. . .The huge pool of labor has a lot to do with the prevailing wage restraint. . .The unemployment statistics don't count the roughly 4 million part–time workers who are eager for full–time jobs. In addition, the explosive increase in the number of temporary workers gives few employees much leverage in negotiating pay raises."

Union jobs provide better wages and benefits than their nonunion counterparts, but they are fast disappearing. Full–time workers who were union members earned median weekly wages of $592 in 1994 compared to $432 for nonunion workers—a wage differential of $8,320 over 52 weeks.

"Few American managers have ever accepted the right of unions to exist," says *Business Week*. "Over the past dozen years, in fact, US industry has conducted one of the most successful antiunion wars ever, illegally firing thousands of workers for exercising their rights to organize." The unionized share of the workforce was just 15.5 percent in 1994.

In the words of the Labor Research Association's *American Labor Yearbook 1993*: "With the possible exception of Hong Kong and South Korea, the US provides workers with less legal protection than any other industrialized country. . .[It] has the smallest proportion of workers covered by collective bargaining agreements." The *Yearbook* continues: "The US has become a cheap labor haven for global capital looking for low wage and benefit costs, high productivity, and a nonunion environment. . .For example, German firms such as BMW, Adidas, Siemens, and Mercedes are moving into the Carolinas, where huge tax breaks are available and the unionization rate is below 5 percent."

Jobs and wages are being downsized in the "leaner, meaner" world of global corporate restructuring. Corporations are aggressively automating and shifting operations among cities, states, and nations in a continual search for lower taxes, greater public subsidies, and cheaper labor. "Cheap labor" does not mean low skill. Computer engineering and software programming are increasingly being "outsourced" to Third World and East European countries. In *Business Week*'s words, "What makes Third World brainpower so attractive is price. . . .In India or China, you can get top–level [computer engineering] talent, probably with a Ph.D, for less than $10,000."

Full–time jobs are becoming scarcer, as corporations shape a cheaper, more disposable workforce of temporary workers, part–timers, and other "contingent workers." More workers are going back to the future of sweatshops and day labor.

Workers are increasingly expected to migrate from job to job, at low and variable wage rates, without paid vacation, much less a pension. How can they care for themselves and their families, maintain a home, pay for college, save for retirement, plan a future? How do we build strong communities? We can't build them in economic quicksand.

Full of Unemployment

While some workers have "jobs without futures," others have "futures without jobs." The prevailing definition of "full employment" has become steadily less full of employment and more full of unemployment.

The US government downsizes the unemployment rate, but not the reality, much as it does the poverty rate. To be counted in the official unemployment rate you must have searched for work in the past *four* weeks. If you've searched for work in the past year, or even the last five weeks—but not the last four weeks— then, presto, you're not officially unemployed. The government doesn't count as "unemployed" the millions of people who are so discouraged from long and fruitless job searches that they have given up looking. It doesn't count as "unemployed" those who couldn't look for work in the month before they were surveyed because they had no child care, for example. If you need a full–time job, but you're working part–time because that's all you can find, you're counted as employed.

As *Business Week* puts it, "Increasingly the labor market is filled with surplus workers who are not being counted as unemployed." Official Black unemployment is more than double the White rate; the Latino rate is almost double the White rate. The official Black unemployment rate averaged 14.1 percent between 1976 and 1993. Real unemployment and underemployment rates are even higher.

The situation is going to get much worse, without a major change in policies. In the late 1940s, Norbert Wiener, the Massachusetts Institute of Technology (MIT) mathematician who established the science of cybernetics, warned of the danger of widespread technological unemployment from automation. The high–tech cyberfuture has arrived. Trends analyst Jeremy Rifkin predicts in *The End of Work* that within a few decades hundreds of millions of people working globally in manufacturing, services, and agriculture could be displaced through automation, artificial intelligence, and biotechnology.

We must start using technological advances to free people for more socially productive work, and for family, community, culture, learning, recreation and so on. Without a change in course, the high–tech world will be a high–oppression world, the kind of world envisioned in stories like *1984, Virtual Light,* and *Blade*

Runner. A world in which some people live in futuristic splendor, and millions live in timeless poverty. A violent world of crumbling cities sprinkled with high–tech gadgets. A world where bosses are organized and workers are not. A world of virtual reality travel and plundered natural wonders. A world in which prisons are the fastest–growing government service. A world of virtual democracy, at best, without real choice, much less accountability. Or an overtly authoritarian world of virulent demagoguery.

The Snake Oil of Scapegoating

As the American Dream has become more impossible for more people, scapegoating is being used to deflect blame from the economic system and channel anger to support reactionary political causes. Talk–show demagogues have built their careers on a rising volume of hate.

The cycle of unequal opportunity is intensifying. Its beneficiaries often slander those most systematically undervalued, underpaid, underemployed, underfinanced, underinsured, underrated, and otherwise underserved and undermined—as undeserving and underclass, impoverished in moral values, and lacking the proper "work ethic."

Scapegoating labels like "underclass" and myths like the "culture of poverty" mask impoverishing economics. "Since 1973," reports the Children's Defense Fund, "most of the fastest increases in poverty rates occurred among young white families with children, those headed by married couples, and those headed by high school graduates. For all three groups, *poverty rates more than doubled in a single generation*, reaching levels that most Americans commonly assume afflict only minority and single–parent families." [Italics in original.] The same was true for college graduates.

Racist and sexist scapegoating make it easier to forget that the majority of poor people are White. Scapegoating makes it easier to treat inner–city neighborhoods like outsider cities—separate, unequal, and disposable. Scapegoating encourages people to think of "the poor" as the "Other America," Them and not Us. That makes it easier to divide people who should be working together to transform harmful social and economic policies. Makes it easier to write off more and more Americans as Untouchables. Makes it easier to leave unjust economic practices untouched.

Many White men who are "falling down" the economic ladder are being encouraged to believe they are falling because women and people of color are climbing over them to the top or dragging them down from the bottom. That way, they will blame women and people of color rather than the system.

Scapegoating makes racism and sexism politically correct. The "reverse discrimination" myth allows Whites to make the generic assumption that Blacks are unqualified, and Whites are qualified. If Blacks *are* hired on the job or admitted to the university, it's affirmative action. If Whites *aren't* hired or admitted, it's reverse discrimination. If, with affirmative action's removal, Blacks and other people of color and women are even less represented in jobs and academia, then that will be taken to show they never deserved to be there to begin with, rather than as a sign of continued discrimination.

Never mind that White males hold 95 percent of senior management positions (vice president and above). Never mind that, as the Urban Institute documented in a 1991 study—using carefully matched and trained pairs of White and Black young men applying for entry–level jobs—discrimination against Black job seekers is "entrenched and widespread." An earlier study documented similar discrimination against Latinos.

Discrimination against women is pervasive from the bottom to the top of the pay scale, and not because women are on the "mommy track." *Fortune* reports "that at the same level of management, the typical woman's pay is lower than her male colleague's—even when she has the exact same qualifications, works just as many years, relocates just as often, provides the main financial support for her family, takes no time off for personal reasons, and wins the same number of promotions to comparable jobs."

Susan Faludi writes in *Backlash*: "In a 1990 national poll of chief executives at Fortune 1000 companies, more than 80 percent acknowledged that discrimination impedes female employees' progress—yet, less than one percent of these same companies regarded *remedying* sex discrimination as a goal that their personnel departments should pursue."

Discriminatory pay for women and people of color is not called robbery, but that's what it is. *The State of Working America 1994–95* reports that a Black worker with less than nine years' experience earned 16.4 percent less in 1989 than an equivalent White worker (in terms of experience, education, region, and so on). The gap has widened greatly since 1973, when Blacks earned 10.3 percent less. "In terms of education, the greatest increase in the black–white earnings gap was among college graduates, with a small 2.5 percent differential in 1979 exploding to 15.5 percent in 1989."

Blacks have been hit hardest by corporate and government "downsizing." During 1992, for example, the federal government fired Black workers at more than twice the rate of Whites. The *San Jose Mercury News* editorialized, "It's not that they have less education, experience or seniority. The difference has nothing to do with job performance. A new federally sponsored study shows that blacks are fired more often because of their skin color." Blacks, who were 17 percent of the executive branch workforce in 1992, were 39 percent of those dismissed.

The *Philadelphia Inquirer* has also commented on federal employment racism: "Add to these findings numerous other studies that show the same, disturbing trends in both the public and private sector and it is clear that something is seriously amiss with race relations in the American workplace."

The US Constitution once counted Black slaves as worth three–fifths of Whites. Today, Black per capita income is three–fifths of Whites. That's an economic measure of racism. The Latino–White ratio is even worse.

Blaming Women for Illegitimate Economics

Women are scapegoated as producers and reproducers of poverty. Never mind that impoverished women don't create poverty any more than slaves created slavery.

Historically, "women have been viewed as the breeders of poverty, criminality and other social problems," observes Mimi Abramovitz, professor of Social Policy at the Hunter College School of Social Work. "From the 'tenement classes' of the mid–1800s and the 'dangerous classes' of the 1880s, to Social Darwinism and eugenics, to Freudian theories of motherhood, to Moynihan's 'Black matriarchy' and today's 'underclass,' society blames women for the failed policies of business and the state."

Liberals have joined with conservatives in the crusade to restigmatize motherhood outside marriage. Secretary of Health and Human Services Donna Shalala told *Newsweek*, "I don't like to put this in moral terms, but I do believe that having children out of wedlock is just wrong."

The awful labeling of children as "illegitimate" has again been legitimized. Besides meaning born out of wedlock, illegitimate also means illegal, contrary to rules and logic, misbegotten, not genuine, wrong—to be a bastard.

Imagine labeling married–couple families as pathological breeding grounds of patriarchal domestic violence, or suggesting that women should never marry, because they are more likely to be beaten and killed by a spouse than a stranger. As the *Journal of Trauma* reported, "Domestic violence is the leading cause of injury to women and accounts for more visits to hospital emergency departments than car crashes, muggings, and rapes combined." Nationally, about a third of all murdered women are killed by husbands, boyfriends, and ex–partners (less than a tenth are killed by strangers); "men commonly kill their female partners in response to the woman's attempt to leave an abusive relationship."

Single mothers and their children, especially Black women and children, have become prime scapegoats for illegitimate economics. "The bodies of black women became political terrain on which some proponents of white supremacy mounted their campaigns," wrote Ricki Solinger in *Wake Up Little Susie: Single Pregnancy and Race Before Roe V. Wade.* And "the black illegitimate baby became the child white politicians and taxpayers loved to hate." So it goes today.

Never mind that "if one compares the actual poverty rate in 1993 to what the poverty rate would have been that year if the proportion of people living in female–headed families had remained at the same level as in 1977, one finds the poverty rate would be little changed." That according to the Center on Budget and Policy Priorities report, *Welfare, Out–of–Wedlock Childbearing, and Poverty.* In 1992, approximately 58 percent of all officially poor children lived in single–parent families—the same figure as 1977.

Being married is neither necessary nor sufficient to avoid poverty. The official 1994 poverty rates for married–couple families with children under 18 were nearly 8 percent for Whites, over 11 percent for Blacks, and 24 percent for Latinos! The overall poverty rate for children in the families of married couples under 30 climbed from 8 percent in 1973 to 20 percent in 1990.

The typical women behind the rise in never–married mothers in the 1980s, explains the General Accounting Office (GAO), "differed from the stereotype: They were not unemployed teenaged dropouts but rather working women aged 25 to 44 who had completed high school." Contrary to image, the *proportion* of Black children born to unmarried mothers has grown because the birth rates of *married* Black women have fallen so dramatically. It's also important to understand that many children born "out of wedlock" are born into two–parent families. There has been a large rise in the number of families composed of unmarried couples, including same–sex couples, with children.

The proportion of households headed by women has been rising in all regions of the world. As of 1991, the number of births to unmarried women as a percentage of all live births was 48 percent in Sweden; 47 percent in Denmark; 30 percent in the UK, France, and the United States; and 29 percent in Canada. None of the other countries have US proportions of poverty. Instead of rooting out discrimination, encouraging adequate wages, promoting full and flexible employment, and implementing the kind of child care and other family supports common in numerous countries, many US policy makers are busily blaming women for their disproportionate poverty. According to the United Nations *Human Development Report 1995*, American women are worse off than those in 30 other countries when it comes to women's non-agricultural wage as a percentage of men's.

While more and more men are being impoverished in the current economy, it is even harder for women to work their way out of poverty. Women working full–time, year round, still earn only 72 cents for every dollar earned by men. They don't pay 72 cents on the dollar for rent, or food, or child care, or anything else.

The fact that many female–headed households are poorer because women are generally paid less than men is taken as a given in much poverty policy discussion, as if pay equity were a pipe dream not even worth mentioning. Back in 1977, a US Labor Department study found that if working women were paid what similarly qualified men earn, the number of poor families would decrease by half. A 1991 GAO study found that "many single mothers will remain near or below the poverty line even if they work at full–time jobs. Problems they are likely to face include low earnings; vulnerability to layoffs and other work interruptions; lack of important fringe benefits such as paid sick leave and health insurance; and relatively high expenses for child care."

Looking at the 1990–92 period, the Census Bureau reported that men who left a full–time job or were laid off, and then found another full–time job, saw their paychecks drop from an average of $456 to $312 per week. Women's wages fell from an average of $321 weekly to an even more meager $197. Among the men, an estimated 37 percent had employer–provided health insurance in their old jobs, but only 25 percent did in their new jobs. Among women, only 23 percent had health benefits in their old jobs, and only 14 percent had health insurance in their new jobs.

Most mothers work outside the home as well as inside. But you wouldn't know that by looking at school hours and the scarcity of after–school programs and affordable day care.

Corporations have made a mockery of women's demand for equal employment by lowering real wages so that it increasingly takes two incomes to support a family. More and more women are being told they must work the double day inside the home and outside it, or be cast to the shelters, the prisons, and the streets. Not enough jobs, much less jobs paying living wages? Tough. The right to have a baby, and the right not to have a baby, are both under assault.

Ending Welfare, Extending Poverty

Racist and sexist scapegoating have come together most viciously in the rollback of welfare. The demonization of the "welfare mother," says Rosemary Bray, a former editor of the *New York Times Book Review* whose family received welfare when she was a child, reinforces the patriarchal notion "that women and children without a man are fundamentally damaged goods" and allows "for denial about the depth and intransigence of racism." It allows those benefiting from rising economic inequality to shift the blame for the system's failures in producing sufficient jobs and income on supposed personal failures, such as deficient "work ethic."

AFDC has lagged way behind the rising pace of people in poverty, especially children. Two–thirds of AFDC recipients are children. The number of AFDC child recipients as a percentage of children living below the official poverty line fell from a high of 81 percent in 1973 to 63 percent in 1992. About 38 percent of families receiving AFDC are White, 37 percent are Black (a lower percentage than 1973), 19 percent are Latino, three percent Asian, and one percent Native American. There are disproportionately more people of color on welfare because disproportionately more people of color are impoverished, unemployed, and underemployed, and they have disproportionately less access to other government income support programs, such as unemployment benefits, workers' compensation, and Social Security.

In the stereotype world, the exceptions make the rule: the stereotypical "welfare mother" is a "baby having babies." For example, in the "Replacing Welfare with Work" chapter of *Mandate for Change*, the Democratic Leadership Council's blueprint for the Clinton presidency, the only age reference is to the "15–year–old welfare mother with a new baby." In reality, *0.1 percent* of mothers receiving AFDC are 15 or younger. That's not 10 percent. Not one percent. But one–tenth of one percent. Less than four percent are 18 or younger. A 1994 US GAO report reviewing the 1976–92 period observes: "In 1992, never–married women receiving AFDC were less likely to be teenage mothers. They were also older and better educated than never–married women receiving AFDC in 1976."

Contrary to "welfare as a way of life" stereotype, the typical AFDC recipient has one or two children and "is a short–term user" of AFDC, in the words of the congressional *Green Book*. Long–term recipients have greater obstacles to getting off welfare, such as lacking prior work experience, a high school degree, or child care, or having poor health or disabilities, or caring for a child with disabilities.

Also contrary to stereotype, most daughters in families which received welfare do not become welfare recipients as adults. The myth of an intergenerational Black matriarchy of "welfare queens" is particularly disgusting since Black women were enslaved workers for over two centuries and have always had a high labor force participation rate and, because of racism and sexism, a disproportionate share of low wages and poverty.

AFDC benefits have been chopped repeatedly as if, once you have too little money, it doesn't matter how little you have. Between 1970 and 1994, the median state's maximum monthly benefit for a family of three was slashed nearly in half (47 percent), adjusting for inflation. As the Center on Budget and Policy Priorities notes, "Combined [1994] AFDC and food stamp benefits for the average AFDC family of three was $664 per month (about $8,000 per year), or about two–thirds of the poverty line." Until 1979, all families receiving AFDC were eligible for food stamps; in 1993, 11 percent received none. And, contrary to common belief, fewer than one out of four families receiving AFDC live in public housing or receive any rent subsidies.

Human service advocates warn of a race to the bottom among states in welfare benefits—at the same time there is a race to the bottom in wages. In the words of Liz Krueger of the New York-based Community Food Resource Center, "New Hampshire is rushing to pass welfare 'reform' for fear that recent benefit cuts in Massachusetts will induce a northward move among potential welfare recipients. Connecticut has announced their goal of having the 'toughest national standards for eligibility.'"

How low can they go? All the way down to Mississippi's $120 maximum monthly benefit for a three–person family—and below. Think about that. A monthly $120 amounts to $1,440 per year for a family of three. When food stamps were added to AFDC in Mississippi, the combined benefit amounted to only 43 percent of the official poverty line. How do you survive on that?

As Robert Kuttner commented in a *Boston Globe* op–ed, "States' rights, once a code word for discrimination and backward social policy, are in vogue again. But Justice Louis Brandeis, author of the phrase that states could be 'laboratories of democracy,' warned simultaneously against a 'race to the bottom.'" If states had been left to their own devices in earlier decades, malnutrition would be common and rivers around the country would still be burning.

Scapegoaters have stoked anti-welfare anger by pretending that AFDC is a major drain on public money. The gap between image and reality is vast. A poll of 1994 voters found that one out of five believed that welfare was *the largest* federal government expense, larger even than defense. AFDC spending since 1964 has amounted to less than 1.5 percent of federal outlays. In 1994, it was about one percent. Soon, it will be far less.

Have They No Decency?

History will record that Clinton promised to "end welfare as we know it," and allowed the right to end welfare. It was Clinton who said that we "shouldn't pay people for doing nothing"—as if raising children is doing nothing. It was the Clinton Administration that "freed 34 states from federal rules," to use Clinton's proud words. States were freed to be more mean and miserly. Free to cut families off after two years whether or not work is available, and to deny any aid to children conceived while the family was receiving AFDC benefits.

You know that "welfare reform" spells disaster when Senator Daniel Patrick Moynihan—who sowed the seeds long ago with his "Black matriarchy" malarkey—sounds like Joseph Welch at the McCarthy hearings. Welch told McCarthy: "Until this moment, Senator, I think I never really gauged your cruelty or recklessness. . . .Have you no sense of decency, sir?"

Speaking from the Senate floor during the welfare bill debate, Moynihan lamented, "Are there no serious persons in the administration who can say, 'Stop, stop right now. No, we won't have this'?"

Moynihan asserted, "If this administration wishes to go down in history as one that abandoned, eagerly abandoned, the national commitment to dependent children, so be it. I would not want to be associated with such an enterprise, and I shall not be." He later added, "There is such a thing as resigning in government, and there comes a time when, if principle matters at all, you resign. People who resign on principle come back; people whose real views are less important than their temporary position, 'their brief authority,' as Shakespeare once put it, disappear." It is long past time for administration officials like Donna Shalala, a former chair of the Children's Defense Fund, to resign on principle rather than use their brief authority to help disappear welfare.

The Democrats have sold out so shamelessly that conservative columnist George Will looks good by comparison. Before the Senate vote, Will wrote: "Phil Gramm says welfare recipients are people 'in the wagon' who ought to get out and 'help the rest of us pull.' Well. Of the 14 million people receiving Aid to Families with Dependent Children, 9 million are children. Even if we get all these free riders into wee harnesses, the wagon will not move much faster. Furthermore, there is hardly an individual or industry in America that is not in some sense 'in the wagon,' receiving some federal subvention. If everyone gets out the wagon may

rocket along. But no one is proposing that. Instead, welfare reform may give a whole new meaning to the phrase 'women and
children first.'"

Actually, that phrase has been employed for quite a while in
the effort to stop the backlash George Will has been a party to. It's
a sad commentary on how far the political spectrum has shifted
rightward that Will can now employ it.

The anti–welfare bill passed the Senate, 87 to 12, with only
one Republican and 11 Democrats (Akaka, Bradley, Kennedy,
Kerrey, Lautenberg, Leahy, Moseley–Braun, Moynihan, Sar-
banes, Simon, and Wellstone) opposing it. Senator Carol Moseley–
Braun remarked, "This bill takes a Pontius Pilate approach to
federal responsibility. We are washing our hands of our responsibility to poor children."

Among those abdicating responsibility were her Democratic
Senate sisters Barbara Boxer, Dianne Feinstein, Barbara Mikul-
ski, and Patty Murray. Like Clinton, they are not only unprinci-
pled, they are deluding themselves if they think it will help in
their reelection. Does anyone think Franklin Roosevelt would
have won reelection with the policies of Herbert Hoover?

"Welfare reform" ends the entitlement to cash assistance for
poor children. AFDC, child care, and other programs will be
folded into severely underfunded block grants to the states. The
lack of entitlement status means that when your state's welfare
budget runs out—tough. If your marriage ends, your ex does not
pay child support, and you need temporary help—tough. If you
just lost a job that doesn't qualify you for unemployment benefits,
and you've got children to provide for—tough. If you are fleeing
an abusive spouse—tough.

"Welfare reform" sets time limits for "moving from welfare to
work." If you can't find a job—tough. Never mind that it is the
policy of the government to keep millions of Americans unemployed. The Federal Reserve Board doesn't care if you have a
great "work ethic" when it raises interest rates to slow down the
economy. As Liz Krueger puts it, "There is no time limit for the
lack of jobs in the economy."

Some 7.5 million people are unemployed according to official
statistics. Remember, that means they are actively seeking work
and not finding it. Millions of other Americans are working part–
time because they can't find full–time employment.

Nearly five million adults, most of them women, receive
AFDC. Where are the jobs? Where is the affordable child care?
Where is the right to paid family leave enabling all workers to
take time off for the birth or illness of children? That's a right in
many other countries, not this one. Here, more and more women
are expected to give birth one day, leave the hospital the next,

leave their children wherever they can, and return to work immediately.

Over 2.5 million people who worked full–time, year round, in 1994 were below the official poverty line—the threshold that supposedly marks subsistence. In reality, as John Schwarz and Thomas Volgy show in their book on the working poor, the poverty line is set way too low to cover basic human needs, such as food and housing, much less child care. Low–income families spend, on average, more than one–fifth of their income on child care; families below the official poverty line spend more than one–fourth. One out of four officially poor children live in families in which parents worked full–time, year round. Many parents with young children cannot work full–time inside the home and full–time outside it.

Greed Surplus, Justice Deficit

There is no reason to sacrifice children to the false idol of the balanced budget, and every reason not to. It is a Trojan Horse from which right–wing reactionaries have insured the bipartisan rule of their slash and burn policies.

The federal budget deficit—produced by skyrocketing military spending and tax cuts for corporations and the rich—has been used as a permanent enforcer of cutbacks in social services and public works. We have a greed surplus and a justice deficit. The result is government that is ever leaner and meaner toward those with the least wealth and opportunity. Social spending will be starved during periods of economic growth and recession; recessions will be transformed into depressions.

As economist Max Sawicky explains in a report for the Economic Policy Institute, *Up From Deficit Reduction*: "The ideology underlying the fiscal doctrine of unlimited, unending deficit reduction is not aimed at stable prices, full employment, and greater private investment. Rather, the motivations are to reduce the size of government, to disassemble the US system of social insurance, and to maintain unyielding downward pressure on the price level. The implied economic policy is one of stagnation: a disproportionate weight is put on low inflation to the detriment of employment, investment, and general economic growth. The policy is also counter–redistributive: it favors wealth–holders at the expense of wage–earners, the elderly, and the poor. If stated outright, these goals would be manifestly unpopular, so the sales pitch for extreme deficit reduction has to focus elsewhere—on creating and perpetuating misconceptions or downright superstitions about the federal budget and the public debt." Sawicky shows why a zero–deficit approach does more harm than good and makes the case for a policy of "sustainable deficit reduction."

Congress is robbing impoverished children to pay for more tax cuts for the rich. So are many states. It's an obscene orgy of greed. Conservatives have managed to confuse the idea of raising taxes on the wealthy with raising taxes in general, so that any attempts to put the tax system back on more of a sliding scale are given the politically unpopular brand "tax hikes." In the guise of populist tax revolt, conservatives insure low taxes for those who can afford to send their kids to private day care, private school, private hospitals, and private colleges. In Europe, where taxes are higher, governments invest much more in social spending and infrastructure to assure basic human needs and more shared economic progress. One result is less crime and violence.

The United States continues to beat plowshares into swords. In the words of the Center for Defense Information (CDI), led by retired military officers, "President Clinton's FY 1996 military budget request is a full $20 billion more in today's dollars than America spent on the military in 1980, a time of great Cold War tension. . . .America's military budget is nearly as large as the military budgets of all the other nations in the world combined."

"Despite the absence of any serious threats," reports CDI, military spending in the United States continues at the astounding rate of $5 billion every week, $700 million per day, $500,000 per minute, and $8,000 per second. Congress wants to make it even higher, giving the Pentagon money for weapons even the generals admit they don't need.

In 1994, the federal government spent $17 billion on AFDC, child support enforcement, and child care. It will cost $31 billion to build 20 additional, unneeded B–2 bombers.

Numerous military and foreign policy specialists have called for bringing the military budget down to $175 billion, including CDI and former Secretary of Defense Robert McNamara. Arms control expert Randall Forsberg, director of the Institute for Defense and Disarmament Studies, goes much further. She proposes a phased 10–year program to build a cooperative international security system with strong mechanisms for peaceful conflict resolution and a commitment to "non–offensive defense," bringing the US military budget to $87 billion, for savings of $989 billion over ten years.

With a sane budget, fair taxes, and fair economic policies, we can invest in children—the nation's future—rather than sacrifice them on the altar of militarism and greed.

We must find a way to draw the line for decency. If we do not, the scapegoating spiral will escalate, and fewer and fewer will escape— until we are left with a country where the majority are working poor, or unemployed, or in rapidly multiplying prison cells.

Locking Up "Surplus" Labor

The United States is Number One in locking up its own people. It imprisons Black men at a much higher rate than South Africa did under apartheid. In the words of the National Center on Institutions and Alternatives, the United States has "replaced the social safety net with a dragnet."

The federal and state prison populations swelled 188 percent between 1980 and 1993—though, contrary to common belief, the crime rate generally went down in that period. The real impact of "three strikes and you're out" legislation has yet to hit. The federal and state prison populations are over half Black and Latino. The racially–biased "War on Drugs" is increasingly responsible.

Nearly one out of three Black men in their twenties is in prison or jail, on probation or on parole on any given day, the Sentencing Project reports for 1995. The great majority have been convicted of a nonviolent offense.

In an unusual editorial shortly after the Los Angeles riots, the *New York Times* quoted a 1990 report by the Correctional Association of New York and the New York State Coalition for Criminal Justice: "It is no accident that our correctional facilities are filled with African–American and Latino youths out of all proportion. . .Prisons are now the last stop along a continuum of injustice for these youths that literally starts before birth." The *Times* observed that it costs about $25,000 per year to keep a kid in prison—not counting the high cost of prison construction. "That's more than the Job Corps, or college," noted the *Times*. A hard search for a job becomes an even harder one after you have a criminal record on your life *résumé*.

Studies have found discrimination in the criminal justice system at all levels. A study of California, Michigan, and Texas by Joan Petersilia, cited by Coramae Richey Mann in *Unequal Justice*, found that controlling "for relevant variables influential in sentencing. . .blacks and Hispanics were more likely to be sentenced to prison, with longer sentences, and less likely to be accorded probation than white felony offenders."

It is impossible to understand why so many people of color, particularly Blacks, have a record—and why so many more will get a record—without understanding the racially–biased "War on Drugs." Three out of four drug users are White (non–Latino), but Blacks are much more likely to be arrested and convicted for drug offenses and receive harsher sentences. The share of those convicted of a drug offense in the federal prison system skyrocketed from 16 percent of inmates in 1970 to 38 percent in 1986 and 61 percent in 1993—and is expected to grow to 72 percent by 1997. The percentage of drug offenders in state prisons grew from 9 percent in 1986 to 23 percent in 1993; among women prisoners, about a third are serving time for drug offenses. Many of those serving time for drug charges are nonviolent, low–level offenders with no prior criminal records. The overall arrest rate for drug possession is twice as high as for sale and/or manufacturing.

As the Sentencing Project reports, Blacks constitute 13 percent of all monthly drug users, 35 percent of arrests for drug possession, 55 percent of convictions, and 74 percent of prison sentences. Almost 90 percent of those sentenced to state prison for drug possession in 1992 were Black and Latino. The American Bar Association found that drug arrests skyrocketed by 78 percent for juveniles of color during 1986–1991, while *decreasing* by a third for other juveniles.

Law officers and judges, reports the *Los Angeles Times*, say, "although it is clear that whites sell most of the nation's cocaine and account for 80 percent of its consumers, it is blacks and other minorities who continue to fill up America's courtrooms and jails, largely because, in a political climate that demands that something be done, they are the easiest people to arrest." They are the easiest to scapegoat. Never mind that, as former drug czar William Bennett puts it, "the typical cocaine user is white, male, a high school graduate employed full time and living in a small metropolitan area or suburb." In the words of a 1993 *USA Today* special report:

> The war on drugs has, in many places, been fought mainly against blacks. . . .
>
> [Police officials] say Blacks are arrested more frequently because drug use often is easier to spot in the Black community, with dealing on urban street corners. . .rather than behind closed doors.
>
> And, the police officials say, it's cheaper to target in the black community.
>
> "We don't have whites on corners selling drugs. . . .They're in houses and offices," says police chief John Dale of Albany, N.Y., where blacks are eight times as likely as whites to be arrested for drugs. . . .We're locking up kids who are scrambling for crumbs, not the people who make big money."

While many of the easily spotted street corner buyers are White, as well as the big money traffickers and money launderers, you don't have to be dealing or buying on street corners to feel the racial bias of the "drug war." A study in the *New England Journal of Medicine* found both racial and economic bias in the reporting of pregnant women to authorities for drug or alcohol abuse, under a mandatory reporting law. The study found that substance abuse rates were slightly higher for pregnant White women than pregnant Black women, but Black women were about 10 times more likely to be reported to authorities. The bias was evident whether the women received their prenatal care from private doctors or public health clinics. Poor women were also more likely to be reported to authorities.

Between 1986 and 1991, the number of Black women incarcerated for drug offenses shot up 828 percent. That's compared with 241 percent for White women and 328 percent for Latinas. A 1994 Department of Justice study of federal prisoners, summarized by the Sentencing Project, found that "women were over-represented among 'low–level' drug offenders who were non-violent, had minimal or no prior criminal history, and were not principal figures in criminal organizations or activities, but who nevertheless received sentences similar to 'high–level' drug offenders under the mandatory sentencing policies."

Looking at federal mandatory minimum sentences, a report to Congress by the US Sentencing Commission found that "whites are more likely than non–whites to be sentenced below the applicable mandatory minimum." One obscene result of federal and state mandatory minimums is that low–level offenders are routinely treated more harshly than high–level offenders because the low–level offenders can't provide the kind of information or forfeited assets wanted by prosecutors in exchange for reduced charges and sentences.

The racial bias of the "drug war" is symbolized by the much harsher mandatory minimums for crack cocaine (for which mostly Blacks are arrested, though Whites are the majority of users) than powder cocaine (mostly Whites arrested). As the Minnesota Supreme Court found in 1991, there is no rational basis for distinguishing between crack cocaine and powder cocaine. Yet, in the words of the Sentencing Project, the US Sentencing Commission has "calculated that a person convicted of trafficking in five grams of crack with a maximum retail value of $750 will receive the same sentence as an offender charged with selling 500 grams of powder cocaine retailing for $50,000."

Racial bias in the "drug war" is also evidenced by the much more lenient and, often, treatment–oriented approach to drunk drivers, most of whom are White males. You would never know that almost the same number of people are killed annually by drunk drivers as are murdered, and alcohol is associated with much more violence and homicides nationally than illicit drugs.

Earlier "drug wars" were also racially biased. As Diana Gordon writes in her book, *The Return of the Dangerous Classes*, "The first drug prohibition law was an 1875 San Francisco ordinance prohibiting opium and aimed at Chinese workers, who were no longer needed to bring the railroad west and who were blamed for taking jobs of whites during a depression." The current drug war begun in the 1980s, says Gordon, is not only "a rearguard action against full equality for racial minorities," but an instrument for "whipping young people (and often cultural liberals) back into line."

The "drug war" has been used to justify the erosion of constitutional protections against unwarranted stops, searches, and seizures, and the rollback of other civil liberties. The rollback has been especially severe for people of color. In the words of the *Los Angeles Times*: "As police have moved *en masse* into poor minority communities...their presence has meant that innocent citizens have been swept up along with the guilty.....Across the nation, blacks—and some Latinos—complain that their neighborhoods are barricaded, that roadblocks are set up for identification checks, that they are rousted from their apartments without warrants, that police target them with 'stop on sight' policies and that they are disproportionately arrested in 'sweep' operations for minor misdemeanors and traffic violations that have nothing to do with the drug war."

Racist self–fulfilling prophecy is evident in the use of racial characteristics in drug suspect profiles, which guide who is stopped and searched in cars, buses, and airports.

The courts, juvenile facilities, jails, and prisons are jammed. Murderers, rapists, and other violent offenders are being released early to make way for nonviolent ones. Many judges, police officers, and prosecutors acknowledge the injustice and insanity of current policies. "Corrections" spending, the fastest growing part of state budgets, is consuming tax dollars that once went to social services such as treatment for drug addiction, education, job training, and housing.

The United States is sentencing more and more people to poverty, prison, and early death.

Democracy or Demagoguery

"Today's Sun Belt represents a confluence of Social Darwinism, entrepreneurialism, high technology, nationalism, nostalgia and fundamentalist religion, and any Sun Belt hegemony over our politics has a unique potential...to accommodate a drift toward apple–pie authoritarianism." So wrote conservative strategist Kevin Phillips in his 1982 book, *Post–Conservative America.*

The failed American Dream can give way to a new American fairness or a neo–fascist nightmare. It can happen in Europe. It can happen here.

As Sinclair Lewis warned in *It Can't Happen Here*, through the voice of newspaper editor Doremus Jessup: "The tyranny of this dictatorship isn't primarily the fault of Big Business, nor of the demagogues who do their dirty work. It's the fault of Doremus Jessup! Of all the conscientious, respectable, lazy–minded Doremus Jessups who have let the demagogues wriggle in, without fierce enough protest."

Clinton's favorite strategy is a well–tested failure: the best defense is a good sellout. Sell out labor; dump Lani Guinier, Joycelyn Elders, and numerous others deemed politically incorrect by rightwingers; scapegoat single mothers; make court appointments courting conservatives; and so on. Clinton and company behave like defense lawyers who plea bargain every case, no matter the particulars of guilt or innocence. Who wants a lawyer with a track record of pleading their clients "part guilty"?

The Democrats have reaped the scapegoating divisions they have sown with their moves to the right on welfare, immigration, and so on. They divide their electoral base of workers, Blacks, and women, and wonder why Republicans conquer. It's an impossible process of multiplication by division.

Right–wing politicians won in 1994 because their base (mostly religious conservative Republicans, but also like–minded Independents and Democrats) was mobilized to turn out in force— and there was no Perot to divert them—while the more liberal and moderate Democratic base was demoralized and turned off.

According to a report by the Roper Center for Public Opinion Research, the proportion of the 1994 electorate (not a representative sample of the larger population) calling themselves conservative increased 7 points nationally. Nearly one in five voters (19 percent) identified themselves as part of "the religious right political movement."

During the 1980s, Reaganites were the shock troops of global corporate capitalism, lowering wages, busting unions, scapegoating Blacks and women, rolling back communism, socialism, and social democracy abroad—and rolling back welfare and social services and democracy at home. In many ways, rightwingers continue to serve that shock troop purpose. But as shock troops and their leaders grow more powerful, they have more power to implement their more radical agenda, an agenda that is not fully shared by global corporate elites—and can ultimately threaten them.

To put it simply, corporate executives want their own oligarchy, not the Christian Coalition's theocracy.

In a 1992 *New York Times Magazine* article, Kevin Phillips reflected on the contemporary "politics of frustration." He noted "the radicalization of the usually nonideological midsection of the population because of cultural and economic trauma," and warned: "This can lead to dangerous politics, the most terrible example being Germany in the 1920s and early 1930s, when hard times and a collapsing center produced Adolf Hitler." Phillips continued:

> One measure of the depth of the current frustration in America is that [David] Duke could win the support of a majority of white Louisiana voters in two straight statewide elections, notwithstanding television advertisements showing him in Ku Klux Klan robes and swastika armbands.
>
> [Presidential candidate Patrick] Buchanan took many of the same positions as Duke on immigration, race, welfare, trade and nationalism, albeit more moderately. And the charges of nativism, fascism, xenophobia and anti–Semitism inspired by his statements had little effect on his support. When a radicalizing middle class regards the establishment as bankrupt and the status quo as intolerable, normal standards fall quite easily.

Scapegoating fuels fear and fear fuels scapegoating. It is not far–fetched to see the seeds of "ethnic cleansing"—the widely–adopted euphemism for genocide in the former Yugoslavia—in the widespread support given California's Proposition 187. Land plundered from Mexico is called Texas, California, New Mexico, and Arizona—while undocumented Mexican immigrants are called "illegal aliens." The anti–"alien" scapegoating is spreading rapidly to legal immigrants. Think about how successful the Big Lie technique has been: how easy it's been to scapegoat women on welfare. How easy it's been to roll back civil liberties with the excuse of fighting the racially biased "War on Drugs." How easy it's become to spend more money on prisons and less on education. How easy it's been to relabel millions of children as illegitimate.

Think about how far to the right the political "center" has shifted. Views once considered extremist far right are now considered ordinary, views once considered centrist are now considered ultraliberal, and views genuinely to the left are largely absent in the mass media. A nation that committed genocide against Native Americans, enslaved Blacks, and imprisoned Japanese Americans should never doubt authoritarianism can happen here.

Today, with little opposition, a right–wing majority in Congress is voting away pieces of the Bill of Rights and cornerstones of 20th-century progress. How would the nation enter the 21st-century with a right–wing president, a right–wing Congress, and a reactionary Supreme Court?

It is time to strip away the camouflage of scapegoating from the upward redistribution of wealth. It is time to stop pretending the problem is people with cultures of poverty and not the current economy of impoverishment. It is time to pose a true alternative to the dangerous false populism of the right.

It is time to stop building more prison cells, and instead build the preventative foundation of income security, child care, and education. It is time to adopt an Economic Bill of Rights.

This article is based on Holly Sklar's latest book, *Chaos or Community? Seeking Solutions, Not Scapegoats for Bad Economics* (Boston: South End Press, 1995) and "Back to the Raw Deal," *Z Magazine,* November 1995. Sklar's other books include *Streets of Hope: The Fall and Rise of an Urban Neighborhood* (co–authored) and *Trilateralism: The Trilateral Commission and Elite Planning for World Management.* © 1995, Holly Sklar.

The Wise Use Movement

Right–Wing Anti–Environmentalism

William Kevin Burke

In the last days of the 1992 presidential campaign, George Bush denounced "environmental extremists" who sought to lock up natural resources and destroy the American way of life. At the heart of this imagined green conspiracy was the "Ozone Man," Senator Al Gore Jr., author of *Earth in the Balance*. Bush's attack on environmentalism failed to save his candidacy, but it was a high water mark for the political influence of the "Wise Use" movement, a network of loosely allied right–wing grassroots and corporate interest groups dedicated to attacking the environmental movement and promoting unfettered resource exploitation.

New organizing opportunities and media exposure of the movement's less savory connections have caused constant splintering within the movement. At present, the best way to recognize Wise Use groups is by the policies they support. Therefore, Wise Use will be used here to describe all organizations that promote the core Wise Use agenda: removing present environmental protections and preventing future environmental reforms in order to benefit the economic interests of the organization's members or funders.

Five years ago Wise Use was just the latest fundraising concept of two political entrepreneurs: Ron Arnold and Alan Gottlieb. Arnold once worked for the Sierra Club in Washington State. He has told reporters that he helped organize teaching expeditions to areas that became the Alpine Lakes Wilderness Area. Alan Gottlieb is a professional fundraiser who has generated millions for various right–wing causes.

Wise Use groups are often funded by timber, mining, and chemical companies. In return, they claim, loudly, that the well–documented hole in the ozone layer doesn't exist, that carcinogenic chemicals in the air and water don't harm anyone, and that trees won't grow properly unless forests are clear–cut, with government subsidies. Wise Use proponents were buffeted by Bush's defeat and by media exposure of the movement's founders' connections to the Rev. Sun Myung Moon's Unification Church network (tainted by charges of cultism and theocratic neo–fascism), but the movement has quickly rebounded. In every state of the US, relentless Wise Use disinformation campaigns about the purpose and meaning of environmental laws are building a grassroots constituency. To Wise Users, environmentalists are pagans, eco–nazis, and communists who must be fought with shouts and threats.

Environmentalists often point to public opinion polls that show most Americans are willing to sacrifice some short–term economic gains to preserve nature. But the Wise Use movement is eroding the environmental consensus that dominated American politics from the Greenhouse Summer of 1988 until shortly after the media overload that greeted Earth Day 1990.

What's in a Name?

The term "Wise Use" was appropriated from the moderate conservationist tradition by movement founder Ron Arnold. In 1910, Gifford Pinchot, first head of the US Forest Service, called for national forestry policies based on the wise use of America's trees and minerals. That triggered a simmering feud between Pinchot and Sierra Club founder John Muir. Muir wanted to see wilderness valued for its own sake, as the spiritual center of the world. In theory, the current US system of combining national forests managed for resource extraction with wilderness areas managed for recreation is a compromise solution to this debate.

But Ron Arnold did not pick the term Wise Use because of an affinity to the moderate conservationism of Pinchot. In 1991, he told *Outside* magazine that he chose the phrase Wise Use because it was ambiguous and fit neatly in newspaper headlines. Such duplicitous and opportunistic tactics are a trademark of the Wise Use movement. "Facts don't matter; in politics perception is reality," Arnold told *Outside*.

For a number of years, Arnold was a registered agent for the American Freedom Coalition, a political offshoot of Rev. Sun Myung Moon's Unification Church. The American Freedom Coalition takes credit for funding the first Wise Use conference in 1988. Aside from telling *Outside* he is willing to ignore facts to achieve his goals, Arnold proclaims at every opportunity that his mission is to destroy the environmental movement. "We're mad as hell. We're dead serious. We're going to destroy them," he told the *Portland Oregonian*. In the spring of 1995, Arnold told a Vermont audience that Wise Users do not want to negotiate with environmentalists.

Ron Arnold's big career break coincided with the coming of the Reagan presidency and Arnold's own rapid swing to the right. In 1981, he co–authored *At the Eye of the Storm*, a flattering biography of James Watt that the former Secretary of the Interior helped edit. Watt's attempts to dismantle environmental regulation and open federal lands to logging and mining produced short–term gains for corporate interests, but the long–term result of such policies was public revulsion and the explosive growth of the environmental movement during the 1980s.

Arnold's movement–building was enhanced when he joined forces with Alan Gottlieb. Gottlieb's Center for the Defense of Free Enterprise (CDFE) reportedly takes in about $5 million per year through direct mail and telephone fundraising for a variety of right–wing causes. Gottlieb seems to possess a genius for dancing along the edge of legal business practices. He purchased the building that houses CDFE's headquarters with money from two of his own non–profit foundations, then transferred the building's title to his own name so he could charge his foundations over $8,000 per month in rent. Gottlieb also spent seven months in prison for tax evasion.

In 1988, Gottlieb published Ron Arnold's book, *The Wise Use Agenda*, which outlines their movement's goals and aims. Few environmentalists would find fault with the spirit behind this quote from *The Wise Use Agenda*: "[Wise Use's] founders [feel] that industrial development can be directed in ways that enhance the Earth, not destroy it." But the *Agenda* itself is basically a wish list for the resource extraction industries. The Wise Use movement seeks to open all federal lands to logging, mining, and the driving of off–road vehicles. Despite much rhetoric about seeking ecological balance and environmental solutions, almost the only environmental problem *The Wise Use Agenda* addresses rather than dismisses is the threat of global warming from the build–up of carbon dioxide in the earth's atmosphere. The solution proposed is the immediate clear–cutting of the small portion of old growth timber left in the United States so that these forests can be re-planted with young trees that will absorb more carbon dioxide.

Although the science cited by Wise Use sources is suspect, and their arguments are mostly retreads of corporate press releases, today nearly everyone on the right wants a piece of the Wise Use movement. Rush Limbaugh, Lyndon LaRouche, the National Farm Bureau Federation, and dozens of other organizations and public figures are adopting their own versions of Wise Use rhetoric.

Much of this popularity can be explained by the lingering economic recession of the early 1980s, which provided a receptive grassroots audience for the Wise Use claim that it is easier to force nature to adapt to current corporate policies than to encourage the growth of more environmentally sound ways of doing business. Wise Use pamphlets argue that extinction is a natural process; some species weren't meant to survive. The movement's signature public relations tactic is to frame complex environmental and economic issues in simple, scapegoating terms that benefit its corporate backers. In the movement's Pacific Northwest birthplace, Wise Users harp on a supposed battle for survival between spotted owls and the families of the men and women who make their livings harvesting and milling the old growth timber that is the owl's habitat. In preparation for President Clinton's forest summit in Portland, Oregon, Wise Use public relations experts ran seminars to teach loggers how to speak in sound bites. Messages such as "jobs versus owls" have been adapted to a variety of environmental issues and have helped spark an anti–green backlash that has defeated river protection efforts and threatens to open millions of acres of wilderness to resource extraction.

While attacking environmentalists, Wise Use statements borrow heavily from environmental rhetoric; this borrowed rhetoric often cloaks a self–serving economic agenda. The Oregon Lands Coalition in effect supports the timber industry by arguing that only people who cut down trees really love the wilderness. At the same time, the Wise Use movement opposes environmentalist efforts to find new careers for unemployed loggers who could be hired to begin restoring the stream beds ravaged by clear–cutting of forests.

Similarly, National Farm Bureau Federation publications repeatedly argue that farmers are the true stewards of the land. But the Farm Bureau lobbies for fewer restrictions on pesticide use and for the clearing of wetlands—not for government support for the alternative farming practices that the National Research Council's 1989 book, *Alternative Agriculture*, showed can reduce farming's impact on the environment while improving farmers' net incomes.

Both the National Farm Bureau Federation and the Oregon Lands Coalition later disavowed any association with Alan Gottlieb's Center for the Defense of Free Enterprise and the term Wise Use. Groups that portray themselves as moderate Wise Users, like the Farm Bureau and Alliance for America, now describe their approach with substitute terms like "multiple use," while still employing Ron Arnold's tactics and inviting him to speak at Wise Use conferences. This distancing is apparently due to Arnold's willingness to make extreme statements to the press and the baggage of his association with Rev. Moon's Unification Church.

"It shouldn't be surprising that there are these terminology wars, given that so much of this movement is about manipulating language and manipulating people's understanding of concepts like environmentalism," according to Tarso Ramos, who monitors Wise Use activity for the Western States Center in Portland, Oregon.

In fact, the Wise Use movement resorts to a bewildering range of subterfuges to mask its agenda. For instance, the developer–funded Environmental Conservation Organization and its member organization, the National Wetlands Coalition, want to make it easier for their funders to drain wetlands to build malls. To that end, Champion Paper and MCI fund the Evergreen Foundation, which spreads the word that forests need only clear–cutting and healthy doses of pesticides to become places of "beauty, peace and mystery."

In a similar example, the Sea Lion Defense Fund is the Alaska fishing industry's legal arm in its fight against government limits on harvests of pollock, one of the endangered sea lion's favorite foods. Oregonians for Food and Shelter and Vermont's Citizens for Property Rights cultivate a folksy grassroots image while promoting the agendas of developers or extractive industries. This was a tactic first advocated by Ron Arnold in a series of articles he wrote for *Timber Management* magazine in the early 1980s.

Alliance for America

Since the first corporate check arrived, the Wise Use movement has been split by debates over who will control organizing strategy and funds. "[Wise Use] is not a disciplined ideological coalition. It is a multifaceted movement. There are factions within it. They fight. The objectives of various players are very different. Coalitions can be tenuous, but they are very effective," says Tarso Ramos. The Oregon Lands Coalition (OLC) is dominated by timber interests but also includes the National Farm Bureau Federation, pro–pesticide groups, and land–use planning activists representing developers.

In 1991, the OLC became a national organization by creating the Alliance for America. The Alliance's stated purpose is to "put people back in the environmental equation." The means to this end is to enlist grassroots groups in each state to fight environmentalists on a wide variety of issues. In 1991 and 1992, the Alliance staged "Fly–ins for Freedom" that brought supporters to Washington, DC, to lobby on behalf of logging, mining, and ranching interests.

From its founding, the Alliance for America's purpose was to unify grassroots anti–environmentalist organizations in all 50 states. In the western states, where the movement was born, the Wise Users tend to be freedom–loving, right–wing libertarians, yet they spend much of their time and energy working to protect government subsidies for ranchers, miners, and loggers.

A well–worn joke describes the typical westerner's attitude toward the federal government as "go away and give me more money." Groups like the Oregon Lands Coalition and People for the West strive to preserve government privileges, such as below–cost sales of timber from federal lands and the 1872 mining law that lets mining companies lease government mineral rights for as little as $2.50.

A more subtle approach was required to build support for Wise Use groups in eastern states, where the Wise Use movement's natural audience, primarily rural landowners, was not so accustomed to government largesse. The Alliance for America quickly found a slogan for its efforts to organize east of the Mississippi: private property rights.

The Theme of Private Property Rights

The Wise Use movement argues that regulations protecting environmentally sensitive areas on private property are unconstitutional "takings." They cite the Fifth Amendment to the US Constitution, which states in part: "nor shall private property be taken for public use, without just compensation." That clause is the basis for the concept of eminent domain, which allows government entities to take land for public projects by paying property owners the land's fair market value.

Across the nation, the Wise Use movement is backing state legislation seeking to expand the legal concept of what constitutes a "government taking" to include all situations where possible profits from developing, mining, or logging private lands are limited by environmental regulations. The movement argues that if a regulatory agency wants to protect a wetland, for example, the agency must pay the wetlands owner what he or she *might* have made if the wetlands were drained in order to become a buildable site.

The private property rights strategy may prove Wise Use's best weapon. Despite their ability to draw attention and corporate money, western Wise Use organizations will remain vulnerable to negative press coverage because they are so often arguing for more government handouts for their corporate backers. But the call to protect private property rights from "government land grabs" or "unconstitutional takings" appeals strongly to rural landowners and small businesspeople, sectors of society that fear economic change and heavy–handed environmental reforms. "As an organizing strategy, takings is a kind of deviant genius," says Tarso Ramos. "It automatically puts environmentalists in the position of defending the federal government and appeals to anyone who has ever had any kind of negative experience with the federal government, which is a hell of a lot of people."

By the end of 1992, private property rights advocates had introduced legislation expanding the definition of takings in 27 states. If passed, these bills would rule that government regulatory actions, such as wetlands protection or even zoning restrictions, are "takings," and require that landowners be paid for the potential value of the land they lost due to government actions. A single lost takings case could bankrupt most state regulatory agencies. The takings movement would, if successful, effectively end environmental protection in the US. The only federal legal test of takings was *Lucas v. South Carolina*. Lucas, a developer, sued the state for the lost value of homes he had planned to build on land that South Carolina subsequently declared sensitive coastal habitat. The 1992 US Supreme Court ruling on the case is often trumpeted as a takings triumph by Wise Users, but was actually a split decision requiring that South Carolina prove the homes would have constituted a public nuisance before enforcing the regulation protecting the sea coast.

In Vermont, a failed takings law was nicknamed the "pout and pay" bill. Opponents argued that the bill would have encouraged owners of low–value properties to imagine fantastic development schemes that conflicted with zoning restrictions or wetlands protection, then present the federal government with the bill.

After a bitter legislative battle, Arizona Governor Fife Symington signed a takings bill into law in June 1992. Delaware also passed a takings bill in 1992. In 1993, Utah passed a takings bill. In Idaho and Wyoming, takings bills passed the state legislatures, but were vetoed by the governors of each state on the grounds that the laws would create unnecessary bureaucracy. Similar bills are pending in a number of states across the country.

It is at the grassroots, city, town, and county level in rural areas that the Wise Use movement has been most effective. State–level takings laws fare better than efforts to convince the federal government it has no right to regulate land use. American industry has never dared advocate total war on the environment, even if the argument can be made that at times standard industry practices have fit that description. But grassroots Wise Users are proving effective shock troops, using tactics inspired by Ron Arnold to reverse decades of environmental compromise and negotiation in a few months.

The private property rights call was first sounded in the Northeast by the John Birch Society. In 1990–91, John Birch Society members helped turn out hundreds of people to protest the Northern Forest Lands study, a joint effort by the federal government and the governments of New York, Vermont, New Hampshire, and Maine to plan for the future of the vast woodland known as the Big North.

Now, New England's private property rights movement has outgrown its John Birch Society origins. Wise Use groups in every New England state have affiliated with the Alliance for America. In Vermont, Citizens for Property Rights has assembled a coalition of developers and far right politicians to crusade for the repeal of the state's progressive land–use laws. The Maine Conservation Rights Institute, based in the state's far northeast (a stronghold of Christian fundamentalism), promotes a typical Wise Use agenda, opposing wetlands and forest protection under the guise of conservation.

A western Massachusetts Wise Use group called Friends of the Rivers (FOR) blocked a US Park Service plan to designate the upper reaches of the Farmington River a federally protected "wild and scenic" river. With assistance from Alliance for America, FOR spread disinformation on the effects of wild and scenic designation. Its literature predicted businesses being forced to close, property values plummeting, and riverbank homes being taken by the government.

Friends of the Rivers' most vocal ally was Don Rupp, who is affiliated with Alliance for America. Rupp previously had led an unsuccessful struggle against wild and scenic designation of the Upper Delaware river in New York. Along the Delaware, Rupp warned of dire effects from wild and scenic designation that were virtually identical to the claims that appeared in Friends of the Rivers' literature. But no homes have been taken or landowners forced to move from Rupp's home territory. And after the Park

Service stepped in to provide protection to the river property, land values along the Upper Delaware rose. Friends of the Rivers' leaders included the Campetti family, owners of an oil distributor and off–road vehicle dealership, and Francis Deming, who operates his 100–acre property as a pay–as–you–go dumpsite. But despite this evident self–serving interest, FOR's claims frightened enough Massachusetts residents to cause three towns to vote against the wild and scenic designation of the Upper Farmington. FOR displayed posters claiming local wild and scenic supporter Bob Tarasuk was a paid government agent. Tarasuk had once spent a summer working for the Bureau of Land Management; he reports that harassing phone calls from opponents of wild and scenic designation eventually forced him to get an unlisted telephone number.

"There is no better tactic than to threaten someone's land. Get someone who lives on their land and that's all they have and then tell them that the government is coming to take it. Fear works. The Alliance for America knows this and I believe they coach [local groups]," Tarasuk said. "Your land has been stolen," read an FOR flier distributed along the Farmington.

In Connecticut, along the lower reaches of the Farmington River, a local river protection group called the Farmington River Watershed Association defeated FOR's efforts to prevent wild and scenic designation. Drawing on its strong local base, the Watershed Association (founded in 1953) rallied local citizens to support wild and scenic designation. Don Rupp's efforts to spread fearful tales about the Park Service were blunted by the fact that the city of Hartford has flooded several branches of the lower Farmington to create reservoirs. Connecticut residents saw wild and scenic designation as Federal protection from future dam projects.

The battle over New England's rivers reached a climax in March 1993, when the New Hampshire Landholders Alliance, an affiliate of the Alliance for America, convinced six of seven New Hampshire towns along the Pemigewasset River to vote against the river's proposed wild and scenic designation. Patricia Schlesinger of the Pemi River Council said that only 15 percent of the registered voters in the seven towns took part in the town meetings that decided the river's fate. "People felt intimidated and abused by fear–mongering and deceit. It was canned stuff, claims that the 'feds are going to take your land.' It was typical Wise Use tactics."

The founders of the New Hampshire Landholders Alliance, Cheryl and Don Johnson, have a profit motive to fight wild and scenic designation along the Pemi. Don Johnson works for Ed Clark, a local businessman who has unsuccessfully sought to build a small hydroelectric dam at a scenic area called Livermore

Falls—a project that would be prohibited if wild and scenic status were secured. As a result of the defeat of the wild and scenic plan, the state of New Hampshire will lose $450,000 in federal aid to develop a park at Livermore Falls.

Free Market Environmentalism

Environmentalists are conditioned by decades of using legislative processes to battle industry over the scale of development and resource exploitation in natural areas. But Wise Users don't contest the scope of environmental protection; they wage war on the notion that any ecological problems exist that cannot be solved by reliance on the free market. David Gurnsey, Maine Conservation Rights Institute's representative to the Northern Forest Lands Advisory Committee, did not criticize the conclusions of the Committee's biodiversity study—he claimed the whole concept of preserving biodiversity was a veiled effort to take land from private owners.

Wise Users often call environmentalists "watermelons": green on the outside, but red to the core. This association of environmentalists with the specter of communism is not mere grassroots name–calling. Corporate–funded, rightist libertarian think tanks like the Cato Institute and the Reason Foundation publish analysis and research supporting the Wise Use claim that green politics are the last vestige of communism's collectivist, One World Government plot to subjugate the planet. In its most extreme forms, this logic surfaces in the claim of Lyndon LaRouche's followers that Greenpeace's activists are eco–terrorists and pawns of the KGB. The Greenpeace–KGB connection, first trumpeted in LaRouche publications, resurfaced in the writings of Kathleen Marquardt, founder of Putting People First and winner of the Best Newcomer Award at the June 1992 Wise Use Leadership Conference.

In some respects, however, free market environmentalism as advocated by Cato's director of Natural Resource Studies, Jerry Taylor, or *Reason Magazine* editor, Virginia I. Postrel, has more merit than many environmentalists want to admit. For example, the biggest source of water pollution in America today is municipal wastewater facilities built with federal assistance. It was only after the end of federal subsidies for wastewater treatment that alternative clean–up methods like engineered wetlands were able to win out over traditional wastewater plants in many areas. But the Wise Use movement is not seeking to open opportunities for small businesses to profit while healing the planet. They want to dismantle government environmental protection while removing restrictions on industrial exploitation.

At the grassroots level, the Wise Users are taking on many of the typical characteristics of demagogic, paranoid right–wing movements, portraying environmentalists as in league with the federal government to destroy families. In Vermont, Citizens for Property Rights decorated a rally with effigies of their opponents dangling from nooses. Massachusetts' Friends of the Rivers claimed that environmental groups had paid off legislators to support wild and scenic designation of the Farmington River. In New Hampshire, opponents of grassroots Wise Users along the Pemigewassett River received threatening phone calls.

Wise Use & the Right Wing

By 1993, the Wise Use movement had begun forming its first links with anti–gay activists and the Religious Right. In his report, *God, Land and Politics*, Dave Mazza of the Western States Center traced the growing association of two grassroots movements in Oregon. "Oregon's electoral process has seen the Wise Use Movement and the Religious Right movement coming together in a number of ways, intentionally or unintentionally pushing forward a much broader conservative social or economic agenda," Mazza concluded.

The Oregon Citizens' Alliance, which achieved a small measure of national fame by its advocacy of a state referendum effectively legalizing discrimination against gays and lesbians (Measure 9), is trying to climb on the state's crowded Wise Use bandwagon by sponsoring an initiative undermining Oregon's land–use planning laws. As the Wise Use movement continues to spread, it is becoming both more vociferous and sophisticated. The leaders of the Wise Use movement have demonstrated that they would rather intimidate environmentalists than negotiate compromises between economic and environmental interests. In practice, Wise Use is proving to be a slick new name for some of democracy's oldest enemies.

William Kevin Burke has written extensively about environmental issues. This article appeared in the June 1993 issue of *The Public Eye*. © 1995, William Kevin Burke.

Regulatory Takings & Private Property Rights

Tarso Ramos

"Regulatory takings" has become the cornerstone of the "Wise Use" movement's legislative agenda as well as the ideology underlying the movement's "property rights" wing. Under the regulatory takings banner, Wise Use leaders have rounded up a broad range of economic and political interests, including developers, small property owners, timber companies, and others into the so—called "property rights" movement. More accurately termed "property primacy" for its subordination of the public good to private financial interests, this is the fastest growing wing of the Wise Use movement.

In their newsletters, journals, books, and presentations, Wise Use leaders routinely object that environmental regulations are destroying private property rights—that the green movement has generated an avalanche of regulatory red tape that threatens to suffocate small property owners and destroy industrial civilization altogether. "If the government wants your land, they should pay for it!" is a common declaration at Wise Use rallies, generally in reference to wetlands laws, "wild and scenic" rivers designations, or other environmental protections. Wise Use national leader Chuck Cushman in particular has led the "property rights" charge against the creation of national parks, and, with Ron Arnold and other leaders, has helped to cultivate a network of local "property rights" groups across the nation. Organizations such as Defenders of Property Rights and the Alliance for America are active at the national level, and former Alliance chairman David Howard shares movement updates and analysis through his publication, *Land Rights Letter.* Corporate–funded "public interest" legal firms, such as the Mountain States Legal Foundation, Pacific Legal Foundation, and the Northwest Legal Foundation, have carried the banner in the courts, while conservative think tanks decry the erosion of property rights in guest editorials that provide support for state–level takings legislation. Regulatory takings doctrine has provided the theoretical and rhetorical basis for much of this activity.

Regulatory takings doctrine holds that government regulatory action that negatively affects the value—actual or potential—of private property constitutes a "taking" of property and, as such, is prohibited under the takings clause of the Fifth Amendment of the US Constitution unless affected property owners are fairly compensated. (The relevant portion of the Fifth Amendment reads, "nor shall private property be taken for public use, without just compensation.") Historically, the courts have interpreted the takings clause as pertaining to cases of condemnation under eminent domain—that is, the government cannot confiscate your land or other property without paying you a fair price for it. However, only in instances where government regulations have been found to eliminate virtually all economic value of property have some Supreme Court justices supported financial compensation for a "regulatory takings." By contrast, regulatory takings doctrine deems a vast array of public interest and regulatory laws to be illegal.

The regulatory takings movement appears to have its origins in the libertarian school of legal thought associated with the University of Chicago and epitomized by professor Richard Epstein. Epstein's 1985 book, *Takings: Private Property and the Power of Eminent Domain,* provided the impetus for a regulatory takings legal and legislative strategy. It is useful to examine Epstein's writings, for although proponents of regulatory takings legislation invariably argue that the scope of such laws would be finite, Epstein openly asserts that his position on regulatory takings "invalidates much of the twentieth century legislation," including the National Labor Relations Act, minimum wage laws, civil rights legislation, virtually all government entitlement programs, and quite possibly Social Security. In fact, Epstein proposes to challenge the entire New Deal as "inconsistent with the principles of limited government and with the constitutional provisions designed to secure that end."

For instance, Epstein argues that minimum wage laws are "undoubted partial takings, with all the earmarks of class legislation, which requires their complete constitutional invalidation."

Under regulatory takings doctrine, employers forced to pay a statutory minimum wage higher than wages set by free market forces suffer from a government takings of their property. "Collective bargaining," Epstein asserts, "is yet another system in which well–defined markets are displaced by complex common pool devices whose overall wealth effects are in all likelihood negative and whose disproportionate impact, especially on established firms, is enormous."

Here Epstein's argument raises the obvious question: for whom are the wealth effects of collective bargaining negative? It also provides the answer: the owners of "established firms." Collective bargaining has increased the economic means of the great majority of working people in the United States by securing decent wages and benefits for union members, and driving wages higher even for the unorganized. Thus, while regulatory takings has come to be deployed in the war against environmental regulations, and, by extension, the environmental movement, it threatens to undo the gains of other great movements for progressive social change of the last century and a half: the labor movement, the civil rights movement, the women's movement, the anti–poverty movement, and others. Indeed, this is part of the strategy of takings advocates, who hope to use anti–environmental campaigns to popularize "property rights" rhetoric and build support for takings legislation, as well as a redefinition of takings by the courts.

Proponents of takings legislation argue that it will provide relief to small property owners who, they say, are increasingly restricted by wetlands ordinances, growth management laws, and other environmental statutes. Such arguments can be persuasive, since government bureaucracy does sometimes generate burdensome, irrational, and even harmful regulations, and as the relationship between, for example, wetlands protection and the public health is somewhat technical, as well as indirect. However, under regulatory takings doctrine, in order to prohibit industrial polluters from fouling air, land, and water, the public would be required to pay the cost of pollution prevention. This quite direct relationship between regulatory takings law, environmental protections, and the public health is either ignored by proponents or is resolved in the manner suggested by Ron Arnold: if a citizen can show a violation of rights by a corporate polluter or anyone else, let her or him sue.

Epstein found allies for his radical legal theories in a most influential place, the White House. In March 1988, President Ronald Reagan signed Executive Order 12630, which codified Epstein's doctrine and advised that "[e]xecutive departments and agencies should review their actions carefully to prevent unnecessary takings and should account in decision–making for those takings that are necessitated by statutory mandate." Executive Order 12630 amounted to a presidential order against regulating industry and an attack on public interest law. In his memoir, Reagan Administration Solicitor General Charles Fried offers the following analysis of Executive Order 12630:

Attorney General [Edwin] Meese and his young advisors—many drawn from the ranks of the then fledgling Federalist Societies and often devotees of the extreme libertarian views of Chicago law professor Richard Epstein—had a specific, aggressive, and, it seemed to me, quite radical project in mind: to use the Takings Clause of the Fifth Amendment as a severe brake upon federal and state regulation of business and property. The grand plan was to make government pay compensation as for a taking of property every time its regulations impinged too severely on a property right—limiting the possible uses for a parcel of land or restricting or tying up a business in regulatory red tape. If the government labored under so severe an obligation, there would be, to say the least, much less regulation.

Following Reagan's second term as president, Idaho Senator Steve Symms (a strong Wise Use ally who, before retiring from the Senate, helped to pass the National Recreational Trails Trust Fund, to date the only successful item on the 25–point Wise Use Agenda) attempted to pass federal legislation codifying Executive Order 12630. With his retirement in 1992, Symms (who now heads Ollie North's Freedom Alliance) passed the takings torch to Senator Bob Dole, who has carried it since. When support for takings, typically introduced as a "Private Property Rights Act," was not forthcoming from the Democrat–controlled Congress, Dole and others managed at times to defeat their opponents' legislation by attaching takings language to, for instance, bills giving cabinet status to the Environmental Protection Agency. Reps. Billy Tauzin (D–La.) and Richard Pombo (R–Cal.), later became visible advocates of regulatory takings in the House, and during the successful 1994 Republican campaign for control of Congress, takings was incorporated into the Republican "Contract with America" as part of the proposed Job Creation and Wage Enhancement Act. Unlike Reagan's takings order—an assessment–type measure that hamstrung regulatory enforcement with bureaucratic red tape—the version of takings now promoted by Congressional Republicans requires financial compensation for "regulatory takings" of property.

At the national level, "takings" legislation has been opposed by labor, environmental, civil rights, religious, and other public interest organizations. Among these groups are the AFL–CIO Industrial Union Department, AFL–CIO Food and Allied Service

Trades Department, Alliance for Justice, Coalition Against Child-hood Lead Poisoning, Defenders of Wildlife, Farmworker Justice Fund, Izaak Walton League of America, League of Conservation Voters, National Audubon Society, National Parks and Conservation Association, National Urban League, National Wildlife Federation, Public Citizen, Sierra Club, United Food and Commercial Workers Union, United Church of Christ, United Steelworkers of America, and the Wilderness Society. As this broad opposition attests, of the various Wise Use efforts, the intersection of the movement's anti–labor, anti–environmental, and anti–civil rights elements are most immediately evident in regulatory takings legislation. This recognition has been critical to blocking passage of federal takings legislation, and has helped to stem the tide of regulatory takings bills at the state level.

As of October 1995, takings bills (a mix of assessment and compensation type measures) had passed in Arizona, Delaware, Florida, Idaho, Indiana, Kansas, Louisiana, Mississippi, North Dakota, Oregon, Tennessee, Utah, Virginia, Washington, and West Virginia, and had been introduced in all the other states in the Union. Some of the new takings laws have been challenged and overturned. In November 1994, the Arizona law was repealed by citizens' referendum with 60 percent of the vote. (A takings measure was removed from the 1994 Florida ballot after a legal challenge, and during the same campaign season, ballot measures were filed but failed to qualify in Oregon and Washington.) The Oregon law which passed in 1995 was later vetoed, and a measure to repeal the Washington law was being considered by voters in November 1995. The rapid and pervasive dissemination of regulatory takings legislation has been facilitated by the American Legislative Exchange Council (ALEC), a national organization of right–wing ideologues and business interests that drafts policy on a wide range of economic and social issues and offers a smorgasbord of model bills to conservative state legislators in all 50 states. The group's model legislation ranges from reactionary AIDS/HIV policy, to telecommunications proposals, anti–labor "right–to–work" bills, and Wise Use regulatory takings legislation. ALEC's task force on natural resources includes representatives from such environmentally sensitive and labor–friendly corporations and organizations as Waste Management, Amoco, Shell, Texaco, Union Pacific Railroad, Chevron, American Petroleum Institute, American Nuclear Energy Council, and Coors, among others. The author of ALEC's model takings bill is Mark Pollot, who also drafted Reagan's takings order and who now heads a division of Ron Arnold's organization in Idaho. ALEC's support for the Wise Use movement is not limited to model bills; the February 1991 issue of the group's newsletter, *The State Factor*, carried a long speech by *Detroit News* columnist Warren Brookes entitled "The Attack of the Killer Watermelons: Flat Earth Science and Zero Risk." Nor is ALEC's anti–labor activity limited to the dissemination of "right–to–work" legislation; ALEC has also spearheaded a national campaign targeting public sector unions as "America's protected class" that facilitated a successful 1994 ballot campaign in Oregon to cut public worker wages by six percent.

The fight against state–level regulatory takings bills has been difficult. Cloaked in the Fifth Amendment, and branded "property rights," the bills are attractive to state legislators unaware of their broad implications and pleased at the opportunity to go on the record with a vote in favor of "property rights." Moreover, entrenched political forces in the form of the Farm Bureau, Cattlemen's Association, National Association of Builders, timber companies, and others have repeatedly put their considerable weight behind takings legislation. Finally, state–level labor and environmental leaders were at first less educated about regulatory takings than their national counterparts; and, to make matters worse, in several states seemingly innocuous takings language has been stealthily incorporated into other bills. Due to the powerful forces marshaled in support of takings bills, broad coalitions have been important to defeating them. In particular, organized labor and environmental groups have worked to block regulatory takings in legislatures and to secure governors' vetoes where bills have passed. Possibly in response to the success of such coalitions, in 1993 the Oregon Wise Use organization Oregonians In Action announced a regulatory takings ballot initiative narrowly restricted to compensation for "takings" resulting from the protection of wildlife habitat. Catered to attract the support of timber unions, as well as pro–timber Wise Use groups, the narrow focus of the initiative might have forestalled a labor/environmental alliance to oppose it. Fortunately, the initiative failed to qualify for the ballot. However, in some states takings forces have successfully pursued a strategy of incrementalism, enacting narrow laws in a given legislative session, and expanding their scope in subsequent years. Also, if the state takings statutes now on the books are upheld by the courts, we may well find ourselves on the slippery slope toward the rollback of the New Deal advocated by Epstein. For, once regulatory takings doctrine is ruled constitutional, there is little to prevent its application beyond wetlands and wildlife protection to minimum wage laws, civil rights statutes, and other public interest legislation.

Due to the increasingly conservative composition of state legislative bodies, some previously successful anti–takings coalitions are finding themselves unable to hold the line, even against progressively onerous takings proposals. Washington State provides an instructive example. In the spring of 1992, Ron Arnold declared that "The future of the property rights issue for the next decade will probably be centered in Washington State." Opponents of Washington's recently enacted Growth Management Act (GMA) had just managed to saddle it with an assessment–type takings provision, and their earlier, successful ballot fight against a more stringent version of the GMA proposed by environmental groups had served to galvanize corporate support for the burgeoning property rights movement. Working to realize Arnold's prediction, and responding to a GMA requirement that counties develop local land–use plans, Wise Use organizers constructed a network of county–level "property rights" groups across the state. Various of these local groups have stymied implementation of the GMA, taken over local governments, launched campaigns to form new counties under their command, and passed Wise Use "county rule" ordinances that claim control of federal lands within county boundaries. With the assistance of the Alliance for America, Washington Wise Use activists formed The Umbrella Group (TUG) as a statewide coalition vehicle. TUG executive director Dan Wood went to work lobbying the strongly Democratic legislature to pass a regulatory takings law, but was rebuffed. Wood formed the Washington Property Protection Coalition and in 1994 tried to place a takings measure (written by the Northwest Legal Foundation) on the Washington ballot, but failed to collect the requisite number of signatures. However, in the 1994 elections Republicans seized control of the Washington House and reduced Democrat's control of the Senate to a one–vote majority. The following spring, Wood again collected signatures for the measure, now in the form of a citizens' initiative to the state legislature (I–164). As the signature deadline neared and Wood again appeared destined for failure, timber, building, and real estate interests rescued the effort with an infusion of more than $250,000, much of it used to pay professional signature gatherers. Despite the discovery that a significant number of the signatures submitted were forgeries, enough of them were found valid to qualify the measure and send it to the legislature. To the astonishment of many political observers, both houses of the Washington legislature passed I–164, the strongest compensation–type regulatory takings law in the nation.

The Washington takings measure was enacted by a legislature financially beholden to the corporate interests that invested over $250,000 in this "citizens'" initiative. Major contributors to the I–164 campaign gave a combined total of more than $309,000 to legislative candidates in the 1994 election cycle alone, with over 87 percent of these dollars supporting Republican candidates. But while the vote for I–164 split largely along party lines, passing by a vote of 28–20 in the Republican–controlled House, the most critical votes cast in favor of I–164 may have been those of Democratic Senators James Hargrove and Brad Owen, who gave takings proponents the majorities they needed to pull the initiative from committee and put it to a vote of the full Senate. Both Hargrove and Owen had received significant contributions from I–164's corporate sponsors in their last election campaigns, when Hargrove's campaign manager had been none other than I–164's Dan Wood. Four other Senate Democrats voted in favor of I–164, three of whom also had taken significant campaign contributions from real estate and natural resource corporations, while two Republicans voted against the initiative. Following the passage of I–164, corporate backers of the measure disclaimed any relationship with the Wise Use movement. By contrast, Ron Arnold told a Seattle newspaper, "How do you help people speak up in a voice that will help big industry? The Wise Use Movement does that. The little people are the real constituency. They do the work of big industry."

In Washington, citizens' initiatives passed by the legislature become law without needing the governor's approval. However, a coalition of environmental, labor, and good government groups gathered enough signatures to force a referendum on the takings law, to be decided in November 1995.

While there is at least active opposition to regulatory takings as a legislative effort, the forces marshaled in favor of takings appear to be gaining, rather than losing, momentum. This is also true outside of the legislative arena, where regulatory takings provides the underpinnings for the expanding "property rights" wing of the Wise Use movement. This focus on "property rights" represents a shift in emphasis away from the movement goals presented in Arnold's 1989 volume, *The Wise Use Agenda*. The 25–point *Agenda* reads like a wish list for natural resource interests on the public lands, and most Wise Use campaigns have centered on public lands issues such as grazing, hard rock mining, timber harvesting, and petroleum exploration. By casting environmental regulations as a threat to individual property rights and economic security, Wise Use has found a means to tap the vast demographic base located in suburban and urban areas (as well as the deep pockets of a new set of corporate sponsors). In contrast, organizing around natural resource industries and control over federal lands generally limits movement support to the rural West. Also, with the regulatory takings approach, Wise Use has discovered powerful populist organizing "handles." Focusing on such issues as wetlands designation, controls on urban growth, and "wild and scenic" rivers designation—rather than industrial contamination of water supplies or minimum wage statutes—the movement has developed "little people" messengers for its big business agenda. Finally, Wise Use strategists have endeavored to use regulatory takings doctrine as a bridge between two distinct and seemingly incompatible movement constituencies: the free marketeer and privatization types, and corporate interests seeking to maintain and expand subsidized access to public lands and resources. Thus, public lands grazing permits have been redefined by the movement as "property rights," and efforts by critics of public lands grazing to bring subsidized permit fees in line with the going rates on private lands are now characterized by some as "takings."

Regulatory takings is by no means the only component of the Wise Use legislative agenda. Other items include measures to free states from federal laws unaccompanied by federal largesse (termed "unfunded mandates") and to turn portions of the public lands over to the states—an old Sagebrush Rebellion demand finding new support among Congressional "devolution" (a new term for "states' rights") advocates. However, "takings" represents the single most comprehensive Wise Use assault on our ability as a society to check the worst excesses of corporate capitalism. Moreover, "property rights" has become a bridge issue linking Wise Use with other right–wing movements. In the Northwest, the multi–state network of the Oregon Citizens Alliance—best known for its campaigns to deny civil rights protections to lesbians and gay men—has declared "property rights" to be one of its top priorities. At the national level, the Christian Right cable television network, National Empowerment Television, broadcasts Wise Use specials on property rights, and in turn, Wise Use publications promote NET as a source of news and commentary. With this expanding base of support, takings may prove to be not only one of most onerous components of the Wise Use agenda, but one of the most viable.

Tarso Ramos is an analyst with the Western States Center in Portland, Oregon. Earlier versions of this article have appeared in several Western States Center publications. To obtain a copy of this article accompanied with footnotes, contact the Western States Center. © 1995, Tarso Ramos.

Culture Wars & Freedom of Expression

David C. Mendoza

The skirmishes over specific artists, projects, and grants that we have experienced since 1990 were only the prelude to the music that we must face now—military bands, not New Music. Those attacks were aimed at destabilizing the cultural establishment and laying a minefield in its midst. Whether you capitalize "culture war" or not, and whether you like their military metaphor or not, the forces that launched it are now in power and can advance from random sniper shots to full–fledged battle.

Their objective is clear. The right—call it religious, Christian, radical, far, whatever—derides contemporary culture because it cannot abide its liberal underpinnings. Despite the marginalized status of artists and intellectuals in our society, the right correctly realizes that art and ideas are powerful symbols of a society and now they desperately want their artists and intellectuals to have center stage in academia, public radio and television, museums, theaters, media and popular culture, *et al.* Their solution: "privatize" the government agencies that support culture.

What exactly does "privatize" mean? The term, used by William Bennett and Newt Gingrich when asked about the future of the National Endowment for the Arts (NEA) and the National Endowment for the Humanities (NEH), can mean only one thing: end government support and eliminate the agencies that contribute to cultural programs. Without government support, the remainder of funding is private; private foundation and corporate grants, private individual donations, and members of the public buying memberships, tickets, and trinkets at museum gift shops.

The growth of public support for culture at the federal, state, and local level since 1960 has promoted an even greater growth in corporate and private support. Although it can be debated whether public funding was the sole impetus for increased private funding, there is no debate that the cultural landscape of the nation today is more diverse and dynamic—i.e., looks much more like America—than before there was public funding. This is the real achievement of public agencies like the NEA, and this is precisely why the right wants to reprivatize culture.

Those of us who recognize this achievement as progress rather than what the right characterizes as a slide into "multicultural mediocrity," celebrate the diversity of cultural expressions now available in every corner of America. The evolution of public arts funding coincided with the civil rights movements, and the right of cultural expression was a part of the prize. Before there was public funding, there was no El Teatro Campesino (San Francisco), Northwest Asian–American Theater (Seattle), Guadeloupe Cultural Arts Center (San Antonio), Dance Theater of Harlem, or Ballet Hispanico (New York City). There was no Next Wave or Off–Off Broadway, no modern dance boom, gay and lesbian film festivals, new music, or folk art revival. And there was no Corpus Christi Arts Council, Bronx Council on the Arts, Orange County Arts Alliance, Kentucky Arts Council, or Virgin Islands Council on the Arts. And Bill T. Jones, an African–American, openly gay, HIV–positive male dancer/choreographer was not on the cover of *Newsweek* and giving dance workshops in Wisconsin. Through one of their many successful language coups, the right has successfully trivialized and undermined the basic concept of multiculturalism, but there, my friends and taxpayers, is what it really is. This array of unabashedly multicultural arts programs was nurtured by your tax dollars, which, through government arts agencies and their systems of citizen peer panels, were awarded on the basis of artistic excellence and a respect for the diversity of the donors: the taxpayers.

By and large, almost everyone is a taxpayer, including non–citizens, and even some illegal immigrants. Contrary to current sound bites, taxpayers are not just the vocal minority who oppose how the NEA makes a few of its grants. The 86 people who buy tickets to see a performance artist in a small non–profit space in Minneapolis or Austin pay taxes, too, and can rightfully expect that if that artist or organization meets the standards of artistic merit as determined by the peer panels, then some of their tax pennies might be thrown back their way in the form of a grant to support the culture they choose to experience. Likewise, it is surely possible for each and every taxpayer (and their families) to find 68 cents worth (the amount of their tax bill that goes to the NEA) of art funded by the NEA they appreciate. This might include "Great Performances" or "American Playhouse" on PBS, books written by writers and published by non–profit presses, or recordings made by non–profit music groups, all funded in part by the NEA and available in virtually every congressional district of all 50 states and territories.

The right further proposes that eliminating public support is really only an end to "welfare for the rich." It is the thesis of George Will and others that "those who want culture can afford to pay for it themselves." Now the rich are also taxpayers, so they might rightfully expect to have some of their nickels and dimes support the art they enjoy, and Will is probably correct in suggesting that the wealthy will not do without the arts if the NEA is axed. However, from his privileged perch among the socio–economic elite, his arrogant classism is astounding. He implies that any folk who want to make or experience art can ante up their own dollars, find a Fortune 500 company and a foundation to give them grants, and if they can't raise enough to cover the costs, then set the tariff accordingly, and expect those who want to attend to pay the price. Right.

No matter what they name it or how they spin it, what they really want is to force many of us back into our respective closets and reestablish the cultural landscape of the 1950s. Such a culture coup is a prize trophy in their "battle for the soul of America." This would be accomplished with a return to private sector support, which they cynically know will not afford the diversity of expression we have begun to experience since 1960. This prize will not be won without resistance, and it is forming as you read this. Even the major arts institutions (and hopefully their corporate board members) are finally taking these guys seriously. Despite this analysis, my own view is they will not ultimately win at all. This battle represents the last desperate gasp of an old world order at the *fin de siécle*. Late 20th–century demographics, the civil rights achievements, and the impact of decades of cultural diversity, will not be erased and pushed back into any closet. However, things may certainly get worse before they get better, while they try to divert our tax dollars from supporting cultural pluralism toward building orphanages for the children of unwed teen mothers or reviving Star Wars.

In 1996, you may have an extra 68 cents in your pocket— maybe it will even be a whopping $3 if they manage to eliminate the National Endowment for the Humanities, the Corporation for Public Broadcasting, as well as the NEA. You might send it to your local National Public Radio station during their fund drive or apply it toward a ticket to a performance or film festival, or a book of poetry. Or you could set it aside for postage stamps, phone calls, and faxes to members of Congress to tell them over and over and over that three dollars doesn't buy much culture, especially for low–income and middle–class families, and that saving every taxpayer three dollars will have an infinitesimal effect on the deficit.

A defense for the preservation of public support for culture does not preclude our efforts to hold agencies such as the NEA accountable to the Constitution and the First Amendment. These two efforts can and will be waged in tandem. Indeed, this accountability itself is a hallmark of public support, one that cannot be enforced on private foundations or corporations.

As we don our battle fatigues, let's at least be clear about what we are fighting for. The battles over culture with the 104th Congress will not be about reducing the deficit, not about ending welfare for the rich, and not about the largesse or responsibility of private philanthropy. These battles will be about the very first contracts with all Americans in all their hyphenated diversity: the Declaration of Independence, the Constitution, the Bill of Rights. And, yes, these battles are indeed about values. The value of respect for individual and cultural diversity in a nation of native peoples and descendants of immigrants that is part of a world with a global economy and instantaneous communication. The value of intellectual freedom, critical thinking, and dissent in a world where fundamentalist militants and totalitarian regimes imprison and/or issue death threats against artists and assassinate journalists. The value of accepting the moral responsibility of caring for children, even if they aren't your own and even if you don't have any. The value of our environment apart from the profit to be made from its natural resources. These values may not be "traditional" for all individuals, families, or politicians. But these are socially redeeming values, and our society is, now more than ever, desperately in need of redemption.

David C. Mendoza is executive director of the National Campaign for Freedom of Expression, based in Seattle, WA, and Washington, DC. This article first appeared in their newsletter, *NCFE Bulletin.* © 1995, David C. Mendoza.

Media Power

The Right–Wing Attack on Public Broadcasting

David Barsamian

The assault on the Corporation for Public Broadcasting and its associated entities, PBS, Public Broadcasting Service, and NPR, National Public Radio, is part of a broad range attack to dismantle and roll back a number of programs, some of them dating to the New Deal. The debate is not just about money but it's about a vision of 21st–century America and the communications needs of a democratic society. The contractors on America tell us that the nation can no longer afford the luxury of tax-payer–supported TV and radio programs. Newt Gingrich wants to "zero out" funding for CPB. The Corporation receives $285 million from Congress. The Speaker of the House says that PBS and NPR users are "a bunch of rich, upper–class people who want their toy to play with it." Public broadcasting, the Georgia Republican says, is "a sandbox for the elite." Before examining the present situation, it is important to give some background.*

The CPB was created in 1967. From its origins, the mission of public TV and radio has been to provide an alternative to commercial stations. The Carnegie Commission Report, which led Congress to pass the Public Broadcasting Act of 1967, argued that public TV and radio programming "can help us see America whole, in all its diversity," serve as "a forum for controversy and

---

* The author is indebted to William Hoynes's book *Public Televison for Sale* for some of the information in this article.

debate," and "provide a voice for groups in the community that may otherwise be unheard." The legislation was introduced and passed within nine months, such was the general support in both houses of Congress.

The Public Broadcasting Act was the last of Lyndon Johnson's Great Society programs and indeed it was the only one dealing with telecommunications. The system, structurally flawed in my view, was designed to be supported but not controlled by the federal government. CPB is private. Its 10–person board is appointed by the President. It disburses monies directly to hundreds of public TV and radio stations. The following is important to note because many people are confused on this point.

Scores of community radio stations and all five Pacifica Radio stations are not NPR members. However, they all receive substantial funding from CPB. In some cases, the loss of CPB monies will jeopardize the very existence of some stations. In most cases, there will be staff layoffs, reduction in news and public affairs programming, and an increase in on–air fundraising and underwriting spots. Alexander Cockburn misses this crucial aspect entirely.

In the March 6, 1995 issue of *The Nation*, he says, "I'm with Gingrich on this one." I share Cockburn's disappointment with PBS and NPR, but there is a larger principle at stake here and I think it deserves our attention and support. Community radio stations are one of the few mechanisms for dissent. We must preserve, protect, and expand them. We should not only resist the cuts, we should demand more money.

It didn't take long for CPB to start taking hits. The newly elected Nixon Administration quickly made known its aversion to the so–called left–liberal media and public television. One documentary in particular set off the President. It was called *Banks and the Poor*. It critically examined banking practices that exacerbated poverty in urban areas. The program closed with a list of 133 senators and congressmen with bank holdings or serving on Boards of Directors of banks. On June 30, 1972, Nixon vetoed CPB's authorization bill. Over the next two months, CPB's chairman, president, and director of TV all resigned. Nixon finally signed the authorization bill at the end of August.

The Nixon episode demonstrated the acute vulnerability of the public media. CPB took steps to protect itself in the future. It reorganized its relationship with local stations in terms of programming and decision–making. The Nixon veto led CPB to turn its attention to securing corporate underwriting, initially from major oil companies, as a new and outside source of funding.

The Carter presidency saw a steady growth in public TV, NPR, and community radio stations. When Ronald Reagan entered the White House, both PBS and NPR faced renewed political and economic pressures. On one level, the Reaganites were philosophically hostile to public broadcasting. It favored deregulation.

On another level, the hostility was more partisan, as the Nixon canard about left–liberal bias in the public media was again resurrected. Reagan cut funding for CPB. The State Department publicly called NPR "Radio Managua on the Potomac." A regular chorus of complainers, Jesse Helms, Patrick Buchanan, and others generated a cacophony of criticism. As despised as NPR is, it is public television by far that has borne the brunt of right–wing vituperation. PBS's *Vietnam: A Television History* was roundly condemned as being too critical of US policy in Indochina. PBS bent over backward to accommodate the right–wingers. A special one–hour response was broadcast. It was hosted by Charlton Heston and produced by Reed Irvine's Accuracy in Media.

In 1986, there was a firestorm of protest over *The Africans*, a nine–part series written and hosted by Ali Mazrui of Kenya. Mazrui advanced the radical idea that imperialism and colonialism had adversely affected the peoples and countries of Africa and that their legacy was having a devastating impact. This was too much for the right. The wogs were out of control. *National Geographic*–like specials, of which there are no shortage of on PBS, featuring zebras, giraffes, and gorillas in the mist, are preferred to anything remotely relating to the reality of Africa.

At PBS, Bill Moyers' documentary about the Iran/Contra scandal, *The Secret Government*, ignited a conflagration of invective abuse. *Days of Rage*, a documentary on the *intifada*, the Palestinian uprising, drew similar near–hysterical criticisms. PBS was now run by an anti–Israeli/anti–Semitic clique. Note how these two concepts are conflated, a great achievement of propaganda.

Another documentary, *Journey to the Occupied Lands*, was strongly criticized in much the same way as *Days of Rage*, by CAMERA, an extreme pro–Israel media watchdog group. CAMERA also went after the Terry Gross "Fresh Air" interview program on NPR, accusing Gross of Israel–bashing. The dubiousness of the charge was illustrated when Gross refused to air an already recorded interview with Robert I. Friedman, author of *Zealots for Zion*, a book that is critical of the Israeli settler movement.

Programs featuring non–heterosexual protagonists are also unacceptable. The right wing vociferously complained about *Tongues Untied*, Marlon Riggs' film about gay, black men. *Tales of the City*, a PBS mini–series about gay life in San Francisco in the 1970s was also raked over the coals by the guardians of public morality. *Tales* was discontinued, despite receiving record ratings. The handful of targeted documentaries demonstrate a clear pattern. Programs that depart from received wisdom and the straight and narrow path of right–wing ideology are not only to be condemned but are cited as proof positive that PBS is dominated by wild–eyed leftists. No amount of servility and subordination is satisfactory for the right wing. Nothing short of 100 percent compliance to their agenda is required. Like the Stalinists that they are, they will tolerate no dissenting voices. Only writers with the irony and imagination of Jonathan Swift, George Orwell, and Lewis B. Carroll could do justice to the right's assertions that public broadcasting leans to the left.

The concerted campaign of vilification and intimidation has had an impact. PBS has gotten the message. Here are just a few examples. It has refused to air *The Panama Deception*, winner of the 1993 Academy Award. *Deadly Deception*, another Academy Award winner, was also turned down. As of this writing, it has refused to broadcast nationally the internationally acclaimed *Manufacturing Consent*. [Some local stations have broadcast these documentaries.] PBS has refused a series on human rights hosted by Charlayne Hunter–Gault. A "Frontline" documentary on Rush Limbaugh that did air in February 1995 was a much–diluted fluff piece.

The intellectual author of much of the right–wing attack is David Horowitz. He was the former editor of *Ramparts* and a New Left figure in the late 1960s and early 1970s. Today, Horowitz espouses extreme right–wing ideas. He is the President of the Center for the Study of Popular Culture in Los Angeles and he publishes *Comint*, a newsletter dedicated to ferreting out the Marxist/Leninists that control public radio and TV.

I saw Horowitz play a prominent role at the Public Radio Conference in Washington, DC, in the spring of 1993. I suspect that he wrote parts of the keynote address delivered by Senator Bob Dole. He used to work for the Kansas senator. Dole used the occasion to attack public radio, specifically Pacifica. He also criticized PBS, saying it was hiding its real agenda behind Big Bird and Barney. Dole's tone was menacing, a harbinger of things to come. The ensuing brouhaha resulted in a bill passed in Congress, ostensibly to punish Pacifica, that took away $1 million from stations. The right wing had its first taste of blood.

Horowitz, like many of his cohorts, does not lack for dollars. His center and newsletter are constantly churning out material attacking public radio and TV. Some choice comments: "PBS has become a subsidiary of the Democratic Party. . . has produced incredibly one–sided programming from the far–left. . . has served the Clinton agenda . . . . NPR has hyped the Black Panthers. . . NPR's sympathies are so much on the left side of the spectrum. . . There are no senior figures at NPR who are conservative. . . PBS programs regularly attack whites. . . CPB for 25 years has been run by Democrats and liberals. It needs to change itself or go down."

Gingrich contends that cable and the market can fill the void left by PBS. Can it? Forty percent of US homes do not receive cable. Beyond that, the commercial market does not seem inclined to produce the types of programming currently being offered by public radio and TV. Why should they? Commercial media are entirely driven by the need to generate ratings in order to sell airtime to advertisers. They are not in the media business for the fun of it. Roy Thompson, the Canadian media mogul, put it succinctly: "I buy newspapers to make money to buy more newspapers to make more money."

Notice that Gingrich does not even make the claim that commercial radio news can replace NPR or community radio. The current attack is about expanding corporate media power specifically by extending its control over valuable frequencies occupied by the hundreds of PBS and public radio stations. These frequencies are to be put on the auction block and will go to the highest bidder. Meetings have been held involving Gingrich and Senator Larry Pressler with Rupert Murdoch of the Fox Network, John Malone of TCI, and executives from Bell Atlantic to discuss the carving up of the public airwaves.

In the Newt world disorder, the notion of a public space or place is non-existent. Comments about the lack of money are transparently absurd. Monies are available to fund the Seawolf submarine, aircraft carrier battle groups, the B-2 bomber, the F-22 fighter, and to fight a two-front war. The US spends more money on the military than the rest of the world combined. Aid to Israel continues at record levels. Billions are available for giant agribusiness subsidies. Tens of billions are available for the bailout of Wall Street investors who are holding Mexican *tesobonos*, junk bonds. Corporations pay fewer taxes today than they did 30 years ago. Is this because there are fewer corporations? Hardly.

The tax code provides numerous loopholes. More and more US capital finds its way into off-shore tax-protected bank accounts in the Bahamas, the Grand Cayman Islands, and Panama. The notion of the market is applied selectively. The political system imposes welfare, tax write-offs, subsidies, and bailouts for the rich, and market discipline for everyone else.

This system, incidentally, is supported by both political parties. Gingrich can sanctimoniously rail against the poor and the evils of welfare while his own district, Cobb County, a rich suburb of Atlanta and home to Lockheed, receives more federal subsidies than all but two counties in the US.

The attack is highly politically charged. On January 27, 1995, Pressler sent a long letter that reeks of McCarthy–like innuendo to the head of CPB demanding to know among other things, "How many NPR staff have previously worked for Pacifica stations? Please list them by name and job category." The South Dakota senator then wanted to know, "How many NPR staff have previously worked for evangelical Christian stations? Please list them by name and job category."

A roll call of regular PBS programs reveals the following left–liberal bias: "Adam Smith's Money World," "Wall Street Week," "Washington Week in Review," "The Bloomberg Business Report," "MacNeil/Lehrer NewsHour," "Tony Brown's Journal," "Ben Wattenberg's Think Tank," "The McLaughlin Group," McLaughlin's "One on One," and the longest–running PBS show of all, William Buckley's "Firing Line."

CPB has just approved funding for a new talk show featuring Reaganite Peggy Noonan. The two main NPR news programs are "Morning Edition" and "All Things Considered." All these programs taken in aggregate definitely constitute a bias, but it's not a left–liberal one. It is a measure of the success of massive right–wing propaganda that anyone could even consider these ludicrous charges and not burst into paroxysms of laughter.

In January 1995, Gingrich was asked if he thought the Republicans were returning to 1933. He said, no, not 1933 but 1760. Why 1760? The Speaker is, as he likes constantly to remind us, a trained historian. 1760 is a chilling thought. What were the social conditions? White male property owners were the only ones with any rights. There were the market wonders of slavery, genocide, child labor, seven–day work weeks, 14–16–18–hour work days, unfettered and unregulated capital control.

It's not just the public airwaves I'm talking about here. The New Right agenda is going to attempt to privatize libraries and schools, but first they want total control of the media. No independent media outside the corporate nexus will be allowed to exist.

There is an urgent need for a concerted effort to safeguard the public radio frequencies and TV channels. As problematic as the programming is, the public interest demands that its airwaves not be sold off. I can predict with certainty that once these frequencies and channels go commercial, they will never come back. The vultures of corporate power, in alliance with their lackeys in Congress, are salivating at the prospect of acquiring new stations and expanding their media monopolies. A democratic society needs a vital and diverse public broadcasting system. It is up to people to organize and defend their airwaves.

David Barsamian is a radio journalist with a syndicated weekly public affairs program, "Alternative Radio." He is a regular contributor to *Z Magazine*, where an earlier version of this chapter first appeared in April 1995. His latest books are *Keeping the Rabble in Line* (with Noam Chomsky) and *The Pen and the Sword* (with Edward Said). A catalog of his interview tapes is available from Alternative Radio. © 1995, David Barsamian.

White Supremacy in the 1990s

Loretta Ross

The notion that racism is a violation of human rights is not a new one, as those who have experienced its effects would testify. The ground–breaking progress gained by the civil rights movement of the 1960s in the United States has steadily eroded over the past decade, and the issues and incidents of racism as well as anti–Semitism, homophobia, and violence against women are ones that need to be addressed with increasing urgency. While the courts are more and more frequently relying on civil rights laws to prosecute racially–motivated violence, the common abuses of basic human rights are often overlooked. In fact, the encroachment of white supremacist ideologies into the social fabric of our politics, our institutions, and our laws means that intolerance is becoming the rule of the day, and the overt violation of the persons and property of individuals and groups is not only easily accepted, but part of the *status quo*.

America has moved into a new era of white supremacy. The new tactics used by white supremacists and far right organizations must be exposed so that we can work together to mitigate their effectiveness. The purpose of this paper is to reveal those strategies in a discussion of the ideologies and practices of white supremacists in the United States today. This includes a discussion of the relationship between three converging and ever–growing factions—the ultra–conservatives, religious fundamentalists, and the far right. In this context, racism cannot stand alone as the sole antagonist of human rights violations. The victims of white supremacist ideologies and politics include immigrants, gays and lesbians, Jews, and women, as well as people of color.

This paper will make clear the connection between racism, homophobia, anti–Semitism, and gender discrimination, both outside and within our social structures and institutions.

When the New Hope Baptist Church in Seattle, Washington was struck by arson in the spring of 1994, it was reportedly because its minister, Rev. Robert Jeffrey, is a progressive activist in the area. Jeffrey, an African American, is involved in fighting several anti–gay initiatives in the state. He is also a sponsor of Black Dollar Days, which organizes the African American community to spend its dollars exclusively with Black businesses. Many believe the attack on his predominantly Black church was intended to drive a wedge between African American and gay and lesbian forces in the region.

At the same time, a new computer bulletin board opened up in the area. Calling itself the "Gay Agenda Resistance," the electronic network offers its subscribers tips on how to stop the gay rights movement in the Pacific Northwest. With the right passwords, it also includes tips on how to target their opponents with violence.

Is this a coincidence? Probably not. What this story illustrates is how the white supremacist movement in America has learned to shift its tactics. No longer able to rely on open racism as an effective recruiting tactic, they have now found a more socially acceptable target for hate—lesbians and gays.

Is this a new white supremacist movement? Does this mean they no longer hate people of color, Jews, feminists, immigrants, etc.? No and No. The number of hate crimes in this country is evidence that hatred still exists as a family value.

Hate groups in the mid–1990s are refocusing their energies. They are worried that they can never convince the majority of white Americans to join them in their netherworld. While many whites may share their prejudices, very few are willing to act on them by openly carrying a Klan calling card or an Uzi. This situation demands a new strategy that combines old hatreds with new rhetoric. White supremacists desperately need to reinvigorate their movement with new recruits by manipulating white fears into action.

White fears of change or difference are exploited by hate groups. At the same time, they are expanding their targets of hate. They have adopted not only homophobia as a prominent part of their new agenda, but are forcefully anti–abortion, pro–family values, and pro–American, in addition to their traditional racist and anti–Semitic beliefs. This broadening of issues and the use of conservative buzzwords have attracted the attention of whites who may not consider themselves racist, but do consider themselves patriotic Americans concerned about the moral decay of "their" country.

From the ranks of homophobes, anti–abortionists, racists, anti–Semites, and those who are simply afraid of a fast–changing world, white supremacists find willing allies in their struggle to control America's destiny. Hate groups cannot be dismissed as no more complex than the virulence of a few fringe fanatics. With the breathless way the media covers hate groups, it is sometimes easier to characterize them simply as misfits or extremists, rather than acknowledge them as part of the larger problem of widespread racism, anti–Semitism, and homophobia.

When they wish, hate groups get lots of free publicity from tabloid talk shows eager to boost ratings with the winning combination of race, guns, and violence. Such hosts may hypocritically hold their noses while racists, particularly skinheads, advertise their toughness and their addresses on national TV.

In this way, many more people are exposed to their message, convinced by their passion, and seduced by their simplistic answers to complex social problems. With time and repetition, white supremacists have fused many "fringe" far right beliefs together into "acceptable" mainstream values. While hate groups have previously relied on violence, their new manipulation of ultra–conservative rhetoric has combined with this to provoke a deadly acceptance of intolerance in this country.

The influence of hate groups is evident in the increase in violent hate crimes across the nation. Most are committed not by actual members of hate groups, but by freelancers trying to halt the social changes around them. Many are trying to form hate gangs of their own.

FBI statistics report that 65 percent of America's hate crimes are committed by whites against Blacks. A good portion of such hate crimes are what we call "move–in" violence, when neighborhoods, schools, churches, or jobs are finally integrated 30 years after the 1964 Civil Rights Act. Terror over the visibility of the lesbian and gay movement lies behind the numerous hate crimes against gays and lesbians (and their allies)—the fastest–growing hate crime category in the country.

Some of the haters, living on the United States' borders, are petrified at the thought that brown hordes of Mexicans, Chinese, or Haitians may swarm over them if they cease their militant rhetoric and violence toward these immigrants. If they live near Native American reservations, the aim of their violence is to challenge the few remaining treaty rights granted native peoples.

Other white supremacists want to save the white race by controlling the behavior of white women—they attack interracial couples, lesbians, and feminists. They join the anti–abortion movement, believing they can prevent white women from getting legal abortions. Racist far right organizations have been quick to glorify anti–abortion violence, making it yet another hot issue to fuel the fires of the white revolution.

There are others who want to save the environment for the white race. They have infiltrated the environmental movement, or have switched sides to join the Wise Use movement. They are frantic to exploit the earth's natural resources to accumulate wealth before that time early in the 21st–century when demographics predict that America will no longer be majority–white. In particular, many new recruits to the movement come from the Religious Right across a bridge of homophobia. Haters robed in clerical black are barely distinguishable from those hiding under white bedsheets, particularly in the eyes of their victims.

Hate groups have decided that they are no longer willing to wait for the white revolution—the violent backlash against human rights movements. They want a fast solution before, as they put it, "the white race is extinct."

Some white supremacists are opting to lead the way as a guerrilla strike force, precipitating the purification of America of all those who are not white, straight, and Christian. In a frank statement about white supremacist strategy, Aryan Nations member Louis Beam wrote:

> We do not advocate segregation. That was a temporary measure that is long past. . . .Our Order intends to take part in the Physical and Spiritual Racial Purification of ALL those countries which have traditionally been considered White lands in Modern Times. . . .We intend to purge this entire land area of Every non–White person, gene, idea and influence. [Capitalization in original.]

These self–described "white separatists" believe that the United States government is controlled by a conspiratorial cabal of non–whites or Jews, or a combination of both. They seek to change this "Zionist Occupation Government" either through terror or violence, or by influencing the political mainstream. They tell their followers that crime and welfare abuse by African Americans, immigration by Mexicans and Asians, or a fictional Jewish conspiracy are responsible for a decline in the status of white people. They accuse civil rights organizations of "hating white people" and brand whites who do not support them as race traitors or self–haters.

These fanatics are terrorists who use bombs, murder, arson, and assaults in their genocidal war. Some skinheads—for example, the Fourth Reich Skins arrested a few years ago in Los Angeles or the Aryan National Front, convicted of murdering homeless people in Alabama—are in the vanguard of this street–level violence. Meanwhile, older survivalists like Randy Weaver, who was acquitted of killing a federal marshall in an Idaho firefight in 1992, are barricaded in mountain shelters with stockpiles of weapons, awaiting the final Armageddon.

Impressionable, often alienated people, both young and old, are natural recruits for this movement. They bring new energy and a willingness to display their hatred aggressively. They also expand the influence of the white supremacist movement—into the anti–abortion movement, into the anti–gay movement, into the English–only movement—opening new avenues for the expression of hate.

Other white supremacists are following a less violent strategy: exchanging bullets for ballots and running for political office. Some attempt to clone David Duke's success. With a little cosmetic surgery on the nose and resume, Duke was able to convince 55 percent of white Louisianians to vote for him when he ran for governor in 1992. Tapping into the resentment of the white backlash, Duke promoted himself as a defender of white rights and, for a brief moment, shook America out of its racial daydream.

Many observers were surprised so many whites voted for Duke since they had lied in pre–election polls. Duke set himself apart from other "klandidates" by convincing the majority of whites to act on their perceived group interests as whites—something that had not been achieved so openly since the 1980s' romance with the Reagan revolution.

What many Americans fail to realize is that, increasingly, white people are being literally scared out of their wits by demagogues like Duke, who crystallize for them their fears of people of color, lesbians and gays, the government, the media, welfare mothers, immigrants, the economy, health care—and the list goes on. Instead of rejecting Duke as a fringe opportunist, they voted for him because of his well–documented racist past. He was serious about white rights; he gave them permission to practice a kinder, gentler white supremacy.

In the 1990s, the image of organized hate is rapidly changing. It is no longer the exclusive domain of white men over 30. It is becoming younger and meaner. Many people join the movement as teenagers, including a remarkable number of young women.

A kind of "Sisterhood of Hate" to procreate white supremacy has emerged. Since the mid–1980s, women have joined the racist movement in record numbers—from the White Nurses preparing for racial holy war to female skinheads producing videotapes on natural childbirth techniques. This new and dangerous increase accounts for nearly one–third of the membership of some hate groups. The increase in the number of women, coupled with a strategic thrust to reform the public image of hate groups, has expanded women's leadership.

These new recruits do not fit the stereotypical image of wives on their husbands' arms. In fact, many of them are college–educated, very sophisticated, and display skills usually found among the rarest of intellectuals in the movement.

Most Americans don't understand the pervasiveness of white supremacists and the importance of their ideology in America's self–definition. Thus, they are unaware of how this ideology has mutated over the years and now blurs the lines between organized racists and their more mainstream counterparts in the Religious Right and ultra–conservative movements.

Of particular concern in the 1990s is a continuing convergence of sections of the white supremacist movement with the radical Christian Right, as represented by Pat Robertson, and nationalist ultra–conservatives, as represented by Pat Buchanan. This alliance is between religious determinists who think that one's degree of Christianity determines one's future, economic determinists who see themselves in a war of the "haves" against the "have–nots," and biological determinists for whom race is everything. All believe they are in battle to save Western civilization (white Europeans) from the ungodly and the unfit (people of color, gays and lesbians, and Jews).

In the 1990s, their cutting edge issue has been homophobia, as anti–gay campaigns have enriched their coffers and also mobilized a conservative current in the African American community. For example, their ability to oppose allowing gays in the military transferred directly to killing or stalling President Clinton's proposals on the budget, health care reform, jobs, and economic recovery. Of the three trends, the ultra–conservatives have the best ability to mainstream their views.

They all oppose the social gains of the 1960s and they share strong elements of racism and national chauvinism that can bridge their differences. Nativist themes favoring the rights of natural born Americans to those of immigrants may widen their appeal. For example, the Rev. Billy McCormack, who campaigned for David Duke in the early 1990s and was prominent in the 1992 Republican National Convention, is now the Louisiana state chair of Robertson's Christian Coalition.

This trend, which the Center for Democratic Renewal (CDR) first noticed in the Duke campaigns, has continued around a series of issues: gay rights, crime and welfare reform, immigration, English–only, America First nationalism, opposition to the North American Free Trade Agreement, and even Holocaust denial. Now, election campaigns featuring isolationist and nationalist themes and ultra–Christianity are an opportunity for rapprochement for all sectors of the right wing. They can march back to the center of power sharing a very big tent. No Special Rights and No

Political Correctness campaigns have their origins in the white supremacist belief that white supremacy is right for America.

White Supremacy as an Ideology

The fact that race relations in the United States are usually presented as a Black/white model disguises the complexity of color, the brutality of class, and the importance of religion and sexual identity in the construction and practice of white supremacy. This simplistic model, which fails to convey many of the important aspects of white supremacy, cannot specifically explain how white supremacy influences American culture and politics.

White supremacy is an ideology that manipulates US politics and affects all relations in American society. It is sustained by rigid ideological categories. The construction of racial categories, although varying greatly over time, has always been based on the economic, social, and political aspirations of people of European descent. Throughout European history, racial definitions have been based on lineage, phrenological characteristics, skin hue, and religion. This system was institutionalized in America through systematic violence, distorted Christianity, and dubious science.

The concept of a white race aggressively struggling against all others to maintain its presumed purity is an expression of the European model of white supremacy, based not necessarily on skin color, but on social stratifications and values assigned by the dominant group.

These categories and values—a series of immunities, privileges, rights, and assumptions that became the foundation for ideological whiteness—are not entirely dependent on skin color or even class status. The creation of racial categories, including "whiteness," affects identity construction and social relationships. Because white supremacy springs from the identity crisis of European nationalism, it is not surprising that it replicates similar identity crises among its victims. Thus, racism, anti–Semitism, homophobia, sexism, and nativism are interdependent in the practice of white supremacy. Other components are national chauvinism and religious fundamentalism.

These categories are not inherent, natural, or biologically determined. Rather they are artificial beliefs created by social, economic, and political conditions. Such beliefs have altered the laws, language, and customs of the United States in the service of regulating social relations.

Helan Page, an African American anthropologist, defines white supremacy in the US as an "ideological, structural and historic stratification process by which the population of European descent. . .has been able to intentionally sustain, to its own best advantage, the dynamic mechanics of upward or downward mobility or fluid class status over the non–European populations (on a global scale), using skin color, gender, class or ethnicity as the main criteria" for allocating resources and making decisions. This complex definition explains the substance of white supremacy and its ability to mutate like a virus to meet constantly changing conditions. Since neither white supremacy nor the European nationalism that is its base is recognized as an expression of group interests, it is difficult for other groups to defend themselves against it. Even many who benefit from its existence fail to recognize its current manifestation as institutionalized racism or homophobia.

These common group interests need no conscious manipulation to be expressed; they are based on color, class, sexual orientation, and Christianity. From far right groups like the Ku Klux Klan to liberals who deny the pervasiveness of anti–Black racism on the left, white supremacy privileges all people of European descent: a sort of affirmative action for whites.

The words of a few defenders of white supremacy make these common interests very clear. Thom Robb, national director of the Knights of the KKK, speaking at a 1993 Klan rally in Pulaski, Tennessee, declared: "Politicians, teachers, professors, religious leaders. . .none of them speak out for the defense of white Christian America."

Robb's speech was no more threatening than the militaristic rhetoric offered by failed presidential candidate Patrick Buchanan at the 1992 Republican National Convention: "If your leaders have lost the stomach and the will to fight, then you go out and find new leaders. . . . Our culture is superior to other cultures, superior because our religion is Christianity."

The connection between a far right marginal figure like Thom Robb and a national mainstream politician like Pat Buchanan is a shared belief in white supremacy. Robb is less successful at disguising his fundamental prejudices. While the Klan is seen as being against all who are not white, radical conservatives like Pat Buchanan or religious leaders like Pat Robertson of the Christian Coalition prefer to advocate for Western civilization and Christianity. All see themselves as threatened by a non–white, non–European–dominated future America.

White supremacist beliefs, though largely invisible to the majority of the American public, regardless of race, are at the heart of the American experience. The persistence of these beliefs suggests that the racial myths and stereotypes common to white supremacy are integral to the maintenance of the US social order.

Sometimes the tenets of white supremacist groups can be helpful when they reflect, epitomize, crystallize, or even clarify the perceptions of a predominantly white Christian society. For example, a December 1990 survey conducted by the National Opinion Research Center revealed that 78 percent of non–Blacks said African Americans are more likely than whites to "prefer to live off welfare" and less likely to "prefer to be self–supporting." Such studies prove the enduring nature and widespread acceptance of white supremacist beliefs. These beliefs help to explain why the majority of white Louisianians voted for David Duke.

Each of these beliefs is a reassertion of European nationalism and its successor, American nationalism. White supremacy, assuming its own universal value and superiority, justifies the aggressive imposition of its own assumptions on other peoples and cultures. This is its response to the movements of people of color, women, lesbians and gays, and minority religions when they defend themselves against the aggression of white supremacy. Robb and Buchanan simply seek to redefine America's Manifest Destiny, to abridge its multicultural reality, and to continue the dominance of white supremacy. As Theodore Allen points out in *The Invention of the White Race*, "in critical times, the thrust for freedom and democracy is thwarted by the reinvention of the white race."

The invisibility of white supremacy masks how violence and the threat of violence guarantee its durability. White people assert their moral right to use violent force whenever their group interests are threatened. People of color have no equivalent moral right to defend themselves against European aggression, especially when such aggression is done in the name of "law and order."

This paradoxical belief has been a powerful weapon with which to steal and exploit land and other natural resources, to defend slavery and racism, to condemn lesbians and gays, and to deride all who are not Christian. Those who are not white or Christian are expected, at best, to merge into the dominant culture and political system, or worst, to remain invisible and not to challenge white Christian hegemony. Outsiders seeking acceptance are constantly pressured to prove themselves, to suppress their indigenous culture, and to assimilate into the "mainstream" to achieve upward mobility.

White supremacist beliefs are perpetuated through a series of social conventions irrespective of political boundaries. Organized white supremacy makes prevailing attitudes of prejudice appear moderate and reasonable: it normalizes everyday injustice. For example, a 1993 study commissioned by the National Science Foundation found that racist attitudes and stereotypes are rampant among whites, regardless of political affiliation. For example, 51 percent of the respondents who identified themselves as conservatives said they think African Americans are "aggressive and violent." For those who identified themselves as liberals, 45 percent felt that Blacks had those attributes. Furthermore, Blacks are "irresponsible" according to 21 percent of the conservatives and 17 percent of the liberals studied.

Excessive tolerance of white supremacist activities threatens the culture of pluralism and impairs the practice of democracy in America. White supremacists are America's deepest nightmare because they attack not only individuals, but they assault the legitimacy of our democratic process itself. Their ideology seeks to overturn civil and human rights achieved through open debate and free elections, one of the cornerstones of democracy.

Because the percentage of whites who actually belong to white supremacist groups is small, there is a general tendency to underestimate their influence. What is really significant is not the number of people actually belonging to hate groups, but the number who endorse their messages. Once known primarily for their criminal activities, racists have demonstrated a catalytic effect by tapping into the prejudices of the white majority.

Recent polls by the National Opinion Research Center reveal that 13 percent of whites in America have anti–Semitic beliefs; another 25 percent are racist. This noticeably impacts public policy concerning central issues of racism, poverty, crime, reproductive rights, civil rights for gays and lesbians, the environment, and more.

White Supremacy in Practice

Most white supremacists in America believe that the United States is a "Christian" nation, with a special relationship between religion and the rule of law. Because racists give themselves divine permission from God to hate, they often don't see that their actions are driven by hate; they claim to "just love God and the white race." If they are religious, they distort Biblical passages to justify their bigotry. A popular religion called Christian Identity provides a theological bond across organizational lines. Identity churches are ministered by charismatic leaders who promote racial intolerance and religious division. Even for those who are not religious, "racist" to them means being racially conscious and seeing the world through a prism of inescapable biological determinism with different races having different pre–ordained destinies.

Only about 25,000 Americans are hardcore ideological activists for the white supremacist movement, a tiny fraction of the white population. They are organized into approximately 300 different organizations. No two groups are exactly alike, ranging from seemingly innocuous religious sects or tax protesters to openly militant, even violent, neo–Nazi skinheads and Ku Klux Klan Klaverns. The basic underpinnings of these organizations may be rooted in religion; they may be paramilitary, or survivalists, or anarchists. Currently, Klan groups are on the decline while more Hitler–inspired groups, like the National Alliance and the Church of the Creator, are growing in number and influence. Swastikas and Uzis are replacing hoods and crosses.

Each group is working to create a society totally dominated by whites by excluding and denying the rights of non–whites, Jews, gays and lesbians, and by subjugating women. The movement's links are global, from the pro–apartheid movement in South Africa and the neo–fascists in Germany to robed Klansmen in the deep South.

Some 150,000 to 200,000 people subscribe to racist publications, attend their marches and rallies, and donate money. Approximately 100 hate–lines are in operation, with recorded messages that propagandize the caller with hate–motivated speeches and publicize upcoming meetings and rallies. Because of their increasingly sophisticated use of the media and electronic technology, there are 150 independent racist radio and television shows that air weekly and reach millions of sympathizers. This estimate does not include commercially–backed broadcasters like Rush Limbaugh who also spew racist vitriol, or the countless mainstream talks shows that regularly feature racists during ratings week sensationalism.

In the 1960s, the Ku Klux Klan was the most infamous of the organized hate groups with an estimated 40,000 members in 1965. But by the end of the 1970s, the majority of white supremacists belonged to organizations other than the Klan. They had evolved from loosely structured fraternal organizations into highly developed paramilitary groups with extensive survivalist training camps, often funded by proceeds from counterfeit money and bank and armored car robberies. In the 1990s, they have transformed themselves from a violent vanguard into a sophisticated political movement with a significant constituency.

Although the Ku Klux Klan is the most notorious, hate groups come in many forms. For example, they organize as religious cults, most predominantly along the Christian Identity model, which asserts that: (1) white people are the original Lost Tribes of Israel; (2) Jews are descendants of Satan; and (3) African Americans and other people of color are pre–Adamic, or beasts created by God before He created Adam, the first white man. Christian Identity followers feel they can attack and murder

Jews and people of color without contradicting their religious convictions because they have been told by their leaders that people of color and Jews have no souls.

Another significant religious cult is the Church of the Creator, founded in 1973. Its members believe they are engaged in a racial holy war (RAHOWA) between the "pure" Aryan race and the "mud races." Adherents are frequently in the headlines for their violence. In 1993, members were arrested by the FBI as part of the Fourth Reich Skinheads who attempted to bomb First AME Church in Los Angeles and assassinate LA motorist Rodney King. Members have also been arrested in numerous murders, violent assaults, and bank robberies across the nation. They believe that they can precipitate the race war by provoking a violent response with attacks upon Jews and people of color.

The Aryan Nations in Idaho has been one of the umbrella organizations seeking to unite various Klan and neo–Nazi groups. Members spread across the country attend annual celebrations of Hitler's birthday at the Idaho encampment in April. In 1979, founder Richard Butler convened the first Aryan Nations World Congress on his property and attracted Klan and neo–Nazi leaders from the US, Canada, and Europe, who gathered to exchange ideas and strategies. This annual summer event has led to greater cooperation among a wide variety of groups.

There are at least 26 different Ku Klux Klan groups in the United States, most of them concentrated in the South. The largest and fastest–growing is the Knights of the KKK, headquartered in Harrison, Arkansas, under the leadership of Thom Robb. The Knights recently held rallies in Wisconsin, Ohio, Louisiana, Indiana, Texas, Tennessee, Arkansas, and Mississippi. Robb's Knights were the first group to recruit skinheads into their ranks, and he has been quick to put promising young leaders like Shawn Slater in Colorado into the national spotlight. It is the most Nazi–esque of the Klans, maintaining strong ties to Richard Butler's Aryan Nations in Idaho.

Robb's group, originally founded by David Duke in the 1970s, has moved into national Klan leadership because of the dissolution of the Invisible Empire Knights of the KKK in 1993. The Invisible Empire's national leader, J. W. Farrands of Gulf, North Carolina, recently lost in a suit filed by the Southern Poverty Law Center (SPLC) against the Invisible Empire for the violent attacks in 1987 on civil rights marchers in Forsyth County, Georgia. Farrands was ordered by the court to pay $37,500 in damages to the plaintiffs in the class action suit. The settlement with the SPLC prohibits use of the Invisible Empire's name or the publication of their newspaper, *The Klansman*. Farrands has reorganized his forces under a new name, the Unified Knights of the KKK, to continue their racist activities.

It is typical for the 1990s Klan, reeling from criminal convictions, to publicly disavow violence while secretly encouraging its followers to commit hate crimes under the cover of darkness. However, they are still known for their "Knight Riders" and the Klan calling cards used to terrorize people the Klan dislikes.

The Holocaust–denial movement is the clearest expression of the anti–Semitic nature of white supremacy. Various institutions within the white supremacist movement are revising the history of Nazi Germany, claiming that the Holocaust against the Jews either did not happen or was greatly exaggerated.

The most sophisticated of these institutions is the Institute for Historical Review (IHR) in California. Founded by longtime racist and anti–Semite Willis Carto, the IHR offers hatred with an intellectual gloss. Although the IHR is currently beset by internal power struggles between founder Carto and Institute staff, it still remains the source of much of the anti–Semitic literature in the hate movement.

Carto also founded the Liberty Lobby in the 1950s, and in 1974 began publishing *The Spotlight*, a weekly tabloid with approximately 100,000 paid subscribers. In 1984, he started the Populist Party, which ran David Duke for US President in 1988.

The most violent wing of the white supremacist movement is the growing neo–Nazi skinhead movement, of which there are about 3,500 members in the United States. They openly worship Hitler and many young people, with ages from 13 to 25, are inducted into their ranks after committing a hate crime as part of the gang initiation. Their youthful appearance is rapidly changing the face of hate. Girls are rapidly rising into skinhead leadership.

Skinhead groups have developed their own leadership and appeal, distinct from adult Klan and neo–Nazi groups. Skinheads have committed over 25 murders and have expanded into 40 states. Most of their victims are African Americans, Latinos, Asian Americans, gays and lesbians, and the homeless. The typical skinhead assault begins with liquor, drugs, and hate. Skinheads are the "urban guerrillas" of the hate movement.

More seasoned adults have abandoned open violence to sanitize their public images. Such adults recruit and encourage young people to commit criminal activities, just as older drug dealers use young kids to push drugs. Unfortunately, this means that hate crimes committed by juveniles are often seen as mere pranks, not the serious assaults on liberty and freedom that they really are. This tactic also frequently allows the adult leaders to escape punishment. For example, the FBI learned of the assassination plots planned by the Fourth Reich Skinheads by monitoring the phone lines of Tom Metzger, leader of White Aryan Resistance (WAR) in California.

Skinheads have firmly established themselves in six to eight national organizations, rather than simply as appendages of adult groups. In 1993, rather than waiting for the race war to start, they were "doing things to start the race war" according to skinheads arrested in June who attempted to bomb a predominantly Black housing project in Toledo, Ohio. On July 20, a pipe bomb was thrown through the front windows of the Tacoma, Washington, offices of the NAACP. A week later, the Sacramento, California, NAACP office was also gutted by a bomb.

While young people commit the majority of hate crimes in America, the adult leaders are forming a series of political organizations with which to spread their message of hate and bigotry. When David Duke left the Klan, he formed the National Association for the Advancement of White People (NAAWP) to serve as a "white civil rights organization" which would oppose integration, affirmative action, welfare, interracial marriages, and scholarship programs for minorities.

Many of the distinctions between various Klan and neo–Nazi groups have dissolved. The membership is extremely fluid: members flow in and out because of internal squabbles and leadership battles. Cross–memberships, in–depth leadership summit meetings, and the use of common periodicals are frequent, indicating considerable organizational cohesion. For example, members of WAR are featured in newspapers from the Church of the Creator; Klansmen often appear at Aryan Nations events; NAAWP activists have been seen at Klan rallies. Their primary point of disagreement is whether to fight for white supremacy through violence, politics, or both.

Coalition Building for Human Rights

Just because white supremacy exists and has done so for a long time, there is no reason for its victims to accept it. This apparent tautology serves as a reminder of the distracting potential for misdirecting our focus into fighting each other rather than understanding the nature and endurance of white supremacy.

In the words of Dhoruba Bin Wahad, "We must prepare ourselves collectively to wage many struggles at once, [and] we must do so with a common sense of mission and purpose." Pride and solidarity prepare individuals to become partners in an alliance against oppression.

Coalition building requires that each group clarify its own identity apart from that created for it by white supremacy.

Learning each other's history is critical to understanding why we cannot set each other's agendas.

Mutual efforts against white supremacy are not just an educational process that teaches each group about the other; this work also addresses the loss of contact and lack of trust between communities.

Oppressed groups need to have separate spaces in which to gain their self–respect, name themselves, and discover their own history. These same groups need to form coalitions with other groups in order to compare, contrast, and identify the connections among different types of white supremacist oppression.

Coalition work is not easy or comfortable; it is hard to be confronted constantly with our own and each other's bigotry which forces us to reevaluate our cherished assumptions. Despite the difficulties, coalitions provide us with a much greater potential to bring about fundamental opposition to white supremacy and advancement of our movements for human rights.

Together, we must hold, not only individuals, but governments accountable. The silence of government equals permission to hate. Local governments must be responsible for the abuse of basic human rights of its citizens. State governments must stand up against intolerance. And the federal government must be the guiding force behind the protection of human rights and human dignity in this country in which we claim that all are created equal. Local, state, and federal legislation must be enacted and enforced to protect individuals and groups from racial, religious, homophobic, and xenophobic intolerance.

The human rights community must also more thoroughly study and analyze the full extent to which white supremacist motivated human rights abuses occur in this country. The cost of racism, homophobia, anti-Semitism, sexism, and nationalism is high, not only to individuals but to whole groups of people who fall into certain "categories." Their victimization leaves them afraid in the streets, in their jobs, and even in their homes. Unable and unwilling to disguise the very essence of who they are, they face abuse ranging from mild intolerance to threat of death.

At the present time, there are not safe places for the victims of this type of violence to turn to. No homeless shelters, no women's shelters, and often even no police departments offer them support. The first step in building these resources is to recognize the magnitude of the problem so that human rights activists can come together to offer help and support to those outside the majority rule.

A concerted, prolonged effort to teach young people about the true impact of white supremacy and its prevalence in American society is fundamental to breaking the cycle. To ignore this issue is to build intolerance into the next generation. An understanding of the historical and institutional effects of racism and the other "isms" that dominate our culture and society is vital to understanding present bigotry and abuse.

When we recognize that racism, homophobia, sexism, anti-Semitism, and xenophobia flow from the same spring, and that they permeate every aspect of the lives of all Americans, we can then take steps together to make the United States a place that respects and honors the dignity of all people.

Loretta J. Ross, a veteran civil rights and feminist organizer, is Program Research Director of the non-profit advocacy and research group the Center for Democratic Renewal (CDR), based in Atlanta, GA. © 1995, Loretta J. Ross.

White Panic

Henry A. Giroux

Incidents of violence in the United States have become so commonplace that they seem to constitute the defining principle of everyday life. Acts of violence ranging from the banal to the sensational dominate the contents of newspaper accounts, television news programs, and popular magazines. More importantly, the never–ending images of violence seem to cancel out the actual experience and suffering caused by violence as the American public is bombarded with daily images of violence, ranging from coverage of the O. J. Simpson trial to reports of serial killers who maim and murder victims with mail bombs. Whether in the popular media or other fact–reporting spheres, the reality of everyday violence is supplemented by a culture of violence produced as entertainment for broadcast and cable television programs, movie theater films, and video games. Within this expanding culture of violence, the relationship between fact and fiction becomes more difficult to comprehend as real life crimes become the basis for television and movie entertainment, and newscasting becomes increasingly formulaic, sensational, and less neutral and objective.

While violence appears to cross over designated borders of class, race, and social space, the representation of violence in the popular media is largely depicted in racial terms. That is, representations of violence are largely portrayed through forms of racial coding that suggests that violence is a black problem, a problem outside white suburban America. In fact, white Americans fancy themselves the new besieged group of the 1990s—voiceless and powerless in the age of "political correctness." No longer safe from the threat of urban violence, they increasingly view themselves as prisoners in their own homes.

Beneath the growing culture of violence, both real and simulated, there lies a deep–seated racism that has produced what I call white moral panic. The elements of this panic are rooted, in part, in a growing fear among the white middle class over the declining quality of social, political, and economic life that has resulted from an increase in poverty, drugs, hate, guns, unemployment, social disenfranchisement, and hopelessness. Expressions of white panic can be seen in the passing of Proposition 187, which assigns increasing crime, welfare abuse, moral decay, and social disorder to the "flood" of Mexican immigrants streaming across the borders of the United States. White panic can also be read in the depictions of crime in national newspapers and magazines. For example, *Time* magazine, following the arrest of O. J. Simpson, presented his jail mug shot on its cover with a much darkened face, feeding into the national obsession of the black male as a dreaded criminal. The magazine had to later issue an apology for this racist gesture. Even more aggressively, the *New York Times Magazine* ran a cover story in June 1993 titled "A Predator's Struggle to Tame Himself" accompanied with a picture of a tall, black male prisoner on the cover. In August 1994, the *Times Magazine* ran another cover story on youth gangs, and put a picture of an Afro–American woman on the cover. Again in December 1994, it ran yet another story titled "The Black Man is in Terrible Trouble. Whose Problem is That?" The story was accompanied by a cover picture of the back of a black man's shaved head, displayed with a gold ring prominently hanging from his ear. The following week, the *New York Times Magazine* ran a lead story on welfare and referenced it with the image of a black woman on the cover. What is reprehensible about the endless repetition of these images is that they not only reproduce racist stereotypes about blacks by portraying them as criminals and welfare cheats, but they remove whites from any responsibility or complicity for the violence and poverty that has become so endemic to American life. Racist representations feed and valorize the assumption that unemployment, poverty, disenfranchisement, and violence are a black problem.

One of the most recent expressions of resurgent racism in the media can be seen in the massive popular news, television, and magazine coverage given to *The Bell Curve* by Richard Herrnstein and Charles Murray, a book that legitimates the position that racism "is a respectable intellectual position, and has a legitimate place in the national debate on race." Furthermore, a silent white majority self–righteously situates itself in the role of moral witness and judge of the fate of black people in this country.

The racial coding of violence is especially powerful and persuasive in its association of crime with black youth. As Holly Sklar points out, "In shorthand stereotype, black and Latino boys mean dangerous, girls mean welfare, they all mean drugs. They are all suspect." The racial coding of crime is also evident in widespread popular media coverage associating black rap music with gang violence, drugs, and urban terror. Motion pictures depicting "realistic" portrayals of black ghetto life add fuel to the fire by becoming a register in the popular mind for legitimating race and violence as mutually informing categories. The consequences of such racist stereotyping produce more than prejudice and fear in the white collective sensibility. Racist representations of violence also feed the increasing public outcry for tougher crime bills designed to build more prisons and to legislate get–tough policies with minorities of color and class. All of this is accompanied by the proliferation of pseudo–scientific studies advocating the creation of a custodial state to contain "some substantial minority of the nation's population, while the rest of America tries to go about its business."

Social and political causes of violence are eluded. The media highlights the simplistic calls of conservative politicians for more prisons, orphanages for the children of poor black and white mothers, and censorship of the arts and media in the interests of managing social inequalities rather than challenging and transforming them. Whether in the portrayal of popular black music or in Hollywood movies, violence becomes the defining attribute for indicting an entire racial group. Of course, violence is not absent from representations of white youth and adults, but it is rarely depicted so as to suggest an indictment of whites as a social and ethnic group.

On the contrary, violence in films about white youth is often framed almost exclusively through the language of pathology, political extremism, or class–specific nihilism. For example, the white youth portrayed in *Natural Born Killers* (1994) become acceptable to white audiences because the possibility for identification never emerges. They are pathological killers, children of grossly dysfunctional families, clearly outside of the parameters of normalcy that prevail throughout white middle class society. Another highly–touted, avant garde youth film, *True Romance* (1993), couples postmodern pastiche, violence, and pop cultural icons. In this film, 1970s retro trash and references inform contemporary white youth culture, including an Elvis character with a gold jacket who dispenses advice in bathrooms, a heroine who enjoys kung fu movies, and a leading character who works in a comic book store.

Youth are isolated and estranged in these films and offer no indictment of American society because they largely embrace a disturbing nihilism, but also because they appear marginal, shiftless, and far removed from Dan Quayle's notion of American family values. They are on the margins, and the hip violence in which they engage has the comfortable aura of low–life craziness about it. You won't find these kids in a Disney film. The portrayal of white youth violence emerges through an endless series of repugnant characters whose saving grace resides in their being on the extreme psychological and economic edges of society. When white youth commit violent acts, anguished questions of agency, moral accountability, and social responsibility do not apply. Agency for white youth is contaminated by a personal pathology that never questions the social and historical conditions of its construction. But in the racially coded representations of violence in black films, questions of agency are untroubled by freak individual pathologies, and serve instead to indict blacks as an entire social group, while legitimating the popular stereotype that their communities are the central sites of crime, lawlessness, and immorality.

In films about violent white youth such as *Laws of Gravity* (1992), *Kalifornia* (1993), and *Natural Born Killers* (1994), the language of hopelessness cancels out any investigation into how agency is constructed, as opposed to simply guaranteed, in the larger political and social sense. But in black youth films such as *Sugar Hill* (1993), *Boys N the Hood* (1991), *Menace II Society* (1993), and *Fresh* (1995), there is the haunting sense that blacks are responsible for reducing their sense of individual and social agency to the degree that they will live out lives of little hope amidst a culture of nihilism and deprivation. In the end, black powerlessness becomes synonymous with criminality. By totalizing the limiting constraints blacks have to face in everyday life, these films avoid altogether how agency functions as a historical and social construction, pointing in turn to larger determinants outside of the language of racism, biology, psychology, and cynicism. Dominant representations of black and white youth violence feed right–wing conservative values of the Newt Gingrich variety but offer no insights into the culture and densely populated landscape of violence at the heart of white, dominant society.

Henry A. Giroux is a regular contributor to *Z Magazine*, where this column first appeared in March 1995. © 1995, Henry A. Giroux.

An International Perspective on Migration

Cathi Tactaquin

There were over 100 million migrants (immigrants and refugees) in the world in 1995. This unprecedented level has prompted widespread concern about the causes and consequences of international migration. Although the United Nations General Assembly recently has taken steps to convene an international conference on migration and development, migrant–receiving countries such as the United States are developing national immigration policies that may seriously jeopardize the basic human rights and economic survival of this growing population.

The United States receives less than 1 percent of the world's migrants on an annual basis. Nonetheless, it has responded to the international crisis in migration by cracking down on undocumented immigrants, tightening border controls, restricting access to political asylum, and threatening immigrant access to public assistance programs. Most policy makers are quick to pander to racist and xenophobic fears and claims that immigration has become a primary source of this country's economic instability.

Despite the ever increasing volume of restrictions and resources devoted to immigration, these measures have had little, if any, impact on the sources and patterns of international migration.

Sources of International Migration

Historically, some factors have consistently influenced migration flows, but dramatic political and economic changes over the last decade have produced new migrant populations and patterns that defy "traditional" immigration controls and have led to a widespread belief that international migration has indeed reached crisis proportions. Many experts consider it one of the most significant global issues of our time, reflecting economic and societal failures to provide adequate jobs and shelter, environmental protection, and the preservation of basic human rights.

The root causes of international migration are several and often intertwined, so that traditional categories, such as labor migration, family reunification, or asylum–seeking, are no longer clear–cut:

• **Economic:** While economics is a major cause of displacement, migrants who come from impoverished conditions are likely to have been affected by other factors, including political and social unrest not formally acknowledged as endangering human rights conditions.

• **Political:** Most of today's refugees are fleeing conditions of generalized violence and hostilities rather than individual persecution. Most current conflicts are taking place within countries rather than between them.

• **Environmental:** Millions of people have been displaced because the land they live on has become toxic or is unable to support them. While some conditions are the result of natural disasters, much environmental degradation is caused by humans—national and multinational business interests that disregard protections or purposely ravage natural resources.

• **Ethnic Tensions:** Many of the highly publicized refugee flows today have been traced to ethnic tensions unleashed by national instabilities and conflicts or fomented by political adversaries. In the process of national consolidation, some minority groups may be viewed as obstacles, breaking up a country's national identity or dividing political loyalties.

The destinations of migrants have also significantly shifted over the last 30 years. Migration patterns have always been affected by such factors as geographic proximity, historical and political ties, culture, language, and so forth. But the dominant flow is South to North, a trend that has significantly increased in the last few decades, with the United States as a particular magnet for migrants from developing countries. However, there is still considerable migration among Northern countries, and more so among countries in the South. Obviously, 99 percent of the world's migrants do not come to the United States, despite current national fears that the country is being overrun by "hordes" of the foreign–born.

Who Are the Migrants?

The International Organization for Migration estimates there may be about 30 million "irregular" migrant workers—those who are undocumented or without legal permission to remain in countries where they live. The United States receives an estimated 300,000 undocumented immigrants annually.

About 20 million migrants are displaced within their own countries and have not crossed international boundaries.

The refugee population has more than doubled since the early 1980s to over 20 million today, compared with an estimated 8.5 million in 1980. Seventy–five percent of these refugees have moved to bordering countries in developing regions, which are most hard–pressed to accept new and often rapid increases in population. Refugees are the most numerous within Asia—about 10 million people—with about 5.5 million in Africa and 4.5 million in Europe. By contrast, advanced countries such as the United States and Canada together receive just over one million refugees.

Because migration has become such an important issue, recent international fora, such as the UN's International Conference on Population and Development (ICPD), held in Cairo in September 1994, have been strongly criticized for their insufficient treatment of the migration question.

Sending countries were especially frustrated at the ICPD by the attitudes of Western nations, typically the receiving countries. A particularly heated debate broke out over the issue of family reunification, which sending countries felt should be preserved in the official conference document as a "right" of migrant people. However, Canada, the United States, and European nations opposed the language, offering a compromise that merely "encouraged" nations to consider family reunification in determining their immigration policies—an action which the sending countries, predominantly composed of people of color, felt was just one more example of the racial hostility of the predominantly white receiving nations.

While the conference made gains in asserting the centrality of the empowerment of women in addressing resolutions to rapidly escalating population growth, the ICPD did not make any headway in confronting the impact of international development policies on population and consequent pressures toward increased migration. Of course, such gross omissions served the political and economic interests of the Western nations that continue to dominate such international gatherings and which resist fetters on their development policies and practices. The debacle over family reunification, however,

stirred sending country delegates to press for an international conference on migration and development, a controversial proposal which
was under consideration at the United Nations in 1995.

Such a conference would likely address long–range measures to
alleviate migration pressures, including: economic growth, investment and cooperative aid programs; easing the developing countries'
tremendous debt burdens; promoting fair trade policies; education,
health care access, and economic opportunities, especially for women
in developing countries; and generally developing more stable economic environments.

Migration, Development & Trade

There is strong feeling among developing countries that as trade
and development policies and agreements are forged, the question of
migration must also be put on the table. This was an especially sore
point in the negotiations over NAFTA, which essentially redefined
the international border between the United States and Mexico by
allowing for the free flow of goods, resources, and capital, but which
omitted discussion of the obvious flow of labor across borders—a permanent and essential element of the global economy.

In the meantime, as the scope of international migration in the
new global economy continues to broaden, considerable concern has
arisen about rights protections for migrants—and for foreign nationals residing temporarily in new countries. Most receiving countries
are taking steps to restrict immigration in ways that have little impact on migration pressures, but which will severely limit the rights
and mobility of immigrants already residing in those countries.

Many countries around the world—not just the major receiving
nations—have growing percentages of foreign nationals living within
their boundaries, and, in many instances, migrants, whether documented or undocumented, have few, if any, rights protections.

Pursuing International Protections

The UN's 1990 Convention on the Protection of the Rights of All
Migrant Workers and Members of their Families was created to
augment existing covenants, further delineating the growing classes
of people not residing in their countries of origin. The Convention
faces an uphill battle before it "comes into force" (it requires full ratification by 20 countries, and only a few have ratified it thus far).
Even when it gains recognition, its provisions are still subject to the
civil laws of each country. However, it does set the basis for promoting international rights standards in this era of the global workforce,
and provides a framework for evaluating national proposals dealing
with immigration. California's anti–immigrant initiative, Proposition

187, for example, certainly violates the spirit and intent of international migrants' rights protections.

The tendency of countries to build higher walls in an attempt to block immigration in no way addresses the complexities of migration, but is a simplistic response to heightening ignorance, racial intolerance, and xenophobia. Migration—not just immigration into any one country—is an international issue, a manifestation of uneven social, political, and economic development and conflict that requires cooperation and collective action among countries and regions.

Cathi Tactaquin is Senior Research Associate at the Applied Research Center and a board member of the Poverty & Race Research Action Council (PRRAC). She is also a member of the International Migrant Rights Watch Committee, headquartered in Geneva. This article first appeared in *Poverty & Race*, Vol. 4, No. 2, March/April 1995, published by PRRAC. © 1995, Cathi Tactaquin.

Pulling Up the Ladder

The Anti–Immigrant Backlash

> *Many persons who have spoken and written in favor*
> *of restriction of immigration, have laid great stress*
> *upon the evils to society arising from immigration.*
> *They have claimed that disease, pauperism, crime*
> *and vice have been greatly increased through the*
> *incoming of the immigrants. Perhaps no other phase*
> *of the question has aroused so keen feeling, and yet*
> *perhaps on no other phase of the question*
> *has there been so little accurate information.*
> Jeremiah Jenks and W. Jett Lauck

Doug Brugge

These words, written in 1912 by Jeremiah Jenks and W. Jett
Lauck, who had been part of the United States Immigration
Commission, sound surprisingly contemporary. In 1995, there is a
popular argument that immigrants are responsible for many, if
not all, of the problems facing our country. This theme has been
struck before in US history. It has arisen now in part because
right–wing organizations have promoted immigrants as a group
targeted for blame. For example, an organization prominent in
this right–wing campaign, the American Immigration Control

Foundation (AICF), in a 1992 mailing, lists immigrants as the culprits behind high taxes, wasted welfare dollars, lost jobs, high costs for education, and rising crime. AICF claims that immigrants are driving up health care costs by grabbing free care while also bringing disease into the US. Interestingly, subsequent versions of the same letter, sent out the following year, reduce their claim of 13 million illegal immigrants to 6–8 million, a number still higher than that cited by *Time* magazine as no more than 5 million. As Jenks and Lauck conclude in the above quote, the debate is still characterized more by angry talk than by facts.

An important ingredient in the success of the right's anti–immigrant campaign is its ability to deflect anger about the negative effects of the current US "economic restructuring" onto the scapegoat of immigrants. This tactic nests within a larger goal of capturing political gain by exploiting a popular issue. This is nothing new, but rather is a practice rooted in a long–standing history of reaction to immigration, nurtured today by a cluster of right–wing political organizations dedicated to this single issue.

The History of US Immigration

It is impossible to understand the current wave of anti–immigrant sentiment without some historical perspective. Indeed, excepting the Native American population, it is often said that the US is a nation of immigrants. Certainly, the role of cheap immigrant labor has been critical in building the US economy. Immigration has been both voluntary and forced. In early US history, territorial and economic expansion was a magnet for persons fleeing poverty and political repression. There was also forced immigration in the form of the slave trade and the annexation of one half of Mexico by the Treaty of Guadeloupe Hidalgo, signed in 1848, at the end of the Mexican–American War. This, not traditional immigration, is the reason that a significant number of Chicanos in the Southwest live in the US rather than in Mexico.

By the turn of the 19–century, territorial expansion was no longer a major force fueling immigration. The new magnet was the industrial revolution, which was in full swing and in need of labor. Today, as the US is going through another economic shift to a service and information–based economy with global reach, immigration is once again a factor.

The US has historically had a complex reaction to immigration. On the one hand, immigrants have been crucial to US economic progress at certain junctures in our economic development. On the other, there has been considerable hate and anger directed toward immigrants, based on xenophobia, religious prejudice, and fear that immigrants will take jobs from native–born workers. It is revealing to take a brief look at some of this history of immigration as told by Howard Zinn in *A People's History of the United States.* In his description of the colonies in the 1700s, Zinn notes that the colonies grew quickly as English settlers and black slaves were joined by Scottish, Irish, and German immigrants. Immigration was causing the larger cities to double and triple in size, but often urban poverty grew apace. "As Boston grew, from 1687 to 1770, the percentage of adult males who were poor . . . .[and who] owned no property, doubled from 14 percent of adult males to 29 percent. And the loss of property meant loss of voting rights." Indeed this often–romanticized period of US history was a time of far harsher immigration conditions than those of today.

Civil War era immigration occurred in an even more hostile environment. The Contract Labor Law of 1864 allowed companies to sign contracts with foreign workers in return for a pledge of 12 months' wages. This allowed employers during the Civil War not only to recruit very cheap labor, but also strikebreakers. Predictably, this resulted in conflict. "Italians were imported into the bituminous coal area around Pittsburgh in 1874 to replace striking miners. This led to the killing of three Italians, to trials in which the jurors of the community exonerated the strikers, and bitter feelings between Italians and other organized workers." It is interesting to note that there was no definition of United States citizenship in the Constitution until the 14th Amendment was added in 1868. A definition was needed, in part to counteract the Dred Scott decision, which held that slaves were not citizens.

At the turn of the century, the immigrant population had changed from largely Irish and German to Eastern and Southern European and Russian, including many Jews. Zinn again describes the impact well, citing the role of immigration of different ethnic groups as contributing to the fragmentation of the working class. He discusses how the previous wave of Irish immigrants resented Jews coming into their neighborhoods. At this time, there was also the added fear that immigrants would bring with them socialist ideas that would undermine the principles of this country.

While nationality, religion, and political ideology were the main basis for resentment of immigrants in urban areas during the first half of the 19–century, race was the issue when Chinese immigrants arrived, brought in to fill a labor gap and then later to work as construction workers on the railroads in the 1860s. Indeed the first anti–immigrant law, passed in California, targeted the Chinese. In 1882, the US passed the Chinese

Exclusion Act, which was not repealed until 1943. Even then, immigration quotas for Chinese were only raised above 105 per year by the Civil Rights Act of 1964. The late 1800s were difficult for Chinese in the US—the growing trade union movement based part of its organizing strategy on advocating deportation of Chinese immigrants. Race riots on the West coast were the response of angry whites who blamed Chinese for their woes.

In 1917 and again in 1942, the US initiated guest labor programs, commonly known as the Bracero programs, that brought Mexican workers into the Southwest to work as non–citizen farm workers and fill an alleged labor shortage. Up to half a million workers were enrolled in the program at its height. The flow of undocumented Mexicans grew during this time, prompting a government effort to stem the tide by "drying out the wetbacks"—an effort to convert undocumented immigrants into Braceros. When that failed, "Operation Wetback" was launched with the deployment of a military style border patrol. The Bracero programs effectively exposed thousands of poor Mexicans to the wealth of the United States and contributed to immigration pressure. It also displaced Chicanos from rural agricultural jobs, fueling their exodus to urban centers.

The role of racism in anti–immigrant sentiment seemed to have dimmed by the late 1970s, at least according to Lawrence Fuchs, who served for two years as director of the Select Commission on Immigration and Refugee Policy. Commenting on hearings held by his committee in 12 major cities from 1979 through 1980, Fuchs stated that "racism [against immigrants] was not nearly as powerful a force as it once was." Fuchs attributed this decline in anti–immigrant racism to the civil rights movement and an expansion of the spirit of pluralism that it forced. This optimistic reading of US tolerance for ethnic, racial, and religious diversity parallels the optimism of that period.

Intolerance, however, was just below the surface of American politics. The appearance of a hospitable melting pot that had an accepting attitude toward immigrants proved illusory. It took only the arrival of immigrants who were politically unwelcome, such as those fleeing the repression in El Salvador, for government policies of exclusion to become explicit again.

As in the case of El Salvador, immigration has sometimes followed a pattern of growth from parts of the world in which the US is heavily involved militarily or economically. In recent years, immigration has increased from South East Asia and the Central America/Caribbean region. This sometimes results from granting entry for persons fleeing official enemies of the US, such as Cuba or Vietnam, but also draws people from countries allied with the US, such as the Philippines, Hong Kong, or El Salvador. It is likely that as global trade relationships grow through treaties such as NAFTA, the coming period will prompt greater immigration.

The Contemporary Anti–Immigrant Campaign

Right–wing anti–immigration groups have placed the 1965 Immigration Act at the center of a campaign to promote anti–immigrant sentiment in the 1980s and 1990s. In the 1965 Act, Congress repudiated the infamous 1952 McCarran–Walter Act, which followed 1920s–era legislation in parceling out immigrants' visas based on country of origin. Under the banner of humanitarian values, Congress decided to allocate visas primarily on the grounds of kinship.

The 1965 law states that 20 percent of all numerically restricted visas will be allocated for skilled workers and 6 percent for refugees, with the remainder split among various family-oriented preference categories. Importantly, spouses, dependent children, and parents of US citizens were exempted from any numerical limits. It is this provision that particularly drew the wrath of the right.

In the 1980s, anti–immigrant sentiment grew during the debate over immigration reform. Supporters of the Immigration Reform and Control Act of 1986 argued that immigrants were stealing jobs and draining the economy, and that political turmoil in Mexico and Central America would spill over into the US. Defenders of immigrants argued that immigrants are, in fact, a positive force in the American workforce and that the US is historically a nation of immigrants.

The final law, authored by Senator Alan Simpson (R–Wyoming) and Representative Romano Mazzoli (D–Kentucky), and promoted by the Reagan White House, was intended to shut the door on the further flow of illegal immigrants, while ostensibly supporting immigrants by offering "legalized" status to undocumented immigrants already in the US.

The Immigration Reform and Control Act contains sanctions against employers who hire illegal immigrants and includes provisions for "guest workers" who are allowed to work in the US, but are denied rights or benefits. (The "guest worker" provisions were touted by Pete Wilson, then a Senator from California.)

Although many immigrants entered the legal citizenship process, despite significant obstacles, the law laid the basis for the current debate over how to effectively seal the border. Further, the guest worker program has contributed to the flow of immigrant workers to the US who have no possibility of becoming citizens.

The most recent piece of major legislation on the issue, the Immigration Act of 1990, reaffirmed the centrality of family reunification, which has been the touchstone of US immigration policy since 1965. However, the concept of family reunification is now under attack.

Rightists Fund Anti–Immigrant Groups

The Federation for American Immigration Reform (FAIR) is directly tied to more virulent racists by the funding it has received from the Pioneer Fund. Between 1985 and 1989, the Pioneer Fund provided eight grants totaling $295,000 to FAIR, and three grants totaling $80,000 to the American Immigration Control Foundation.

Pioneer Fund documents indicate that FAIR received another $150,000 in 1992, making it the largest recipient of Pioneer grants that year. And FAIR clearly has no qualms about receiving such funding. The Pioneer Fund also funded *The Bell Curve.* *

It is also of note that heiress Cordelia Scaiffe May supports FAIR, US English, the Center for Immigration Studies, and others to the tune of $2.5 million. May's political agenda is made clearer by her foundation's underwriting in 1983 of the distribution of *The Camp of the Saints* by Jean Raspail, a book in which immigrants from the Third World invade Europe and destroy its civilization.

Raspail's novel was the emotional touchstone for a recent article in the *Atlantic Monthly* titled "Must It Be the Rest Against the West?" in which the authors ultimately propose rather pragmatic solutions in response to the global division between rich and poor that they perceive as "dwarf[ing] every other issue in global affairs."

The Atlantic Monthly article quotes directly from *The Camp of the Saints,* a copy of which they obtained from the American Immigration Control Foundation. It is instructive to read even a short passage from that book. It describes the masses threatening the white, and naturally civilized world as:

> All the kinky–haired, swarthy–skinned, long–despised phantoms; all the teeming ants toiling for the white man's comfort; all the swill men and sweepers, the troglodytes, the stinking drudges, the swivel–hipped menials, the womenless wretches, the lung–spewing hackers. . . .

These "five billion growling human beings" are threatening the "seven hundred million whites."

---

* The Federation for American Immigration Reform (FAIR) should not be confused with Fairness and Accuracy in Reporting (FAIR) through guilt by acronym.

Immigration, Today & Yesterday

Today there is a tendency to revise history, to extol the virtues of past immigration, specifically that which includes our ancestors, while saying that now the country is full and can hold no more. But as we have seen, the pattern of resistance to immigration was, if anything, more severe during earlier waves of arrivals. Indeed immigration today does not equal, in absolute numbers, the peak of entries around 1910. And immigration as immigrants per 1,000 residents of the US (the rate) is several times lower than at any time during the period 1850–1930.

Anti–immigrant groups have had to endorse historical immigration because the vast majority of non–native US citizens are descended from immigrants. What they do not state directly, but imply in cleverly constructed arguments, is the one thing that clearly is different today. In 1900, 85 percent of immigrants came from Europe (only 2.5 percent came from Latin America and Asia combined). In 1990, Latin and Asian immigrants accounted for more than two–thirds of all immigrants. Indeed, the population of Hispanics in the US is projected to reach 80 million by the middle of the next century, while the Asian population will rise to about 40 million.

The US has been a majority–white country and immigrant labor in the early part of this century was white, although, as we have seen, ethnic, national, and religious distinctions were critical in that time as the basis for defining immigrants as different, inferior morally and intellectually and, thus, threatening. The current influx from Third World countries faces the added dimension of race, a powerful factor throughout US history. Thus the current sentiment is as much the political twin of the racist history of exclusion of the Chinese as it is the resistance to white immigration.

The recent US military action in Haiti is yet another sign of the depth of impact that race has on immigration policy. Haitian immigrants have been widely and falsely disparaged as bringing AIDS into the US. President Clinton, however, promised fair treatment for Haitian refugees during his campaign, only to renege on that promise once in office. When intense economic sanctions failed to force the Haitian military junta out and the flow of boat people continued, pressure mounted to do something and Clinton sent in the troops. In the process, the issue of halting immigration of poor black people was elevated to the level of national security.

The Message of the Right Wing

Dan Stein, Executive Director of FAIR, writes that a public consensus has emerged "in the face of Haitian boats, the World Trade Center bombing, Chinese boats, international immigrant–smuggling and crime syndicates, persistent illegal immigration from Mexico and high profile tales of immigrant–related welfare rip–offs." Stein states that in the face of this assault we need to cut the total number of immigrants, legal and illegal: "the country needs a break to absorb and handle its critical social and internal problems. . . .We have to limit immigration significantly to preserve the nation."

In its advertisements in mainstream magazines, FAIR claims that "nowhere are the effects of out–of–control immigration more acutely felt than in the labor market. The original intent of our nation's immigration laws. . .was to protect the American Worker." In their mailings, FAIR plays on fears by telling a story of Mexicans crossing the US border "with the sole intention of having a child who is automatically an American citizen." In a brochure, FAIR writes:

> Today's challenges are very different from those faced by earlier generations. We no longer have a vast frontier to tame. In fact, we must protect shrinking forests, wetlands and farm lands. . . .We no longer need to encourage an influx of new workers as we did to fuel the industrial revolution.

Overall, the message of the anti–immigrant forces is that things have changed. At one time immigration was a good thing for this country, but no more. There is, in this view, no longer enough to go around and immigrants are cutting into the share of what could be had by good patriotic Americans. Furthermore, anti–immigrant advocates raise the specter of new immigrants failing to assimilate and forcing their culture on everyone else—a prospect that, they argue, could lead to separatist scenarios like the disaster in what was once Yugoslavia.

For instance, *Chronicles*, a rightist monthly cultural magazine, devoted its June 1993 issue to the subject of cultural breakdown in the US resulting from immigration. The cover, a cartoon depiction of the Statue of Liberty, features immigrant characters (with pointed ears to indicate their demon status) clawing their way to the top of the statue, whose face is grimacing in pain and alarm. The thrust of the article is the dual threat of cultural adulteration of the Anglo–Saxon American heritage and the overwhelming inferiority of Third World alternative cultures. Feature writer Thomas Fleming writes, "Arab and Pakistani terrorists, Nigerian con artists, Oriental and South American drug lords, Russian gangsters—all are introducing their particular brands of cultural enrichment into an already fragmented United States that increasingly resembles Bosnia more than the America I grew up in." This message pervades not just right–wing anti–immigrant rhetoric, but the mainstream media and the rhetoric of both political parties.

Public Opinion is Against Immigrants

Today public opinion has been swayed by such arguments and the enormous access that anti–immigrant organizations have to the national media. A *Business Week*/Harris Poll in 1992 found that while 59 percent of those surveyed thought immigration has been good for the US historically, 69 percent of non–blacks and 53 percent of blacks thought present–day immigration was bad. Among the reasons cited were taking jobs away from American workers (60 percent) and using more than their fair share of government services (about 60 percent). black views may be prompted by different reasons than those of whites, since it is likely that blacks are resentful of the success of recent immigrants appearing to overtake them economically, while whites see immigrants threatening what they already have.

There is a clear lack of a sense of the history of immigration in the current out–cry. Nothing so exemplifies the lack of historical connection as a story in the *Boston Globe* New Hampshire Edition, headlined "Son of Immigrants Offers English Bill." The legislation offered by Bernard Raynowska, a state representative from New Hampshire and of Lithuanian descent, would restrict the state's use of bilingual ballots or forms. While Raynowska's father came up the hard way after immigrating, his son now feels, "[i]n the year 2000 wo'ro all going to be speaking Spanish, dressing Spanish [sic] and eating Spanish food." A letter to the editor in the November 10, 1991 *Tampa Times* echoes that sentiment when the writer recalls, through rose–colored glasses, his experience with immigrants in an earlier era. "There was no special consideration given those people, and their children required little time to become proficient in English."

What are the actual statistics to back up this anti–immigrant rhetoric? In fact, less than 1.5 percent of the US population is undocumented, according to the US Census. One quarter of immigrants in the US are undocumented. Most of these do not sneak across the border, but arrive legally and stay beyond the expiration of their visas. Only one–third of undocumented immigrants come from Mexico.

Nothing is as fiercely contested or as wildly divergent in their conclusions as studies on the impact of immigration on the economy. Anti–immigrant organizations point to a study by Dr.

Donald Huddle that shows that immigrants cost the US $44 billion more than they contributed in 1993. Immigrant advocates point to the Urban Institute study that shows that immigrants contributed from $25 to $35 billion more than they took out in 1992. A study by Los Angeles County found that immigrants cost the county almost $1 billion, but give back four times that amount in taxes. The problem, however, for Los Angeles County is that the taxes go to the federal government instead of the county. *Business Week* estimated that immigrants pay $70.3 billion in taxes annually and receive $5 billion in welfare benefits, and another $11.5 billion in primary and secondary education benefits.

The Urban Institute reviewed a number of contemporary studies that "document" the draining effect of immigrants on the US economy in order to find underlying biases. They found that the studies vary in quality, but "the results invariably overstate the negative impact of immigrants for the following reasons: 1) they systematically understate tax collections from immigrants, 2) they systematically overstate service costs for immigrants, 3) none credit immigrants for the impact of immigrant–owned businesses or the full economic benefit generated by consumer spending from immigrants, 4) job displacement impact and costs are overstated, 5) they omit the fact that parallel computations for natives show natives use more in services than they pay in taxes too, and 6) the size of the immigrant population—particularly the undocumented immigrant population—tends to be overstated."

The Immigration Debate & the Issue of Race

It is helpful to take a step back and consider the development of race as a concept. Race is intimately associated with both the development of the US and with immigration policy. This is not surprising since this country was built on dislocation of the indigenous population and the enslavement of Africans. Such deeds are hard to justify against persons that you hold as equals. In the 19th–century, the dominant view was that Africans, Asians, and Native Americans were separate and inferior species. This was based variously on interpretation of the Christian scriptures and on "scientific" comparisons of cranial capacity. According to Gould:

"Louis Agassiz, the greatest biologist of mid–nineteenth–century America, argued that God had created blacks and whites as separate species." On the other hand, Gould noted that, head measurements "matched every good Yankee's prejudice—whites on top, Indians in the middle, and blacks on the bottom; and, among whites, Teutons and Anglo–Saxons on top, Jews in the middle and Hindus on the bottom." Drawings showing that African's heads appeared half–way between those of whites and chimpanzees were common.

Actually, race is an artificial construct. Andrew Hacker writes, "there is no consensus when it comes to defining 'race,' the term has been applied to a diversity of groups. The Irish have been called a race. . .as have Jews and Hindus. . . . In the United States, what people mean by 'race' is usually straightforward and clear, given the principal division into black and white. Yet. . .not all Americans fit into a racial designation." Most obviously, racial designations usually include Hispanic as an option—despite the fact that Hispanic covers many races. On another level, for most Asians and Hispanics, "images of their identities are almost wholly national"— Chinese or Japanese, Puerto Rican or Mexican for example.

In the early part of this century, the terrain of defining racial differences shifted to measurement of IQ, and this was used to justify differential restriction of peoples in immigration. These tests, in particular those by psychologist, "R. M. Yerkes, who persuaded the army to test 1.75 million men in World War I, thus establish(ed) the supposedly objective data that vindicated hereditarian claims and led to the Immigration Restriction Act of 1924, with its low ceiling for lands suffering the blight of poor genes," writes Gould.

In the 1970s, the Pioneer Fund underwrote research by William Shockley and Arthur Jensen, who set the next stage for the IQ and race issue. They proclaimed that blacks have lower IQs than whites. It is not surprising to note the resurgence once again of this idea in the publication of *The Bell Curve* in 1994 by conservative social scientist Charles Murray and the late Harvard Professor Richard Herrnstein. The book develops an argument that intelligence is largely hereditary. Since blacks score below whites on such tests, this leads the authors to draw conclusions in favor of, "ending welfare to discourage births among low–IQ women, changing immigration laws to favor the capable and rolling back most job discrimination laws."

It is bitterly ironic that this was published in the same year that the movie "Forest Gump" became a smash hit by showing the basic humanity and common sense wisdom of a low IQ white man. *The Bell Curve* has been reviewed by sociologist Christopher Jencks as "highly selective in the evidence they present and in their interpretation of ambiguous statistics." And psychologist Richard Nisbett states that their work "wouldn't be accepted by an academic journal—it's that bad."

Indeed, along with the political climate, there already "is a police state that has developed in the southwestern United Stated since the 1980s. No person, no citizen is free to travel without the scrutiny of the Border Patrol," writes Leslie Marmon Silko of the Laguna Pueblo after describing her personal harassment at the hands of the Border Patrol in New Mexico. Significantly, undocumented immigrants from Latin America are primarily "Native Americans or mestizos (mixed–bloods) from Mexico and Guatemala," often driven out by government repression backed by the US government, while "economic refugees from Cuba (mostly white) and from the former Soviet Union (all white) are admitted to the US 'legally.'"

The Republican Party's Use of Anti–Immigrant Themes

The Republican Party has scapegoated immigrants for some time, but now immigration has moved to the center of the party's agenda and has become a platform to advance its political fortunes. David Nyhan, writing in *The Boston Globe,* points to California Governor Pete Wilson's reelection campaign as the flash point of the rise of immigrants as an official enemy in the Republican's electoral strategy. Nyhan writes, "Wilson looked done in by a combination of recession. . .defense cuts, population growth, job loss. . .and a plague of natural calamities. . .and the Los Angeles riots." Then Wilson found a way to invigorate his political prospects. "He pursued an increasingly harsh policy toward illegal immigrants and was reinforced at nearly every turn of the media page by the increasingly polarized electorate."

Nyhan accurately predicted that Wilson's reelection "will nationalize the anti–immigrant debate, which is becoming the most incendiary issue in presidential megastates like Texas, Florida and New York." Indeed, Wilson briefly ran as a candidate for the 1996 Republican presidential nomination, promoting California's anti–immigrant policies as a national "solution."

In fact, the Republican–controlled Congress in 1995, rallying behind the "Contract With America," has taken up immigration. HR 4, the Personal Responsibility Act, would withdraw the safety net from virtually all immigrants, legal and illegal, who are not citizens by excluding them from 60 listed programs. Excepting only emergency medical services, the Republicans call for cutting off Medicaid, food stamps, welfare, school children's meals and immunizations, housing loans, job training, higher education assistance, and child care to a population of tax–paying people who have done nothing illegal.

This would fundamentally shift the relationship between citizens and legal immigrants. Historically, immigrants have been viewed as future citizens. That link between immigrant status and citizenship potential would be broken by the Personal Responsibility Act, accomplishing a major goal of the right–wing anti–immigrant forces. Clearly, "public animosity to illegal aliens has been spilling over into the attitudes toward legal migrants," notes R. Pear in the *New York Times*.

With liberal and progressive organizations weak at this time, anti–immigrant views are raising the fear of "others" who are "different." This sort of scapegoating—explaining away fears and social problems by blaming an unpopular group—has proved an effective strategy in dividing people and confusing them about the source of their problems. Further, the Republican claim that the Personal Responsibility Act would save the voters $21 billion over five years masks the vindictive and short–sighted nature of the bill with a promise of tax–saving budget reduction.

Proposition 187 in California

Closely linked to the 1994 gubernatorial election in California is Proposition 187, a statewide referendum that is a paradigm of the state–level strategy of the anti–immigrant movement. When the voters of California approved Proposition 187 by a margin of 59 to 41 percent, they mandated that teachers, doctors, social workers, and police check the immigration status of all persons seeking access to public education and health services from publicly funded agencies, and deny services to those in the US illegally. Those who voted in the 1994 election were 80 percent white, despite the fact that 45 percent of California's potential voters are people of color, and despite widespread protests from the Latino community.

The proposition, championed by an organization called Save Our State (SOS), was promoted as a cure–all that would reverse the many crises facing California. Despite the possibility that the initiative could cost the state $15 billion in federal funding because it violates federal privacy and eligibility laws, it enjoys widespread support. While Governor Wilson staked his successful reelection bid on endorsing the initiative, prominent Democratic elected officials voiced only muted opposition, and offered up their own plans to strengthen the Border Patrol.

Elizabeth Kadetsky has analyzed the organization behind California's anti–immigrant movement. She finds that SOS itself is "a ragtag movement replete with registered Greens, Democrats, Perotists, distributors of New Age healing products and leaders of the Republican Party." There is little question that SOS has a grassroots base that "right–wing figures have shown up to exploit." Among key financial backers were Rob Hurtt, a millionaire who helped bankroll the Christian Right's campaign for the state legislature, and state legislator Don Rogers, who is associated with the white supremacist Christian Identity movement. But SOS raised most of its modest budget from small donations.

While FAIR and SOS did not work together, FAIR did endorse the measure and was linked to the issue by Alan Nelson, a former INS director under Reagan, who later wrote anti–immigrant legislation in California for FAIR before writing Proposition 187. Kadetsky finds that "SOS's visible advocates personify either fringe populism or cynical manipulation of public sentiment for political gain."

After the passage of Proposition 187, reports of discrimination against Hispanics have been rampant. The Hispanic Mayor of Pomona was stopped by the INS and told to prove his citizenship. In Bell Gardens, a teacher asked students for their immigration papers. In Los Angeles, a bus driver yelled at passengers that they could no longer speak Spanish or Armenian. And a car accident victim was denied emergency services when he couldn't prove his legal status, to name just a few examples. Columnist Jose Armas called this "one of the most hate–charged laws ever passed" and called for support of the growing boycott of California products and tourist and convention visits.

Groundwork for Proposition 187 was laid in 1986 by Proposition 63, a successful referendum to make English the official language of the state. A local affiliate of US English, the California English Campaign, led the campaign in California. US English provided the campaign with between $800,000 and $900,000 for the initial signature drive, and continued to heavily fund the campaign. Other national organizations collaborated to coordinate the campaign, with US English taking the lead. It was an early use of the statewide referendum to tap anti–immigrant sentiment and was a precursor to 187.

English Only
as a Linchpin of Anti–Immigrant Hate

Language is a key issue in the immigration debate. At the same time that there is concern that students are not learning second languages, there are attempts to make sure that young immigrants do not retain their native language. A plausible explanation is that immigrants have the wrong language: Spanish, rather than French or German. The opposition to "other" languages seems to reflect both disdain of foreign cultures and fear of the loss of English as the dominant US language and is closely associated with the racist aspects of immigrant bashing.

The language issue is often falsely framed as a concern that immigrants are not learning English and are not integrating into society. In fact, immigrants today are learning English as rapidly as previous generations of immigrants, despite longer and longer waiting lists for English classes due to government cutbacks. The hidden political agenda of English Only advocates is clear in their attacks on bilingual education and bilingual ballots. When English Only laws have passed, it has emboldened employers to restrict non–English languages at work and cities to outlaw commercial signs in various languages. It has fueled anti–immigrant sentiment, extending to citizens, legal residents, and the undocumented alike, as long as they "look like immigrants."

The danger of official English initiatives comes from their subtlety and ability to win over middle Americans who are unaware of the larger agenda. In fact, US English is a flagship organization of the right's anti–immigrant campaign. Because US English is occasionally characterized as seeking to designate a state or national language that is no more threatening than an official bird or flower, liberals are sometimes puzzled or shocked to read claims that the English Only movement is racist.

John Tanton wrote a memo in 1988 that dirtied the clean public image that US English has sought to maintain. In the memo, Tanton writes, "[a]s Whites see their power and control over their lives declining, will they simply go quietly into the night?. . . .Will Latin Americans bring with them the tradition of the mordida [bribe]?" And, "[o]n the demographic point: perhaps this is the first instance in which those with their pants up are going to get caught by those with their pants down!" The ensuing uproar led to the resignation of then–director Linda Chavez and board member Walter Cronkite.

US English has made a strong comeback in the wake of that crisis. They have hundreds of thousands of members across the US thanks to their ability to reach huge numbers of persons through mass mailings, and they can point to some 17 states that have passed official English laws. Their prime objective today is to change the US Constitution and they have legislation that has gathered some support in Congress. In addition, they have continued to oppose transitional bilingual education.

Immigration and the New Economy

One aspect of economic restructuring today involves a shift from local or national economies to a global economy. US business is moving freely without being tied to local labor forces; consequently, corporations are relocating overseas to find cheaper labor and lax environmental laws. The rise of an information—and

service—based economy has contributed significantly to the dislocation of workers, since it generates a two–tier class structure of
low–income jobs for most and high–income jobs for the few with
the right skills and knowledge. The low–paying jobs that are being created are often jobs that new immigrants are willing to take
but are unacceptable to middle class workers who are seeking jobs
that allow a more affluent and secure lifestyle.

Since 1972, real average weekly earnings have fallen 18.6
percent. blacks have been particularly hard hit, seeing their
family income plummet by one–third since 1973. On the other
hand, in just one year, from 1992 to 1993, after–tax corporate
profits increased by more than $44 billion. Between 1960 and
1988, manufacturing employment fell from 26 percent to less than
19 percent of civilian employment, while jobs in the service–
providing industries (including transportation, real estate,
wholesale and retail trade, service, finance, and public utilities)
climbed from 56 percent to 70 percent. This has caused an
uncharacteristically large–scale displacement of millions of blue
collar middle class workers, as well as professionals and middle
managers.

Displaced workers, along with others who fear for their
livelihood, are fertile ground in which to sow anti–immigrant
sentiment, since angry and frustrated people often seek some
target on which to blame their problems. The right wing has
organized and manipulated such anger and resentment, turned it
away from corporations, and directed it against the government,
decrying high taxes and the inability of the state to solve
problems such as social deterioration, homelessness, crime, and
violence. In addition to the target of "failed liberal policies,"
immigrants make a convenient scapegoat and a very tangible
target for people's anger. Racial prejudice is often an encoded part
of the message.

Right–wing populist themes are particularly effective at
attracting working people disenchanted with the system. A
cartoon in the October 1993 issue of *Border Watch,* a publication
of the American Immigration Control Foundation, depicts "US
Business Interests, Inc." as being pro–immigration. "We hire
aliens cheap," reads a sign in the cartoon, implying that US
corporate interests are promoting immigration and costing US
workers their jobs. Under the headline, "Immigration Takes Jobs
from Americans," an April 1994 issue of *Border Watch* claims that
native born workers are being displaced from both janitorial jobs
and white collar professional positions. An anonymous letter in
Border Watch, identified as from a worker, captures the anti–
immigrant sentiment: "[w]hen the Mexicans get powerful enough
in a job situation, they kick out the 'gringos' so their buddies can

take over." The anonymous writer goes on, "Just wait until they can work their way up the economic ladder, and middle class Americans will feel the sting of Mexican racism."

The Ambivalence of Liberals

Republicans and Democrats are not cleanly divided on the issue of immigration. Ideological positions on the issue are murky, among other reasons because the economic and political problems we are facing were created by both dominant political parties; thus, a popular scapegoat is useful to both. Gregory Defreitas, writing in *Dollars and Sense,* identifies an example of ideological divergence within conservatism: nativist Republicans want to curtail or stop immigration, while conservative libertarians endorse open borders. On the liberal side, a significant number of unionists and environmentalists see immigration as a threat to jobs and the environment.

It is the issues of jobs and the environment that provide the right's anti–immigrant campaign its strongest entree into mainstream attitudes. An indication of the success of this argument is the adoption by the Sierra Club in California of immigration restriction as an environmental cause. Population control is a related issue that can give the anti–immigrant message an acceptable mainstream spin.

The Carrying Capacity Network (CCN) specifically includes "immigration limitation" as a part of this agenda. Among the "Initiatives & Resources" offered in a 1994 publication of the CCN are an incongruous mix of ecology and anti–immigrant titles. These include "American Solar Energy Society," "Immigrants, Your Community, and US Immigration Policy," "Planned Parenthood," and "The Ordeal of Immigration in Wausau."

On the National Board of Advisors of the CCN are the names Anne and Paul Ehrlich, important figures in population control circles. They recently outlined their version of the relation of environment, population growth, and immigration limitation in the January 1991 issue of *The NPG Forum,* published by Negative Population Growth. First they claim that the US is actually the most overpopulated nation in the world because we have a greater per capita environmental impact than any other nation. They conclude that "[t]he first step, of course, is for the United States to adopt a population policy designed to halt population growth and begin a gradual population decline."

Naturally, immigration restrictions are a part of the Ehrlichs' plan. Although they consider immigration to add "important variety to our population," they worry that to maintain "reasonable" immigration rates will mean that others will have to pay too high a price in terms of restricting their family size. Ultimately they view immigration as environmentally destructive because immigrants come from poor nations where they consume little, only to "quickly acquire American superconsuming habits." They also bring unfortunate "reproductive habits" that go against the grain of population control. They conclude that "[t]he immigration issue is extremely complex and ethically difficult, but it must be faced," if we are ever to reach the "optimum" US population size of "around 75 million people." Since this is less than a third of our current population, it raises the question of where all the rest of us will go.

Negative Population Growth has outlined the history of growing competition for jobs in the US. They tie the problem to the effort to "bring blacks into the economic and social mainstream." They point out that the addition of blacks to the workforce after the civil rights movement was compounded by the baby boom and the influx of young women into the paid labor force. The answer? Limits on immigration and "reducing unwanted pregnancy among the poor" stand out to NPG. Thus, they put a liberal spin on the anti–immigrant debate, trying to align civil rights and feminist activists with anti–immigrant themes.

Former Congresswoman Barbara Jordan, who is head of the 1994 Commission on Immigration Reform, is at the more moderate end of the debate. Nonetheless, she recommends cutting immigration and limiting family reunification. To her credit, she has argued for depoliticizing the discussion. Says Jordan, "Now when economic conditions become a little stringent we look around for someone to blame. Right now, the immigrant is the one getting the blame for whatever the social ill is." She goes on to ask, "[n]ow, if we are what we claim to be in our mottoes, then why don't we reinforce our identity as an accepting and caring people and try to deal reasonably and rationally with the real issues?"

The ambivalence of liberals over the issue of immigration has allowed the views of the political right to become mainstream. As has been said earlier, liberals were part of setting economic policy, and can no more explain away what they have done than can the right. Upper–level workers, primarily white and unionized, are often a base for liberalism's themes of tolerance and diversity, but are not immune from lapses of racism and have blamed "foreigners," such as the Japanese, for economic problems in the past. In fact, there has been a recent shift from Japan–bashing and "Buy American" efforts to blaming immigrants. Further, because relatively few recent immigrants are voters and immigrants do not have their own PAC's, they are not widely feared or respected by liberals in the electoral arena.

Final Words

A competitive mentality and a sense of increasingly scarce resources create a fertile soil for anti–immigrant advocates who raise the fear that newcomers will take your job, your home, and your culture—things very central to a secure life. Fear is very real, and the decline in the economic position of the average American is an understandable motivator for fear. But to blame immigrants as the source of that decline is to scapegoat an easy, unpopular target and divert responsibility from more culpable parties. Unfortunately, the message that immigrants are the problem has been all too successful.

Doug Brugge is an occupational and environmental health scientist who serves on the Board of Directors of the Massachusetts English Plus Coalition and co–chairs Unity Boston, a multiracial, grassroots political organization. Call or write PRA for footnotes to this article. This article originally appeared in *The Public Eye* in the Summer 1995 issue. © 1995 Doug Brugge.

The Roots of the I. Q. Debate

Eugenics & Social Control

Whatever the Jukes stand for, the Edwards family does not. Whatever weakness the Jukes represent finds its antidote in the Edwards family, which has cost the country nothing in pauperism, in crime, in hospital or asylum service.

Albert E. Winship,
Heredity: A History of the Jukes–Edwards Families
Boston, 1925

Margaret Quigley

During the first three decades of this century, a small but influential social/scientific movement known as the eugenics movement extrapolated from the new science of human genetics a complex set of beliefs justifying the necessity for racial and class hierarchy. It also advocated limitations on political democracy. The eugenicists argued that the United States was in immediate danger of committing racial suicide as a result of the rapid reproduction of the unfit coupled with the precipitous decline in the birthrate of the better classes. They proposed a program of positive and negative eugenics as a solution. Positive genetics would encourage the reproduction of the better–educated and racially superior, while a rigorous program of negative eugenics to prevent any increase in the racially unfit would include compulsory segregation and sterilization, immigration restriction, and laws to prohibit inter–racial marriage (anti–miscegenation statutes).

I will argue that the eugenics movement of the early 20th–century was primarily a political movement concerned with the social control of groups thought to be inferior by an economic, social, and racial elite. I reject the contention that the movement was primarily scientific and apolitical. I have looked here primarily at the organized eugenics movement and its leading figures, rather than at the average rank–and–file follower within the movement.

My interest in the eugenics movement stems from my fear that the basic principles of the eugenics debate, even its most discredited aspects, are resurfacing in the 1990s. To revisit the eugenics movement of the early 20th–century is to be reminded of the harm the movement intended toward those members of society least able to defend themselves. History, in this case, may help to provide an antidote to contemporary manifestations of eugenicist arguments— the I. Q. debate and the right's anti–immigrant campaign.

Any historical appraisal of the eugenics movement needs to step carefully to avoid imposing the values of the late 20th–century upon eugenicists, especially concerning the question of motivation. The legitimate, scientific framework of the eugenics movement, a mainstream view at the beginning of the century, has been for the most part abandoned by scientists in the years since then.

Similarly, to a great extent, racialist thinking, and in particular white supremacy, was neither questioned nor challenged among the white–dominated intelligentsia of the time. At the same time, the fact that white supremacist views were more acceptable in white society at the turn of the century still allows for gradations of focus and virulence; the question of the extent to which hereditarian arguments may have functioned as a pretext for a movement primarily concerned with the continuation of social and political dominance by upper–class, Protestant men of Anglo–Saxon background is unavoidable.

The roots of the eugenics movement have been traced variously to social Darwinism; social purity, voluntary motherhood, and the perfectionists; the naturalist tradition; Malthus and the neo–Malthusians; and the Progressive political and social movement.

This paper emphasizes instead that the roots of the eugenics movement can be traced to the 19th–century scientific racism movement. "Scientific racism" is a term capable of diverse definitions. For this discussion, I have adopted a slightly modified version of historian Barry Mehler's definition:

[Scientific racism is] the belief [often based on skin color, country of origin, or economic class] that the human species can be divided into superior and inferior genetic groups and that these groups can be satisfactorily identified so that social policies can be advanced to encourage the breeding of the superior groups and discourage the breeding of the inferior groups.

It is possible to argue that notions of control by a racial and economic elite were key to the eugenics movement without embracing reductionist or conspiratorial theories that do damage to the diversity and scope of the movement.

It has been the diversity of the eugenics movement—the wide range of followers it was able to encompass—that has proved most difficult to explain. The eugenics movement was not monolithic: conservatives, progressives, and sex radicals were all allied within a fundamentally messianic movement of national salvation that was predicated upon scientific notions of innate and ineradicable inequalities between racial, cultural, and economic groups.

These scientific notions tended to maintain the status quo by obscuring the racial and class basis of poverty and advancement in the United States. The middle– and upper–class professionals of Anglo–Saxon descent who were leaders in the eugenics movement acted in and out of their own interests.

Those interests led to the development of a political program in which an extreme economic conservatism was marked by a virulent anti–communism linked to an embrace of the untrammeled, unregulated capitalist state. Some eugenicist leaders rejected democracy in favor of the corporate state and, in the 1920s and 1930s, several leaders of the eugenics movement were active in the promotion of German and Italian fascism.

The eugenics movement put forth a coherent, consistent social program in which eugenical sterilization, anti–immigrant advocacy, and anti–miscegenation activism all played crucial roles in the primary eugenicist goal of advancing social control by a small elite. Particularly now, when familiar eugenicist arguments echo within contemporary scientific and political circles, questions of motivation and intent are compelling.

Background of the Movement

The American eugenics movement came into being primarily through the efforts of Charles Benedict Davenport, a biologist with a Ph.D. from Harvard University. While at Harvard as an instructor in the 1890s, Davenport became familiar with the early eugenicist writings of two Englishmen, the independently wealthy Francis Galton and his *protégé* Karl Pearson.

By 1869, Galton had published several articles and a book, *Hereditary Genius*, which argued that human traits, and particularly great ability, can be inherited from previous generations.

It was not until 1883 that Galton coined the term "eugenics," and it was 1904 before he formulated his classic definition of eugenics as "the study of agencies under social control that may improve or impair the racial qualities of future generations, either physically or mentally."

Galton had been tremendously influenced by his cousin, Charles Darwin, whose study of human evolution, *The Origin of Species*, was published in 1859. The eugenicists, led by Galton in England and Davenport in the US, were fascinated more by the idea of the inheritability of human traits than by Darwin's focus on the evolution of species over time.

Charles Darwin thought highly of his cousin's book on the inheritance of genius; he wrote, "I do not think I ever in all my life read anything more interesting and original."

Eugenicists originally believed in the inheritability of virtually all human traits. Charles Davenport's work provided a typical list of hereditary traits: eye color, hair, skin, stature, weight, special ability in music, drawing, painting, literary composition, calculating, or memorizing, weakness of the mucous membranes, nomadism, general bodily energy, strength, mental ability, epilepsy, shiftlessness, insanity, pauperism, criminality, various forms of nervous disease, defects of speech, sight, hearing, cancer, tuberculosis, pneumonia, skeletal deformities, and other traits.

Davenport is reported to have hypothesized that thalassophilia, love of the sea, was a sex–linked recessive trait because he only encountered it in male naval officers.

For the most part, the eugenicists emphasized inheritance and trivialized the importance of environment. Stanford University president David Starr Jordan, an important American eugenicist, was typical in his dismissal of environmental arguments:

> No doubt poverty and crime are bad assets in one's early environment. No doubt these elements cause the ruins of thousands who, by heredity, were good material of civilization. But again, poverty, dirt, and crime are the products of those, in general, who are not good material. It is not the strength of the strong, but the weakness of the weak which engenders exploitation and tyranny. The slums are at once symptom, effect, and cause of evil. Every vice stands in this same threefold relation.

In the same vein, another eugenicist wrote:

> The. . . .social classes, therefore, which you seek to abolish by law, are ordained by nature; that it is, in the large statistical run of things, not the slums which make slum people, but slum people who make the slums; that primarily it is not the church which makes people good, but good people who make the Church; that godly people are largely born and not made. . . .

The US eugenics movement grew out of the American Breeders' Association (later the American Genetics Association), which was founded in 1903 to apply the new principles of inheritance to the scientific breeding of horses and other livestock. In 1906, at Davenport's urging, the ABA established a Eugenics Section (later the Committee on Eugenics). Stanford University president David Starr Jordan chaired the committee and Davenport was its secretary. These men and others active in the Committee on Eugenics (including the founders of the Nativist Immigration Restriction League, Robert DeCourcey Ward and Prescott F. Hall; Henry H. Goddard and Walter E. Fernald, who both joined a subcommittee on feeble–mindedness; Alexander Graham Bell; and Edward L. Thorndike) would form the core of the eugenics movement for the next 25 years.

The organized eugenics movement revolved around Davenport's Station for Experimental Genetics, at Cold Spring Harbor on Long Island, New York, which itself came increasingly to focus on eugenical studies. In 1910, the Eugenics Record Office was established with Davenport as director and Henry H. Laughlin, key eugenicist and leader of the eugenical sterilization movement, as its superintendent. Two other important eugenics organizations were the Eugenics Research Association (with Davenport and Laughlin as its key members) and the American Eugenics Society (AES).

The Eugenics Research Association described itself as a scientific rather than political group and the AES, established in 1921, was visualized as the propaganda or popular education arm of the eugenics movement.

The eugenics movement advocated both positive and negative eugenics, which referred to attempts to increase reproduction by fit stocks and to decrease reproduction by those who were constitutionally unfit. Positive eugenics included eugenic education and tax preferences and other financial support for eugenically fit large families. Eugenical segregation and, usually, sterilization (a few eugenicists opposed sterilization); restrictive marriage laws, including anti–miscegenation statutes; and restrictive immigration laws formed the three parts of the negative eugenics agenda.

Virtually all eugenicists supported compulsory sterilization for the unfit; some supported castration. By 1936, when expert medical panels in both England and the US finally condemned compulsory eugenical sterilization, more than 20,000 forced sterilizations had been performed, mostly on poor people (and disproportionately on black people) confined to state–run mental hospitals and residential facilities for the mentally retarded. Almost 500 men and women had died from the surgery. The American Eugenics Society had hoped, in time, to sterilize one–tenth of the US population, or millions of Americans. Based on the American eugenical sterilization experience, Hitler's sterilization program managed to sterilize 225,000 people in less than three years.

Eugenics' Racial Bias

From the beginning, the eugenics movement was a racialist (race–based) and elitist movement concerned with the control of classes seen to be socially inferior. In proposing the term eugenics, Galton had written, "We greatly want a brief word to express the science of improving the stock. . .to give the more suitable races or strains of blood a better chance of prevailing speedily over the less suitable than they otherwise would have had."

Galton believed that black people were entirely inferior to the white races and that Jews were capable only of "parasitism" upon the civilized nations.

Karl Pearson, Galton's chief disciple, shared his racial and anti–Semitic beliefs. For example, in 1925, Pearson wrote "The Problem of Alien Immigration into Great Britain, Illustrated by an Examination of Russian and Polish Jewish Children," which argued against the admission of Jewish immigrants into England.

In the US, the eugenics movement started from a belief in the racial superiority of white Anglo–Saxons and a desire to prevent the immigration of less desirable racial stocks. In 1910, the Committee on Eugenics solicited new members with a letter that read, "The time is ripe for a strong public movement to stem the tide of threatened racial degeneracy. . . .America needs to protect herself against indiscriminate immigration, criminal degenerates, and. . .race suicide." The letter also warned of the impending "complete destruction of the white race."

Eugenical News, which was published by the Eugenics Research Association and edited by Laughlin, welcomed racist and anti–immigrant articles. At the Second International Congress on Eugenics in 1921, one of the five classifications of exhibits was "The Factor of Race."

Similarly, the American Eugenics Society's "Ultimate Program," adopted in 1923, placed "chief emphasis" on three goals:

- a brief survey of the eugenics movement up to the present time;
- working out and enacting a selective immigration law;

- securing segregation of certain classes, such as the criminal defective.

The Eugenics Research Association included among the major issues its members addressed "[im]migration, mate selection. . .race crossings, and. . .physical and mental measurement."

When the World War I–era IQ testing of all soldiers indicated that almost half of all white recruits were morons according to the newly developed Stanford Binet test, as were 89 percent of all black recruits, the eugenics movement seemed more important and believable.

Although some commentators questioned the validity of the test, and noted that questions on such topics as the color of sapphires and the location of Cornell University might reflect qualities other than intelligence, the statistics, when released, created great anxiety and gave the eugenics movement a substantial boost.

19th–Century Scientific Racism

The scientific racism movement of the mid–nineteenth century provided a number of important legacies to the eugenics movement. American scientific racism was primarily preoccupied with the attempt to establish that blacks, Orientals, and other races were in fact entirely different species of "man," which the scientific racists claimed should be seen as a genus, rather than a species. The theory that the integrity of the human species derived from the creation of one Adam and one Eve was called monogenism or specific unity; monogenists believed that the races arose as a result of the degeneration of human beings since creation. The separate races were essentially the same human material, but different races had degenerated to different extents. Polygenists, by contrast, believed that the races were created separately in a series of different creations. The separate races were entirely different animals. The mid–century theory of polygenism, or specific diversity, was one of the first scientific theories largely developed in the US and was approvingly called "the American School of anthropology" by European scientists.

Harvard Professor Louis Agassiz, a prominent natural historian of the 19th–century, was the most important promoter of polygenism. Agassiz, an abolitionist, insisted that his adoption of polygenism was dictated by objective scientific investigation. Nevertheless, historian Stephen Jay Gould's translation of Agassiz's letter to his mother in 1846 shortly after his emigration to the US, reveals a profound, visceral aversion to blacks.

Not surprisingly, Agassiz was also passionately opposed to racial miscegenation. He believed that racial inter–mixture would result in the creation of "effeminate" offspring unable to maintain American democratic traditions. Agassiz wrote:

> The production of half–breeds is as much a sin against nature, as incest in a civilized community is a sin against purity of character. . . .No efforts should be spared to check that which is abhorrent to our better nature, and to the progress of a higher civilization and a purer morality.

In part because the classic definition of a species revolved around the ability to mate and produce children with each other but not with others, and in part because of a drive toward racial hierarchy, the questions of hybridization and fecundity were of great import to the early American scientific racists. For the eugenicists, these questions were also tremendously important. Much of the early scientific racist rhetoric on hybrids later reappeared in eugenicist writings where it came to form the basis of eugenicist arguments against racial miscegenation. The early concern with fecundity fueled later eugenicist claims that differential racial fecundity was leading to white racial suicide.

The eugenicist recapitulation of earlier scientific racist arguments was not cursory, but deep and enduring. In one of many examples, a 1925 bibliography on eugenics published by the American Eugenics Society recommended the book, *Uncontrolled Breeding, Or Fecundity versus Civilization.*

At the First International Congress of Eugenics in 1912, author V. G. Ruggeri, despite his concern with race–mixing, put forth Mendel's monogenism to bolster his own argument in favor of monogenism; and Lucien March spoke on "The Fertility of Marriages According to Profession and Social Position." The opening of Raymond Pearl's lecture on "The Inheritance of Fecundity" made clear his position within this tradition:

> The progressive decline of the birth rate in all, or nearly all, civilized countries is an obvious and impressive fact. Equally obvious and much more disturbing is the fact that this decline is differential. Generally it is true that those racial stocks which by common agreement are of high, if not the highest, value to the state or nation, are precisely the ones where the decline in reproduction rate has been most marked.

Family Studies, Social Darwinism, and Race Suicide

Eugenical family studies were an important component in the movement's political development; family studies functioned as an objective, scientific basis for the twin myths of a feeble–minded menace and an impending white race suicide. The invention of feeble–mindedness, typically used as a term of art to cover broader issues related to social control, allowed the eugenicists to claim that social (and racial) classes were biological and hence immutable.

The first important eugenicist works in the US were a series of studies of American families supposedly plagued by hereditary feeble–mindedness, beginning with Richard Dugdale's exposition of the Jukes family, published in 1877.

All of the family studies claimed to prove that a single feeble–minded ancestor could (and did) result in generations of poverty-stricken and degenerate offspring. The families in the studies were rural families, of Anglo–Saxon, Protestant descent, and for the most part, their lineage dated to the colonial settlers. The families were remarkably similar to the eugenicist activists in these traits; the main difference between the two was the poverty of the rural families. The equation by the eugenicists of poverty with degeneracy was quite explicit. Eugenicists believed that poverty was no more than a manifestation of inner degeneracy. Charity was therefore unlikely to lead the pauper out of poverty and, in fact, misguided charity might prove very costly to society. In the heightened tone that is common to writers in the family studies, one eugenicist wrote, "It is impossible to calculate what even one feeble–minded woman may cost the public, when her vast possibilities for evil as a producer of paupers and criminals, through an endless line of descendants is considered."

Another writer said, for example, "A habit of irregular work is a species of mental or moral weakness, or both. A man or woman who will not stick to a job is morally certain to be a pauper or a criminal."

In the same vein, a third wrote, "Pauperism and habitual criminality are respectively passive and active states of the same disease."

Feeble–mindedness for the eugenicists was a designation that created a difference between the eugenicists and the families they studied. One group of social reformers described in detail the nature of the feeble–mindedness which they had found characterized prostitutes:

> The general moral insensibility, the boldness, egotism and vanity, the love of notoriety, the lack of shame or remorse. . .the desire for immediate pleasure without regard for consequences, the lack of fore-thought or anxiety about the future—all cardinal symptoms of feeble–mindedness—were strikingly evident.

Thus the prostitute's failure to adhere to social conventions of behavior for women is here called feeble–mindedness.

The deliberate and even fraudulent misrepresentations of the people in the family studies have been established. Stephen Jay Gould, for example, has shown that H. H. Goddard, author of *The Kallikak Family*, retouched photographs to make the Kallikaks appear mentally retarded.

Family studies were used to support the myth of the "feeble–minded menace," which claimed the US was in imminent danger of being swamped by the degenerate and dangerous masses of the feeble–minded. When the feeble–minded menace was linked at the end of the 19th–century to the idea that the better stocks were failing to produce enough children, the idea of race suicide emerged. Race suicide captured the US imagination and lent support to the entire eugenics agenda.

The "race suicide" theory which developed during the first decade of the new century claimed that the greatly lowered birthrate of the better classes, coupled with the burgeoning birthrates of immigrants and the native–born poor, endangered the survival of "the race." "The race" was clearly a term that referred to the white, Anglo–Saxon race and a deep racism permeated the racial suicide period from its beginning in 1900 to 1910. One classic racial suicide work is Robert Reid Rentoul's *Race Culture; or, Race Suicide? (A Plea for the Unborn)*, published in New York and London in 1906. Rentoul speaks of the "terrible monstrosities" created by racial intermarriage and points out that the Americans are "poor patriots" for repealing their racial miscegenation statutes.

The concept of the feeble–minded menace provided a way to make the rural families, who were neither institutionalized, foreign, nor "colored," into people who were "different" from the eugenicists. Underlying the family studies and the myth of the feeble–minded menace was the theory of Social Darwinism, which assumed the existence of a struggle between the individual and society, and of an adversarial relationship between the fit and unfit classes. Eugenical family studies and social Darwinism both involved a transmutation of nature into biology and the eugenics movement frequently acknowledged its debt to Social Darwinism.

The deeply conservative implications of such philosophies included the rejection of government welfare programs or protective legislation on the grounds that such reforms as poorhouses, orphanages, bread lines, and eight–hour days enabled the unfit to survive and weakened society as a whole. From the beginning, the eugenics movement accepted the regressive implications of Social Darwinism. Karl Pearson believed that "such measures as the minimum wage, the eight–hour day, free medical advice, and reductions in infant mortality encouraged an increase in unemployables, degenerates, and physical and mental weaklings."

Pearson's friend, Havelock Ellis, known as a sex radical and free thinker, shared Pearson's elitist views, writing in his 1911 eugenicist book, *The Problem of Race Regeneration*, "These classes, with their tendency to weak–mindedness, their inborn laziness, lack of vitality, and unfitness for organized activity, contain the people who complain they are starving for want of work, though they will never perform any work that is given them." Ellis suggested in the same book that all public relief be denied to second generation paupers unless they "voluntarily consented" to be surgically sterilized.

One American eugenicist said harshly:

> The so–called charitable people who give to begging children and women with baskets have a vast sin to answer for. It is from them that this pauper element gets its consent to exist. . . . So–called charity joins public relief in producing stillborn children, raising prostitutes, and educating criminals.

The economic conservatism of the movement was very clear. Faced with a social problem, the eugenicist leapt to the conclusion that it was the individual who must change to accommodate society (which is one reason why conservative commentators frequently argued that eugenics was a liberal movement committed to the supremacy of the community over the individual). The prevalence of the appeal to economics in eugenics writings led G. K. Chesterton to claim that the eugenicist was, at heart, the employer. Chesterton wrote:

> [N]o one seems able to imagine capitalist industrialism being sacrificed to any other object. . . . [the eugenicist] tacitly takes it for granted that the small wages and the income, desperately shared, are the fixed points, like day and night, the conditions of human life. Compared with them, marriage and maternity are luxuries, things to be modified to suit the wage–market.

The eugenicists' family studies were one aspect of the movement's domestic program of scientific racism. The eugenics movement concentrated on differences: its roots in scientific racism looked to the differences between the white and other races, while the family studies created a distinction between fit and unfit white folks. At the same time, eugenicists and other scientific racists were discovering many different "races" among the foreign immigrants, all previously conceived as members of a single, "white" race.

The Eugenicist Role in Anti–Immigrant Organizing

The involvement of the organized American eugenics movement with the advocacy of immigration restriction was deep and long–standing. Although the organized anti–immigrant movement predated eugenical organizations by a few years, immigration restriction was from the beginning a key component of the eugenics program. For example, the American Eugenics Society published a wide variety of materials on immigration restriction and the 1923 "Original Ultimate Program to be Developed by the American

Eugenics Society" listed immigration restriction as one of the top three goals of the society.

The first organized anti–immigrant group, the Immigration Restriction League, was founded in 1894 in Boston by a small group of Harvard–educated lawyers and academics; Prescott Hall and Robert DeCourcey Ward were the driving forces behind the League. The Immigration Restriction League was based on a belief in the superiority of the white races. Ward summed up the group's philosophy when he wrote "the question [of immigration] is a race question, pure and simple. . . .It is fundamentally a question as to what kind of babies shall be born; it is a question as to what races shall dominate in this country."

Most eugenicists agreed, and Yale Professor and prominent eugenicist Irving Fisher's comment that "The core of the problem of immigration is. . .one of race and eugenics" was typical of the eugenicist position.

In the first decade of the century, the men of the Immigration Restriction League became active members of the Eugenics Section of the American Breeders' Association and other eugenics organizations, focusing their attention primarily on immigration issues. The connection was so compatible that the Immigration Restriction League almost changed its name to the Eugenic Immigration League. Hall and Ward even had sample stationery drawn up with the new name, but found the Board of Directors was unwilling to adopt the name of a movement younger than its own.

In 1918, Davenport and his fellow eugenicist, and virulent racist, and anti–immigration activist Madison Grant (author of *The Passing of the Great Race* and *The Alien in Our Midst*) set up the Galton Society. The Society was established for "the promotion of study of racial anthropology" and from the beginning, immigration restriction was "a subject of much interest."

As John Higham has noted, one strand of nativism in the US derived from a conviction that the immigrant was a political and social radical, importing communistic or anarchistic ideas into the United States. Grant and Davenport both shared this conviction and established the Galton Society in part to bar such foreign radicals. The independently wealthy Grant wrote to the other organizers, "My proposal is the organization of an anthropological society. . .confined to native Americans, who are anthropologically, socially, and politically sound, no Bolsheviki need apply."

Other prestigious members of the Galton Society included Henry Fairfield Osborn (who wrote the introduction to Grant's book) and Grant's friend and *protégé*, Lothrop Stoddard. Like his friend Grant, Stoddard was a strong anti–communist. His book *The Rising Tide of Color* argued that Bolshevism was a dangerous theory because it advocated universal equality rather than white supremacy.

H. H. Laughlin, of the Eugenics Research Association and Eugenics Record Office, was also very involved in anti–immigrant work. He produced many pamphlets on immigration, including "Biological Aspects of Immigration," "Analysis of America's Melting Pot," "Europe as an Emigrant–Exporting Continent," "The Eugenics Aspects of Deportation," and "American History in Terms of Human Migration." Because Laughlin had been appointed the Expert Eugenics Agent for the House Committee on Immigration and Naturalization by the committee's chair, Congressman Albert Johnson, many of these nativist pamphlets were published by the Government Printing Office in Washington, DC. In 1923, Johnson, a confirmed eugenicist, was appointed to the presidency of the Eugenics Research Association, a post held before him by Grant.

The immigration restrictionists were motivated by a desire to maintain both the white and the Christian dominance of the US. A year after the eugenicists' victory in securing passage of the 1924 Immigration Restriction Act, which established entry quotas that slashed the "new immigration" of Jews, Slavs, and southern Europeans, Davenport wrote to Grant, "Our ancestors drove Baptists from Massachusetts Bay into Rhode Island but we have no place to drive the Jews to. Also they burned the witches but it seems to be against the mores to burn any considerable part of our population. Meanwhile we have somewhat diminished the immigration of these people."

Similarly, the racial nature of the anti–immigration position was not veiled. In 1927, for instance, three years after the restrictive act of 1924 was passed, Grant, Robert DeCourcey Ward, and other eugenicists were still anxious to cut non–white immigration further. They signed a "Memorial on Immigration Quotas," urging the President and Congress to extend "the quota system to all countries of North and South America...in which the population is not predominantly of the white race."

The early 20th–century eugenics movement, often dismissed as a fad, provided a coherent and consistent political program to enforce the racial, class, and sexual dominance which was perceived to be under attack in American society. Its program has, in large part, reasserted itself in the late 20th–century, at a time when racial and economic elite dominance of US society is again under attack. The continuing vigor of scientific racism in the United States is in part a testimony to its strong, deep roots.

The late Margaret Quigley was, until her untimely death, an analyst at Political Research Associates. Call or write PRA for footnotes for this article. This article originally appeared in *The Public Eye* in March 1995. © 1995, the estate of Margaret Quigley.

In the Land of White Supremacy

June Jordan

I used to think I was up against racist belief and behavior. But then, about a year ago, I began to focus on white supremacy. Whatever that might mean, I didn't have Aryan Nation–type in mind. I was watching and listening to an everyday, casual kind of mental disorder: something real homespun and regular, like my (white) doctor saying she'd eaten Chinese food twice last week, but the rest of the time, she'd opted for "American."

Or it might be something ordinary like media references to "The Heartland" as "true" America, even though very few of us live in North Dakota, Minnesota, or, for that matter, Oklahoma, and even though the majority of Americans reside on the East or West Coast. And California, for example, is the most populous as well as the most heterogeneous (non–"Heartland") state in the Union.

These were the kinds of things I began to hook up inside my head. I came to recognize media constructions such as "The Heartland" or "Politically Correct" or "The Welfare Queen" or "Illegal Alien" or "Terrorist" or "The Bell Curve" for what they were: multiplying scattershots intended to defend one unifying desire—to establish and preserve white supremacy as our national bottom line.

Racism means rejecting, avoiding, belittling, or despising whatever and whoever differs from your conscious identity.

White supremacy means that God put you on the planet to rule, to dominate, and to occupy the center of the national and international universe—because you're "white."

Anything or anyone appearing to challenge your center—stage position and its privileges becomes ungodly, or the Devil, or the Devil Incarnate, as in "The Jews," "The Niggers," "The Wetbacks," "The Chinks."

White supremacy moves beyond racist formulations of "superior" or "inferior." White supremacy takes hatred of the unfamiliar to the level of religious war between "good" and "evil." Underlying such a world view is an infantile mentality as obviously infantile as it is "normal" in these United States.

And so the catastrophe of Oklahoma City becomes a possible, and, for some, a reasonable, carefully planned event. Nothing and no one—not a one–year–old baby, not a two–year–old child, not unremarkable American workers going about their boring but useful routines, not mothers or fathers or day–care teachers or any number of the simply living—could interdict or mitigate the murder–crazy determination of white supremacists to declare their hatred of "the government" and their hatred of anyone who fails to mirror their faces set, killer resolute, against us.

It has taken me until the tragedy of Oklahoma City to understand that "The Aryan Nation" is not the name of an organization of some sort. "The Aryan Nation" is the goal of the Christian Coalition and the Patriot Militias and the Contract with America and Governor Pete Wilson. "Come unto me all ye who suffer and who seek asylum and an open road, and I will blow you away! I will efface you from my territory, my Aryan Preserve!"

To impose an Aryan Nation upon these United States would require bodily and juridical and legislative assault upon the constitutional liberties and the constitutional protection that defines basic citizenship here. But Aryan Nation wannabes feel fine about that because only the godly deserve to be free.

To impose an Aryan Nation upon these United States would require overthrow of our government and that's also OK because, as some of us may remember, it's supposed to be a government of and by and for "the people"—and, at last count, "the people" have begun to look less and less like Clint Eastwood playing an unemployed Marine at a Christian Revival meeting

And, besides, the only democratic justification for centralized, federal government is its provision for the security of the population it presumes to represent. But you cannot provide for the security of a people without justice, without equality, without food, without education, without gainful employment, without housing. And so we pay taxes to "the government" expecting that, in return, we will receive these goods fundamental to our personal security and to the security of our society.

Hence, affirmative action, for example, is a federal government policy. Hence, the viciously orchestrated attack on "affirmative" for the sake of "angry white men" who, statistics inform us, continue to occupy 95 percent of all senior management positions.

I guess that was the picture of one of those angry white men, that photograph of blond, white Timothy McVeigh. Is that the guy who bombed the federal office building and killed 167 human beings because something truly pissed him off? Is he one of those guys "affirmative action" irritated like, so to speak, crazy?

And he wasn't really "Middle Eastern looking," was he? What a shock! He looked "American," one of the sheriffs remarked.

And then there was the President droning on about our task is to cleanse ourselves of this "dark" force.

"Dark," Mr. President?

On the contrary. White. White. American white–supremacist white. The monster is an "American–looking" white man. This violent, paramilitary hatred is absolutely homegrown and growing.

Do not be misled. There is no difference between hating "the government" and hating "the Jews" and "the Niggers" in the mind–mesh of the Christian–white–rights crusade.

And forget about Negro clowns in the tradition of Clarence Thomas—clowns like the University of California regent Ward Connerly, who has risen to national stature by attacking affirmative action, or the Negro head of a right–wing militia group in Alameda, California. There have always been fools who have flared into infamy almost like an awful amusement before the curtain lifts.

Oklahoma City has lifted the curtain.

If we do not see ourselves, at last, stripped of all excuse and scapegoat, if we do not recognize the weakness of our connections to other—all of us different, and different–looking Americans—as the wellspring for white supremacy, then we may as well admit that we are ready to submit to Timothy McVeigh's final agenda for our country: to achieve an Aryan Nation by any means necessary.

June Jordan, the poet, is professor of African–American Studies at the University of California–Berkeley. This chapter originally appeared as her regular column, "Just Inside the Door," in *The Progressive*, June 1995. © 1995, June Jordan.

The Rise of Citizen Militias

Angry White Guys with Guns

Daniel Junas

Winter is harsh in western Montana. Short days, bitter cold, and heavy snows enforce the isolation of the small towns and lonely ranches scattered among the broad river valleys and high peaks of the Northern Rockies. But in February 1994—the dead of winter—a wave of fear and paranoia strong enough to persuade Montanans to brave the elements swept through the region. Hundreds of people poured into meetings in small towns to hear tales of mysterious black helicopters sighted throughout the United States and foreign military equipment moving via rail and flatbed truck across the country, in preparation for an invasion by a hostile federal government aided by United Nations troops seeking to impose a New World Order.

In Hamilton (pop. 1,700), at the base of the Bitterroot Mountains dividing Idaho and Montana, 250 people showed up; 200 more gathered in Eureka (pop. 1,000), ten miles from the Canadian border. And 800 people met in Kalispell, at the foot of Glacier National Park. Meeting organizers encouraged their audiences to form citizens' militias to protect themselves from the impending military threat. Most often, John Trochmann, a wiry, white-haired man in his fifties, led the meetings. Trochmann lives near the Idaho border in Noxon (pop. 270), a town well–suited for strategic defense. A one–lane bridge over the Clark Fork River is the only means of access, and a wall of mountains behind the town makes it a natural fortress against invasion. From this bastion, Trochmann, his brother David, and his nephew Randy run the Militia of Montana (MOM), a publicity–seeking outfit that has organized militia support groups and pumped out an array of written and taped tales of a sinister global conspiracy controlling the US government. MOM also provides how–to materials for organizing citizens' militias to meet this dark threat.

Militia Mania

It is difficult to judge from attendance at public meetings how many militias and militia members there might be in Montana, or if, as is widely rumored, they are conducting military training and exercises. The same applies across the country; there is little hard information on how many are involved or what they are actually doing. But the Trochmanns are clearly not alone in raising fears about the federal government nor in sounding the call to arms. By early 1995, movement watchers had identified militia activity in at least 40 states, with a conservatively estimated hard–core membership of from 10,000 to 30,000 and growing.

The appearance of armed militias raises the level of tension in a region already at war over environmental and land–use issues. A threat explicitly tied to militias occurred in November 1994, at a public hearing in Everett, Washington. Two men approached Ellen Gray, an Audubon Society activist. According to Gray, one of them, later identified as Darryl Lord, placed a hangman's noose on a nearby chair, saying, "This is a message for you." He also distributed cards with a picture of a hangman's noose that said, "Treason = Death" on one side, and "Eco fascists go home" on the other. The other man told Gray, "If we can't get you at the ballot box, we'll get you with a bullet. We have a militia of 10,000." In a written statement, Lord later denied making the threat, although he admitted bringing the hangman's noose to the meeting.

Militias, Patriots & Angry White Guys

As important as environmental issues are in the West, they are only part of what is driving the militia movement. The militias have close ties to the older and more broadly based Patriot movement, from which they emerged, and which supplies their world view. The militia movement consists of loosely linked organizations and individuals who perceive a global conspiracy in which key political and economic events are manipulated by a small group of elite insiders.

On the far right flank of the Patriot movement are conscious white supremacists and anti–Semites, who believe that the world

is controlled by a cabal of Jewish bankers. This position is represented by, among others, the Liberty Lobby and its weekly newspaper, the *Spotlight*. At the other end of this relatively narrow
spectrum is the John Birch Society (JBS), which certainly is
Eurocentric, but has repeatedly repudiated overt anti–Semitism
and biological racism. The JBS hews to its own paranoid vision.
For the Birchers, it is not the Rothschilds and Jewish banking
elites but "liberal" and internationalist institutions such as the
Council on Foreign Relations, the Trilateral Commission, and the
UN which secretly call the shots.

This right–wing milieu is home to a variety of movements,
including Identity Christians, Constitutionalists, tax protesters,
and remnants of the semi–secret *Posse Comitatus*. Members of
the Christian Right who subscribe to the conspiratorial world
view presented in Pat Robertson's 1991 book, *The New World Order*, also fall within the movement's parameters. Some experts
claim that as many as five million Americans consider themselves
part of or allied with the Patriot movement.

While the Patriot movement has long existed on the margins
of US society, it has grown markedly in recent years. Three factors have sparked that growth.

One is the end of the Cold War. For over 40 years, the
"international communist conspiracy" held plot–minded Americans in thrall. But with the collapse of the Soviet empire, their
search for enemies turned toward the federal government, long an
object of simmering resentment.

The other factors are economic and social. While the Patriot
movement provides a pool of potential recruits for the militias, it
in turn draws its members from a large and growing number of
US citizens disaffected from and alienated by a government that
seems indifferent, if not hostile, to their interests. This predominantly white, male, and middle– and working–class sector has
been buffeted by global economic restructuring, with its attendant
job losses, declining real wages, and social dislocations. While under economic stress, this sector has also seen its traditional privileges and status challenged by 1960s–style social movements,
such as feminism, minority rights, and environmentalism.

Someone must be to blame. But in the current political context, serious progressive analysis is virtually invisible, while the
Patriot movement provides plenty of answers. Unfortunately,
they are dangerously wrong–headed ones.

Ruby Ridge & Waco

Two recent events involving government excessive force in-
flamed Patriot passions and precipitated the formation of the mi-

litias. The first was the FBI's 1992 confrontation with white supremacist Randy Weaver at Ruby Ridge, Idaho, in which federal agents killed Weaver's son and wife. The second was the federal government's destruction of David Koresh and his followers at the Branch Davidian compound in Waco, Texas, in April 1993. Key promoters of the militia movement repeatedly invoke Ruby Ridge and Waco as spurs to the formation of militias to defend the citizenry against a hostile federal government.

The sense of foreboding and resentment of the federal government was compounded by the passage of the Brady Bill (imposing a waiting period and background checks for the purchase of a handgun) followed by the Crime Bill (banning the sale of certain types of assault rifles). For some members of the Patriot movement, these laws are the federal government's first step in disarming the citizenry, to be followed by the much dreaded United Nations invasion and the imposition of the New World Order.

But while raising apocalyptic fears among Patriots, gun control legislation also angered more mainstream gun owners. Some have become newly receptive to conspiracy theorists and militia recruiters, who justify taking such a radical step with the Second Amendment:

A well–regulated Militia, being necessary to the security of a free State, the right of the people to keep and bear Arms, shall not be infringed.

Right–wing organizers have long used the Second Amendment to justify the creation of armed formations. The Ku Klux Klan began as a militia movement, and the militia idea has continued to circulate in white supremacist circles. It has also spread within the Christian Right. In the early 1990s, the Coalition on Revival, an influential national Christian Right networking organization, circulated a 24–plank action plan. It advocated the formation of "a countywide 'well–regulated militia' according to the US Constitution under the control of the county sheriff and Board of Supervisors."

Like the larger Patriot movement, the militias vary in membership and ideology. In the East, they appear closer to the John Birch Society. In New Hampshire, for example, the 15–member Constitution Defense Militia reportedly embraces garden variety UN conspiracy fantasies and lobbies against gun control measures. In the Midwest, some militias have close ties to the Christian Right, particularly the radical wing of the anti–abortion movement. In Wisconsin, Matthew Trewhella, leader of Missionaries to the Preborn, has organized paramilitary training sessions for his church members.

And in Indianapolis, Linda Thompson, the self–appointed "Acting Adjutant General of the Unorganized Militia of the USA," called for an armed march on Washington in September 1994 to demand an investigation of the Waco siege. Although she canceled the march when no one responded, she remains an important militia promoter. While Thompson limits her tirades to US law enforcement and the New World Order, her tactics have prompted the Birch Society to warn its members "to stay clear of her schemes."

Despite slight variations in their motivations, the militias fit within the margins of the Patriot movement. And a recurring theme for all of them is a sense of deep frustration and resentment against the federal government.

Nowhere has that resentment been felt more deeply than in the Rocky Mountain West, a hotbed of such attitudes since the frontier era. The John Birch Society currently has a larger proportional membership in this region than in any other. Similarly, the Rocky Mountain West is where anti–government presidential candidate Ross Perot ran strongest.

And nowhere in the West is anti–government sentiment stronger than along the spine of wild mountains that divide the Idaho panhandle from Montana. In the last two decades, this pristine setting has become a stomping ground for believers in Christian Identity, a religious doctrine that holds that whites are the true Israelites and that Blacks and other people of color are subhuman "mud people."

In the mid–1970s, Richard Butler, a neo–Nazi from California who launched a self–described war against the "Zionist Occupational Government," or ZOG, relocated to the Idaho panhandle town of Hayden Lake to establish his Aryan Nations compound. He saw the Pacific Northwest, with its relatively low minority population, as the region where God's kingdom could be established. Butler also believed that a racially pure nation needs an army.

Butler is aging, and his organization is mired in factional disputes, but he has helped generate a milieu in which militias can thrive. In May 1992, one of his neighbors and supporters, Eva Vail Lamb, formed the Idaho Organized Militia. During the same year, Lamb was also a key organizer for presidential candidate Bo Gritz (rhymes with whites), another key player in the militia movement.

Bo Gritz & the Origins of the Militias

A former Green Beret, Ret. Lt. Col. Gritz is a would–be Rambo, having led several private missions to Southeast Asia to search for mythical US Prisoners of War. He also has a lengthy Patriot pedigree. With well–documented ties to white supremacist leaders, he has asserted that the Federal Reserve is controlled by eight Jewish families. In 1988, he accepted the vice–presidential nomination of the Populist Party, an electoral amalgam of neo–Nazis, the Ku Klux Klan, and other racist and anti–Semitic organizations. His running mate was ex–Klansman David Duke. Gritz later disavowed any relationship with Duke, but in 1992, Gritz was back as the Populist Party's candidate for president.

Gritz has emerged as a mentor for the militias. During the 1992 campaign, he encouraged his supporters to form militias, and played a key role in one of the events that eventually sparked the militia movement, the federal assault on the Weaver family compound at Ruby Ridge, Idaho.

In the mid–1980s, Randy Weaver, a machinist from Waterloo, Iowa, moved to Ruby Ridge in Boundary County, the northernmost county in the panhandle. A white supremacist who subscribed to anti–government conspiracy theories, he attended Richard Butler's Aryan Nations congresses at least three times. And acting on the long–held far right notion that the county ought to be the supreme level of government, he even ran for sheriff of Boundary County. But in 1991, after being arrested on gun charges, Weaver failed to show up for trial and holed up in his mountain home. In August 1992, a belated federal marshals' effort to arrest him led to a siege in which FBI snipers killed Weaver's wife and son, and Weaver associate Kevin Harris killed a federal marshal. Gritz appeared on the scene and interposed himself as a negotiator between the FBI and Weaver. He eventually convinced Weaver to surrender and end the 11–day standoff. The episode gave Gritz national publicity and made him a hero on the right.

He moved quickly to exploit both his new–found fame and the outrage generated by the Weaver killings. In February 1993, Gritz initiated his highly profitable SPIKE training—Specially Prepared Individuals for Key Events. The 10–part traveling program draws on Gritz's Special Forces background and teaches a rigorous course on survival and paramilitary techniques. Gritz—who has already instructed hundreds of Christian Patriots in Oregon, Washington, Idaho, California, and elsewhere—recommends the training as essential preparation for militia members.

MOM

The Randy Weaver shootout also led directly to the formation of the Trochmanns' Militia of Montana (MOM). In September

1992, during the Ruby Ridge standoff, John Trochmann helped
found United Citizens for Justice (UCJ), a support group for his
friend Weaver. Another steering committee member was Chris
Temple, who writes regularly for the *Jubilee*, a leading Christian
Identity publication. Temple also worked as a western Montana
organizer for Gritz's presidential campaign. One of the earliest
mailing lists used to promote MOM came from UCJ.

But despite Trochmann's links to their adherents, white supremacist and Christian Identity rhetoric is conspicuously absent
from MOM literature. Instead, Trochmann purveys the popular
UN/New World Order conspiracy theory with an anti–corporate
twist. The cabal, he claims, intends to reduce the world's population to two billion by the year 2000. At public events, he cites
news accounts, government documents, and reports from his informal intelligence network. Trochmann also reports on the mysterious black helicopters and ties them to the UN takeover plot. In
one of his lectures, distributed on a MOM videotape, he uses as
evidence a map—found on the back of a Kix cereal box—which
divides the United States into ten regions, reflecting, he implies,
an actual plan to divide and conquer the nation.

The Trochmanns give talks around the country and are part
of a very effective alternative media network which uses direct
mail, faxes, videos, talk radio, TV, and even computers linked to
the Internet to sustain its apocalyptic, paranoid world view. The
Trochmanns use all these venues to promote MOM materials, including an organizing manual, *Militia Support Group*, which
provides a model military structure for the militias and lays out
MOM's aims:

> The time has come to renew our commitment to high moral val-
> ues and wrench the control of the government from the hands of the
> secular humanists and the self–indulging special interest groups includ-
> ing private corporations.

It also reveals that MOM has recruited Militia Support
Groups throughout the nation into its intelligence network, which
provides MOM with a steady stream of information to feed into its
conspiracy theories. Consequently, the Trochmanns were well
aware when trouble was brewing in another remote corner of the
West.

The County Rule Movement

In Catron County, New Mexico, the militia movement has
converged with some other strands of the anti–government right
to create a new challenge to federal power. Catron, located in the
desolate southwest of New Mexico and with a population of less
than 3,000 people, has been the site of a novel legal challenge to

federal control of public lands. In what has become known as the "county rule" movement, Catron was the first county to issue a direct legal challenge to the federal government over those lands. It grew out of a conflict between local ranchers and federal land managers over federal grazing lands. County attorney James Catron, whose ancestors gave the county its name, joined forces with Wyoming attorney Karen Budd, a long–time foe of environmental regulation, to produce the Catron County ordinances. These purport to give the county ultimate authority over public lands—making it illegal for the US Forest Service to regulate grazing, even on its own lands.

But such regulations also serve the interests of natural resource industries. Since it is relatively easy for those industries to control county governments, the ordinances provide them with a convenient end run around federal environmental laws and rules. The Catron County legislation has since been disseminated throughout the West—and recently into the Midwest—by the National Federal Lands Conference of Bountiful, Utah, which is part of the anti–environmental Wise Use movement.

Over 100 counties in the West have passed similar legislation, despite the ordinances' shaky legal foundations. The Boundary County, Idaho, ordinances have been overturned in state court, and federal court challenges to county rule legislation in Washington State are expected to succeed; the US Supreme Court has consistently upheld federal government authority over federal lands.

Nevertheless, the county rule movement has succeeded in shifting the balance of power between the counties and the federal government, if through no other means than intimidation. In Catron County, the sheriff has threatened to arrest the head of the local Forest Service office. And the county also passed a resolution predicting much physical violence if the federal government persists in trying to implement grazing reform.

In fact, a climate of hostility greets environmentalists throughout the West. Author David Helvarg writes that there have been hundreds of instances of harassment and physical violence in the last few years. Sheila O'Donnell, a California–based private investigator who tracks harassment of environmentalists, concurs that intimidation is on the rise.

Catron County has been the scene of at least one such incident. Richard Manning, a local rancher, planned to open a mill at the Challenger mine, on Forest Service land in the Mogollon mountains. Forest Service and state regulators want to determine if toxic mine tailings are leaching into watercourses. According to several Forest Service and state officials, Manning threatened to meet any regulator with "a hundred men with rifles." Manning denies having made the threat.

Militias & the Power of the County

The county rule movement and the militias share an ideological kinship, revolving around the idea, long popular in far right circles, that the county is the supreme level of government and the sheriff the highest elected official. *Posse Comitatus*—the name for a far right, semi–secret anti–tax organization—literally means the power of the county. *Posse Comitatus* is also a mainstream legal term relating to law enforcement and local autonomy.

A militia has formed in Catron County, quickly sparking an incident that demonstrates the high level of paranoia in the area. In September 1994, two days after the militia held its first meeting, FBI and National Guard officials arrived in Catron County to search for the body of a person reportedly killed a year earlier in the nearby Mogollon mountains. Several militia members refused to believe the official explanation and fled their homes for the evening. Catron County may be a bellwether: the county rule and militia movements are apparently converging. In October 1994, the monthly newsletter of the National Federal Lands Conference featured a lead article that explicitly called for the formation of militias. The article, which cited information provided by the Militia of Montana and pro–militia organizations in Idaho and Arizona, closed by saying:

> At no time in our history since the colonies declared their independence from the long train of abuses of King George has our country needed a network of active militias across America to protect us from the monster we have allowed our federal government to become. Long live the Militia! Long live freedom! Long live government that fear [sic] the people!

Smoke On the Horizon

Such incendiary rhetoric, commonplace in the Patriot/militia movement, makes an armed confrontation between the government and militia members seem increasingly likely. If past behavior is any guide, federal law enforcement agencies are all too ready to fight fire with fire.

Obviously, militias do not pose a military threat to the federal government. But they do threaten democracy. Even though many in the militia and Patriot movement seem unaware of it, the core theories of the movements emerge from historic segregationist legal arguments and anti–Jewish conspiracy theories. Armed militias fueled by paranoid conspiracy theories could make the democratic process unworkable, and, in some rural areas of the West, democracy is already under siege. As ominously, the militias represent a smoldering right–wing populism—with real and imagined grievances stoked by a politics of resentment and scapegoating—just a demagogue away from kindling an American fascist movement.

The militia movement now is like a brush fire on a hot summer day, atop a high and dry mountain ridge on the Idaho panhandle. As anyone in the panhandle can tell you, those brush fires have a way of getting out of control.

Daniel Junas is a freelance journalist and investigator based in the Pacific Northwest. He is an expert on the theocratic demagogue Rev. Sun Myung Moon, and has written extensively about other right–wing movements. This is a revised version of an article that originally appeared in the Spring 1995 issue of *CovertAction Quarterly*. © 1995, Daniel Junas.

America Under the Gun

The Militia Movement & Hate Groups in America

Jonathan Mozzochi

At the Coalition for Human Dignity we conduct research into right–wing social and political movements and analyze trends and events involving these groups in the Pacific Northwest. We provide support to civil rights groups, journalists, and communities targeted by the extreme right. Our work monitoring the growth of so–called "citizen militias" and the self–described "Christian patriot movement" extends back to 1989, when we first began actively investigating rural networks of anti–Semitic tax protesters in Oregon and Idaho. Much of the militia activity in the Pacific Northwest can be traced back to these rural, far right networks of the 1980s and previous decades.

This article will focus on two prominent militia supporters and their efforts to recruit from the ranks of law enforcement. These individuals are Gerald "Jack" McLamb and Retired Army Lt. Col. James "Bo" Gritz.

Bo Gritz is one of the most important leaders of the paramilitary right wing in America today, whose influence is felt throughout the white supremacist movement. Gritz is a former Army Green Beret who retired from the military in 1979 and has since been involved in numerous private missions to search for American Prisoners of War in Southeast Asia. He tells the story of these and other exploits in his 1991 autobiography, *Called to Serve*. In his book, Gritz also endorses explicitly anti–Semitic conspiracy theories about the Federal Reserve banking system, claiming, "Eight Jewish families virtually control the entire FED—only three are American Jews." (sic).

In 1988, Gritz accepted the nomination of the racist, anti–Semitic Populist Party as the vice–presidential running mate of former Ku Klux Klan leader David Duke. Gritz's bigotry is evident in this quote from a speech he delivered in 1991 at an annual "Bible Camp" run by Pastor Pete Peters, a promoter of the racist, anti–Semitic religion known as Christian Identity:

> The enemy you face today is a satanic overthrow where he would change the United States of America, a nation under God, into USA, Incorporated with King George as chairman of the board. And a Zionist group that would rule over us as long as satan might be upon this earth, that is your enemy. (sic)

Gritz became more prominent in hate group circles when, in August 1992, he negotiated an end to the siege on Ruby Ridge, in Boundary County, Idaho, involving Randy Weaver and federal authorities. The Weaver siege has been cited frequently as being one of the principal events leading to the formation of militia groups.

Since 1993, Gritz has organized a 10–part paramilitary training course and recruited thousands of individuals to participate. An average of 100–200 attendees per session is not unusual. These SPIKE training programs—the acronym SPIKE stands for "Specially Prepared Individuals for Key Events"—recruit participants through gun shows, tax protest meetings, "patriot" gatherings, and the racist lecture circuit. The training involves such topics as lock–picking, counter–intelligence maneuvers, cryptography, and weapons combat.

Among other things, SPIKE trainings are designed to enable participants to create so–called "Christian Covenant Communities," which are essentially self–sufficient, paramilitary enclaves within which patriots can enact their own laws and dispense their own brand of justice, separate from what they believe to be illegally constituted authority [the legitimate authority of lawmakers]. Gritz and his colleague, Gerald "Jack" McLamb have begun major construction on one such community in central Idaho, near the small town of Kamiah.

Called "Almost Heaven" by Gritz and McLamb, this "community" sits adjacent to land owned by the Nez Perce tribe in Idaho County, Idaho. Tribal members have repeatedly expressed their concern with the potential for violence developing from the presence of Almost Heaven, as have other well–meaning people in that community. To the people of Idaho County, Idaho, the patriots, militia organizers, and so–called constitutionalists who may soon flock to Almost Heaven are not merely "withdrawing," or "separating" from society, as they often claim. Rather, they are engaging it, close to home.

McLamb, a retired Arizona police officer and former chemical salesman from California, has been active helping Gritz plan and lead the SPIKE trainings. McLamb is a particularly important figure on the paramilitary right because of his role as the self–appointed ambassador to the law enforcement community. His *Aid & Abet Police Newsletter* and the various reports issued by his American Citizen and Lawmen Association (ACLA) and "Police Against the New World Order" target police officers and military personnel, attempting to "re–educate" them in the ways of bizarre and often thinly veiled anti–Semitic conspiracy theories.

McLamb's primary training manual, *Operation Vampire Killer 2000,* is a 75–page booklet designed to "enlighten" active duty officers in the way of the conspiracy. The booklet is widely distributed at militia meetings and gun shows. Literally hundreds of copies have been delivered to police departments and law enforcement personnel by militia activists nationwide. In Washington State, we know of at least four counties where the booklet has been distributed: Stevens, Pierce, Whatcom, and King.

Like many activists in the militia movement and in the paramilitary right, certain of McLamb's ideas could well be characterized as racist. For example, McLamb has stated that "The globalists. . .[are] promoting interracial marriage" and "You can be white, you can not have interracial marriage, in working to save America, you don't have to do that type of a thing." Both McLamb and Gritz play prominent roles in the frequent "Preparedness Expos" held throughout the nation in such places as Florida, Los Angeles and San Jose, California, Utah, and Arizona. These gatherings attract hundreds—sometimes thousands—of right–wing extremists, militia supporters, white supremacists, Christian Identity followers, conspiracy theorists, and military surplus vendors.

It is worth noting that it was at gun shows and meetings such as these, for example, that Oklahoma City bombing suspect Timothy McVeigh could often be found, thumbing his well–worn copy of the *Turner Diaries*, the fictional account of neo–Nazi revolution. Playing on themes that have been developed over the years in the so–called Christian Patriot movement, both McLamb and Gritz tell audiences at these events that they need to prepare for the "coming storm," and encourage participants to recruit law enforcement officers and military personnel into the movement. Both have encouraged the formation of citizen militias.

For McLamb, and many other militia proponents, "storm preparation" invariably means preparing for apocalyptic scenarios, including the imminent declaration of martial law by the United States government. Gritz and McLamb's SPIKE trainings are designed to enable patriots to establish their own independent government structures, and to prepare for armed confrontation, if necessary, with a treasonous government and its agents.

Both McLamb and Gritz recognize that if they are to make headway with their efforts to disregard civil rights laws, tax laws, and a host of other legal responsibilities that others must abide by, they must cultivate support within law–making and law–enforcing bodies. Hence their efforts to convince law enforcement personnel to serve the interests of the patriot movement. Thankfully, their efforts and those of others in the militia movement to recruit support from county sheriffs throughout the Northwest have largely been rebuffed. But that does not mean that they have been without success.

One prominent supporter of the militia movement and the far right from the ranks of law enforcement is Sheriff Richard Mack from Graham County, Arizona. Mack has sued the federal government over the Brady Bill, which he refuses to enforce. Mack is widely featured on the militia speaking circuit.

McLamb and Gritz, and by extension, the militia movement as a whole, are attempting to lay the groundwork for legitimizing their paramilitary organizing. For example, in Stevens County, Washington, at least one county commissioner is sympathetic to the militias and is a promoter of the *Posse Comitatus* and the racist religion of Christian Identity. Ironically, this commissioner sits on a county advisory committee that provides guidance for local authorities in their dealings with federal land use bodies such as the Bureau of Land Management.

Often the first target of militia supporters is the county sheriff. According to the traditional ideology of the *Posse Comitatus*, the sheriff is the highest law enforcement official. Of course, according to the same ideology, if the sheriff is not enforcing the law as the *Posse* sees fit, it is duly empowered to "discipline" the sheriff. In the 1980s, *Posse* leaders distributed literature threatening to "hang the sheriff at high noon at the county courthouse" if the edicts of tax protestors and their bogus "common law courts" were not carried out.

We see an almost identical approach toward county sheriffs by those in the militia movement today. The concept of the so–called "unorganized militias" is really no different from the bogus notion advanced by the *Posse Comitatus*—the idea that every able–bodied, white, male resident over the age of 18 is automatically a deputized member of county law enforcement, the veritable "Posse Comitatus," the "power of the county."

When paramilitary hate groups find supporters in the ranks of law enforcement, the results can be devastating: important information stored in police computers can be accessed, confidential contingency plans developed by law enforcement can become compromised, and valuable police and military hardware is placed at risk. When militia activists and their allies in the white supremacist movement gain influence among law enforcement, what becomes of our capacity to provide equal protection under the law consistent with the Fourteenth Amendment?

When political figures, law enforcement professionals, and others support some of the programs and ideas advocated by militia groups there is a significant danger of conferring legitimacy upon the broader, more extreme program of white supremacy, anti–Semitism, and racism which many militia groups have, likewise, embraced.

One profound irony, of course, is that the vision of government advanced by many leaders of the militias is not necessarily a vision for substantially less government, but it is certainly a vision for a much different form of government—one in which religious freedom, racial equality, and individual liberty would be severely at risk.

Jonathan Mozzochi is the Executive Director of the Coalition for Human Dignity based in Portland, Oregon. This article is adapted from his testimony at an informational congressional hearing held in Washington, DC, on July 11, 1995. © 1995, Jonathan Mozzochi.

Guns, Ammo & Talk Radio

Jeff Cohen and Norman Solomon

It's no secret that talk radio has long been dominated by conservative hosts—even in liberal cities. But most Americans are unaware of frightening new trends in radio talk shows.

Ask members of the public to describe the right edge of talk radio, and they're likely to mention Rush Limbaugh. Not even close. The spectrum has moved so far to the right that in many markets Limbaugh sounds like a moderate.

The shift is not just to the far right, but the armed right—with open conversation about doing away with "traitors."

And major media companies are behind some of the extremists.

Meet Chuck Baker, who follows Limbaugh for three hours on KVOR Radio in Colorado Springs. While Limbaugh speaks to the conservative movement, Baker speaks to the "patriot" movement about forming guerrilla squadrons and taking out the "slimeballs" in Congress.

"Patriots" rail against Bill Clinton and the plot toward global government known as the "New World Order"; they see gun control as a Big Brother conspiracy.

In Colorado, Baker has used his show to promote patriot militia groups. For months, he accompanied his rants against the government by mimicking the sound of a firing pin in action: "kching, kching." Attacking Senator Howard Metzenbaum over the Brady (gun control) Bill, he said that you wouldn't be rid of the senator until you could stand over his grave, "put the dirt on top of the box, and say, 'I'm pretty sure he's in there.'"

Baker has regularly interviewed leaders of the armed right, including Rev. Pete Peters, who believes that God wants gays dead and pontificates against race–mixing with Jews and minorities.

In August 1994, Linda Thompson of the Unorganized Militia of the United States came on Baker's show to advocate an armed march on Washington to remove the "traitors" in Congress: "We have two million US troops, half of them are out of the country. . . .All of the troops they could muster would be 500,000 people. They would be outnumbered five to one, if only 1 percent of the country went up against them."

Baker, broadcasting from a gun shop, responded positively— telling his guest that soldiers "would come over to our side."

A week later, a caller urged the formation of "an orchestrated militia," saying: "The problem we have right now is who do we shoot. Other than Kennedy, Foley and Mitchell, the others are borderline traitors. They're the kingpins right now, besides the Slick One [Clinton]. . . .You've got to get your ammo."

Baker's response was sympathetic: "Am I advocating the overthrow of this government?. . . .I'm advocating the cleansing." Citing the power of the "masses in rebellion," he asked: "Why are we sitting here?"

Later that day, a caller accused Baker of advocating "armed rebellion." The talk host corrected her: "An armed revolution."

Weeks later, in October, a Baker listener Francisco Martin Duran fired nearly 30 bullets at the White House. Nearby, Duran's abandoned pickup sported a bumper sticker: "Fire Butch Reno"—a favorite Baker nickname for Attorney General Janet Reno.

Inspired by Baker, Duran and scores of other listeners had called a local congressional office in August to oppose a ban on assault weapons. So many calls were irate or obscene that Duran's threat to "go to Washington and take someone out" went unnoticed.

As a talk–show host, Baker accepts no responsibility for Duran: "If he thinks I and Rush Limbaugh are the reasons he went there, then the man needs psychiatric counseling."

Is Baker an isolated, rogue element in the talk industry? Hardly. He remains on the air (toned down slightly) and on the advisory board of the National Association of Radio Talk Show Hosts.

Reporting for *EXTRA!*, the magazine of the media watch group Fairness in Accuracy and Reporting (FAIR), Colorado journalist Leslie Jorgensen interviewed the executive director of the talk show host association. Jorgensen was told: "You're trying to put a muzzle on free speech. . . .Chuck Baker is a good host and knows how to talk to people and calm them down."

No one muzzles nationally syndicated talk host G. Gordon Liddy, who has also expressed sympathy for right–wing militias. Three days before Baker's show touted an armed march on Washington, Liddy told listeners how to kill federal Bureau of Alcohol, Tobacco and Firearms agents: "They've got a big target on there, ATF. Don't shoot at that because they've got a vest on underneath that. Head shot, head shots." Later in the program, Liddy said: "Kill the sons of bitches." Liddy's show is distributed by Westwood One, the country's biggest syndicator of radio programming.

In many cities, right–talk is not enough; the new marketing device in radio is "hot talk"—but it might be renamed "hate talk." In Phoenix, KFYI "hot talk" host Bob Mohan declared that gun control advocate Sarah Brady "ought to be put down. A humane shot at a veterinarian's would be an easy way to do it."

In liberal San Francisco, KSFO—owned by the ABC/Capital Cities media giant—recently abandoned its diverse lineup of talk hosts, and switched to "hot talk": all right, all the time. Now San Franciscans can hear hosts who speak of "lynching a few liberals" and encourage listeners to "shoot illegal immigrants who come across the border" for reward money.

Let's face it: there's something wrong with the talk radio spectrum when Rush Limbaugh is starting to sound tolerant.

Jeff Cohen and Norman Solomon are the authors of *Adventures in Medialand: Behind the News, Beyond the Pundits* (Munroe, Maine: Common Courage Press). Cohen is Executive Director of the media watchdog group Fairness and Accuracy in Reporting (FAIR), and Solomon is on FAIR's Board of Advisers. © 1995, Jeff Cohen and Norman Solomon.

What is Fascism?

Some General Ideological Features

Matthew N. Lyons

I am skeptical of efforts to produce a "definition" of fascism. As a dynamic historical current, fascism has taken many different forms, and has evolved dramatically in some ways. To understand what fascism has encompassed as a movement and a system of rule, we have to look at its historical context and development—as a form of counter-revolutionary politics that first arose in early twentieth-century Europe in response to rapid social upheaval, the devastation of World War I, and the Bolshevik Revolution. The following paragraphs are intented as an initial, open-ended sketch.

Fascism is a form of extreme right-wing ideology that celebrates the nation or the race as an organic community transcending all other loyalties. It emphasizes a myth of national or racial rebirth after a period of decline or destruction. To this end, fascism calls for a "spiritual revolution" against signs of moral decay such as individualism and materialism, and seeks to purge "alien" forces and groups that threaten the organic community. Fascism tends to celebrate masculinity, youth, mystical unity, and the regenerative power of violence. Often, but not always, it promotes racial superiority doctrines, ethnic persecution, imperialist expansion, and genocide. At the same time, fascists may embrace a form of internationalism based on either racial or ideological solidarity across national boundaries. Usually fascism espouses open male supremacy, though sometimes it may also promote female solidarity and new opportunities for women of the privileged nation or race.

Fascism's approach to politics is both populist—in that it seeks to activate "the people" as a whole against perceived oppressors or enemies—and elitist—in that it treats the people's will as embodied in a select group, or often one supreme leader, from whom authority proceeds downward. Fascism seeks to organize a cadre–led mass movement in a drive to seize state power. It seeks to forcibly subordinate all spheres of society to its ideological vision of organic community, usually through a totalitarian state. Both as a movement and a regime, fascism uses mass organizations as a system of integration and control, and uses organized violence to suppress opposition, although the scale of violence varies widely.

Fascism is hostile to Marxism, liberalism, and conservatism, yet it borrows concepts and practices from all three. Fascism rejects the principles of class struggle and workers' internationalism as threats to national or racial unity, yet it often exploits real grievances against capitalists and landowners through ethnic scapegoating or radical–sounding conspiracy theories. Fascism rejects the liberal doctrines of individual autonomy and rights, political pluralism, and representative government, yet it advocates broad popular participation in politics and may use parliamentary channels in its drive to power. Its vision of a "new order" clashes with the conservative attachment to tradition–based institutions and hierarchies, yet fascism often romanticizes the past as inspiration for national rebirth.

Fascism has a complex relationship with established elites and the non–fascist right. It is never a mere puppet of the ruling class, but an autonomous movement with its own social base. In practice, fascism defends capitalism against instability and the left, but also pursues an agenda that sometimes clashes with capitalist interests in significant ways. There has been much cooperation, competition, and interaction between fascism and other sections of the right, producing various hybrid movements and regimes.

Matthew N. Lyons is an independent scholar and freelance writer who studies reactionary and supremacist movements. His articles have appeared in the *Progressive* and other periodicals. These paragraphs are adapted from *Too Close for Comfort: Right Wing Populism, Scapegoating, and Fascist Potentials in US Politics* (Boston: South End Press, 1996), which Lyons co-authored with Chip Berlet. © 1995, Matthew N. Lyons.

Encountering Holocaust Denial

*The SS guards took pleasure
in telling us that we had no chance
of coming out alive,
a point they emphasized with particular relish
by insisting that after the war
the rest of the world would not believe
what happened.*

Survivor of Dachau, quoted in Terence DesPres,
The Survivor: An Anatomy of Life in the Death Camps

Lin Collette

In 1991, college students across the country were confronted with a shocking form of bigotry against Jews: full–page ads in college papers purchased by Bradley Smith, founder of a California organization called the Committee for Open Debate on the Holocaust (CODOH). In the ads, CODOH and its supporters question Holocaust history as presently understood and taught by historians and others. Denial that the Holocaust has been accurately represented is called by critics Holocaust denial or Holocaust revisionism, and by proponents is called Historical revisionism.

The decision whether to run the ads was made by the students running the papers, since most college newspapers are independent of their school's administration. Those papers that chose to run the ad usually defended their decision as respecting First Amendment guarantees; they were uncomfortable with taking any actions that might be construed as suppressing open debate on this or other issues. As writer Carlos Huerta explains in a 1992 article on the issue of Holocaust revisionism on campus, even several newspapers with a large Jewish presence on the staff chose to run the ads. Although they found the ads offensive, these Jewish students tended to see the issue in terms of freedom of expression.

Papers that chose not to run the advertisement, on the other hand, did so because they found it offensive, inaccurate, or both. Campus and public reaction to either decision was swift—usually set squarely against the decision to publish. Papers that chose to publish the ads were often vilified by their communities and attacked for being anti–Jewish or ignorant of the actual mandate of the First Amendment.

The traditional response to Holocaust revisionism within much of the institutional Jewish community has been either to ignore it or to expose the neo–Nazi connections of deniers, often wishing to avoid engaging in open debate with them, or even acknowledging their existence for fear of lending revisionists any form of legitimacy. In this case, however, many students felt that in choosing to run the revisionist ads, Holocaust revisionism would be more effectively counter–attacked.

Jewish experience has been profoundly shaped and reshaped across the centuries by historical experiences of salvation above all, but also of destruction. A deep sense of identity and mission, coupled with the genius of historical memory, have preserved not only for Jews but the rest of the world, the root experiences of the Jewish people. The act of denying the Holocaust, however, diminishes not just Jews but the experiences of all people; hence it is important to understand the phenomenon of Holocaust revisionism and the role it plays in promoting not only anti–Jewish bigotry but a cynical conspiratorial analysis that encourages the acceptance of scapegoating and demonization.

Holocaust denial is not new; it has been a fringe activity since World War II. However, a combination of shrewd organizing by Holocaust revisionists and the aging of Holocaust survivors has allowed deniers to begin to enter the Western mainstream. This is particularly alarming since it seems that every possible document and eyewitness account exists to prove the truth of the Holocaust, even if the actual totals of those executed can never be known. Yet Holocaust revisionism seems to be growing in acceptance—at least among some members of the public.

What is Holocaust Revisionism?

Revisionism is a major function of serious historians, whose goal is to seek an accurate record of history wherever they find it. Some historians review and reinterpret the Holocaust and genocide in a manner that is not a subterfuge for attacking Jews. This type of historical analysis, although sometimes controversial, is generally regarded by scholars and critics as the only credible form of revisionism regarding the Holocaust. Essentially this is, at its most basic and benign level, the rewriting or reinterpretation of Holocaust history in a manner that argues: "It happened, but there are still things we need to learn about it." Such scholars usually have little difficulty getting their theories published in books and reputable journals and are frequently cited as reliable sources. Historians such as Lucy Dawidowicz, Charles Maier, Michael Marrus, Arno Mayer, and Christopher Simpson are found in this group.

Within Holocaust revisionism that involves a strain of anti–Jewish bigotry, there are three distinct schools of thought. These can be described as: "It happened, but far from the extent to which they say it did"; "It happened, but other groups suffered just as much as the Jews"; and "It didn't happen at all."

The first school, when it is taken seriously at all in academia, is considered to be of questionable credibility by most scholars; members of this school go to great lengths to downplay the Holocaust's historical significance or imply that the impact and extent of the Holocaust have been magnified to accomplish particular ends, such as justification of US aid to Israel or aid to Jewish refugees from the former USSR. David Irving, author of a number of books on World War II, the accuracy of which are consistently challenged, could be considered a member of this school, although he sometimes drifts into the more nasty schools of Holocaust revisionism.

The second school is a relative of the first. While admitting that the Holocaust did in fact occur, members of this school argue that Jews were only one of several groups of victims. This is a cynical use of other victim groups. For example, these researchers will claim that the non–Jewish Poles or Germans were equal victims to the Jews, and often minimize the impact Nazi policies had on European Jews by emphasizing the impact of those policies on other groups. An example of equalizing the victims of the Holocaust is the comments of former President Ronald Reagan when he visited a cemetery in Bitburg, Germany in which SS members, German soldiers, and Jewish victims of the Holocaust are buried. The visit caused a furor; Reagan's explanations "compounded his error" by making "no distinction between the fallen German soldiers and the murdered Jews; indeed, he suggested that both were 'victims of a Nazi oppression whose responsibility was abdicated through the madness of one man, Hitler.'"

The third school, the most unconscionable, is the one that has attracted media attention in the past few years. Proponents of this school completely deny that a conscious attempted genocide of Jews occurred. They generally argue that the Holocaust as a policy of genocide was a fabrication by the Jews. Although its advocates deny they are anti–Semitic, much of the material found in this category vilifies Jews and Judaism. Although their materials have no credibility among serious scholars, the credibility of the actual deniers within the general public is somewhat higher, if only because of ignorance.

To be noted is that some neo–Nazis are Hitler proponents who do not deny the Holocaust but openly bemoan the fact that it was not more effective. While grotesque, they are not Holocaust revisionists.

It should also be noted that there is a legitimate and subtle debate over the use of the word holocaust (Sho'ah) to describe the attempted genocide of the Jews. The word is sometimes adopted to describe an instance of mass murder or ethnocide and has been used by the media to describe large–scale killing in Cambodia or Bosnia. The term holocaust has also been expropriated by anti–abortion protesters to describe the number of abortions since *Roe v. Wade* in 1973.

Who Denies the Holocaust?

A November 1992 survey (now in dispute) conducted by the Roper Organization for the American Jewish Committee found that fully 22 percent of American adults and 20 percent of high school students thought it was possible that the Holocaust never happened. Another 12 percent weren't certain whether it was possible or impossible. Because the wording of the questions asked in this poll was flawed, however, Roper conducted a second poll for the AJC in March 1994, using revised questions and a new cohort. Results of the new poll, delivered to the AJC in May 1994, have not yet been released, but it seems certain that the previous poll overestimated the number of people who think the Holocaust never happened. A January 1994 Gallup Poll found that a much lower percentage, approximately 4 percent, of those it surveyed "have real doubts about the Holocaust; the others (19 percent) are just insecure about their historical knowledge or won't believe anything they have not experienced themselves," says Frank Newport, Editor of the Gallup Poll.

Contrary to popular belief, Holocaust denial exists not only on the political right, but also among some individuals characterized as moderate or left, although it is the right that is most prominent in the effort to present "another side" to Holocaust history. Most obvious on the right are the predictable suspects: neo–Nazis, skinheads, and members of the various Ku Klux Klans. The most prominent revisionist organizations are the Institute for Historical Review (IHR) and the Liberty Lobby, publisher of *Spotlight*, a radical right–wing newspaper published in Washington, DC. IHR, Liberty Lobby, and *Spotlight* magazine will be discussed in greater depth elsewhere in this article.

A nationally known Holocaust revisionist is David Duke, elected a Louisiana state representative although a former Klan leader, who ran as the 1988 presidential candidate of the extreme right–wing Populist Party and as a Republican candidate for President for a brief period in 1991–1992. Although he claims to have put his Klan and neo–Nazi past behind him, as late as 1993 he continued to sell IHR publications through his Louisiana State Assembly office, as well as a tape entitled "The Jewish Question II," in which he questions the Holocaust "myth." In addition, he has been reported by Louisiana Republicans as openly asserting that the Holocaust is a hoax dreamed up by Jewish–controlled Hollywood.

A current star of the revisionist lobby is Massachusetts resident Fred Leuchter. His lengthy *Leuchter Report* publicized his studies of "alleged gas chambers" at Auschwitz and other camps, and asserted that no execution chambers existed there. These theories claiming the impossibility of mass gassings were central to his testimony as an "expert witness" at the 1988 trial of Ernst Zundel, a German–Canadian revisionist and neo–Nazi, on trial for violating Canadian laws against publishing and distributing hate propaganda. Although Leuchter does not possess the engineering credentials with which he is often publicly credited, his report quickly became a best–seller on the far right.

Leuchter's *Report* has been discredited by Jean–Claude Pressac, a French writer who himself was a Holocaust revisionist at one time. In his most recent book, *The Auschwitz Crematoria: The Machinery of Mass Slaughter*, Pressac uses documents from recently opened KGB archives to supplement those on file at the Auschwitz Museum archives to illustrate exactly how Nazi extermination techniques worked.

Another segment of the extreme right that continues to claim that the Holocaust is a myth is the Christian Identity movement, which claims that contemporary Jews are not related to the original tribes of Israel, but rather impostors descended from the historic Khazars, a now–dispersed people whose leaders adopted Judaism as a religious belief hundreds of years ago. Identity theology maintains that contemporary Khazar–descended Jews concocted the Holocaust in an effort to cement their reputation as God's Chosen, while Identity Christians are the real descendants of the tribes of Israel and thus the real Chosen People, not contemporary Jews. IHR and Liberty Lobby publications are distributed through many Identity Christian ministries, book houses, and publications, and members of the movement have approvingly discussed the Holocaust denial movement in their periodicals.

In recent years, some segments of the African American community have also come to question the Holocaust's relative importance in history, arguing that the genocidal aspects of slavery and the Middle Passage affected more lives and that genocidal policies in the form of racism still continue today. While this debate can be handled with seriousness and sensitivity, and arguments can be made that slavery was a form of "Black genocide," some proponents use the debate as a cover for anti–Jewish bigotry. This is the case with the most prominent proponents, the Nation of Islam, headed by Minister Louis Farrakhan. Farrakhan himself has been accused of fostering anti–Jewish bigotry through his speeches and by refusing to condemn completely the anti–Jewish rhetoric of his spokespersons, particularly Khallid Abdul Muhammed, who has been giving incendiary speeches at various colleges around the country.

Although Farrakhan has been called a "problem for a broad range of American blacks who rightly fear that his anti–Semitic rhetoric erodes the moral authority of his appeals against racism," a 1994 *Time*/CNN poll of 504 African Americans found that 62 percent of those familiar with him said that he was good for the Black community and that 63 percent believed that he spoke the truth. Only a fifth of those questioned considered him anti–Semitic.

Because other aspects of the Nation's message strongly appeal to the African American community, such as an emphasis on self–reliance, cultural pride, and personal responsibility, many Blacks are prepared to look past Farrakhan's other, more controversial stands on Jewish relationships with Blacks, and racism against whites. For Jews, however, it is harder, if not impossible, to overlook those stands. Further, many aspects of Farrakhan's political ideology are so authoritarian, repressive to women, and homophobic that they are perceived as threatening to groups other than Jews.

Four Jewish groups withdrew their sponsorship of the Parliament of the World's Religions held in Chicago in September 1993, when it was learned that Farrakhan had been invited to speak. In response to an October 1992 Farrakhan visit to Atlanta, Georgia, the Anti Defamation League of B'nai B' rith (ADL) said, "The fact that the Nation of Islam does some good in the Black community is not a rationale for forgiving its scapegoating of Jews and Judaism."

Farrakhan, of course, is not the only Black leader to have exhibited anti–Jewish tendencies. A number of rap musicians have also been condemned for including anti–Jewish lyrics in their works. In addition, several Black scholars specializing in Afrocentric studies have sparked comment because their books and articles allege disproportionate Jewish complicity in slavery. One of the most recent incidents involved a book written by Wellesley College professor Tony Martin that chronicles a campaign of alleged persecution against him by Jews at Wellesley. The book was condemned by the school's president in a letter mailed to faculty, alumni, and students.

A prominent journalist and media personality who has openly questioned and belittled the extent of the Holocaust is Patrick Buchanan, 1992 Republican presidential candidate. Buchanan is known to have "mocked the feelings of Holocaust survivors as 'group fantasies of martyrdom and heroics,'" and has questioned the capability of the Treblinka concentration camp to have engaged in mass gassings of inmates.

Buchanan also appeared to go out of his way to anger Jews by arguing "the innocence of accused and convicted Nazi executioners." He has also "suggested that in any case the hunt for old, enfeebled men was of dubious moral value." For his unwavering support of John Demjanjuk, whose 1988 war crimes conviction was overturned on appeal by the Israeli Supreme Court, Buchanan (as well as Ohio Congressman James Traficant) were praised and embraced in an editorial in the *Journal of Historical Review*, published by the Institute for Historical Review. During the months leading up to the Persian Gulf War, Buchanan repeatedly referred to war hawks as being in Israel's "amen corner."

Buchanan's friends and colleagues find it difficult to believe he could be a "card–carrying anti–Semite" and, indeed, Buchanan has characterized anti–Semitism as a singular "disease of the heart" in his newspaper column. The problem, his friends say, is his "preference for journalistic swagger over editorial precision."

Mel Elfin, writing in *US News and World Report*, commented that in calling Congress "Israeli–occupied territory" and advising that the US not "cave in to 'Jewish' pressures," Buchanan displayed a "callous ignorance" of Nazi–style demagoguery. Elfin concludes: "If [Buchanan] really believes anti–Semitism is a 'disease of the heart,' he would be well–advised to avoid providing aid and comfort to those who still consider the Holocaust a myth and for whom group hatred has become a way of life."

The Institute for Historical Review

The chief organization promoting Holocaust denial is the Institute for Historical Review, a California organization founded in 1978 by Willis Carto, who also founded the extreme right–wing Liberty Lobby. IHR styles itself in fundraising letters as a "voice for historical truth" and a "champion of historical knowledge" because "we have the knowledge, and because we have the determination to see the truth prevail."

IHR was particularly gleeful over the acquittal of John Demjanjuk by the Israeli Supreme Court in the summer of 1993, claiming that the case is an important vindication of the cause of

Holocaust revisionism. Revisionists felt they had been confirmed in their decades–long insistence that eyewitness testimony—even of Jewish Holocaust survivors—must be regarded with the greatest skepticism. As part of its efforts to gain a mainstream following, IHR publishes the *Journal of Historical Review*, once a quarterly but now bimonthly. Previously geared to an academic audience, the *Journal's* format changed in 1992 from a 5x8 inch library–sized format to a more glossy, 8½x11 format, using more photographs and a less turgid editorial style. The *Journal* is now intended to appeal to all "intelligent" readers, and now carries articles on ancient history, culture, art, religion, philosophy, and social issues, as well as its old standby themes of racial issues and World War II history.

An important IHR function is to hold annual private conferences, usually in California, at which the elite of the Holocaust revisionist community are invited to present their "research." Guests are usually *Journal* subscribers and IHR donors. The 1990 conference featured a coup: one of the presenters was John Toland, author of several respected and authoritative books on World War II history, who is not considered to be a revisionist along the lines of the IHR.

IHR first came to public attention in 1980, when it offered a $50,000 reward to anyone who could conclusively prove that Jews had been gassed at Auschwitz. Mel Mermelstein, a survivor, accepted the challenge and submitted voluminous proof, including his own personal testimony. When the evidence was ignored by IHR, Mermelstein sued IHR for the reward.

During the trial, Mermelstein used the same evidence that had been submitted to IHR. The suit was finally settled in Mermelstein's favor in July 1985, with IHR ordered by the Los Angeles Superior Court to pay the $50,000 reward plus an additional $40,000 for pain and suffering caused to Mermelstein. According to a member of the staff of the Auschwitz Study Foundation, founded by Mermelstein in Huntington Beach, California, IHR did, in fact, pay the judgment.

In 1986, Mermelstein also won a $5.25 million default judgment against former IHR Editorial Advisory Committee member Ditlieb Felderer, a Swedish revisionist who had used his *Jewish Information Bulletin* to personally attack and libel Mermelstein. In retaliation for both suits, IHR and Liberty Lobby sued Mermelstein in 1986 for libel, but dropped the charges in February 1988. Mermelstein filed yet another lawsuit in October 1988, in response to the Liberty Lobby/IHR suit, charging malicious prosecution on the part of IHR. Although that suit was dismissed in September 1991, Mermelstein filed an appeal in August 1992, with no results to date.

IHR has often been mistaken for other, more credible organizations such as the London–based Institute for Historical

Research, whose ideology is far from that of IHR. Organizations with little knowledge of IHR's work have sometimes been hoodwinked into selling ad space or mailing lists to IHR. For example, IHR was able to get a "Call for Papers" published in the newsletter of the American Historical Association in 1993, which caused an uproar when IHR's mission was revealed. As a result, the AHA decided to donate the money paid for the ad to the Simon Wiesenthal Center.

In 1980, IHR bought part of the membership list of the Organization of American Historians in order to send every OAH member a sample issue of the *Journal of Historical Review*, which ultimately caused the OAH to make its policies concerning purchase of its mailing list more restrictive. Ten years later, in 1991, the OAH agreed to publish an IHR "Call for Papers" in its newsletter, a move that enraged many members. OAH editors justified their decision by citing the First Amendment, and stood by it.

IHR presents a public face that avoids overt anti–Jewish bigotry. However, its fundraising letters, mailed to "supporters of truth in history," reveal its directors' prejudices quite clearly, as shown in a quote from a March 1992 letter:

> The powerful interest groups opposed to historical awareness will not stand idly by while the suppressed facts of 20th century history continue to gain an ever widening audience. With millions of dollars at their disposal, for every dollar we spend to correct the historical record, they'll spend a thousand more building Holocaust museums and memorials, agitating for school indoctrination programs, backing Hillel groups on college campuses, and funding their vast web of professional snoops, censors, slanderers and media manipulators.

This text embodies a conspiratorial impression of Jewish power and control that reflects a major strain of historic anti–Jewish prejudice.

IHR claims that its founding goal was to follow in the footsteps of Harry Elmer Barnes, once a well–known and respected World War I historian and revisionist whose obsession with conspiracy theories led him to virulent anti–Jewish bigotry and support for Nazi policies during World War II and to a later belief that the Holocaust was a hoax.

In a "fact sheet," the IHR claims to shed light on suppressed information about key chapters of history, especially 20th–century history, that have special relevance today. It goes on to firmly support the First Amendment right of free speech. In fact, as aptly stated by Deborah Lipstadt, IHR's actual goal was "to move denial from the lunatic fringe of racial and anti–Semitic extremism to the realm of academic respectability. The IHR was designed to win scholarly acceptance for deniers."

Mermelstein's victories have been major defeats for IHR's cause. Nevertheless, IHR has managed to survive since paying out a

$90,000 settlement to Mermelstein, as well as ever–increasing attorneys' fees. There is some evidence of cost–cutting, however—most notable in the *Journal of Historical Review*, which lost much of its bulk in 1992. There also are rumors that the IHR is losing donors; and this was before the split with Carto.

Another major setback was a firebombing attack in 1984 that destroyed most of IHR's files and office equipment at its Torrance, California warehouse and office, and prevented it from publishing the *Journal* for several years. Because it had been experiencing some harassment from several alleged members of the Jewish Defense League, IHR's leaders accused JDL of the arson, but no evidence was found linking JDL to the attack.

In October 1993, Willis Carto was forced out of the Institute for Historical Review in an apparent dispute over funding and ideology. Carto has filed suit in Los Angeles Superior Court to resume control of IHR.

Liberty Lobby/Noontide Press

Often those who get involved with IHR are unaware of its historic connection to Liberty Lobby, a connection which IHR itself is slow to reveal, presumably for the sake of its credibility. Indeed, only Liberty Lobby publicizes the connection, often publishing Holocaust revisionism in *Spotlight* and even devoting entire issues of that newspaper to the "Holocaust hoax." In addition, Noontide Press, a Carto/Liberty Lobby outfit, has been run in previous years by Tom Marcellus, current director of IHR. Fundraising letters for IHR have been printed on Noontide Press stationery; both organizations are usually based in the same California cities. If IHR moves, so does Noontide.

A legal connection has also been established. An appeal filed by Liberty Lobby, IHR, and the League for the Survival of Freedom, in an effort to present themselves as separate entities, was dismissed by the United States Court of Appeals in 1988. The appeal was part of Carto's attempt to sue the *Wall Street Journal* for calling him an anti–Semite. As Judge Robert Bork (soon to become famous in the failed attempt by the Reagan/Bush Administration to elevate him to the Supreme Court) stated in his opinion, the tactic was designed merely to disassociate the three groups from each other, in order to save their individual reputations. In addition, it probably was done as a financial move, to ensure that suits filed against one would not affect the other two, so that at least one group would survive should there be a legal defeat, as there was in the Mermelstein lawsuit.

Liberty Lobby's central role in promoting Holocaust revisionism dates to the 1960s, although associates such as Francis Yockey dabbled in this area in the early 1950s. Its involvement seems to have begun with its publication of *The Myth of the Six Million*, a book which "has become a staple item in the Liberty Library and in the wares of various racist–paramilitarist groups." In the 1960s it published discussions of Zionism and the Jews in *Spotlight* whenever possible, and on occasion it attacked ADL. While some criticisms of ADL deserve debate—such as whether or not its close relationship to law enforcement and intelligence agencies has led it to violate the privacy rights of dissidents, or if its high–profile attacks on Black anti–Jewish bigots are disproportionate—the Liberty Lobby critique of ADL falls into the classic pattern of conspiracy theories regarding Jewish power.

In later years, Liberty Lobby published at least two problematic tracts on the Middle East, one written by author Issa Nakleh (who has been a featured speaker at IHR conferences) expounding theories such as "Zionist intrigue as a factor in America's 1917 intervention," "dispute of the Holocaust statistic of six million Jewish victims," and "a conception of East European Jews as Khazars rather than Palestinian semites."

The Liberty Lobby's intention to support Holocaust revisionism became clearer in the early 1970s when it began to distribute *The Hoax of the Twentieth Century*, by Northwestern University professor Arthur Butz. Since then, it has often used *Spotlight* to promote the IHR, rail against Jewish groups, and protest the opening of the United States Holocaust Museum.

After Carto's ouster from IHR, he immediately began to plan a new revisionist publication to be published in October 1994. Called *The Barnes Report,* after revisionist historian and longtime Carto friend Harry Elmer Barnes, the journal is clearly intended as a challenge to the *Journal of Historical Review.* In an advertising blurb in the August 29, 1994 issue of *Spotlight,* the newspaper's Senior Editor Vince Ryan claims that *The Barnes Report* would be an incorruptible source *you know you can trust.*

CODOH

Another Holocaust revisionist organization is the Committee for Open Debate on the Holocaust. Its efforts to place full–page newspaper ads in college newspapers (most recently *The Good 5¢ Cigar*, the student newspaper of the University of Rhode Island in Kingston, Rhode Island) has garnered extensive news coverage. Essentially a one–man operation, CODOH is run by Bradley Smith, a Korean War veteran and high school graduate who, as a bookseller, was prosecuted and convicted in the 1960s of disseminating obscene material because he sold Henry Miller's *Tropic of Cancer*. At the time, he portrayed himself as a fervent believer in freedom of speech and expression, and it is that philosophy, he says, which prompts him to fight so hard for the cause of Holocaust revisionism.

Smith claims to have believed in the Holocaust "myth" until 1979, when someone gave him a copy of an article from the French newspaper *Le Monde*, written by French Holocaust revisionist Robert Faurisson. The article so impressed him that he underwent a "conversion," and has since self–published the first two parts of his autobiography, *Confessions of a Holocaust Revisionist*. He has also been working with the IHR as its spokesman and media director.

Smith founded CODOH in 1987 along with Mark Weber, who is now the editor of IHR's *Journal of Historical Review*. In an effort to promote his beliefs, he has appeared on well over 300 radio and television talk shows and began the college advertising effort. According to Smith, accounts of the Holocaust are akin to the stories found in the *National Enquirer* and other supermarket tabloids.

Smith's demeanor as a calm, kindly, elderly gentleman helps to sell his message. He is a far cry from the stereotypical alienated fanatic that one typically associates with anti–Jewish and neo–Nazi beliefs. Unfortunately, his opponents often become emotionally overwrought when confronting Smith's confident lies, and can seem more fanatical than he does.

International Revisionism

Revisionist groups also exist in other countries, notably the Historical Review Press in Great Britain. There are also many individuals who have devoted their lives and careers to attacking the "myth" of the Holocaust. Some of the more famous include the British popular historian David Irving, Canadian high school teachers James Keegstra and Malcolm Ross, right–wing publisher Ernst Zundel, and French university professors Robert Faurisson and Bernard Notin. Both Keegstra and Faurisson have lost their teaching positions because of their beliefs, while Ross still teaches English and mathematics in a Moncton, New Brunswick high school, despite challenges by opponents.

Zundel has been tried twice on the same charges in Canada, for publishing "false news" through the printing and distribution of revisionist books and tracts such as *Did Six Million Really Die?* He was convicted both times, but each time his conviction was dismissed by the Canadian Supreme Court, most recently in August 1992, on the grounds that the law against spreading false news was too vague and might be used to limit legitimate forms of speech.

Two years after the verdict against Zundel was overturned, he is still publishing his revisionist literature. One of the newest offerings is a 567–page condensation of evidence presented at his trials. In addition, he has begun a satellite television program, as well as short–wave radio broadcasts in English and German, with the latter aimed at his ever–increasing right–wing audience in Germany. Although Zundel is reportedly under investigation by Canadian authorities, no admissible evidence of "hate crimes" has been found. A member of the Ontario Provincial Police commented in a 1993 interview that "Mr. Zundel is very knowledgeable about what he can say."

Keegstra, a former history and shop teacher, as well as Mayor of Eckville, Alberta, lost both jobs after a long struggle by opponents to oust him. Parents, disturbed by the anti–Jewish tone of their children's notes from Keegstra's classes, objected and sought to have him dismissed. They eventually succeeded, but encountered a great deal of opposition from his supporters, who ran the gamut from fellow teachers coming to the aid of one of their own to right–wing ideologues whose views were akin to Keegstra's.

Keegstra, like Zundel, was tried twice on charges related to spreading hatred and violating the "false news" law. Although an earlier conviction was overturned by the Canadian Supreme Court in 1991, after the second trial in July 1992 Keegstra was convicted of "promoting hatred by teaching his high school students that Jews have conspired to gain control of the world."

According to a 1985 article in the Jewish monthly *Midstream,* the frightening aspect of the entire affair was not so much that it happened, but that Keegstra poisoned the minds of his students for 14 years, that he induced them to hate Jews, and that this did not bother the high school principal, who said that Keegstra was a "good teacher" and that he would be "happy to see Keegstra reinstated." It did not stop one of his antagonists from thinking she could work with him in "trying to make Eckville a decent place to live," and it failed to disturb the equanimity of the school superintendent, who found Keegstra "most convincing" at the hearing where it was decided to keep him on for another year.

That his teachings had somehow been able to muscle aside the standard history found in mass media and school curriculum on the Holocaust and World War II was also alarming to Jigs Gardner, author of the *Midstream* article. But for Holocaust revisionists and revisionist sympathizers, mainstream media and Hollywood productions are run by special interest groups (usually meaning Jews) and therefore programming is controlled to convey only the message these groups want the public to hear.

Finally, the neo–fascist cult leader Lyndon LaRouche has questioned the Holocaust by claiming that most Jews died of disease and overwork, a stock–in–trade argument of Holocaust revisionists. Followers of LaRouche and Farrakhan have been making joint appearances in recent months.

These are only a few of the many deniers who have received public attention recently. Unfortunately, their message is sparking increased "debate" over the Holocaust, and the numbers of their supporters seem to be increasing.

Why Holocaust Denial?

Moderate Holocaust denial/revisionism generally takes the form of "wanting to hear both sides of the story," or questioning the extent of the Holocaust, in the spirit of not wanting to believe something on the scale of the Holocaust could happen. Carlos Huerta believes that the reason for this may be simply that people want to be tolerant, even of the most crackpot opinions. Such individuals, he says, have a sense of American fair play and have difficulty in understanding what they perceive as personal, slanderous attacks against revisionists. They ask the obviously simple question that if revisionism is so wrong and absurd, why not simply expose it as such and end the issue.

As mentioned earlier, however, a number of Holocaust scholars and Jews have declined to debate Holocaust deniers/revisionists, based on their fear that to do so would indicate that Holocaust denial is an acceptable theory. Deborah Lipstadt, a noted author and historian specializing in the Holocaust, explains:

> The existence of the Holocaust [is] not a matter for debate. I would analyze and illustrate who they were and what they tried to do, but I would not appear with them. To do so would give them a legitimacy and a stature they in no way deserve. It would elevate their anti–Semitic ideology—which is what Holocaust denial is—to the level of responsible historiography—which it is not.

Lipstadt cites the case of a television program on which she refused to appear but viewed at a later date:

> When the show aired, in April 1992, deniers were given the bulk of the time to speak their piece. Then Holocaust survivors were brought on to try to "refute" their comments. Before the commercial break the host, Montel Williams, urged viewers to stay tuned, so that they could learn whether the "Holocaust is a myth or is it truth."

Unfortunately, the refusals of experts and survivors to confront the revisionists, while understandable, may allow Holocaust denial a virtually unchallenged forum. This is especially true in the case of call–in talk shows, which pit deniers (who are, ironically, well–prepared and well–read in standard Holocaust history) against well–meaning opponents who may not be well–versed in the subject, but know, through whatever means—experience or reading—the truth of the Holocaust. Such programs can become an exercise in emotionalism, with callers and even talk show hosts losing their tempers as they attempt to confront the deniers with the facts about the Holocaust.

It is not surprising that Holocaust deniers are taking full advantage of most Americans' tolerance for eccentrics. Brian Siano, in a column in *The Humanist*, comments:

> With nearly any subject we learn about in school, we retain only the broad outlines. Relatively few of us understand the Holocaust in intimate, working detail. Most people know of Hitler, camps, gas, maybe the number *six million*, and the vague understanding that the United States put a stop to it. It's not hard to imagine such a person; lots of them graduate high school every year.
>
> Now imagine someone coming up to this person and saying, "That Holocaust stuff is just silly, unscientific nonsense. Have you ever wondered how the Nazis could possibly gas so many people to death? Especially when the gas they used was only an insecticide?"

Often, in our zeal to hear both sides of an issue, we are eager to question established truths, sometimes *in toto*. Americans have a fascination with conspiracy theories and so are often willing to entertain even the most crackpot theories in the belief that everyone deserves a fair hearing. On the other hand, we are often too willing to believe "authorities" who claim to be experts on one thing or another and to take what they say as the certified truth. These contradictory behaviors work in the revisionists' favor.

The increasing numbers of those who engage in Holocaust denial is perhaps emblematic of our own lack of memory of our past, and our preference for dealing with the present and future, rather than the past. As Geoffrey Hartman reflects:

> As events "pass into history," and they seem to do so more quickly than ever, are they forgotten by all except specialists? "Passing into history" would then be an euphemism for oblivion, though not obliteration. That something is retrievable in the archives of a library may even help us to tolerate the speedy displacement of one news item by another. The storage capacity of the human memory is, after all, very limited. But what of the collective memory, with its days of celebration and lamentation, and the duty to keep alive a community's heritage?

This desire to let the unpleasant past slip away has contributed to controversy in Germany, where the *Historikerstreit*, or "Historians' Debate" over the meaning of Germany's Nazi past, has prompted bitter dissension among that country's scholars. The process of *vergangenheitsbewaltigung*, or "mastering the past," is a difficult one, forcing scholars to face the evil caused by the Nazis before and during World War II. Unfortunately, such questioning of the past has given rise to a new form of revisionism, in which many Germans are asking why their country should be held solely responsible for what happened 50 years ago and, indeed, why Germans today should be held responsible for "the sins of the fathers."

The debate in Germany has been prompted by an increase in commemorations of Hitler's seizure of power and of defeat in World War II as anniversaries reached the 40–and 50–year mark. Charles Maier, in his book exploring the *Historikerstreit, The Unmasterable Past*, says that although the current historical debate focuses on objections raised by conservative politicians and scholars concerning Germany's level of blame for the Holocaust, "the right did not open Pandora's box alone." Rather, as Jürgen Habermas, a prominent social philosopher, comments in Maier's book, "the memories [are accumulating] of those who for decades could not speak about their suffering," and must be spoken. In other words, Holocaust survivors arc increasingly talking about their ordeal, forcing us to confront what they endured.

Such confrontations have often prompted those who have little or no interest in world events to question why the Jews seem obsessed with the Holocaust. Says Geoffrey Hartman, "Many think they already know about the Holocaust, and that it has received too much attention. But their attitude is a sign that they have no direct memory of the events and learn about them mainly from ceremonies and the media." Further, he says, "Life is characterized by a contradictory effort: to remember and to forget, to respect the past and to acknowledge the future."

What is troubling to all of those who have suffered through the Holocaust, but particularly to Jews, who werc the prime targets, is the "careless or calculated rewriting of history" that "prevents many of them from laying their own ghosts to rest." But, most Jews are determined to keep memory alive, in spite of comments such as those made by Reagan at the Bitburg cemetery, comments that treated the young World War II German conscripts as if their suffering were equal to that of the victims of the Holocaust. Jews "saw the remark as only underscoring the tendency of history to blur the reality of their suffering—an inclination that is also visible in revisionist histories that have held the Jews partly to blame for their own slaughter."

The experience of the Massachusetts public education group, Facing History and Ourselves (FHO), is an example of this tendency. In 1986, FHO applied for grants from a special program of the Department of Education, the National Diffusion Network, to support its work educating high school students and adults about the forces that can lead to genocide, using the Holocaust and the Armenian genocide as examples. Its grant applications were reviewed by a special panel and rejected on the grounds that "[T]he project itself lacks balance; will former Nazis, etc. be allowed to speak?" After several other attempts, the organization was finally awarded a four–year grant in October 1990.

Holocaust Revisionism & Anti–Semitism

It is possible that Jewish efforts to understand and study the Holocaust are suffering from a backlash effect, similar to the backlash against feminism or even the Black civil rights movement. It takes the form of an attack against ideas that are described as being "pushed down one's throat," and perhaps many of those who resent frequent reminders of the Holocaust, but who are not active revisionists, are simply viewing the demands of Holocaust victims as "going too far" and "dwelling too much on the past."

The deniers play on a desire to avoid that which is unpleasant, and to forget the past and concentrate on the present. Holocaust denial also plays on conscious and unconscious anti–Semitic belief structures. Anti–Jewish sentiment and social prejudice has been a consistent presence in the US and other parts of the world, fostered by negative images of Jews in popular culture, often underestimated by historians.

Although overt prejudice and discrimination against Jews has declined, a covert form still survives, and so may be an important factor in fueling a tendency and/or desire to forget the facts of the Holocaust. Some may reason that the Jews (and other "undesirables") got their "just deserts" for perceived crimes committed against humanity, such as the murder of Christ or other alleged offenses, including support for socialism or communism or usury. This was in fact the attitude of many while the Holocaust was occurring, and it still is given voice by members of the extreme right. Indeed, Bradley Smith has been quoted as saying, "if God does love the anti–Semites, it might have something to do with way He feels about how some of you guys [Jews] behave."

But one doesn't have to be right–wing to believe anti–Jewish conspiracy theories or hold prejudiced views about Jews. As events unfolded during the course of the Keegstra affair, the unconscious prejudice of many Canadians came to the surface. This was usually embodied in the tendency for Christian communities to "denounce the anti–Semitic teachings of a self–proclaimed devout Christian" but to shy away from providing "outspoken moral leadership" on the question of prejudice against Jews.

Post–World War II America frowns on the open display of prejudice against Jews, although polls done in the 1980s indicated that one–third of all Americans believed that "Jews have too much power in the business world; 20 percent that they have too much power in the United States," opinions which echo the classic beliefs of most bigots.

Vice President Spiro Agnew once complained that the Jews controlled the banks and the media. In addition, there is still a perception that all or most Jews put the interests of Israel and

American Jewry ahead of those of the United States, illustrated by the comment of Senator Ernest Hollings, who once referred in debate to Senator Howard Metzenbaum (D–Ohio) as "the Senator from B'nai B'rith."

In its annual audit of anti–Semitic incidents, the ADL reported that the total number of incidents in 1993 (1,867) is the second highest in the audit's 15–year history, and an eight percent increase over the 1992 total of 1,730. Acts of a personal nature—harassment, threats, or assaults—increased by 23 percent, while vandalism against properties declined by 8 percent. According to the ADL, "this trend would seem to dovetail with the sense of many observers across the nation that confrontational, 'in–your–face' acts of violence, intimidation, and incivility, have been growing and spreading in recent years."

The audit, however, is but an annual account of overt acts of anti–Jewish bigotry or hostility, not a measure of actual prejudice present in the US today. Other observers say that, although the figures uncovered by the 1993 audit are alarming, they should be taken in perspective. J. J. Goldberg, writing for the *New Republic*, argues that in reality:

[Anti–Semitism] is on the decline. Discrimination in housing, jobs, and schooling, once endemic, has all but disappeared. State–sponsored anti–Semitism, long a defining fact of European life, is virtually unknown here. Hostility toward Jews, measured in public opinion polls, has been declining steadily for two generations. Events that seemed sure to provoke broad anti–Semitism, from the Arab oil boycott to the arrests of Israeli spy Jonathan Pollard and Wall Street cheat Ivan Boesky, came and went without a blip.

The only increase, Goldberg claims, has been in incidents.

While a disturbing number of Americans may not believe or be sure that the Holocaust did happen, 83 percent of adults and 81 percent of students felt that "the main lesson to be learned from the Holocaust is that firm steps must be taken to protect the rights of minorities." Of note is that 60 percent of adults and 53 percent of high school students agreed that the Holocaust "makes clear the need for the state of Israel as a place of refuge for Jews in times of persecution."

While the extent and effects of anti–Jewish prejudice in the US are matters of ongoing debate, the ability of Holocaust revisionists to unleash or create anti–Jewish prejudice seems amply demonstrated.

What Should Be Done About Holocaust Denial?

There is no consensus at the moment on how to respond to Holocaust revisionism. Those who see the deniers as virulent anti–Jewish bigots eager to gain a respectable foothold for their distorted interpretations of history cannot agree whether the deniers should have the same First Amendment protections to which others are entitled. Recently, the German government has taken the position that Holocaust denial is forbidden speech. It presented a broad package of bills to combat right–wing violence that includes harsher jail terms for right–wing thugs and punishment for those who deny the Holocaust happened.

Two Rutgers faculty members who published an op–ed piece in the *New York Times* argue against publishing deniers' material in student newspapers:

> [The Editors'] decision to print [CODOH'S] ad is based on principle: an aversion to censorship or a belief that hate material should be aired and publicly refuted. Surely their right to publish such ads should not be questioned. They alone must decide what good purpose, if any, is served by printing ads that are intentionally hurtful and obviously false. [Yet] the ads should be rejected.

Their assertion later in the essay that "if the Holocaust is not a fact, then nothing is a fact" is well taken. Yet, while they defend the students' right to make their own decision about what should be published, they strongly advise that the ads be rejected. There have been similar discussions in other venues, even on computer bulletin boards and the Internet. One Internet computer node site based in British Columbia is host to the "Holocaust, The" and "Fascism" electronic mailing lists and the "Holocaust FAQ's," a text file repository of several sets of "Frequently Asked Questions" about the Holocaust, Holocaust denial, and the Carto/Liberty Lobby empire.

In early 1993, the "Holocaust" list moderator, Ken McVay, sparked a discussion of this same issue by mentioning that he had been asked to post articles from *Spotlight* that denied the Holocaust, but with refutation, and asked for input from bulletin board subscribers. A number of subscribers vehemently opposed the idea, arguing that it would be a travesty for the list to become another means of distributing revisionist propaganda. Others, including McVay, understood the concerns but focused on the education issue, as does the following posting by David Mandl:

> We're talking not about helping to spread these documents, but about refuting the wild claims of the 'revisionists' whenever necessary. It's been the subject of some debate whether 'we' should just ignore them, thus denying them valuable exposure, or address these claims and expose their lies; I've wavered on this question myself. But I think this group is here to confront these 'people' head–on and deal with their texts. Do you just stuff your garbage in a closet and ignore it, pretending that the fairy garbageman will take it away some day?

Eventually, the discussion ended with the posting of the disputed article from *Spotlight*, with commentary by a subscriber.

Allowing deniers space and time to present their views may indeed be the lesser evil. If such material is suppressed, it takes on the appeal of suppressed "information," becoming more desirable. The public cannot help wonder what is dangerous about the prohibited material and so try to obtain it any way possible.

It seems, then, that a major challenge posed by Holocaust revisionists lies in determining the most effective response to them. Neither ignoring their existence nor suppressing their speech will make them go away. A middle course, acknowledging and allowing the publication of their theories and swift, calm, and thorough refutation, seems a stronger strategy in confronting revisionist distortions. As expressed by the student editors at Rutgers—how can one fight a devil one cannot see? How, indeed.

Lin Collette is a doctoral candidate in Religious Studies at the Union Institute in Cincinnati, Ohio. She is writing her dissertation on media depictions of right–wing Christian groups. Footnotes in the original version, which appeared in the September 1994 issue of *The Public Eye,* are available from Political Research Associates. © 1995, Lin Collette.

Divisions that Kill

The Enemy Without & Within

Suzanne Pharr

When the decision to acquit the cops who brutally beat Rodney King was announced and people began burning their communities and attacking each other, I thought to myself, the right wing is achieving its goal to divide and conquer us as a people.

Then, when the media immediately turned away from an analysis of the injustice of the verdict to focus solely upon the violent response, and when George Bush told the nation that what was happening in Los Angeles was not about civil rights or protest or equality but the "brutality of the mob," I thought, the Christian Right is victorious in its strategy to strip events from their political context and to frame them as morality. They frame these events not as a matter of justice and injustice but of good and evil behavior of certain groups of people.

My outrage pounded in my temples as I sat riveted to the TV, and I saw my own face mirrored everywhere: in those who stole goods and torched buildings, in the white truck driver beaten nearly to death, in the Asian grocers armed to defend their shops, in the women who cried for the loss of their community. I felt torn apart. Horrified, I thought, these divisions are killing us, and they did not come to us by chance or through the natural order of things. These divisions have been encouraged and manipulated for decades by those who oppose our liberation.

As I watched buildings burn and people die during the long May Day weekend, I thought of other miscarriages of justice: the 1978 verdict to sentence Dan White to only six years of prison for killing gay San Francisco Supervisor Harvey Milk and Mayor George Moscone. And then there was the 1991 refusal of California Governor Pete Wilson to sign into law legislation providing civil rights protection to lesbians and gay men. As with the Rodney King verdict, these actions came to symbolize decades of injustice and our people took to the streets in outrage. As Martin Luther King, Jr. said, riot became the language of the unheard.

In the riots that followed these actions, we found ourselves without the leadership and vision for uniting our people to turn our rage against the source of our oppression. Instead, we turned much of it against each other. Our disunity had for too long been manipulated by our enemies pitting us against one another for the crumbs of access, resources, and privileges; disrupting our work by FBI infiltration of our movements; destroying our leaders through police attacks such as those directed at the American Indian Movement and the Black Panthers; and through the relentless shifting of blame from those who benefit from oppression to those who suffer from it. Angry, frustrated, and on the defensive, we have been led to adopt their values and tactics and to oblige them by doing part of their destructive work.

While we turn upon each other in our frustration, pain, and rage, the Christian Right's "foot soldiers of the Lord," who oppose our very existence, march on to increasing successes on every front. Creating a climate of division and hatred, they shape public opinion to oppose our liberation and, in the end, to kill us. It was not just coincidental that the Rodney King verdict came after a year of highly publicized racist campaigning by Pat Buchanan and David Duke and Bush's sniping against the 1990 Civil Rights Restoration Act.

Since the early 1970s, the Christian Right has launched a political attack against lesbians and gay men, people of color, and feminists that has affected every adult and child in this country. It has made significant headway in dismantling the gains of the Civil Rights movement and has become a major threat to the fundamental principles of democracy. The Christian Right is united through homophobia, racism, and sexism in pursuit of their goal of merging church and state, institutionalizing a narrow view of morality, and maintaining social control by eliminating rights and freedoms.

This broad coalition of highly organized Christian fundamentalists and evangelicals, politicians, and businessmen has been a major force in creating the political climate we know today. It is backed by conservative think-tanks like the Heritage Foundation and legal and legislative strategy centers such as the Rutherford Institute. Its message is delivered and funds are raised by Pat Robertson's Christian Broadcasting network, and hundreds of thousands of "foot soldiers" are provided by Operation Rescue, Eagle Forum, and Concerned Women for America. Working on a variety of fronts, this network has created strategies to infiltrate and control all our institutions, from school boards to the Supreme Court.

While our racism, sexism, and homophobia have often separated us from one another, these religious conservatives lump us together because they see people of color, feminists, lesbians, and gay men as standing in the way of their goal to merge church and state—to give legislated dominance to white Christian males who receive their authority from Biblical scriptures. Indeed, they see us as being the cause of the breakdown of the social order. According to their logic, those rights and protections which give us voice in a democratic society are the cause of immorality and social chaos and must be thwarted or dismantled. The Civil Rights movement's demand that power be shared by all is a block to their authoritarian vision.

Attacking the idea that some people are inferior by race and must be dominated, the Civil Rights movement issued a call to conscience and to reason. It said that true democracy calls for justice, participation, and freedom. For most of us, indoctrinated to believe in a democracy that supported the interests of wealthy white males, this was a new and profoundly moving idea. Imagine: a demand for justice, participation, and freedom. The words rang in our ears.

The call was heard by African Americans, and other people of color: Asians, Latinos, Native Americans. Other movements were born. It occurred to women that if racial discrimination prevented participation in democracy, so then must discrimination based on sex. It was a heady, movement–building idea. Lesbians and gay men looked at our lives, and everywhere we looked, we saw an absence of justice, open participation, and freedom to be who we are. Then Stonewall gave us the historic, symbolic moment to move toward liberation.

The Civil Rights movement not only marked the way for other great liberation movements, but its very successes led to a reaction to it and all who embarked upon the long and arduous path to equal rights. It was not by coincidence that it was in the late 1960s, during the presidential campaign of George Wallace of Alabama, that we began to feel the impact of the organized Christian Right.

Over the past two decades, the Christian Right claimed victories in a campaign against homosexuality led by singer and orange juice promoter, Anita Bryant; the effort to defeat the Equal Rights Amendment led by the Eagle Forum's Phyllis Schlafly; a highly organized coalition of evangelical groups led by Pat Robertson to elect Ronald Reagan; a widespread attack led by Operation Rescue to dismantle abortion rights piece by piece; and an assault upon affirmative action laws led by Jesse Helms, among others. These are only a few of their efforts. The Christian Right has created "armies of God" to infiltrate all of our institutions in pursuit of their goal of institutionalizing their narrow vision of morality. They have been at the center of the effort to restrict AIDS funding and prevention education; the attack on the battered women's movement as "anti–family"; the crusade for teaching creationism rather than evolution; and the drive to limit freedom of speech. Their efforts to infiltrate and dominate institutions have touched the lives of every person in the US.

Perhaps the worst danger to our liberation is that our fear, anger, and defensiveness lead us to take on the tactics of the enemy. As the right wing attacks our dignity and worth, we respond by attacking those within the movement who are different from us; as they invade our right to privacy, we respond by outing our own people; as they pit us against each other for the crumbs of benefits, we fight each other for recognition that our particular issue (AIDS funding, breast cancer research, civil rights legislation, hate crimes laws, domestic partnership recognition) is the most important; as they attack our leadership, we attack and refuse to support our leaders; as they distort and silence the voices of oppressed people, we shout down and silence those we disagree with; as they block equality and participation for oppressed people, we subordinate the concerns of women, people of color, and people with disabilities in our movement. In the end, we have to ask, who is served by our tactics? Who benefits most?

Our inability to agree on the answers to these questions fractures our vision and strategy. Each of us, still invested in making change, continues our participation in some way in "the movement," while fighting in disunity and horizontal hostility among ourselves. In particular, we have been divided by sexism and racism, with lines drawn between men and women, between white people and people of color. I fear that our disunity and lack of connection will kill us.

We must begin a process of doing what we jokingly call "getting over ourselves" so that we can develop a vision and leadership that brings us together. This means that we will have to stop shouting, "Me, me!" and learn to harmonize on "Us, us." Developing the politics of inclusion will not be easy because we have many barriers to overcome and because we have no model for it.

But I am convinced that this is the only road to both survival and liberation.

The Christian Right, on the other hand, has an easier time in creating its politics of exclusion. Recognizing that most people are disturbed by the social and political chaos in the US, they offer us a vision of the past. They ask us to look in the rear view mirror to the 1940s and 1950s, when white soldiers returned from the war with the G. I. Bill to go to school, finding jobs plentiful and housing available, and there was a sense of stability and order. What they call for, of course, is a racist, sexist, and homophobic vision, for this was a time of legalized segregation, when male authority was unchallenged by women, abortion was illegal, and lesbians and gay men were invisible. They speak of this as the time of "traditional family values." For many of us, it was the time of family horrors, when rape, battering, incest, and alcoholism were kept as secrets within the family. Nevertheless, the Christian Right is able to unite frightened and uninformed people in a nostalgia for the past—when social order and benefits for the few were bought at the expense of women, people of color, lesbians, and gay men.

Our vision of inclusion is built on the future, not the past; we are creating that which has not been before. If we can understand that the right uses divisiveness to destroy our vision of inclusion, then we can learn that our most effective work of resistance and liberation is to make connections, both politically and personally. Making true connections may be the most cutting edge work for the 1990s.

I have seen this work taking place in rural Oregon communities this spring where people are coming together to talk about claiming their communities. Lesbians and gay men, people of color, feminists, ministers, social workers, labor unionists, domestic violence workers, blue–collar workers, etc., are gathering in common cause to say to each other that this attack by the Christian Right against the lesbian and gay community is actually a fundamental threat to democracy that affects everyone. These rural Oregonians are sick of the Christian Right framing the issues and controlling the public debate for the past two decades. It is clear to them from looking at their school boards, for example, that the right has infiltrated deeply into their communities, and they are scared. Instead of allowing the right to create the rules of community life and to determine who gets to participate, these community people want to work together for a common vision that includes everyone. This means that people who have traditionally had little to do with each other are now sitting side by side and learning about each other's lives. This process gives me great hope. I think people are hungry for true information and for a way to work together for justice in every community.

While many progressive people agree that we must work against racism, sexism, homophobia, anti–Semitism, etc., I'm not sure that we always understand how intricately these oppressions are linked and how deeply they are connected to our very survival. For instance, do white lesbians and gay men truly understand that fighting against racism is key to our freedom? As we pursue liberation, we will have to build politics of connection from those glimpses we get of our shared destiny with other oppressed people.

Sometimes I feel our work is like celestial navigation. Before directional instruments were invented, sailors navigated the seas by fixing their compass on the North Star; however, if they fixed on the wrong star, then everything thereafter was off course. We are working against years of a society fixing on the wrong star. This nation has built all its institutions and policies from the starting point of a fundamental lie: that certain groups of people are inferior to others and hence should be subordinated to them. Every direction taken from this fundamental lie puts us off course, and group after group gets lost. If one begins with the lie that people of color are inferior to white people, then it makes equal sense that women are inferior to men. And so it goes. It is our work to fix upon the truth: that all people are of equal worth and deserve justice.

We must do this work as though our lives depend on it. Because they do—all of them, no matter what sex or race or sexual identity or class. There must be justice for all of us or there will be peace for none.

Suzanne Pharr is an organizer, strategist, and writer, working with the Women's Project based in Arkansas. Author of *Homophobia: A Weapon of Sexism*, she is currently working on a book about the rise of the right and our response to it. This chapter originally appeared in the NGLTF publication, *Fight the Right Action Kit*. © 1995, Suzanne Pharr.

Blacks & Gays

Healing the Great Divide

<u>Barbara Smith</u>

Perhaps the most maddening question anyone can ask me is "Which do you put first: being Black or being a woman, being Black or being gay?" The underlying assumption is that I should prioritize one of my identities because one of them is actually more important than the rest or that I must arbitrarily choose one of them over the other for the sake of acceptance in one particular community.

I always explain that I refuse to do political work and, more importantly, live my life in this way. All of the aspects of who I am are essential, indivisible, and pose no inherent conflict. They only seem to be in opposition in this particular time and place, living under US capitalism, a system whose functioning has always required that large groups of people be economically, racially, and sexually oppressed, and that these potentially dissident groups be kept divided from each other at all costs.

As a Black lesbian feminist, I've devoted many years to making the connections between issues and communities and to forging strong working coalitions. Although this work is far from finished, it has met with some success. In 1993, however, two essential aspects of my identity and two communities whose freedom I've always fought for were being publicly defined as being at war with one another.

For the first time, the relationship between the African American and gay communities was being widely debated both within and outside of movement circles. One catalyst for this discussion has been gay leaders cavalierly comparing lifting the military ban with racially desegregating the armed forces following World War II. The NAACP and other Black Civil Rights organizations' decisions to speak out in favor of lesbian and gay rights and to support the April 1993 March on Washington have met with protests from some sectors of the Black community and have also spurred the debate.

Ironically, the group of people who are least often consulted about their perspectives on this great divide are those who are most deeply affected by it: Black lesbian and gay activists. Contradictions that we have been grappling with for years, namely homophobia in the Black community, racism in the gay community, and the need for both communities to work together as allies to defeat our real enemies, are suddenly on other people's minds. Because Black lesbians and gays are not thought of as leaders in either movement, however, this debate has been largely framed by those who have frighteningly little and inaccurate information.

Thanks in part to the white gay community's own public relations campaigns, Black Americans view the gay community as uniformly wealthy, highly privileged, and politically powerful—a group that has suffered nothing like the centuries of degradation caused by US racism. Rev. Dennis Kuby, a civil rights activist, states in a letter to the *New York Times*: "Gays are not subject to water hoses and police dogs, denied access to lunch counters, or prevented from voting." Most Blacks have no idea, however, that we are threatened with the loss of employment, of housing, and custody of our children, and are subject to verbal abuse, gay bashing, and death at the hands of homophobes. Kuby's statement also does not acknowledge those lesbians and gays who have been subjected to all of the racist abuse he cites because we are both Black and gay.

Because we are rendered invisible in both Black and gay contexts, it is that much easier for the Black community to oppose gay rights and to express homophobia without recognizing that these attacks and the lack of legal protections affects its own members.

The racism that has pervaded the mainstream gay movement only fuels the perceived divisions between Blacks and gays. Single issue politics, unlike gay organizing that is consciously and strategically connected to the overall struggle for social and economic justice, does nothing to convince Blacks that gays actually care about eradicating racial oppression. At the very same time that some gays make blanket comparisons between the gay movement and the Black civil rights movement, they also assume that Black and other people of color have won all our battles and are in terrific shape in comparison with gays.

In an interview in the December 1992 *Dallas Voice*, lesbian publisher Barbara Grier states: "We are the last minority group unfairly legislated against in the US." Grier's perception is, of course, inaccurate. Legislation that negatively affects people of color, immigrants, disabled people, and women occurs every day, especially when court decisions that undermine legal protections are taken into account.

In 1991, well before the relationship between the gay community and the Black community was a hot topic, Andrew Sullivan, editor of *The New Republic,* asserted the following in *The Advocate*:

> The truth is, our position is far worse than that of any ethnic minority or heterosexual women.
>
> Every fundamental civil right has already been granted to these groups: The issues that they discuss now involve nuances of affirmative action, comparable pay, and racial quotas. Gay people, however, still live constitutionally in the South of the '50s....
>
> We are not allowed to marry—a right granted to American blacks even under slavery and never denied to heterosexuals. We are not permitted to enroll in the armed services—a right granted decades ago to blacks and to heterosexual women.
>
> Our civil rights agenda, then, should have less to do with the often superfluous minority politics of the 1991 Civil Rights Act and more to do with the vital moral fervor of the Civil Rights Act of 1964.
>
> A better strategy to bring about a society more tolerant of gay men and women would involve dropping our alliance with the current Rainbow Coalition lobby and recapturing the clarity of the original civil rights movement. The point is to rekindle the cause of Martin Luther King, Jr. and not to rescue the career of Jesse Jackson.

Sullivan's cynical distortions ignore that quality of life is determined by much more than legislation. Clearly, he also knows nothing about the institution of slavery. Joblessness, poverty, racist and sexist violence, and the lack of decent housing, health care, and education make the lives of many "ethnic minorities" and "heterosexual women" a living hell. But Sullivan doesn't care about these folks. He just wants to make sure he gets what he thinks he deserves as an upper class white male.

Lesbians and gay men of color have been trying to push the gay movement to grasp the necessity of anti–racist practice for nigh onto 20 years. Except in the context of organizing within the women's movement with progressive white lesbian feminists, we haven't made much progress.

I'm particularly struck by the fact that for the most part queer theory and queer politics, which are currently so popular, offer neither substantial anti–racist analysis nor practice. Queer activists' understanding of how to deal with race is usually limited to their including a few lesbians or gay men of color in their ranks, who are expected to carry out the political agenda that the white majority has already determined.

In October 1993, Lesbian Avengers from New York City traveled to several states in the Northeast on what they called a "freedom ride." Lesbians of color from Albany, New York pointed out that the appropriation of this term was offensive because the organization had not demonstrated involvement in anti–racist organizing and has made no links with people of color, including non–lesbians and gays in the communities they planned to visit. Even when we explained that calling themselves "freedom riders" might negatively affect the coalitions we've been working to build with people of color in Albany, the group kept the name and simply made a few token changes in their press release.

These divisions are particularly dangerous at a time when the white right wing has actually targeted people of color with their homophobic message. As white lesbian activist Suzanne Pharr points out in an excellent article, "Racist Politics and Homophobia," which appeared in the July/August 1993 issue of *Transformation*:

> Community by community, the Religious Right works skillfully to divide us along fissures that already exist. It is as though they have a political seismograph to locate the racism and sexism in the lesbian and gay community, the sexism and homophobia in communities of color. While the Right is *united* by their racism, sexism, and homophobia in their goal to dominate all of us, we are *divided* by our own racism, sexism, and homophobia. [Italics added.]

The right's divisive strategy of enlisting the Black community's support for their homophobic campaign literally hit home for me in June. A Black lesbian who lives in Cleveland, Ohio, where I grew up, called to tell be that a group of Black ministers had placed a virulently homophobic article in the *Call and Post*, Cleveland's Black newspaper.

Entitled "The Black Church Position Statement on Homosexuality," the ministers condemn "HOMOSEXUALITY (including bisexual as well as gay or lesbian sexual activity) as a lifestyle that is contrary to the teachings of the Bible." Although they claim to have tolerance and compassion for homosexuals, their ultimate goal is to bring about "restoration," i.e., changing lesbians and gays back into heterosexuals in order "to restore such individuals back into harmony with God's will." One of the several sources they cite to prove that such "restoration" is possible is the *Traditional Values Foundation Talking Points, 1993*, a publication of the Traditional Values Coalition.

The ministers also held a meetings and announced their goals to gather 100,000 signatures in opposition to the federal civil rights bill, HB 431, and to take their campaign to Detroit and Pittsburgh. A major spokesperson for the ministers, Rev. Marvin McMichol, is the minister of Antioch Baptist Church, the church I was raised in and of which the women in my family were pillars. Antioch is on a number of levels one of the most progressive congregations in Cleveland, especially because of the political leadership it provided at a time when Black people were not allowed to participate in any aspect of Cleveland's civic life.

McMichol states, "It is our fundamental, reasoned belief that there is no comparison between the status of Blacks and women, and the status of gays and lesbians." He explains that being Black or being female is an "ontological reality. . . .a fact that cannot be hidden," whereas "homosexuality is a chosen lifestyle. . .defined by behavior not ontological reality."

By coincidence, I met Rev. McMichol just a month before this time when Naomi Jaffe, an activist friend from Albany, and I did a presentation on Black and Jewish relations at the invitation of Cleveland's New Jewish Agenda. Antioch Baptist and a Jewish synagogue co–sponsored the event. My cousin had informed me that McMichol was a very important person in Cleveland and that he had just stepped down as head of the NAACP. Naomi and I were struck by his coldness to us throughout the evening in sharp contrast to the kind reception we received from both the Black and Jewish participants who were mostly elder women. We guessed that is was because of his homophobia and sexism. Little did we know at the time how right we were.

When I first got news of what was going on in my hometown, I was emotionally devastated. It would have been bad enough to find out about a major Black–led homophobic campaign in any city in this country, but this place wasn't an abstraction, it was where I came from. It was while growing up in Cleveland that I first felt attraction toward women and it was also in Cleveland that I grasped the impossibility of ever acting upon those feelings. Cleveland is a huge city with a small–town mentality. I wanted to get out even before I dreamed of using the word lesbian to describe who I was. College provided my escape. Now I was being challenged to deal with homophobia, dead up, in the Black community at home.

I enlisted the help of the National Gay and Lesbian Task Force (NGLTF), Scot Nakagawa, who runs their Fight the Right office in Portland, Oregon, and members of the Feminist Action Network (FAN), the multi–racial political group to which I belong in Albany. Throughout the summer we were in constant contact with people in Cleveland. FAN drafted a counter petition for them to circulate and in early September several of us went there following NGLTF's and Stonewall Cincinnati's Fight the Right Midwest Summit. Unfortunately, by the time we arrived, the group that had been meeting in Cleveland had fallen apart. We had several meetings primarily with Black lesbians, but found very few people who were willing to confront through direct action the severe threat right in their midst. Remaining closeted, a reluctance to deal with Black people in Cleveland's inner city, and the fact that Cleveland's white lesbian and gay community had never proven itself to be particularly supportive of anti–racist work were all factors that hampered Black lesbian and gay organizing. Ironically, racial segregation seemed to characterize the gay community, just as it does the city as a whole. The situation in Cleveland was very familiar to me, however, because I've faced many of the same roadblocks in attempts to do political work against racism and homophobia in my own community of Albany.

I cannot say that our effort to support a visible challenge to the ministers in Cleveland was particularly successful. The right wing's ability to speak to the concerns and play upon the fears of those it wishes to recruit; the lack of visionary political leadership among both Black and white lesbians and gays both nationally and locally; and the difficulty of countering homophobia in a Black context, especially when it is justified by religious pronouncements, makes this kind of organizing exceedingly hard. But we had better learn how to do it quickly and extremely well if we do not want the pseudo–Christian right wing to end up running this country. Since returning from Cleveland we have been exploring the possibility of launching a nationwide petition campaign to gather at least 100,000 signatures from Black people who support lesbian and gay rights. One Black woman, Janet Perkins, a heterosexual Christian who works with the Women's Project in Little Rock, Arkansas, has already spoken out. In a courageous article entitled "The Religious Right: Dividing the African–American Community" (*Transformation*, September/October 1993), Perkins takes on the ministers in Cleveland and the entire Black church. She calls for Black church members to practice love instead of condemnation. She writes:

> These African–American ministers fail to understand they have been drawn into a plot that has as its mission to further separate, divide and place additional pressure on African–Americans so they are unable to come together to work on the problems of the community. . . .
>
> What is needed in our community is a unity and bond that can't be broken by anyone. We must see every aspect of our community as valuable and worth protecting, and yes we must give full membership to our sisters and brothers who are homosexual. For all these years we have seen them, now we must start to hear them and respect them for who they are.

This is the kind of risk-taking and integrity that makes all the difference. Perkins publicly declares herself an ally who we can depend upon. I hope in the months to come the gay, lesbian, and Black movements in the country will likewise challenge themselves to close this great divide, which they can only do by working toward an unbreakable unity, a bond across races, nationalities, sexual orientations, and classes that up until now our movement has never had.

Barbara Smith is a Black feminist writer and activist. She is the editor of *Home Girls: A Black Feminist Anthology* and is currently a scholar–in–residence at the Schomburg Center for Research in Black Culture, where she is researching the first book–length history of African American lesbians and gays. This is a revised version of an article that first appeared in the special Fall 1993 issue of *Gay Community News*. © 1995, Barbara Smith.

Race, Religion & the Right

Scot Nakagawa

The long history of right-wing activism against the rights of people of color is reflected in their choice of tactics in all of their campaigns. Racist ideology and rhetoric are underpinnings of current anti–gay propaganda and strategy used in the right wing's latest attempts to subvert democratic potential in American society.

Activists organizing against the Religious Right's anti–gay attacks must come to understand how racism and sex oppression are connected in right–wing rhetoric and strategy. This is especially important because the struggle to overcome race–based discrimination provides the legal and ideological foundation for our gay and lesbian liberation struggle and for the larger movement to realize the promise of full civil equality for all people. Any attempt to undermine the civil rights gains made by African Americans and other people of color will undermine the ability of all groups to achieve civil equality.

The History of Race and US Racism

The struggle for multi–racial democracy in the US is a fight against both interpersonal and institutional forms of discrimination that have deep roots in slavery. Racism in the US, as experienced by all people of color, is largely based on the justification for and institutionalization of slavery. Despite the abolition of slavery and the contributions of African Americans to the establishment of a more democratic society during Reconstruction, its legacy persisted both on an interpersonal and institutional level into the 1960s. The historical effects of slavery continue even now to be a critical element of American social, cultural, political, and economic life.

Prior to slavery, Native Americans, Africans, Latinos, and Asians were regarded as subhuman based on religion. To white Americans and Europeans, the world's people existed in two categories: Christian or heathen. The human worth of any individual was defined according to their relationship to a Christian god.

The problem this presented to slaveholders and to those involved in the project of pacifying and destroying Native American nations is that the evangelical nature of Christianity allowed for people of color to "find religion." Hence, the development of the concept of race as a biological or "natural" determinant of human worth, and the subsequent development of a racial hierarchy in the US. Both the science of racialism and the institutionalization of racial hierarchy were constructed as more permanent answers to white America's presumed need for slave labor.

The civil rights movement of the 1960s and the continuing struggle against race–based discrimination is rooted in the struggle against slavery. In the 1960s, African Americans led a fight to remove the legally codified vestiges of slavery from the Constitution and from state and local laws. Most odious among these were Jim Crow laws that required racial segregation.

The right wing has popularized the misconception that the African American–led civil rights movement defines civil rights in the United States. In truth, the civil rights movement of the 1960s was a movement against only one kind of civil rights *violation*—race–based discrimination. Right wing attempts to promote the myth that only people of color have civil rights are based in racism.

The right wing repeatedly states that "legitimate minority status" may only be conferred to those who can be identified as minorities because of "innate, natural characteristics" such as race. However, the concept of race in the US was largely invented, and justified through pseudo–science, by white Americans to rationalize the exploitation and slavery of Blacks.

In short, the concept of race in the American context is a socially constructed system for placing people in a hierarchical structure of social and economic relations. There is nothing "innate" or "natural" about "race."

A Legitimate Minority?

There is no such a thing as "legitimate minority status" as defined by the Religious Right. People of color are not defined as a minority on the basis of income or morality. In fact, right–wing definitions of "morality" have been an obstacle to the achievement of equality for people of color throughout the history of the US.

The right wing has argued that gays and lesbians, and in some cases bisexuals, are not eligible for consideration for "minority status and all the privileges thereof." This argument promotes the myth, popularized by the right wing, that *being a minority in a majority rule society comes with privileges.* As New Right leader Paul Weyrich of the reactionary Free Congress Foundation has stated, "The politicians have been scared because the homosexual lobby, like the civil rights lobby, has exaggerated importance in Washington." When we hear the right wing taking about "minority privileges" and "minority rights," we need to ask just what those privileges and rights are, and whether poor education, substandard housing, and low life expectancy are part of this "special" benefits package.

Acting Affirmatively

Affirmative action has been associated with quotas and called a "special right" by the Religious Right. We need to understand just what affirmative action does and does not do.

Affirmative action is not a "special right." No one has a right to affirmative action. Instead, it is a program that is intended to remedy some problems associated with a historical pattern of discrimination. Because affirmative action is a remedy and not a right, it is not intended to be permanent.

Affirmative action does not mandate quotas that require hiring unqualified people of color to take jobs away from white men. No quotas are associated with affirmative action. Instead, some employers are required to review the racial and gender composition of the qualified applicant pool when hiring new employees. The percentage of those eligible for affirmative action in the qualified applicant pool and the actual applicant pool set a standard intended to prevent discrimination. It is neither true that all people of color are employed because of affirmative action, nor that people of color are the only people to benefit from affirmative action.

More Right–Wing Myths

The Religious Right claims that people of color "deserve" civil rights protections on the grounds that racism has resulted in disproportionate levels of poverty in communities of color.

Leaders of the Religious Right have simultaneously made the claim that racism no longer exists, and have even gone so far as to claim that racism has been reversed and whites are the new victims.

They further claim that Blacks, Latinos, Native Americans, or Asians with higher than average incomes are indices that those people of color who are poor, particularly Blacks, are suffering from a lack of moral rectitude.

Facts They Ignore

How rich or poor someone or some group may be, all have civil rights and the option of making claims of discrimination and demanding government redress of our grievances. While poverty is frequently the result of discrimination, the presence of poverty is not a test for whether any group may enjoy civil rights.

Not all people of color are poor. The proportion of African American families with incomes over $50,000 increased over the last two decades from 10.0 to 13.8 percent.

While the total number of African American families earning more than 50,000 dollars has increased, the median income for Blacks overall has decreased since the 1970s.

These statistics are indicative of the lack of real civil rights protection and enforcement in the 1970s and 1980s. Over this period, there has been a rapid erosion of the gains of the civil rights movement. One key force behind this erosion is the new religious right wing.

Recognizing Connections

The history of racism and the struggle for civil equality of people of color in the United States is far broader and more complex than can be covered in this brief overview. It is critical that we come to understand this history and its impact on contemporary society in order to effectively combat a right-wing movement that has been an integral force in that history, and has as one of its goals a return to the "traditional values" of openly expressed and overtly institutionalized racism.

It is simply not enough for us to "honor diversity." We must recognize that we are the products of a history steeped in racism and sexism, and that our oppression as gay, lesbian, bisexual, and transgendered people is one product of this history. Rather than simply honoring diversity we must build democracy.

Scot Nakagawa is an organizer with the National Gay and Lesbian Task Force's Fight the Right project. This article previously appeared in the NGLTF publication, *Fight the Right Action Kit.* © 1995, Scot Nakagawa.

Assault on Affirmative Action

Adolph Reed, Jr.

Not long ago I rode on the train back from Detroit within earshot of a white, freelance electrician who works for an international corporate temp agency. In the course of chatting about his work with another white passenger, he complained that his Detroit job had been hampered by the rest of his crew. He knew from the time they showed up that they would be a problem, he said, because, "First of all, one of them was Puerto Rican." Nearly everyone else on the car was black, so he may have felt constrained to let the Puerto Rican stand in for other minorities. He then talked disparagingly about how the crew members comported themselves raucously in hotel restaurants and bars— saying nothing at all about the quality of their work.

Later in the conversation, the electrician recounted an incident from a different job, in which a co-worker and buddy locked a donkey in a hotel room as a practical joke. The result was considerable property damage, but he narrated the tale with good humor, as boys–will–be–boys hijinks.

This anecdote underscores a problem that permeates American society and has consequences for many public debates— ranging from affirmative action to capital punishment to welfare: the same or comparable actions are judged differently, depending on the racial identities of the actors.

Now that the Republicans and their right–wing Democratic allies have chosen to make affirmative action their racist "wedge" issue of the year, constructing a reasonable, honest, and progressive perspective on affirmative action is particularly important.

Fundamental to the argument against affirmative action is the view that it makes tradeoffs between merit and quotas.

This view rests on two key premises:

• that it is possible to isolate in the practical world of human choices some pure or absolute notion of merit; and

• that the criteria that determined access to jobs and schools before the advent of affirmative action depended on such a notion of pure merit.

Of course, there is no idea of merit that is innocent of prejudice. Despite all the blather about "reverse discrimination," the closer we get to real cases, the clearer it is that work, school, and our public spaces are still full of precisely the sorts of exclusionist behavior that civil rights enforcement seeks to overcome.

Employers and supervisors base their decisions on considerations that include the extent to which they feel comfortable with a given candidate, their sense of how an individual would "fit" in the workplace situation, and on vague feelings and prior assumptions about candidates' general abilities.

As with the electrician, those assumptions are likely to be influenced by racial or gender stereotypes. Not surprisingly, several studies using discrimination "testers" (pairs of applicants matched on all obviously pertinent characteristics except race) recently have demonstrated that, when black and white candidates are identically qualified on paper, blacks are likely to be rejected in favor of whites for jobs, housing, even automobile purchases.

There is no objective measure that exists entirely apart from human prejudice and ideology.

Early psychometricians interpreted the finding that women performed better than men on some components of IQ tests as evidence of flawed design and adjusted the tests accordingly. Why? Because they presumed from the outset that men are smarter than women and that, therefore, a test result that showed the opposite had to have been structured poorly.

Similarly, Stephen Jay Gould's *Mismeasure of Man* documents the history of "race" researchers' revisions, often inversions, of their indicators of biological superiority upon finding that blacks seemed to score higher than whites on some tests. Pure, "scientific" reasoning decreed that the measures—say, relative lack of body hair—couldn't really indicate preeminence because blacks were clearly inferior.

Women are no longer (at least for the moment) presumed automatically to be less intelligent than men. In fact, intelligence testers have for some time crafted tests to correct for gross gender differences in results. But race differences don't set off the same alarms, because the idea of racial equality in intelligence hasn't yet attained the status of an automatic, incontrovertible assumption. This distinction is highlighted by the fact that the eugenicist book *The Bell Curve* within four months of publication sold 400,000 copies, and has been treated as respectable science by all too many pundits and academics.

The lesson here with respect to affirmative action is that even ostensibly neutral measures can be freighted with prejudice. That is why the US Supreme Court in the 1971 *Griggs v. Duke Power* decision ruled that employers can use hiring and promotion standards that disproportionately exclude blacks only if they can demonstrate that those standards specifically measure the ability to get the job done. (*Bell Curve* authors Charles Murray and Richard Herrnstein attacked the *Griggs* decision early and often.)

It is unquestionably true that until the 1960s blacks directly and explicitly on racial grounds were denied access to public contracts and commercial credit. The effect was that whites enjoyed a competitive advantage that facilitated success in general and gave them a racial monopoly on public contracting in particular.

The same holds for many categories of employment. A white police officer, hired before affirmative action, as likely as not owed his employment and subsequent promotions in part to the existence of a racial and gender monopoly that limited the field against which he had to compete. A white carpenter who belonged to a union that didn't allow black or female members was in the same position.

The benefits accruing from this preferential access to desirable employment, moreover, extend through other aspects of life—from ability to accumulate capital in the form of home ownership and education to, beginning with the New Deal, eligibility for those forms of social welfare targeted to stably employed whites. Employment discrimination intensifies housing inequality, which reinforces unequal access to the political system and public policy, which reinforces unequal access to social resources, which intensifies income inequality, and so on and on. That beneficiaries of these preferences may have worked hard for their attainments does not negate the equally significant fact that their efforts have been aided by the direct, indirect, and cumulative effects of the exclusion of others no less worthy than they.

Still, affirmative action's foes argue that specific efforts to correct for racial bias fly in the face of "fairness." The relative absence of minorities and women from attractive jobs, and the fact that they are clustered in unattractive positions should not, they say, be taken as evidence of discrimination. The logic of this view is that equal opportunity is guaranteed simply by proclaiming a policy of non–discrimination. Anything beyond that—like setting specific goals and standards to overcome discrimination—amounts to mandating quota systems, they say. And quotas reject "merit."

This complaint has a long, nefarious history. Supreme Court Justice Joseph Bradley's opinion in the 1883 decision overturning the 1875 Civil Rights Act proclaimed—18 years after the end of slavery and in the midst of the terrorist reimposition of white supremacy in the South—that it was time that the black American "takes the rank of a mere citizen, and ceases to be the special favorite of the laws."At bottom, this perspective assumes that the real–world dynamics that concentrate advantages among whites or men don't mean a thing about equal opportunity. Systemic white or male privilege is presumed to be a reasonable, natural expression of merit. This at least verges on an assumption of inherent white, male superiority. The acceptance of white, male social privilege as natural lay behind Reagan and Bush Administrations' lawsuits challenging affirmative action plaintiffs to show an actual intent to discriminate—a requirement that is practicably impossible to satisfy.

The Supreme Court majority in recent years has relied on an intent standard and has disregarded history and social context in a number of civil rights rulings. *The City of Mobile v. Bolden* ruling in 1980 upheld the city's use of an at–large electoral system, even though no blacks had been able to win seats on the city council. The court held that black underrepresentation could not be taken as sufficient evidence of discrimination. Alabama's—and Mobile's own—segregationist history, according to this interpretation, is irrelevant. The burden lay with those claiming exclusion to prove discriminatory intent.

The 1989 *Richmond v. Croson* ruling extended this logic to affirmative action in municipal contracting. In throwing out the city's minority set–aside program, the Supreme Court ruled that a pattern of extreme under-representation (blacks made up more than 50 percent of the population, and fewer than 1 percent of contractors) doesn't constitute evidence of entrenched patterns of exclusion sufficient to justify extraordinary measures to create equality of opportunity.

The 1992 *Shaw v. Reno* ruling made a comparable argument in throwing out the Congressional-reapportionment scheme that made it possible to elect the first black representatives in this century from North Carolina–a state that as recently as the late 1960s was home to more Ku Klux Klansmen than any other. And in its current session, the court—in ruling for white firefighters claiming reverse discrimination as a result of a municipal hiring and promotion plan aimed at approaching parity in black representation—treated as irrelevant even the particularly sordid white–supremacist history of Birmingham, Alabama.

To defend these illogical decisions, opponents of affirmative action have seized on a set of misleading arguments that revolve around the theme that affirmative action actually is self–defeating. One such claim is that affirmative action stigmatizes its beneficiaries as unqualified and therefore *creates* racist stereotypes, resentment, and thus discrimination. Another is that it instills in those beneficiaries debilitating doubts about both their competence and their white, male colleagues' perceptions of their abilities. Yet another is that affirmative action restricts opportunity for minorities and women by slotting them into narrow quotas. The notion that affirmative action creates racism is an old chestnut; it has been applied to every initiative undertaken in support of racial equality from the Fourteenth Amendment to the *Brown* decision and the 1964 Civil Rights Act. It collapses before the simple fact that widespread racist practices prompted anti–discrimination efforts in the first place.

The claim that affirmative action is intended to compensate for past suffering—a kind of reparations—has become conventional and is even bandied about by ostensibly progressive pundits. This formulation gives rise to diatribes about how much whose immigrant grandparents suffered themselves and how many of them owned slaves and other such pointless blather. But the purpose of affirmative action is to remove fetters on equality of opportunity by attacking *existing* patterns of inequality that originate from current discrimination and the cumulative results of past exclusion and discrimination.

Opponents now often claim that affirmative action is ineffective because it mainly benefits the well–off. But studies by Martin Carnoy (in his 1994 book, *Faded Dreams*) and Jonathan Leonard (in the *Review of Economics and Statistics* and the *Journal of Human Resources*) find a significant positive effect of anti–discrimination efforts for *all* skill levels among black Americans. And anecdotal information certainly supports those findings.

In the academic world, anti–discrimination policies have induced admissions committees to look more closely at pools of students who would earlier have been dismissed out of hand. And affirmative action guidelines for faculty hiring practices have been largely responsible for proliferation of open, nationally advertised searches and regularized procedures that break down nepotism and inbreeding.

The most visible recent "reverse discrimination" controversy illustrates the weakness of the anti–affirmative action position in academia. In *Cheryl J. Hopwood v. University of Texas Law School*, it turns out that race was not a salient factor. The alleged victims were unlikely to have been admitted even if no blacks or Latinos had applied. Their academic records, in fact, were medio- cre. The plain fact is that the charge of special preferences is a smokescreen. The options are not affirmative action or some pris- tine world in which "merit" is its own reward, but affirmative ac- tion or naked discrimination and exclusion.

Adolph Reed, Jr. teaches at Northwestern University and is co–chair of the Coalition for New Priorities. He writes frequently on issues of class, race, and social justice including a column for the Progressive where this chapter first appeared in June 1995. © 1995, Adolph Reed, Jr.

Black Conservatives

Deborah Toler

For most African Americans the notion of a Black conservative is an oxymoron. The overwhelming majority of us reject conservative political positions because we understand in concrete, everyday, practical terms what conservative policies are and who conservatives are, and we know both are racist. Conservative policies are Republican vetoes of civil rights bills, opposition to affirmative action, and Willie Horton campaign ads. Conservatives are Ronald Reagan, George Bush, Jesse Helms, David Duke, and Pat Buchanan. Enough said. *

Unlike the majority of African Americans, Black conservatives generally oppose affirmative action and government minority business set–aside programs, oppose minimum wage laws and rent control laws, oppose any increase in social welfare spending, and oppose vigorous enforcement of voting rights and desegregation regulations. Black conservatives favor the death penalty, privatization of government services, deregulation of business, and voucher systems for public housing and for education.

---

* The term racist and racism in this paper refer to the most pernicious form in this country, an ideological outlook or system of beliefs by an individual or institution that incorporate one or more of the following conscious or unconscious premises: that the core values that define America are inextricably linked to the white northern European middle and upper class experience; that the problems in communities of color are primarily due to flawed individual characteristics of the people of color themselves; that racial tensions in America are primarily due to the unreasonable demands of people of color; and that people of color, especially African Americans, are biologically inferior to white Americans in terms of mental capacity, moral character, or ambition.

Also out of step with the Black majority are Black conservatives' right–wing foreign policy views. Rabidly anti–communist, in the 1980s Black conservatives supported US–backed, right–wing governments and guerrilla movements throughout Central and South America. In Africa, they support right–wing factions such as UNITA in Angola, RENAMO in Mozambique, and the Inkatha Freedom Party in South Africa. Black conservatives are often unquestioning supporters of Israel and, more important, are anti–Palestinian.

Politically conservative African American notables traditionally have been an anomaly in the African American community; examples are Booker T. Washington, Zora Neale Hurston, George Schuyler, and Joe Black. Prior to the Clarence Thomas Senate Judiciary Committee hearings' televised parade of Black conservatives, most African Americans outside the academy and policy–making circles were not aware that a number of well–known and influential African–Americans make the same imperialist, classist, and, most particularly, racist arguments made by white conservatives.

Academic and media discussions of Black conservatives focus on the specific merits or flaws of their arguments and policy positions. But the more interesting and instructive question which will be explored here is: how can Black conservatives echo the fundamentally racist arguments of white conservatives and, further, be institutionally and organizationally allied with the sector of white America that is historically most racist?

Black conservatives, of course, deny that the policy positions of white conservatives are racist. They claim African Americans' fear of self–criticism blinds us to what is only principled racial criticism. Black conservatives choose to ignore, or consign to "water over the dam" status, Martin Kilson's trenchant observation that "at no point in the 20th–century have the claims of Black folks for political and social parity gained active support or sympathy from mainstream American conservative leaders, organizations, and intellectuals, whether religious or secular." Indeed, conservative whites are often active opponents of African American civil rights.

I will argue that Black conservatives are able to engage in delusions regarding the racist orientations and activities of their white conservative intellectual mentors and allies because of a congruence between white conservative interpretations of African Americans and the Black bourgeoisie's long–standing negative interpretation of who Black people are. These Black bourgeois attitudes, which denigrate poor African Americans, are very much the result of the socioeconomic development of the Black bourgeoisie within the context of white cultural oppression.

These negative attitudes toward poor members of the community have historically been shared by the liberal and conservative Black bourgeoisie alike. At the turn of the century, for example, both Booker T. Washington and a young W. E. B. DuBois shared the view that, in DuBois's words, the way to alleviate "the present friction between the races" was to correct the "immorality, crime, and laziness among Negroes themselves" ("The Conservation of Race," 1897).

The difference between liberal and conservative Black bourgeois attitudes is that Black liberals also recognize the structural obstacles to Black progress. Black liberals believe the primary focus ought to be on creating "a new America." Today's Black conservatives adopt the classic Black conservative view of Booker T. Washington, one focusing on creating "a new Negro." Like Washington, they view African Americans as a somehow "unfinished" product of slavery, still needing to prove ourselves worthy of the rights of other American citizens. This subtle and subversive aspect of Black conservative intellectuals' arguments has gone largely unnoticed and unanalyzed.

Black conservatives echo white conservatives' racist arguments and ally themselves with white conservative racist elements because they share similar views of African Americans and of the causes of Black oppression and Black poverty.

It is Black conservative *intellectuals* who have consistently received media attention and have been most influential in policy formulation. Therefore, Black conservative intellectuals will be the focus here, specifically six men who received the greatest attention throughout the 1980s: Glenn Loury, Thomas Sowell, Walter Williams, Robert Woodson, Shelby Steele, and Stephen Carter.

But it is important to recognize that we have yet to see a Black conservative movement per se, not only because there are only a limited number of African Americans who hold conservative political views, but also because the same kinds of philosophical splits that divide the white right also divide the Black right.

Black Conservative Factions

A small group of conservative Black intellectuals and political officials have defined the intellectual parameters of the Black conservative argument. Like neoconservatives, almost all were once liberal/left Democrats. Like neoconservatives, they are pro–Israel and anti–affirmative action. They are to the left of ultraconservatives like Patrick Buchanan, but the boundary between the ideological positions of Black conservatives and ultraconservatives is often porous. Blacks who are philosophically similar to neoconservatives share most of the traditional values movement's positions and are more than willing to take advantage of the financial and organizing power of more extreme Religious Right conservatives, such as Pat Robertson.

The best known of Black conservative intellectuals are Thomas Sowell, an economist at the conservative Hoover Institution on War, Revolution and Peace, and Walter Williams, economics professor at George Mason University in Alexandria, Virginia. Sowell and Williams are conventional "free market" conservatives in the mold of Milton Friedman. Slightly more moderate Black conservatives include: Glenn Loury, an economist formerly at Harvard University's Kennedy School of Government and currently professor of economics at Boston University; Shelby Steele, English professor at San Jose State College; Stephen Carter, law professor at Yale University; and the only activist in the group, Robert Woodson, founder and president of a research and development organization in Washington, DC, the National Center for Neighborhood Enterprise.

Throughout the 1980s, a group of younger Black conservatives was touted in the media as the "next generation" of Black conservative intellectuals. Representative of this group are Joseph Perkins, a former aide to Vice–President Dan Quayle and the second youngest journalist ever hired by the *Wall Street Journal*, now on the staff of the *San Diego Union Tribune*; Deroy Murdock, who served as an aide to conservative Republican Senator Orrin Hatch of Utah and was the subject of a front page cover story in the Style section of the *Washington Post*; and Kevin Pritchett, former staffer and editor of the infamous right–wing student newspaper at Dartmouth College, the *Dartmouth Review*.

Few women appear in Black conservative ranks. It is unclear whether this reflects Black women's rejection of conservative ideas or if this is due to the combination of racism and sexism that diminishes and obscures all Black women's contributions, or a combination of both. Prominent among the few identifiable Black conservative women intellectuals are Illinois State University sociologist and Ayn Rand disciple Anne Wortham, and Harvard–trained Eileen Gardener, a researcher at the ultra–conservative Heritage Foundation in Washington, DC. Wortham is better known than Gardener because her book, *The Other Side of Racism*, has received attention. This harangue against basic precepts of modern human rights and civil rights campaigns is too extreme, however, even for most Black conservative intellectuals. Wortham is nonetheless influential in some far right circles. Another Black conservative, Heritage Foundation's Minority Outreach Director Claudia Butts, served briefly as the Bush Administration's White House liaison to Blacks.

Another group of Black conservatives who captured media attention in the 1980s were officials and appointees from the Reagan and Bush Administrations. In the Reagan Administration, the best known were White House staffer William Keyes, State Department appointee and twice–failed Senate Republican candidate Alan Keyes (no relation to William), the late Clarence Pendleton, Reagan's Chairman of the US Civil Rights Commission, Samuel Pierce, the scandal–ridden director of Housing and Urban Development (HUD), and William B. Allen, appointed to the US Civil Rights Commission in 1987.

In the Bush Administration, Michael L. Williams, Department of Education Assistant Secretary for Civil Rights, was known for his independent 1990 ruling that college scholarships awarded on the basis of race were illegal. Supreme Court Justice Clarence Thomas, formerly a member of the Reagan Administration, is not only the best known of all Black conservatives, but within the African American community is the only Black conservative whose name is both widely known and is immediately equated with conservative politics.

There is a mistaken tendency to lump all Black Republicans into the Black conservatives category. Representative Gary Franks, for example, is the only Republican in the Congressional Black Caucus and is also a well–known Black conservative. But Franks and other Black conservative Republicans are atypical. It is true that most Black Republicans are generally conservative on business–related tax and regulation policy issues and are typically more socially conservative than Black Democrats. But the majority of Black Republicans are also admitted beneficiaries and staunch supporters of affirmative action programs and, as such, are located in the vanishing moderate wing of the party. During the Reagan and Bush Administrations, numerous skirmishes erupted between liberal and conservative Black Republicans as both vied for the ear of the White House and fought alongside their respective white counterparts for the soul of the Republican Party.

There is also a cluster of Blacks, former civil rights leaders, and entertainers, whom most African Americans recognize but do not necessarily associate with conservative causes. Of these, Tony Brown, host of the popular PBS talk show "Tony Brown's Journal," is the most influential. Brown, very much in the mold of Black conservative intellectuals Thomas Sowell, Walter Williams, and Robert Woodson, preaches "self–help" capitalism as the solution to Black problems. Many of Brown's African American fans remain unaware that he became a Republican in 1991.

Former National Football League star Roosevelt Grier works with World Impact, a Los Angeles–based evangelical Christian organization, and is a prominent Republican celebrity figure. Other Black conservative media stars include Marva Collins, whose Chicago West–side Preparatory School was the subject of a "60 Minutes" story and a made–for–television movie, and Joe Clark, the baseball–bat–wielding principal of Patterson, New Jersey's Eastside High School. Clark became a favorite of then–Secretary of Education William Bennett and his exploits provided the storyline for the feature film "Lean on Me."

African Americans, especially those of us old enough to remember the civil rights era, have been shocked by the conservative turn taken by such former civil rights stalwarts as James Meredith, Roy Innis, the Rev. James Bevel, and the late Rev. Ralph Abernathy. In 1962, James Meredith became the first Black student to integrate the University of Mississippi. In 1989, Meredith became the first Black professional on the staff of North Carolina Republican Senator Jesse Helms. Most recently, he ran unsuccessfully for the Mississippi House seat vacated by President Clinton's Secretary of Agriculture, Mike Espy. Although most African Americans know that Abernathy, Innis, and Bevel all adopted conservative politics, few are aware of just how far right these former civil rights leaders have turned, or that they have ties to authoritarian, right–wing organizations. Abernathy worked until his death with Rev. Sun Myung Moon's Unification movement. Innis has worked in alliance with Lyndon La Rouche's organizations. And Rev. Bevel now works closely with groups controlled by both Moon and LaRouche.

Ties with the Traditional Values Movement

A more narrowly focused group of Black conservatives comes out of the right–wing traditional values movement within the Black community. This group merits special attention. Notwithstanding the occasional secular group, it is primarily made up of Black Christian fundamentalist groups, and its followers differ significantly from Black conservative intellectuals and bureaucrats. Unlike the former, the traditional values people are part of a movement and, as such, engage in constituency–building activities. Whereas conservative Black intellectuals and political officials uniformly scoff at Afrocentrism, some of the Black fundamentalist groups adhere to strongly Afrocentric orientations. Indeed, the combination of hard–core Christian fundamentalism with Afrocentrism contains the potential for schisms within Black Christian fundamentalism and certainly with the notoriously racist elements of the white Christian fundamentalist movement as a whole.

The larger, predominantly white traditional values move- ment is well placed to receive more attention as the right gears up to fight the Clinton Administration's policies on abortion, AIDS, and sex education in schools. Indeed, as the right–wing Christian fundamentalist and traditional values movements continue to or- ganize to overtake the Republican Party at the local level, and as their influence on US politics spreads, those Black Americans af- filiated with the positions of the traditional values movement are positioned to garner as much attention in the 1990s as the Black conservative intellectuals did in the 1980s. This is particularly true given that the African American community, while tradi- tionally liberal on political issues, is also traditionally conserva- tive on social issues, such as abortion rights and homosexual rights.

Dr. Mildred Jefferson, a physician who was the first Black woman to graduate from Harvard Medical School, has long been a star in the traditional values movement. Dr. Jefferson was a founder and former chairman of the National Right to Life Com- mittee, and served three terms as the organization's president. She is currently chair of the National Right to Life Crusade. Jef- ferson is joined by several other lesser lights who are asserting themselves as movement spokespeople: Los Angeles school teacher Ezola Foster, Rev. Cleveland Sparrow in Washington, DC, Greg Keath in Michigan, and Rev. Edward V. Hill in Los Angeles.

Keath is the leader of two groups, Rescue Black America (RBA) and the Alliance for Family, both staunch opponents of abortion. Rescue Black America uses tactics similar to those used by anti–abortion groups such as Operation Rescue. Like Keath, Washington, DC minister Cleveland Sparrow is also adamantly opposed to abortion, but his organization, the National Coalition for Black Traditional Values (NCBTV), increasingly is targeting homosexual civil rights issues and AIDS anti–discrimination laws. Sparrow was formerly head of the Moral Majority chapter in the District of Columbia, and is gathering increasing political clout in the white conservative establishment. Sparrow aligned himself with Senator Jesse Helms (R–NC) and Representative William Dannemeyer (R–CA) in an effort to overturn a Washington, DC, City Council ordinance that bars insurance companies from refus- ing coverage to people who test positive for the HIV virus.

Ezola Foster's Los Angeles–based Black Americans for Fam- ily Values (BAFV) also opposes homosexual rights and AIDS anti– discrimination laws, as well as a woman's right to abortion, AIDS education, and sex education in schools. Arguing in 1988 that the issue was whether Republicans want to send voters the message that "it is the party of the family. . .[or] the party of perverts," Foster has repeatedly supported efforts by Representative William Dannemeyer and other right–wing Republicans to get the California GOP to ban gay Republican clubs from the party. Edward V. Hill is pastor of the 2,000–member Mount Zion Missionary Baptist Church in the Watts section of Los Angeles. He is a close friend of Jerry Falwell and was a member of Falwell's now–defunct Moral Majority. Hill once dismissed protesters picketing his church during a Falwell visit, saying the protesters were "Muslims, homosexuals, and abortionists."

The Lincoln Institute & Clarence Thomas

In terms of institutional structures for disseminating Black conservative ideas, the Lincoln Institute for Research and Education in Washington, DC, is *the* bastion of Black conservatism. Founded by Jay A. Parker in 1978, the Institute illustrates the typically overlooked importance of Black conservatives to conservative US foreign policy agendas.

Since its founding, the Lincoln Institute has had close ties to the extreme rightist World Anti–Communist League (WACL). WACL aggressively supported right–wing governments and military movements in Central America and Southern Africa, such as the Contras in Nicaragua, the ARENA Party in El Salvador, UNITA in Angola, RENAMO in Mozambique, and the Inkatha Freedom Party in South Africa, among others. Parker served on the Board of the US WACL affiliate and Lee Edwards, another Lincoln Institute founder, was a principal WACL organizer in the United States and WACL's registered agent in 1982.

Clarence Thomas, widely portrayed as a neoconservative, is a classic illustration of the murkiness of the dividing line between mainstream conservatives and ultra–conservatives. Clarence Thomas and Jay A. Parker served together on Ronald Reagan's 1980 transition team for the Equal Employment Opportunity Commission (EEOC). According to Parker, the team "argued strenuously" against affirmative action, which they viewed as "a new racism." By March 1981, Parker had become a registered agent for the South African homeland of Venda. In June 1981, Clarence Thomas joined the Advisory Board of the Lincoln Institute's quarterly publication, *The Lincoln Review*. At the same time, Thomas became an Assistant Secretary of Education. Parker's Justice Department filings state that soon after he began representing Venda, he held discussions with US Department of Education officials about his client.

In 1985, Parker and William Keyes, the former Reagan aide (and a contributing editor for *The Lincoln Review*), founded a lobbying organization called International Public Affairs Consultants, Inc. (IPAC). That same year, IPAC began representing the

South African Embassy. Clarence Thomas was listed as one of a handful of guests attending an IPAC dinner for the South African Ambassador in 1987. In 1984, Keyes started Black PAC, with Parker serving as treasurer, to work for Jesse Helms's re-election, and to oppose the "terrorist outlaw" African National Congress (ANC) and "extremists" such as Jesse Jackson and the Congressional Black Caucus. In June 1987, the conservative weekly *Human Events* reported that Thomas, then of the EEOC, and Clarence Pendleton, who was then Reagan's chair of the US Civil Rights Commission, attended a Black PAC strategy session to plan for important political battles being waged in Congress.

Also in June 1987, Thomas made a well-known speech at the Heritage Foundation, in which he said: "A few dissidents like Thomas Sowell and J. A. Parker stand steadfast, refusing to give in to the cult mentality and childish obedience that hypnotize black Americans into a mindless political trance. I admire them, and only wish I had a fraction of their courage and strength." Thomas remained on *The Lincoln Review*'s Advisory Board throughout the period Parker and Keyes represented the South African government, resigning at the time he was appointed to the Federal Court of Appeals in March 1990.

Black Conservative Publications

The Lincoln Review and the quarterly *Issues and Views*, published and edited by Elizabeth Wright of New York City, are the most prominent Black conservative publications. Both quarterlies publish articles by and about Black conservatives. *The Lincoln Review* focuses on both domestic and foreign policy. During the Cold War, the *Review* was known for its rabid anti-communist editorial line. The *Review* is anti-choice, pro-death penalty, anti-affirmative action, pro-defense spending, anti-Martin Luther King national holiday, pro-school prayer, anti-Washington, DC statehood. It is also unreservedly and uncritically supportive of Israel.

Issues and Views focuses on "self-help" and entrepreneurial activity in the Black community. Jay Parker and Walter Williams are advisors to *Issues and Views*. Lesser-known publications include Emmanuel McLittle's *Destiny* magazine, published in East Lansing, Michigan, and Earl Ofari Hutchinson's bi-monthly newsletter. Hutchinson is a Pacific News Service commentator and owner of IMPACT! Publications.

Black Conservative Thought

Given how widely lauded they are in mainstream media, it is disappointing to actually read Black conservatives' work. What comes to mind is Lewis A. Coser's comment in his 1974 edited book, *The New Conservatives*: "These new conservatives do not give the impression of having reflected in a sustained and systematic manner on political philosophy. They express a mood and a fashion rather than a deeply felt political stance. They seem to be sustained by a desire to seize the shifting Zeitgeist by its tail, and they batten on the mood of disillusionment that has seized the country after the hopes of the early 1960s."

Black conservatives' work does not exhibit a sustained and systematic examination of conservative political philosophy and its potential usefulness for Black Americans. Nor do the Black conservatives, most of whom are trained social scientists, engage in credible social science research. They ignore reams of data contradicting their underlying assumptions and fail to produce reliable statistical evidence or to generate ethnographic research to support their positions.

Contrary to the impression, presented in mainstream media accounts, that Black conservatives offer "new," "innovative," and "advanced" ideas, there is little new in what Black conservative intellectuals have to say. For the most part, they merely repeat long–standing white conservative and neoconservative arguments. They build on a philosophical foundation borrowed from Booker T. Washington, and incorporate self–help bromides of Black cultural nationalist rhetoric. What is new in Black conservatives' analyses is that it is Black people developing an implicitly racist rationale for placing limits on social policies.

In somewhat simplified form, Black conservatives' explicit analysis rests on five fundamental points:

• Although lingering racism still exists, thanks to the victories of the civil rights struggles, racial discrimination is no longer a critical obstacle to Black progress. We can speak of a racist American past, but not of a racist contemporary America.
• African American demands for equal opportunity made during the civil rights era now go too far in demanding equal *outcomes*. A non–discriminatory America does not ensure equal outcomes. Capitalism maximizes skill and talent and any differences among ethnic groups, or between genders, is a function of each group's particular strengths and weaknesses.
• Today's problems of race relations and Black poverty cannot be remedied by government policy alone. The roots of today's problems are located first and foremost within African Americans: in our inability to successfully compete in a free market system, in the poor values and irresponsible and offensive behavior of poor Blacks, in our psychological hang–ups about group identity and past victimization, and/or in our failure to take full advantage of existing opportunities. In this light, not

only are government social welfare and legal remedies, such as affirmative action programs, unnecessary, they are detrimental to the development of Black people. Social welfare programs destroy Black families, foster debilitating dependency, and reward irresponsible behavior.

- Affirmative action programs lower Black self–esteem since whites will always diminish Black accomplishment as reflecting only affirmative action imperatives and Black beneficiaries of affirmative action programs can never be fully confident that their success stems from their talent. These programs are also detrimental to Blacks because of the white (male) resentment they engender. Affirmative action has, in any case, only benefited more advantaged Blacks.

- The appropriate strategy for African Americans is one focusing on self –help. First, we need to de–emphasize racial identity and loyalty in favor of an *American* identity. Second, African Americans should compete on the basis of merit only. Third, we need to de–emphasize government programs and civil rights legislation in favor of racial self–help. Blacks need to focus on Black entrepreneurship, building and supporting Black business, particularly in poor Black neighborhoods. And, most important, the Black middle class needs to teach poor African Americans appropriate values and behavior.

Black Conservatism & White Conservatism

Black conservative thought is related to two analyses of African American oppression promoted by white conservatives: the idealized Free Market School and the Culturalist School. In other words, the grounding for Black conservative thought is found in the work of white conservatives.

Economists Thomas Sowell and Walter Williams come out of the market–centered school of economic thought dominated by Milton Friedman and Gary Becker. This school argues that it is not in the interest of white employers and white workers to oppose Black employment opportunities. Such racist behavior is against market rationality, and therefore prevents the maximization of profits. The best policy is to educate and persuade white employers and white workers to be rational, to function in their own best interest. The market school advocates "pure" market mechanisms to undermine "racist" tastes, without government intervention. Freedom, in the market view, is defined as the extent to which capital is left unfettered in its drive to maximize profit.

Thomas Sowell, a student of Friedman and the intellectual progenitor of today's Black conservatives, promotes this idealized free market approach. In his 1975 book, *Race and Economics*, and in more than eight books that followed, Sowell has argued that government intervention, in the form of anti–discrimination laws and other employment regulations, has had negative consequences for disadvantaged people. Sowell insists that because racism is inefficient and economically irrational, market mechanisms alone are sufficient to erode racist behavior.

Sowell has introduced a market version of today's "culture of poverty" argument. He argues that variations in racial and ethnic success are a function of a differential distribution of values, attitudes, and other cultural traits among different racial and ethnic groups. He argues that a "culture of poverty" hampers Blacks' ability to successfully play the game of market capitalism. "The point," Sowell says in his 1983 book, *Economics and the Politics of Race*, "is not to praise, blame or rank whole races and cultures. The point is simply to recognize that economic performance differences are quite real and quite large."

Walter Williams goes to extreme and bizarre lengths to develop what is, in effect, a defense of racism under the cover of protecting freedom of choice and capitalist rationality. In doing so, Williams makes selective and unscientific use of data, and changes language and definitions to meet his specific needs. In Williams' definition, "prejudice" is simply a process of pre– judging, making a judgment based upon existing knowledge. Hence, if employers refuse to hire young Black males, it is due not to prejudice, but to their pre–existing knowledge about young Black males' low levels of education and/or poor work habits. Discrimination is informed preference, similar to being discriminating in one's taste.

Most Black conservatives are grounded in a second white conservative analysis of the nature of Black oppression and Black poverty, the culturalist school. Black conservatives' culturalist arguments repeat the implicitly classist, sexist, and racist arguments first developed by Daniel Patrick Moynihan, Edward C. Banfield, Charles Murray, and many other white conservatives and neoconservatives to explain Black poverty. Like these white conservatives, Black conservatives locate the most significant causes of Black poverty in African American culture, particularly in the culture of Black, female–headed households.

In their claims that poor African Americans are somehow inherently and generically defective, culturalist arguments come perilously close to a third conservative analysis, the overtly racist claim that Blacks are genetically inferior, made by conservative white sociobiologist theorists such as Arthur Jensen and Richard Herrnstein.

The Negro Family: The Case for National Action, published in 1965 and popularly known as *The Moynihan Report*, is the most significant early statement of the current crop of "culture of poverty" and "underclass" theories. Drawing selectively from Black sociologist E. Franklin Frazier's methodologically flawed study, *The Negro Family in the United States* (1966), Moynihan's central thesis was that the Black family is immersed in a weak and unstable subculture. In this subculture, matriarchy is the dominant form, severe unemployment exaggerates the situation, the weak Black family produces children who are incapable of enjoying educational and employment opportunities, and no meaningful change is possible until that family is strengthened "from within." Government programs, argued Moynihan, are useless until such changes take place. It was *The Moynihan Report* that made it respectable to place the source of Black poverty within the Black community itself.

Edward C. Banfield's 1970 book, *The Unheavenly City*, developed the class aspects of the "culture of poverty" argument. Banfield concluded that the character and content of low–income groups' culture inhibits them from competing with others in American society. Banfield claimed that, "The lower–class forms of all problems are at bottom a single problem: the existence of an outlook and style of life which is radically present–oriented and which therefore attaches no value to work, sacrifice, self–improvement, or service to family, friends, or community. Social workers, teachers, and law enforcement officials. . .cannot achieve their goals because they can neither change nor circumvent this cultural obstacle."

Charles Murray's 1984 book, *Losing Ground*, goes further, claiming that because Moynihan's and Banfield's theories were correct, government social welfare programs have not only failed to work, but have exacerbated the problem by rewarding "antisocial" and irresponsible behavior, such as having children outside of marriage, and have promoted a crippling dependency on government hand–outs. Murray advocated, as do some Black conservatives, eliminating every federal benefit program for the non–elderly poor.

Economist Glenn Loury has most consistently and coherently repeated the Moynihan/Banfield/Murray culturalist arguments, in a series of articles and in his 1987 book, *Free at Last? Racial Advocacy in the Post Civil–Rights Era*. According to Loury, "What is important to the alleviation of black poverty and racism is not the economic structure of the United States nor the racist behavior of whites, but African–Americans' behavior. Further progress toward the attainment of equality depends most crucially at this juncture on the acknowledgment of the dysfunctional behaviors which plague black communities and so offend others."

Similarly, Shelby Steele reckons, "There was much that [President Ronald] Reagan had to offer blacks, his emphasis on traditional American values—individual initiative, self-sufficiency, strong families—offered what I think is the most enduring solution to the demoralization and poverty that continue to widen the gap between blacks and whites in America. Even his de–emphasis of race was reasonable in a society where race only divides."

Black conservatives maintain, as did Booker T. Washington, and as do white conservatives such as Moynihan, that African Americans emerged from slavery "not ready for prime time." Slavery, they argue, left us ill–equipped for full participation in either the economic or political life of the country. As Shelby Steele says, "But, though it [the Emancipation Proclamation] delivered greater freedom, it did not deliver the skills and attitudes that are required to thrive in freedom. . . .Oppression conditions people away from all the values and attitudes one needs in freedom—individual initiative, self–interested hard work, individual responsibility, delayed gratification. . . .These values. . .were muted and destabilized by the negative conditioning of [our] oppression. I believe that since the mid–sixties our weakness in this area has been a far greater detriment to our advancement than any remaining racial discrimination."

Thomas Sowell puts it more bluntly in his analysis that African Americans came out of slavery with ". . .the enduring stigma of hard manual, or menial labor," which "has produced an anti–work ethic handicapping blacks. . . ." In other words, African Americans are lazy.

In order to understand Black conservatism, it is important to understand the character of the Black bourgeoisie. Developing as it did within the context of white cultural oppression, it is not surprising that the values identified by Black conservative intellectuals such as Shelby Steele and Thomas Sowell as "traditional American values" are hallmarks of both American conservative mythology and Black bourgeois mythology. The ethic of "individual initiative" and "strong families" are values intimately related to the stereotypes that locate Black poverty in the misbehavior of those Blacks who do not make progress.

Black bourgeois mythology is a powerful theme in the African American community, one that exists on two layers. First, like the conservative Horatio Alger myth, Black bourgeois mythology asserts that values and behavior determine economic success. Second, the myth maintains that middle class African Americans are different from other African Americans. The development of the

Black bourgeoisie is rooted in its apartness from the Black mass majority.

Prior to desegregation, African Americans of all socioeconomic groups lived in the same segregated communities. The economic and political position of the Black bourgeoisie depended on the business and political support of poorer Blacks living under segregated circumstances. Nonetheless, most of the Black bourgeoisie historically has seen itself (even when white America has not) as different from the Black masses, in attitude and behavior, as well as in economic success.

Histories of the socio–cultural development of the Black middle class emphasize the pivotal role played by schooling for newly freed slaves, schooling which often would make them members of an incipient Black bourgeoisie in the immediate post–Civil War era. Initially, most of this schooling was carried out by white missionaries and abolitionists from the North, and later by Black graduates of their schools. These white instructors were intent on imparting the Puritan work ethic and morality prevalent in white schools of the day. Thus, among other things, the schooling emphasized "proper" sexual behavior. Schools demanded that students be chaste, especially the girls, and all students were expected to marry and live "conventional" family lives.

The emphasis on "moral" sexual behavior had special significance in the case of Black students. White Northern teachers emphasized it because, using paternalistic and implicitly racist reasoning, they believed it the best way to disprove Southern white racists' belief that the Negro's "savage instincts" prevented him from conforming to puritanical sex behavior.

"Moral" sexual behavior resonated with newly freed slaves for a number of reasons—among them, the sexual exploitation and denial of the right to family life under slavery, and the teachings of the Black Church.

In addition to insisting on high moral standards, schooling for the incipient Black middle class added the classist and racist concept that only "common Negroes" engaged in "unconventional" sexual behavior and a wide array of other "dysfunctional," "primitive" behaviors, such as laziness, boisterousness, improvidence, and drunkenness. Thus, it was their values and their behaviors that made Black elites elite and set them apart from the Black masses.

It is no accident that today both liberal and conservative Black elites are preoccupied by what is, in reality, a nonexistent "epidemic" of Black teen pregnancies, or that poor, female–headed households receive special opprobrium. In part, this stems from the overall patriarchal character of US culture—one in which white ethnic groups' poverty is also largely blamed on female–

headed households. But sexual behavior has long been a touchstone of Blacks' civilized status.

Indeed, it is important to recognize that a historical strain in Black political agitation was that elite Blacks were being denied the rights they deserved by virtue of having proved themselves "civilized," i.e., better than and separate from "common Negroes." In the words of Adolph Reed, Jr., "Race spokespersons commonly have included in their briefs against segregation (or discrimination in other forms) an objection that its purely racial character fails to differentiate among blacks and lumps the respectable, cultivated, and genteel in with the rabble."

I emphasize this because far too little attention has been paid to the extent to which Black conservatives' arguments—whether delineating the causes of Black oppression, locating the causes of Black poverty, or (as will be seen) making the case against affirmative action—all come back to issues of distinguishing middle class from poor Blacks. This holds also for Black conservatives as individuals, and their need to distinguish themselves, their status, and their identity from negative Black stereotypes.

The Role of Internalized Oppression

Apart from their classic Black bourgeois perspectives, Black conservative intellectuals also consistently demonstrate they have personally internalized negative stereotypes about poor African Americans and about African American culture. The evidence for this lies in the underlying assumptions of their written work, the descriptions of poor African Americans in that work, and their personal biographies.

In 1986, Glenn Loury wrote: "But it is now beyond dispute that many of the problems of contemporary black American life lie outside the reach of effective government actions and these can only be undertaken by the black community itself. These problems involve at their core the values, attitudes, and behaviors of individual blacks. They are exemplified by the staggering statistics on pregnancies among young, unwed black women and the arrest and incarceration rates among black men."

Yet Loury's personal history includes fathering two out–of–wedlock children, a jailing for non–payment of child support, and 1987 arrests for cocaine and marijuana possession and for assaulting the young mistress he had established in a separate household. Referring to that past history, Loury has said: "I thought if I hung out in the community and engaged in certain kinds of social activities, in a way I was really being black."

English professor Shelby Steele complains that African Americans suffer from a collective self–image that prefers victimization to success and imposes a suffocating racial conformity that ostracizes nonconformists like him. He discusses his own dissociation from images of lower–class Black life when it was represented by an imaginary character named Sam, created by his childhood family. Sam embodied all the negative images of Blacks his father had left behind because "they were 'going nowhere.'"

Steele succinctly states his concern about being confused with poor Blacks when he admits: "The stereotype of the lazy black SOB is common, and the fear is profound that I'll be judged by that stereotype. They will judge our race by him [an unemployed young Black man]—and they'll overlook me, quietly sitting on that bus grading those papers."

Nowhere in the array of Black conservatives' positions are the themes of traditional Black bourgeois attitudes and personal individual status and identity more prevalent than in Black conservatives' opposition to affirmative action. As we have seen earlier, in their analyses of Black oppression and the Black culture of poverty, the foundation of their arguments comes from white conservatives and neoconservatives.

Black Conservatives & Affirmative Action

Nathan Glazer's 1975 book, *Affirmative Action, Ethnic Inequality and Public Policy*, summarized white neoconservatives' objections to affirmative action: that, by the end of the 1960s, discrimination was no longer a major obstacle to minorities' access to employment, education and other social mobility mechanisms; affirmative action has not benefited the poor who need it most, but has primarily benefited middle class Blacks and other minorities; and affirmative action fuels white resentment against minorities.

In his 1984 book, *Civil Rights: Rhetoric or Reality?*, Thomas Sowell repeats each of Glazer's basic objections. Quoting statistics from the *Moynihan Report*, Sowell insists: "The number of blacks in professional, technical, and other high level occupations more than doubled in the decade preceding the Civil Rights Act of 1964. . . .The trend was already under way." Also, like Glazer and other white conservatives, Sowell maintains that "The relative position of disadvantaged individuals within the groups singled out for preferential treatment has generally declined under affirmative action."

Sowell and the other Black conservatives insist affirmative action programs violate whites' "constitutional rights" in general and those of white males in particular. Not only is this seen as unfair, but, like Glazer, Black conservatives worry about the resulting white resentment. In Sowell's words: "There is much reason to fear the harm that it is currently doing to its supposed beneficiaries, and still more reason to fear the long–run consequences of polarizing the nation. . . .Already there are signs of hate organizations growing in more parts of the country and among more educated classes than ever took them seriously before."

What is most interesting about Sowell's affirmative action critique, however, is not that he repeats the standard white conservative critique, but that he adds a self–esteem component to that critique. It is this self–esteem component that reflects the personal status concerns of Sowell and other Black conservatives.

Sowell argues that while accomplishing few positive results, affirmative action actually undermines the efforts of successful minority individuals by creating a climate in which it will be assumed that their achievements reflect not individual worth, talent, or skill, but special consideration. "Pride of achievement is also undermined by the civil rights vision that assumes credit for minority and female advancement. This makes minority and female achievement suspect in their own eyes and in the eyes of the larger society."

Other Black conservative intellectuals follow Sowell's position, first making the same criticisms as white conservatives but adding self–esteem, personal diminishment, and status issues. Shelby Steele complains that affirmative action has reinforced a self–defeating sense of victimization among Blacks by encouraging us to blame our failures on white racism rather than on our own shortcomings. He too worries that affirmative action "makes automatic a perception of enhanced competence for the unpreferreds and of questionable competence for the preferreds—the former earned his way. . .while the latter made it by color as much as by competence."

In *Reflections of an Affirmative Action Baby*, Stephen Carter denies being a conservative. But his discussion of affirmative action is a mirror image of the standard neoconservative critique. Like Glazer, Carter argues that "What has happened in America in the era of affirmative action is this: middle–class black people are better off and lower class black people are worse off." Carter's "best black syndrome" is the most quoted Black conservative status/self–esteem statement about affirmative action: "The best black syndrome creates in those of us who have benefited from racial preferences a peculiar contradiction. We are told over and over that we are the best black people in our profession. And we are flattered. . . .But to professionals who have worked hard to succeed, flattery of this kind carries an unsubtle insult, for we yearn to be called what our achievements often deserve: simply the best—no qualifiers needed!"

Carter and the other Black conservative intellectuals say they object to the fact that affirmative action benefits those minorities who are already middle income. They do not produce convincing statistical evidence to support this contention. Nor do they recognize that affirmative action was designed to address discrimination, not economic disadvantage, or that most government programs benefit middle and, especially, high income groups. Nor do Black conservatives ever recommend that affirmative action become a program for all poor people, including the more than ten million poor whites in this country.

What Black conservatives do argue for is that Blacks compete on merit and merit alone. Their "merit only" policy is clearly an idealized paradigm. It ignores the fundamental reality that any selection process is always a combination of some imperfect assessment of merit (skills and talent) and purely personal filtering processes. To assume that race and/or gender considerations are neutral at the level of personal filtering is naive to say the least.

What is clear in Black conservatives' defense of merit as the sole criterion for selection or advancement is their own sense of personal diminishment by affirmative action labels. Indeed, Black conservatives fret a great deal about proof of their personal talent. And their comments, focused as they are on white's judgments of them and their capabilities, demonstrate that, ironically, they remain very much the captives of white racism.

A genuinely confident African American does not care if whites see her/him as the beneficiary of affirmative action imperatives, knowing that racism *ipso facto* dictates that success on the part of Blacks be seen as the result of unfavorable advantages. Thomas Sowell adamantly denies ever having been an affirmative action beneficiary and reportedly resents being identified as a "Black" anything.

Glenn Loury blasted white liberal Hendrik Hertzberg for saying he'd never met a well–informed, unbigoted Black who did not agree we have to be twice as talented and twice as hardworking to achieve the same degree of success as our white counterparts: "How quickly he [Hertzberg] forgets! We've met more than once, and in the course of our encounters never did I confirm, and often did I contradict the sentiments he ascribes to all 'well informed, unbigoted' blacks. I can only conclude that my earnest denunciation of affirmative action failed to register as the legitimate sentiments of a black intellectual. . .Perhaps he simply dismissed my opinions as a shockingly familiar neoconservatism in blackface."

Given that Black conservatives associate negative racial attributes with low–income Blacks, it is not surprising that much of Black conservative analysis seeks to distinguish middle class from lower class Blacks. An unstated but clear objective throughout Black conservatives' arguments is the attempt to recast the current American identification of "Black" with (in Steele's words) "the least among us" to one in which "Black" is identified with their positive stereotype of middle class Blacks.

Glenn Loury captures this point: "The fact that the values, social norms, and social behaviors often observed among the poorest members of the black community are quite distinct from those characteristic of the black middle class indicates a growing divergence in the social and economic experiences of black Americans." Loury produces no supporting evidence for this observation.

The Theme Of Self–Help

Black conservative intellectuals' solutions for improving race relations are very much tied to the classic attitudes of the Black bourgeoisie, and to issues of identity and status. Further, their solutions always assign leadership roles to the Black middle class. Consistent with their analysis of the causes of Black oppression and Black poverty, they return to the "slavery damaged" theme, and locate the solutions within individual Blacks and the Black community. The reasoning behind their proposed solutions represents some of the most reactionary of their thinking.

Loury and the other Black conservatives insist "self–help" is the only viable solution to Black dilemmas. They argue we have to rely on ourselves because, as Loury states, referring to Booker T. Washington, "[Washington] understood that when the effect of past oppression has been to leave people in a diminished state, the attainment of true equality with their former oppressor cannot much depend on his generosity but must ultimately derive from an elevation of their selves above the state of diminishment."

In addition, Loury and others have developed the profoundly subversive notion, as described by Adolph Reed, that "it is somehow illegitimate for black citizens to view government action and public policy as vehicles for egalitarian redress." Unlike all other American citizens, African Americans, according to Black conservatives, must win white approval by proving ourselves worthy of the rights of citizenship.

"The progress that must now be sought is that of achieving respect, the equality of standing in the eyes of one's political peers, of worthiness as subjects of national concern," Loury argues. Loury frequently acknowledges his intellectual debt to Booker T. Washington's controversial philosophy. He concedes Washington's approach may not have been entirely appropriate for the political and social contexts of his time, but Loury firmly believes the Washington approach is relevant in the post–civil rights era. "The point on which Booker T. Washington was clear, and his critics seem not to be, is that progress of the kind described above must be earned, it cannot be demanded."

Consistent with their belief in the superiority of the Black middle class, Black conservatives argue that instead of relying on government programs and civil rights legislation, middle class Blacks should make economic investments in Black communities; Blacks should support Black businesses; and, most important, the Black middle class needs to teach poor African Americans proper behavior and values. This self–help language, cloaked as it is in Black cultural nationalist rhetoric, has been among the most warmly received of the Black conservative messages in the African American community.

This is not surprising. First of all, self–help literally defines how African Americans have managed to survive slavery, Reconstruction, and a series of trials and travails right up through the present day. Black conservatives and those praising them on this point sound as though African American history has not always included such famous proponents and practitioners of self–help as Martin Delaney, Edward Blyden and Alexander Crummel, Marcus Garvey, the Nation of Islam, the Black Panthers, Jesse Jackson's Operation PUSH, and the thousands of Black women's clubs, Black Greek and professional associations and Black church–based organizations, among others. But African Americans' long heritage of self–help activities has tended to see self–help as a supplement to, not a replacement for, deserved government services and full employment at family–sustaining wages.

In addition to its historical resonance for African Americans, the Black conservative promotion of self–help flatters the Black middle class, casting it as the salvation for poor African Americans. It is noteworthy that even some liberal and progressive middle class Blacks have endorsed the Black conservatives' "culture of poverty" analysis and their call for self–help to address the problem.

What is missed about Black conservatives' self–help advocacy is that, unlike the cultural Black nationalist tradition whose rhetoric they borrow, theirs is neither an organic, collective model of self–help, nor one intended to enhance Black unity and Black cultural integrity. It is based on a savage individualism, advocating a *laissez–faire* formula for Black progress through the commitment of individual Blacks to economic wealth and cultural assimilation.

As stated by Shelby Steele: "The middle class values by which we [the Black middle class] were raised—the work ethic, the importance of education, the value of property ownership, of respectability, of 'getting ahead,' of stable family life, of initiative, of self reliance, *et. cetera*—are, in themselves, raceless and even as-similationist. They urge us toward participation in the American mainstream, toward integration, toward a strong identification with the society, and toward the entire constellation of qualities that are implied in the word individualism."

Steele's comments illustrate another subversive aspect of Black conservatives' proposed solutions—the call to subsume our racial identity and to forgo collective racial action in favor of in-dividualistic pursuits and a nationalistic American identity. Black conservatives issued this call during the 1980s, at a time when overt racist (and frequently violent) attacks on Blacks were at a post–civil rights era high, when the national political leadership of the country implicitly signaled its approval of racist attitudes, and when government and corporate policies were decimating poor and middle class African Americans alike with last hired/first fired policies. Given the political climate of the 1980s, Black conservatives were calling for no less than Black acquies-cence and appeasement in their own oppression.

Black Conservatives' Ties to White Conservatives

Black conservatives are few in number, with few exceptions have no name recognition in the African American community, have little to no institutional base in our community, have no significant Black following, and have no Black constituency. In-deed Black conservatives' highest visibility is in the white, not the Black community. It is due primarily to their ties to white conser-vative institutions that Black conservatives have come to be viewed as spokespersons for the race, despite lacking a base in the African American community. Conservative think tanks such as the Hoover Institution on War, Revolution, and Peace, the Ameri-can Enterprise Institute, and the Heritage Foundation (which has even implemented a minority outreach program), and conserva-tive foundations such as the Olin Foundation, the Scaife Founda-tion, and the Bradley Foundation sponsor Black conservatives in numerous ways.

White conservative institutions award Black conservatives fellowships, consultant work, directorships, and staff positions. They also provide public relations services which get Black con-servatives television and radio appearances, help get editorials, opinion pieces, and articles by Black conservatives into main-stream, even liberal, newspapers and magazines, publish articles and books by Black conservatives, and sponsor workshops and conferences by and for Black conservatives.

Conservative and neoconservative publications such as *The Wall Street Journal, Human Events, The Washington Times,*

Commentary, The Public Interest, The National Interest, American Scholar, and *The New Republic* have played a major role in promoting Black conservatives' visibility, publishing articles by and about them. And finally, the Republican Party, especially during the years of the Reagan Administration but also during the Bush Administration, rewarded Black conservatives with high–visibility government appointments and with financing for Black conservative electoral campaigns.

The Institute of Contemporary Studies, a conservative research organization established by former aides to Ronald Reagan after Reagan left the statehouse in Sacramento, sponsored the first conference of Black neoconservatives in San Francisco in December 1980. Called the Fairmount Conference, it attracted about 125 conservative Black lawyers, physicians, dentists, Ivy League professors, and commentators. It remains the best–known gathering of Black conservative thinkers and policy makers.

A review of prominent Black conservatives' careers reveals the extent to which they have benefited from their corporate–funded presence in white conservative foundations, think tanks, and publications.

Thomas Sowell is a senior fellow at the conservative Palo Alto think tank, the Hoover Institution on War, Revolution, and Peace. Sowell is the most prolific of the Black conservative intellectuals; his 14 books have been widely reviewed in conservative and mainstream publications alike. Conservative publications such as *Commentary, The American Spectator, Human Events, Wall Street Journal, Barron's,* and *Business Week* consistently provide the most glowing reviews. Articles by and/or about Sowell have appeared in numerous mainstream publications such as *Time, Newsweek, The Washington Post,* and *The New York Times,* among others.

When Sowell decided in 1981 to start a (short–lived) organization explicitly intended to counter the NAACP, the Black Alternatives Association, Inc., he reportedly received immediate pledges $1 million from conservative foundations and corporations.

Glenn Loury's reputation and influence rest on only one book and a series of articles that have appeared in most of the major mainstream publications, as well as the conservative *Wall Street Journal, Commentary,* and *The Public Interest* The Heritage Foundation published one of his best–known essays, "Who Speaks for American Blacks," as a monograph in *A Conservative Agenda for America's Blacks.* Boston University's rightist President John Silber hired Loury when Loury left Harvard University's Kennedy School of Government.

Robert Woodson has served in several capacities at the American Enterprise Institute. Woodson is also an adviser for the Madison Group, a loose affiliation of conservative state–level think tanks, launched in 1986 by the American Legislative Exchange Council (ALEC). ALEC is an association of approximately 2,400 conservative state legislators and is housed in the Heritage Foundation's headquarters in Washington, DC. The conservative John M. Olin Foundation gave $25,000 to Woodson's National Center for Neighborhood Enterprise. Woodson's 1987 book, *Breaking the Poverty Cycle: Private Sector Alternatives to the Welfare State*, was published by the conservative National Center for Policy Analysis in Dallas, then reissued in 1989 by the conservative Commonwealth Foundation, on whose board he sits.

Walter Williams is the John M. Olin Distinguished Professor of Economics at George Mason University, has been a fellow at the Hoover Institution and at the Heritage Foundation, and received funding for one of his books from the Scaife Foundation.

The importance of these ties is not white conservative patronage *per se*. Black liberals benefit from similar ties to liberal institutions. A critical intellectual difference, however, is that Black liberals' analyses and policy ideas originated in their experiences in the civil rights and Black Power movements, movements that emerged from the African American community. Black liberals' analyses, limited though they are, continue to be shaped by their Black constituents, who help fund civil rights organizations and elect them to office. It is important to question the implications of the fact that Black conservatives' arguments originate in white conservatives' arguments and that Black conservatives are in no way answerable to a Black constituency.

The historical distinction between white liberals and white conservatives is also a critical one. White liberal patrons and allies have historically allied themselves with, not against, Black interests. During the civil rights struggles, the only place white conservatives could be found was implicitly or explicitly beside Bull Connor, Strom Thurmond, Lester Maddox, and George Wallace. The white conservatives with whom Black conservatives are allied tried to obstruct the very civil rights legislation which even Black conservatives concede was necessary to create what they insist is now a largely discrimination–free America.

Today, Black conservatives belong to a Republican Party thoroughly tainted by racism, whose leadership openly pursues a "southern strategy," employing racially polarizing tactics. Ironically, even today white conservatives remain ambivalent over the desirability of attracting more Blacks to conservative causes and to the Republican Party. Those favoring outreach to Blacks and other minorities have various motives. Pragmatic Republican strategists want to capture at least some of the solid Black support for the Democratic Party. Further, many conservatives recognize that sometime in the 21st century a majority of the US population will be people of color. Given the historical role played by the traditionally politically liberal African American community as a catalyst for change, many mainstream white conservatives believe conservatism must become more inclusive if it is to survive.

Additionally, many Jewish conservatives seek an alliance with Black conservatives, who represent a sector within the African American community that will unite with them in support of Israel. The result is to diminish African American support for Palestinian and Arab causes and the related criticism of military ties between Israel and South Africa.

The more extreme conservatism of Patrick Buchanan and the extreme right wing of the Republican Party is, however, explicitly racialist. As Margaret Quigley and Chip Berlet detail in their oveview article in this anthology, the right has always seen the African American civil rights movement as part of a secular humanist plot to impose communism on the United States. This faction identifies sexual licentiousness and "primitive" African American music with subversion.

Patrick Buchanan wrote a well-known column titled "GOP Vote Search Should Bypass Ghetto" in which he argued that Blacks have been grossly ungrateful for efforts already made on their behalf by Republicans, who had already done more than enough to obtain their support.

It says much about his willingness to "sleep with the enemy" that, even after this notorious column and after Buchanan's outspoken racism during his 1992 run for the Republican Party's presidential nomination, Thomas Sowell could still write in a 1992 column: "If and when he [Buchanan] becomes a viable candidate on his own, perhaps in 1996, that will be time enough to start scrutinizing his views and policy proposals on a whole range of issues."

As crucial as white conservative patronage has been to the careers and visibility of Black conservatives, it should not be viewed as their sole support. Mainstream, liberal, and even progressive institutions also have promoted them to their present-day status and levels of influence.

Robert Woodson's most notable award came from the moderately liberal MacArthur Foundation, which awarded him a $320,000 "genius" grant in 1990. Walter Williams is a featured commentator on National Public Radio's "All Things Considered." Both Williams and Sowell are syndicated columnists. Shelby Steele produced and hosted a public television documentary on

Bensonhurst in 1990. Articles by or about Sowell, Loury, Steele, and Carter appear regularly in such established outlets as *The New York Times, The Boston Globe, Dissent, Time,* and *Newsweek.* Shelby Steele, Glenn Loury, and Tony Brown were among those featured in the January/February and the March/April 1993 issues of *Mother Jones* magazine, in a two–part article on urban poverty.

It is similarly noteworthy that while Black conservatives received an exceptional amount of publicity throughout the 1980s, the most intellectually sophisticated and nuanced group of African–American scholars and theorists—progressives such as bell hooks, Angela Davis, June Jordan, Manning Marable, Adolph Reed, Jr., and Cornel West—received next to none.

Between January 1980 and August 1991 three prominent newspapers, *The New York Times, The Washington Post,* and *The Philadelphia Inquirer,* published 11 op–eds, 14 articles, and 30 reviews by or about Thomas Sowell, Shelby Steele, and Walter Williams. However, during this same period, three prominent progressive African–American scholars, bell hooks, Manning Marable, and Cornel West, had no op–eds, no articles, and no stories by or about them in these same three newspapers.

This is, in part, a reflection of the conservatism that pervaded the political culture of the United States throughout the 1980s. But the question remains: how and why did a group of African Americans so unrepresentative of Black majority political opinion and so uninvolved in the affairs of the African American community come nonetheless to be anointed as race spokespeople, even by white institutions claiming to reflect liberal democratic ideals? From the perspective of the African American community, there is nothing democratic about the ascendancy of Blacks who demand that we acquiesce in fundamentally racist interpretations of who we are.

Conclusion

The principal complaint of most African Americans against Black conservatives, particularly the intellectuals featured here, is that they provide cover for policies that do grievous harm to Black people. But the potential harm inherent in Black conservatism is a danger to all Americans.

June Jordan has observed that problems which first appear in poor African American communities—substandard schools, AIDS, violent crime—always eventually appear in middle–income white communities. At that point they leave the realm of the "culture of poverty" and become an "American problem."

The United States has never allowed full citizenship rights for all its citizens. It has never built a social culture devoid of racism, sexism, anti–Jewish bigotry, homophobia, or classism. Our economic system has never provided full employment at a sustainable wage. As a nation, we have never committed ourselves to providing as basic human rights a quality education for each and every child, universal high–quality health care, and a decent place to live for all people.

So long as the devastating inequities that characterize American society persist, and racism continues to exacerbate these inequities, there is absolutely no way to make meaningful, much less provable, statements correlating peoples' values with their socioeconomic status.

By tying poor African Americans' poverty to race and our supposed slavery–flawed culture, Black conservatives insult African Americans. They also divert attention from June Jordan's observation that Black problems inevitably become problems of the larger society. At some point, white Americans and middle–income Americans in general are going to be forced to confront the fundamental problems caused by this country's severe maldistribution of resources and its intolerance of diversity. Black conservatives delay that confrontation and in so doing, they do the entire country a grave disservice.

By uncritically promoting Black conservatives, liberal and progressive institutions not only undermine their own stated principles, they exhibit a not–so–subtle form of racism. As Adolph Reed, Jr. points out: who would listen if the word "Italian" or "Jew" were substituted in Black conservatives' characterizations of African Americans? We should be clear that stereotyping and victim–blaming is not more respectable because it is done by a member of the group being demeaned.

Deborah Toler holds a Ph.D. in political science. She is currently senior research analyst at the Institute for Food and Development Policy (Food First), in Oakland, California. Call or write Political Research Associates for footnotes for this article, which originally appeared in *The Public Eye* in the September 1993 and December 1993 issues. © 1995, Deborah Toler.

A Call to Defend Democracy & Pluralism

Blue Mountain Working Group

We are a group of individuals interested in joining with others to rebuild a multi–issue movement for progressive social change that can assist in informing and organizing broad coalitions to reverse the ominous right–wing backlash currently sweeping the United States. In May 1993, we came from across the nation to the conference center in Blue Mountain, New York to share our concerns about the growing prejudice and scapegoating being provoked by intolerant and anti–democratic religious and secular movements of the hard right.

A wide range of individuals participated in the three–day meeting, including organizers, activists, journalists, academics, and researchers. Some had institutional affiliations, others did not. All the participants had been involved in educating about or organizing against right–wing campaigns at the local or national level, and had shown a commitment to respecting diversity and valuing cooperation. The goal of the gathering was to meet and discuss our experiences and ideas, develop a national perspective, and begin to outline a strategic response that reflected the diverse communities where we work and live. We carried out our discussions with a sense of purpose, a knowledge of history, a commitment to thoughtful and thorough discussion, a desire to learn from each other, and a humility born of painful experience heightened by an apprehension of peril. This statement is one result of our ongoing discussions during the past 18 months.

We see the current general right–wing backlash as one of the most significant political developments of the decade, combining well–funded national institutions with highly motivated grass–roots activists. To effectively counter this movement, we believe it is essential to understand the specific and complicated components of the political right wing across its many forms, and the often conflicting and competing aspects of right–wing theory and practice.

While the political right in the US can be bewildering in its complexity and shifting identities and allegiances, its players historically have assembled their core tenets and shared agendas from the same set of beliefs. They include conscious or unconscious support for white privilege; male supremacy; subservience of women and people of color; hierarchical religious and family structures; the protection of property rights over human rights; preservation of individual wealth; a rapacious form of unregulated free market capitalism; aggressive and unilateral military and foreign policies; and authoritarian and punitive means of social control. They also include opposition to the feminist movement and abortion rights; democratic pluralism and cultural diversity; gay rights; government regulations concerning health, safety, and the environment; and minimum wage laws and union rights.

The most activist segments of the US political right working within the electoral system are distinct from traditional conservatism, with its support for the status quo, as well as distinct from the far right or ultra right, with its overt theories of racist biological determinism and open support for individual and collective violence. We see some overlap among these tendencies, especially in local campaigns, but contend that the current coalition effort uniting diverse right–wing activist groups around specific common themes represents a historic phenomenon that has appeared before in US history during times of economic and social stress. Various activist right–wing movements have historically been called the hard right, intolerant right, authoritarian right, regressive right, reactionary right, nativist right, populist right, radical right, extremist right, moralistic right, orthodox right, traditionalist right, nationalist right, exclusivist right, self–righteous right, elitist right, zealous right, theocentric right, theonomic right, and theocratic right.

We feel the phrase that best describes the essence of the contemporary activist right–wing movement is "anti–democratic right." The main goal of the anti–democratic right is to craft a reactionary backlash movement to co–opt and reverse the gains of the progressive social movements of the 1960s and 1970s which sparked the ongoing civil rights, student rights, anti–war, feminist, ecology, and gay rights movements.

To achieve this goal, the anti–democratic right works in many arenas—cultural, social, artistic, electoral, legislative, legal, political, academic, journalistic, religious, and theological. It has an infrastructure that engages in research, strategic analysis, media outreach, fundraising, education, community organizing, and direct action. The specific segment of the anti–democratic right that most concerns us is a growing coalition of well–funded reactionary political activists working with authoritarian religious zealots to define what it means to be an American in narrow, spiteful, and exclusionary terms.

The leaders of the anti–democratic right recognize that many persons have real grievances over various social and economic problems in our society, but these leaders cynically divert attention away from a serious discussion of these complex issues toward targeted scapegoats such as African Americans, Asians, Arabs, and other people of color, Spanish–speaking residents, feminists, lesbians, gay men, immigrants, welfare recipients, Jews, Muslims, the disabled, and other persons, many of whom are still seeking equal access to the promised benefits of our society.

In a country confronting complex problems, the anti–democratic right offers simple slogans. In a society of many cultures, the anti–democratic right offers a monocultural vision of citizenship. In a society struggling for participatory democracy, the anti–democratic right offers elitism, exclusivity, and submission to authority.

The leaders of the anti–democratic right are deeply troubled by critical thinking, cultural diversity, and dissent; and they warn about the chaos of mass democracy and pluralism, and the evils of liberalism and secular humanism. When they speak of traditional family values, they often speak only of those values which traditionally have reinforced disproportionate access to power and privilege for certain segments of our society—the upper class, males, whites, heterosexuals, northern Europeans, and Christians.

Many leaders of the anti–democratic right depend on fundraising through direct mail and televangelism, where using divisive and polarizing scare tactics to raise money has become commonplace. We have seen some leaders of the anti–democratic right use deception, false or unreliable statistics, pseudo–science, and pseudo–academic research. They opportunistically promote stereotypes, scapegoating, objectification, and irrational conspiratorial analyses alleging secular humanist treachery. They gracelessly exploit divisiveness, dehumanization, demonization, and demagoguery. They smugly act in a moralistic, self–righteous, even sanctimonious manner. They seek to impose their rigid and uncharitable views on every American. The danger they pose to democratic pluralism is real. The anti–democratic right seeks to control what we read, the music we hear, the images we see, how we learn, what happens to our bodies, how we worship, and whom we love.

The rise of the anti–democratic right in our country occurs at a time when racial nationalism is sweeping Europe. We have witnessed the murders of immigrants, people of color, and religious minorities in Germany, and the spread of anti–Jewish bigotry across the continent. Who could have predicted the brutal ethnic cleansing in the former Yugoslavia or the election victories of neo–fascists in Italy? In our own country, hate crimes and physical assaults on persons in targeted groups are on the increase. We have seen the shootings of abortion providers and bombings of clinics. We should not be complacent and dismiss the possibility that an economic or social crisis in the US could serve as a trigger for some hard–right religious zealots or reactionary racial nationalists to engage in paramilitary activity or unleash a campaign of intimidation and violence that could destabilize our own country.

It may seem a remote possibility, but it *can* happen here. We know from history that authoritarianism, theocracy, demagoguery, and scapegoating are building blocks for fascist political movements—and that people mobilized by the cynical, regressive, populist–sounding sentiments sown by a Ross Perot can be harvested by the angry, divisive, racial nationalist rhetoric of a David Duke or Pat Buchanan. We also know the paradox of fascism is that when most people finally are asking whether or not it is too late to stop it. . .it is. Better that resistance be early and preventative rather than late and unsuccessful.

Because we believe the anti–democratic right is a growing social movement, we see three immediate tasks to protect democratic values:

- defending diversity within a pluralistic society.
- maintaining the separation of church and state.
- protecting the right to privacy for all people.

We share a sense of urgency. Time is of the essence. We must stop the hard right anti–democratic backlash movement before it inflicts more damage on our society.

In defending democracy and pluralism, we must refrain from using the same polarizing techniques of scapegoating, demonization, and demagoguery that have been so successful for the anti–democratic right. As we fight intolerance, we will consciously strive to resist using the same intolerant tactics we oppose. We will respect diversity while defending democracy. We recognize that many of the individual grassroots activists being mobilized by the leadership of the anti–democratic right are sincere and honest people with real fears concerning jobs, family, schools, and personal safety. They are not our enemies, they are our neighbors—and potentially our allies.

We defend the right of all persons to hold religious beliefs and moral codes without government restriction or interference. But we insist that in a constitutional democracy the arguments for legislation and regulation be based on rational debate and factual evidence that demonstrate a useful purpose and a compelling government interest. The leaders of the anti–democratic right wave the flag, wrap themselves in the cloak of religion, and claim they speak for God and country. We are not attacking God when we confront those who pridefully presume to speak for God. We are not attacking religion when we challenge those who imply that only persons who share their specific narrow theological viewpoint can claim religious or moral values. We are not attacking our country when we rebuke those who peddle a message of fear, prejudice, and division.

To stop the right–wing backlash we must help to build broad popular coalitions that include at the core all the communities under attack by the anti–democratic right in its many incarnations; and we must also include in these coalitions all persons of good conscience willing to defend democratic pluralism. Our allies are all persons who oppose theocracy and control by an authoritarian elite, and all persons who are willing to stand up for a real, dynamic, and vibrant democracy.

As progressives, we believe there are many values we must uphold in building any principled coalition. Our method of work as a progressive coalition must reflect diverse styles, perspectives, and goals. We must speak with many different voices representing the many different threads that weave the social fabric of our nation. We see progressive social change as an ongoing process involving persons from many constituencies and issues working together whenever possible in an alliance for democracy and pluralism.

Our alliance embraces the struggles for racial and ethnic justice, especially for persons who trace their identity to Africa, South America, Central America, Mexico, the Caribbean, Asia, the Middle East, and the Pacific Islands. Our alliance embraces the struggles for fairness and tribal rights for the native peoples of this continent.

Our alliance embraces the movements seeking equal rights and safety for women. Our alliance embraces groups promoting a woman's right to control her own body, defending abortion rights, advocating comprehensive sexuality education and family planning, and seeking implementation of gay–positive curricula and AIDS awareness education. Our alliance embraces the equal rights movements defending the lesbian, gay male, bisexual, and transgender communities.

Our alliance embraces those seeking social and economic justice for African Americans and the eradication of the vestiges of slavery and second–class citizenship. Our alliance embraces the struggles against scapegoating of immigrants, people of color, and welfare recipients. Our alliance embraces groups challenging racism, sexism, homophobia, and anti–Jewish prejudice.

Our alliance embraces the impoverished seeking dignified work and a living wage. Our alliance embraces residents of the inner city seeking control and revitalization of their communities. Our alliance embraces those in rural areas seeking to preserve the family farm and fighting for fair agricultural and land–use policies. Our alliance embraces persons opposing the anti–regulatory Wise Use, sovereignty, counties, and states rights movements. Our alliance embraces groups fighting for a decent minimum wage, accessible child care, compassionate welfare regulations, and meaningful job training. Our alliance embraces alienated youth and the isolated homeless.

Our alliance embraces movements championing artistic freedom and fighting censorship in schools and libraries. Our alliance embraces persons learning to overcome physical, emotional, and psychological challenges to independence. Our alliance embraces movements for a sound environment, better schools, bilingual education, and universal health care. Our alliance embraces persons decrying religious bigotry against Jews, Muslims, Catholics, and other belief systems. Our alliance embraces groups resisting militarism, ultra–nationalism, fascism, and genocide.

We come from churches, synagogues, mosques, and other places of spiritual worship and secular reflection. We come from labor unions, non–profit agencies, progressive businesses, foundations, membership organizations, and social clubs. We come from farms and ranches, industrial worksites, office buildings, schools, colleges, factories, and the streets. We come from cities, suburbs, and rural areas. We are organized and unorganized, and work inside and outside the home. And we yearn to build a true alliance that unites all of us on the basis of mutual respect as we defend democracy and pluralism.

We see a synergistic interactive relationship among activists, organizers, researchers, journalists, and academics from these various movements and constituencies as resulting in the most informed and useful analyses, strategies, and tactics to bring about effective action for social change. We believe there must be two–way interaction between the national and local levels. The needs and specific issues of local partners must inform and shape national strategies, and, at the same time, the resources developed by national groups must be made available to grassroots organizers to stimulate informed discussion of various strategies and tactics. At the leadership level, there has not yet been sufficient cooperation among potential progressive allies, and many people in national organizations still need to be educated about the serious nature of the threat posed by the anti–democratic right.

Hard experiences have taught us that short–term tactics that divide communities for the sake of individual electoral victories are short–sighted, frequently backfire, and even when successful, weaken the type of long–term coalition building that is necessary for eventual victory. It is essential to develop an analysis that bridges issues, helps communities understand the threat to them, and pulls together diverse constituencies and issues. The anti–democratic right has been successful in reframing the public debate over key issues such as family, morality, and children. We must participate in and reclaim this debate.

We believe in full equality for everyone—nothing more, but nothing less.

Ours is a vision of democracy where all have an equal voice. Of a democracy where progressive populism encourages active participation by all residents in open, full, and honest debates over legislation and government policies. Where we elect our government representatives on the basis of ideas, not images. Where the consent of the governed is informed consent, not manipulated consent. Where the wealth of wisdom possessed by a political candidate is more important than the reach of their wallet. Where elections offer real choices rather than rotating elites. Where the majority sets policies while consciously respecting the rights of the minority; and both the majority and the minority have their grievances carefully considered, and have access to representation. This is the promise of our nation. We must work to see this promise achieved, rather than see it eroded by the regressive populist–sounding demagoguery of the anti–democratic right.

Our goal is twofold: we must stop the hard right; and we must pursue the unfulfilled promises of a healthy pluralistic democracy: justice, equality, security, and fairness—the real American Dream.

Many of us who met at Blue Mountain have continued working together as an informal network, and this has helped us gain the perspective we need to be more effective in our individual tasks fighting the right in cities and states across the country. It is vital that we all share information, advice, criticisms, and assistance as we learn to work together. The anti–democratic right has a multi–issue strategic agenda, but its tactic is to focus its attacks on one high–visibility target constituency at a time. No single segment of our society has demonstrated an ability to resist these attacks alone. We must learn to work together. We urge everyone who desires to defend and extend democracy to join together in forming broad and diverse, locally based coalitions to resist the rollback of rights; to block the backlash; to fight the right.

The leaders of the anti–democratic right say their movement is waging a battle for the soul of America. They call it a "culture war." We believe the soul of America should not be a battleground but a birthright, and that culture should be celebrated not censored. We believe America is defined by ideas and values, but not those limited by religious beliefs, biology, bloodlines, or birthplace of ancestors.

The time has come to stand up and vigorously defend democracy and pluralism against the attacks orchestrated by cynical leaders of the anti–democratic right. History teaches us that there can be no freedom without liberty, no liberty without justice, and no justice without equality; and we look forward to success because we know it is through the never–ending struggle for equality, justice, liberty, and freedom that democracy is nourished.

- **Russ Bellant**
  Journalist/researcher
  Author:
  The Coors Connection
  Detroit, Michigan
- **Chip Berlet**
  Journalist/activist
  Political Research Associates
  Cambridge, Massachusetts
- **Anne Bower**
  Executive Director/Editor
  The Body Politic Magazine
  Binghamton, New York
- **Robert Bray**
  Fight the Right organizer
  National Gay & Lesbian Task Force
  San Francisco, California

- **Mandy Carter**
  Director, A National Call to Resist Campaign
  National Black Gay and Lesbian Leadership Forum
  Washington, District of Columbia
- **Frederick Clarkson**
  Journalist/researcher
  Co–author: *Challenging the Christian Right*
  Northampton, Massachusetts
- **Marghe Covino**
  Co–Founder, Project Tocsin
  Sentinel Institute for Research & Education
  Sacramento, California
- **Elias Farajaje–Jones**
  Howard University
  School of Divinity
  Washington, District of Columbia

- **Suzanne B. Goldberg**
  Staff Attorney
  Lambda Legal Defense
  New York, New York
- **Kate Harris**
  Reproductive rights organizer
  Consultant to non-profit
  groups
  California
- **Barbara J. Hart**
  Legal Director,
  Pennsylvania Coalition Against
  Domestic Violence
  Reading, Pennsylvania
- **David C. Mendoza**
  Director, National Campaign
  for Freedom of Expression
  Arts activist
  Seattle, Washington
- **Scot Nakagawa**
  Activist/Organizer
  National Gay & Lesbian Task
  Force
  Portland, Oregon
- **David Nimmons**
  Social justice activist
  Gay and lesbian community
  New York, New York

- **Suzanne Pharr**
  Writer/organizer
  Women's Project
  Portland, Oregon
- **Skipp Porteous**
  President, Institute for First
  Amendment Studies
  Research & Education
  Great Barrington,
  Massachusetts
- **Tarso Ramos**
  Researcher/activist
  Western States Center
  Portland, Oregon
- **Loretta Ross**
  Program Research Director
  Center for Democratic
  Renewal
  Atlanta, Georgia
- **Barbara A. Simon**
  Gen. Counsel, Institute for First
  Amendment Studies
  Research & Education
  Massachusetts
- **Urvashi Vaid**
  Organizer/author
  Human rights activist
  Provincetown, Massachusetts
- **Thalia Zepatos**
  Writer/organizer
  Campaign Consultant
  Portland, Oregon

Organizations, when listed, are for identification only. Drafts of earlier versions of this statement were circulated among selected activists and researchers for their comments. This final version reflects the substantial and thoughtful input of many persons other than those whose names appear on this page.

How to Fight the Right

Center for Democratic Renewal

Since 1979, the Center for Democratic Renewal (CDR) has been in the forefront of the struggle against the injustice of white supremacy. Our experience in research, organizing, and training was developed through work with more than 1,000 communities faced with Klan marches, Holocaust denial, or hate crimes. Even though the lines distinguishing the far right, the Religious Right, and ultra–conservatives have blurred, many of their themes are the same. Their ideological and organizational overlap must be exposed. We offer the following strategies for consideration by the progressive movement:

• Build strong think tanks for progressives so that the ideology and strategies of the right can be countered.

• Increase the use of media, especially talk shows and talk radio, to get our message out to the majority of the public that gets its information this way.

• Establish strong relationships with mainstream religious groups and churches to counter the sanctimonious claim that only the Religious Right are people of faith.

• Democratize access to the information superhighway, such as the Internet. This valuable resource is under–utilized by people who share our perspectives and is inaccessible to a large part of our constituency, yet over three million Americans now use the Internet.

• Start grassroots voter education about the true policy implications of the right; don't let them get away with clever sound-bites without exposing the policy consequences of their proposals.

For example, unfunded mandates would mean that many environmental regulations would be thrown out of the window.

- Decouple their sweet talk from their meanness. Make the right talk about real issues, not just slogans on moral values. Religious groups shouldn't act, or sound, like hate groups.

- Use a human rights analysis to link progressive issues together and offer a strategy for holding our government and individuals accountable to international standards.

- Work in broad–based coalitions that unite all of those affected by the right. Single–issue and identity–based politics have their limits and are inadequate for tackling the complexities of the right.

Understand that the key to combating the right is at the grassroots level, so build and strengthen local organizations that can mobilize people community by community and block by block. Don't get discouraged. The backlash politics of the right are just that—a response to the success of our movements for social justice. We will win again!

The Center for Democratic Renewal in Atlanta, Georgia is a national organization assisting community–based groups fighting prejudice and hate crimes. This article first appeared in the CDR newsletter *The Monitor*, in March 1995. © 1995, Center for Democratic Renewal.

Challenging the Campus Right

Advice from the University Conversion Project

Common Questions & Answers

Rich Cowan & Dalya Massachi

Do you mean to prohibit expression of ideas that are not "politically correct"?

There is nothing wrong with trying to influence opinions. There is nothing wrong with trying to establish new standards of decency different from those of our parents' generation. As peace activists, our challenge is to influence people by non–violent methods, by persuasion rather than coercion. We also recognize that people who have historically been ignored in the political process may at first need to speak louder or more often in order to be heard. Or they may need to meet by themselves within a "safe space" in order to find their voices. [*]

All of these activities are attacked as "censorship" by those who are accustomed to monopolizing the stage and dominating the decision–making process. It is both ridiculous and dangerous to compare these activities to the historical legacies of colonialism and white male supremacy. The danger in the "anti–PC" cam-

---

[*] The authors thank Ron Francis for discussions which improved this article.

paign is that privileged groups will view challenges to their privilege as "fascism" in order to justify responding to these challenges with violence.

Conservative groups have repeatedly indicated a goal of eliminating the left (or liberalism). Jack Abramoff, former national chair of the College Republicans, went so far as to say, "we are not just trying to win the next election. We're winning the next generation. . . .It's not our job to seek peaceful co–existence with the left. Our job is to remove them from power permanently."

By talking so much about the right, aren't you labeling people and creating an "Us vs. Them" dynamic that only breeds violence?

Identifying and naming the oppressor is fundamentally different from using the oppressor's coercive tactics as an instrument of rebellion. We would favor the former, and oppose the latter. As long as power hierarchies exist, it is necessary to name them if we want to understand and/or change the world. Those who commit acts of violence must be held accountable for their actions.

For example, it is OK for women to say that men have the vast majority of power in our society or for people of color to talk about the pervasiveness of white supremacy. It is OK for people in the Third World to identify the First World nations that use the majority of the world's resources.

The discomfort caused by questioning these power relationships inevitably brings charges of "us–them" thinking or coercion, but it cannot be compared to the violence involved in enforcing those relationships.

Tactically, there are reasons to avoid alienating those who hold power. But this alienation can only be avoided if people "within the system" (or members of "oppressor groups") take some responsibility for continuing this dialogue.

Aren't you lumping together "legitimate" conservative political activity with hate groups such as neo–Nazis?

No; we are not equating the two groups. Harassment and coercive political activity are quite different from non–coercive persuasion. But to limit our focus to extreme groups would assume that these groups are the sole protectors of inequality: if they were to dissolve tomorrow, everything would suddenly get better. This is not the case.

More mainstream conservative groups—whose audience is much larger—preach an ideology that assumes the "free market" can rectify social inequality. If "it takes money to make money," as capitalists claim, are we to believe that those groups who tend to have more money deserve it because "they are more intelligent," "they work harder," or "they were here first"? Challenge racist and sexist assumptions.

Shouldn't professors be free to be spontaneous in class?
Of course. The problem occurs when professors don't realize what may be offensive assumptions they make about the students in their classes. When they do not use inclusive language or are not sensitive to the new perspectives brought by their students of diverse backgrounds, they are not opening their classrooms to the rethinking of "traditional" scholarship and ideas. Learning and open–mindedness does not end when you are no longer a student—as the student body changes, so must professors.

To be fair, shouldn't student activity boards refrain from funding political activities, or from funding "left" activities more than "right" ones?
Student fees were established at many schools so that student activities can be controlled democratically by students alone, and not be limited to those which support the policies of the university administration.

With or without funding from student fees, many student governments have enacted policies which forbid the use of student funds for "political activities." While the university's non–profit status justifies a ban on supporting partisan (e.g., Democratic or Republican) political campaigns, a ban on all student funding of political activities—as approved recently by the California Supreme Court—is anti–democratic.

This policy plays into the strategy of the right by forcing student groups to rely on funding external to the university. Such a policy is hardly "apolitical." It biases student expression to reflect the existing order, thus perpetuating the inequities of our society. In other words, students whose views coincide with the interests of corporations, wealthy individuals, or the Defense establishment find it easy to obtain funds to express their views. But students with alternative viewpoints will be financially limited, even if their views are popular.

Tips on Responding to the Right Wing

Rich Cowan

Progressive groups on campus who are attacked from the right basically have three options. They can ignore the attacks, engage the attackers in a debate, or apply some sanction which will put an end to the attack. Keep in mind that an attack is not necessarily a bad thing. As in a game of chess, if your opponent's attack is weak, you may wind up way ahead after the exchange. Instead of losing support, a progressive group can expose the history, tactics, and funding of the right, turning this right–wing disruption into an embarassing scandal.

Sometimes the best course of action will be obvious; often not. The debate about what to do will be a contentious one, and has split many progressive groups. If we do not quickly mend these splits, we will fall into the traps set for us by the right. This article offers a framework for discussion so that our groups can more quickly reach a consensus.

These guidelines may also help you respond to a sectarian left group that attacks you for not following their "party line" closely enough.

In such discussions, it is important to evaluate whether the right's provocations reflect a sincere desire to present an alternative point of view, or whether the agenda is primarily to disrupt your campaign. It is also very important to monitor the tide of student opinion: do not lose touch with your constituency.

Ignoring the Attack

Many students today have a disdain for politics because they view it as a shouting match between two extreme points of view. Since the right has money, not numbers, this situation works to their advantage by discouraging mass political involvement. At all costs, avoid mudslinging that merely puts a bad taste in people's mouths.

When the young Republicans wanted to co–sponsor a debate with a peace group I was in, we refused in order to avoid a mudslinging fest that would only speak to the converted on both sides. We agreed to a debate only if it was sponsored by the student government.

Sometimes an attack is so low that no response is necessary. Disclosing the nature of the attack alone will build sympathy to your cause even without discussion of the issues. If the attack is personal, try to have someone else respond other than the person attacked; an injury to one is an injury to all.

Levels of Engagement

The following are some possible ways to respond, from a minimal level of engagement to greater levels. In general, we recommend minimizing the engagement; if a right–wing group has a tiny audience, you only increase that audience by engaging them. However, one or two people can spread one or two points that may cause potential supporters to question your entire campaign. In this case, you will be better off if you are ready with a response. A few ideas:

- Don't bring yourself down to their level. A minimal level of engagement might be making a public statement as to why you do not intend to get into a harangue with the group. Perhaps you could shoot down just one of their arguments as an example of why you think students should not take the rest of their arguments seriously.

- We know what you're against, but what are you for? For example, many right–wing groups question affirmative action. Granted, affirmative action laws do not result in perfect decisions. But do the conservatives have any constructive plan to rectify historic inequality?

- Question the arguments directly. If the right is well–trained and reaches a large audience, your best defenses will be a good political line. Keep in mind some vulnerabilities of the right:

  - The PC label is not as effective as it once was; it is now a "tired argument."

  - The leftist campus climate that is often alleged by the right simply does not exist; if you can demonstrate how right–wing interests dominate your school's governance, people won't take the right's charges seriously.

  - The right has often used anecdotal evidence and bad science.

  - The interests of students making $10,000 a year are really not the same as those of corporate sponsors of the right, making $300,000 per year.

- Question their "Americanism." Part of what makes the US attractive is the right of citizens to oppose their government. If the right is so patriotic, why do they oppose our involvement in dissent? Remind people that McCarthyite tactics designed to ruin faculty careers are hardly "American."

- Question their independence. Use the UCP *Guide* to show how your local right–wing group is not an independent grassroots initiative, but part of a nationally coordinated strategy. Ask the group who trained them. At least one Madison Center paper has had its funds cut off after printing liberal ideas. Is there a connection between the right's funding and the arguments they present, on health care for instance?

"There is no defense against ridicule," wrote Saul Alinsky *in Rules for Radicals*. Ridiculing someone's arguments can be very effective—especially in those cases where the right's arguments are, well, ridiculous.

Exclusion: The Free Speech/Harassment Debate

The right may deliberately operate in a gray zone between legitimate political activity and harassment. The best advice we can give to a group is to establish clear, justifiable definitions of disruption, harassment, and hate literature in advance, so that you can defend a decision to take action when your political opponents cross that line. Free speech is not without limits; if your school fails to respond to harassment, your group could organize a response.

All progressive groups that have succeeded over the long haul have established mechanisms to prevent disruption by individuals, right–wing or not. See the excellent book *The War at Home*, by Brian Glick.

Rich Cowan & Dalya Massachi are with the University Conversion Project. This article may be photocopied and distributed at no charge provided that the article and this notice are included in their entirety. For a full 52–page guidebook which includes 38 graphics and 8 charts, please send $6 plus $1 postage to University Conversion Project, Box 748, Cambridge, MA 02142. Outside the USA the cost is $10. For information on memberships ($25/$20/$10) and a complete publications list, send e–mail to ucp@igc.apc.org or call 617–354–9363. © 1994, University Conversion Project.

Immigration & the Civil Rights Movement's Response

Bill Tamayo

The civil rights movement in the United States is confronted by numerous social issues of unprecedented complexity: concerted attacks on affirmative action, increasing racial violence and hatred, questions about the "genetic ability" of African Americans to excel, and the lack of political leadership in government to address these issues.

Passage of California's Proposition 187 (the so-called "Save our State" initiative) in November 1994 drove home the message that immigrants, like many others in America, are a drain on society. The public's perception of this community—non-white, undocumented, criminally bent, welfare abusers—was fueled by public officials and the media. Not surprisingly, while many African Americans, Latinos and Asian-Americans voted against 187, most whites voted for it 2–1.

The general alignment of all civil rights groups in California against Proposition 187 was positive. However, that alignment does not yet reflect a common view on the broader questions of undocumented immigration, immigrants rights, and immigration policy overall.

As recently as spring 1990, the NAACP supported the employer sanctions provisions of the Immigration Reform and Control Act (IRCA) of 1986, which bars the hiring of undocumented persons and requires some verification of work authorization. While IRCA was being debated in Congress, Latinos, Asians, and members of the Congressional Black and Hispanic Caucuses condemned the measure as discriminatory. But the NAACP's Washington lobbyist in 1985 asserted that because of job competition between the undocumented and African Americans, the organization supported sanctions. And the Leadership Conference on Civil Rights—the nation's premier coordinating mechanism for civil rights advocacy before Congress and the executive branch, representing some 185 national organizations—did not oppose employer sanctions because of sharp division in its ranks.

A 1990 General Accounting Office (GAO) study confirmed the predictions of discrimination in its finding and found that nearly 20 percent of employers admitted discriminating against Asians and Latinos (citizens and lawful permanent residents) because of IRCA. Armed with this evidence, Latinos and Asians, joined by the Lawyers Committee for Civil Rights Under Law and the NAACP Legal Defense and Educational Fund (LDF) and many others, convinced the NAACP to revisit the question. Then NAACP Director Benjamin Hooks successfully urged his membership to reverse its position. The Leadership Conference eventually came around, but only after Latino groups publicly voiced their consideration of withdrawing membership.

Immigration-Bashing = Racism

Racism has dominated and continues to dominate immigration policies in the United States and other Western nations. As recently as 1993, in response to a World Bank report that over 100 million people have left their home countries and to a related report by the United Nations High Commissioner for Refugees, the G–7 countries (United States, Germany, France, Italy, Canada, Japan, and Great Britain) adopted policies to restrict immigration and deny quick access to asylum. These efforts were designed to stem immigration from Africa, Latin America, and Asia. The racial component of these policies was vividly illustrated as immigrants from Turkey, the Middle East, Africa, and Asia were victims of racial violence throughout Western Europe in the early 1990s.

In the United States, these policies translated into proposed curbs on the political asylum process, rapid deportation, increased border enforcement (without provisions for oversight) and efforts to deny undocumented immigrants public services, such as Proposition 187. In 1993, California Governor Pete Wilson proposed denial of citizenship to US–born children whose parents were undocumented. Wilson chose to turn back the clock to an era when US–born African Americans and Native Americans were denied citizenship by law.

While this effort was unsuccessful, Wilson touched an extremely hot button and realized that fanning the flames of xenophobia was not only popular but provided the key element for his re-election.

The Personal Responsibility Act, introduced in Congress by Republicans as part of the "Contract with America," would deny legal permanent residents over 40 social services and benefits, including Social Security Insurance, Aid to Families with Dependent Children, and lawyers funded by the Legal Services Corporation. Since its introduction, some of these measures have been incorporated into other welfare reform proposals. By October 1995, the Personal Responsibility Act had been passed by both the House and the Senate and was in conference committee prior to being sent to the President for signing or a veto.

The Task for Civil Rights Groups

What should the civil rights movement do amidst this cacophony of hate, racism, and nativism? Foremost, the movement must draw out the commonalities among the communities it seeks to represent and on whose behalf it is advocating. Allowing to go unchallenged the pattern of blaming similarly situated victims of racism for one's plight would be a striking setback. If anything, the current heightened racialized climate serves as a painful reminder that many of us are in the same boat and need not blame each other for being there. Even perceptions that non-white but non-black minorities who may or may not be citizens should not be at the table of civil rights debate do an injustice to the vision of civil rights leaders like Dr. Martin Luther King, Malcolm X, and others who approached the issue of civil and human rights with a global and internationalist perspective.

While the history of the movement has been inconsistent on the issue of immigrants' rights, there have been proud moments. The American Civil Liberties Union (ACLU) was formed out of challenges to the roundups and deportations of immigrant labor activists during the Palmer Raids of 1919–1920 and continues to represent immigrants in civil rights matters. In 1915, the NAACP successfully defeated a Senate amendment to deny admission to persons of African descent, and in 1952 argued for defeat of the dangerous McCarran–Walter Act, which maintained the racist national origins quotas in our immigration laws. During the Proposition 187 campaign, the Urban League, NAACP LDF, Mexican American Legal Defense & Educational Fund, and Asian organizations vociferously opposed the measure. These experiences lay the foundation for a more concerted effort to protect the rights of immigrants and beat back the racism that underlies anti–immigrant measures. More important, that joint practice serves to build a common vision about who is responsible for this climate of hate and racism, and leads to a decrease in inter–ethnic hostilities.

Civil rights groups have an important mission in this period. They must be able to articulate more forcefully the issues of the im-migrant population, including the undocumented, and assert that this community is part of the civil rights community. They must as-sert that working together and drawing the lessons are the main ways in which we can survive this period of vitriolic scapegoating and "racialized patriotism" in which non–whites and non–citizens are be-ing jointly demonized without mercy.

Bill Tamayo is the former Managing Attorney of the Asian Law Caucus, a public interest, civil rights organization in San Francisco, California. He is a board member of the Poverty and Race Research Action Council (PRRAC). This chapter was slightly updated from a version that first ap-peared in PRRAC's newsletter, *Poverty & Race*, Vol. 4, No. 2, March/April 1995. © 1995, Bill Tamayo

Religious Conservatives & Communities of Color

A Roundtable of Activists

Michelle Garcia

Interview participants:

Gwenn Craig, Lesbians and Gays of African Descent for Democratic Action: San Francisco, California. Scot Nakagawa, Fight the Right: Portland, Oregon. Mandy Carter, National Black Gay and Lesbian Leadership Forum: Los Angeles, California. Steve Takemura, Gay Asian Pacific Alliance: San Francisco, California. Stephanie Smith, National Center for Lesbian Rights: San Francisco, California. Evelyn White, *San Francisco Chronicle,* San Francisco, California. Erna Pahe, American Indian AIDS Institute: San Francisco, California. Carmen Chavez, Latino/a Lesbian and Gay Organization: Washington, DC.

Led by the Christian Coalition, religious conservatives aim to push a fundamentalist agenda that includes opposition to abortion, favors school prayer and "creationist science," and is explicitly anti–homosexual. In some areas, as reported in *Third Force* magazine, the Religious Right is actively recruiting religious leaders of color, often on the basis of an anti–gay and lesbian political platform.

What can activists in communities of color do to develop a gay–positive alternative to these recruitment efforts? *Third Force* posed this question recently to a number of individuals active in gay and lesbian rights struggles. The interviews were conducted separately and woven together for this article.

Third Force: How can people of color address how the right wing uses an anti–gay agenda to infiltrate communities of color?

Gwenn Craig: We need to open up ongoing dialogues. People on both sides are willing to clear up misunderstandings of the past. The gay community's "taking power" is often seen as a gain at the expense of African Americans, which means we fight each other instead of looking at the real enemy: those who refuse to share power with us.

Scot Nakagawa: Folks need to run inoculation strategies: use church bulletins, newsletters, house meetings/parties, and community newspapers to inform everyone. We must inoculate people with information to prevent the right wing from penetrating our institutions.

The right is basically disseminating propaganda, something they can carry into communities. They're not organizing, building constituencies, or pulling people of color into their groups—that would require accountability. Right–wing organizations don't want to be accountable to us because they can't count on our support. What's going to happen when they work against immigration so our relatives can't come here, or undermine AFDC when disproportionate numbers of our people are on it?

Erna Pahe: We need to cooperate more, to get away from disputes between minority groups for funding. All people deserve access to resources. Agencies can learn to see each other as members of a network.

Steve Takemura: Perceptions of homosexuals in the media are not positive. We need to show the human sides of lesbians and gay men. We are your sons, daughters, aunties, etc. The mainstream media must be responsible about how they portray us. Most of us are average people just like anybody else, over our credit limits just like anybody else.

Third Force: What actions have you taken? What new strategies can we develop for the future?

Evelyn White: Community and political organizations need to exert pressure on the church. That's where change comes from. Mandy Carter is doing it—a front–line response to the problem's source. Get people on Sunday at 11 a.m. before they walk into church. If I were organizing a group, we'd be going to Mount Zion, to Ebenezer Baptist Church. We'd sit there, make our presence known, address the congregation, talk to the minister.

Carmen Chavez: We're organizing the first national Latina lesbian conference on September 16–18 [1994] in Tucson. Our goal is to build our own institutions for Latino/a lesbian/gay organizing. We solidify what already exists to build up those that are still fragile. Ultimately, we'll create a network of information for a national movement. Seed monies in the context of HIV prevention are invested in Latino/a lesbian/gay organizing.

Mandy Carter: NBGLLF's annual conference brings together African American lesbian/bi/gay/transgender people throughout the country. On August 5–7 [1994] we're holding a first–time ever national strategy conference in St. Louis.

We plan to confront Focus on the Family, one of the wealthiest radical right groups with a $150 million yearly budget, a staff of 900, a chapter in every state, and a volunteer pool of two million. They have 1,800 radio stations with daily political broadcasts. Right before the NBGLLF conference they're holding a three–day basketball camp for boys 13 to 18 with single parents (mostly women). While their sons are playing basketball, parents attend "classes" on FOF's anti–gay, anti–choice, and anti–immigration agendas. NBGLLF plans a national press conference that Monday on the site of the FOF camp, a predominantly Black junior college. We've asked for a meeting. We will relay the message: "Do not exploit us for your purposes. NBGLLF intends to be on the front lines of this movement. Notice is hereby being served."

Steve Takamura: I'm really proud of a pro–gay resolution the JACL (Japanese American Citizens League) adopted. The JACL, a national organization with headquarters in San Francisco, is the largest Asian civil rights group in the US, with 114 chapters. The Honolulu chapter voted first to support this resolution supporting same–sex marriages as a civil right. The vote was 10–3, with two abstentions. There was an uproar from the Salt Lake City chapter, and the legal counsel resigned over this issue. The next vote will be at the JACL national convention in Salt Lake City. For Japanese American lesbians and gay men it's a win–win situation. Whether the resolution passes or not, it brings our issues to the forefront.

Erna Pahe: Mothers come up to me saying, "I sent my son away because he was 'like that.'" I answer, "But he is your son. You loved him when he was a baby and he is still your son today." We can't send people away because we don't understand them! AIAI counsels HIV–positive Indians who are deathly afraid of coming out to their families. They act out telling their families in groups. We also contact groups of mothers and grandmothers in their tribes and do sensitivity workshops on the reservations. Mothers can explain things to each other. These strategies work to re–educate people about traditions of honoring two–spirit people.

What organizing can we do? We can hold townhouse meetings for everyone, not just Indian organizations. I compare it to squaw dances on the rez [reservation]—three–day ceremonies. Everyone from the surrounding area comes and shares. They talk about their lives, what's going on, what's bothering them. Everyone is blessed, doctored by the medicine man. We look at the community as a whole.

Gwenn Craig: We need to move into mainstream politics, to gain our rightful place in both lesbian/gay and African American civil rights movements. We want to end the marginalized, schizophrenic existence experienced by many of us—bring our selves together. We're proud of our efforts to create coalitions with other people of color: gay Asian and Latino/a groups. There's a new gay Southeast Asian group. We want to network with all of the groups of color in the lesbian/gay community. LGADDA initiated legislation banning discrimination in bar and dance club admissions. There was a long–standing practice in gay clubs of asking for multiple photo IDs to dissuade people of color from coming in. Many people of color testified that they had been asked for three IDs at certain clubs, while whites were not asked at all. We got the idea from efforts by groups in Chicago and Washington, DC.

Stephanie Smith: One counter–organizing tactic is promoting visible leadership of lesbians of color. With NCLR's Lesbians of Color Project, we go into cities and work on community education with existing grassroots organizations for lesbians of color. We show the video *Gay Rights, Special Rights*, stop the film at key points and talk about it. We discuss strategies for each community: specific threats and what needs to be done about them, what support they need. People come to realize that they're not alone. We can start dialogues in the Black community with church leaders and people of conscience of all orientations. Study the problem. Our congressional caucus has the highest percentage on the Hill for pro–gay votes: 90 percent. At the 1993 March on Washington, Coretta Scott King, Rev. Jesse Jackson, and Rev. Ben Chavis, executive director of the NAACP, spoke supporting civil rights for gays. It's important to reject the premise that the Black community is homophobic.

Third Force: Why do right–wing groups have more success than lesbian and gay groups reaching out to communities of color, as during the fight over Measure 9 in Oregon?

Scot Nakagawa: I don't think the right wing actually had more success, but people assume that they did. That assumption is based on racism. The white lesbian/gay community rarely works with communities of color, so by comparison right–wing activity looms large. The reality is that Black organizations such as the NAACP, the Black United Front, the Albina Ministerial Alliance, and African Americans Voting No on 9 were successful in blocking right–wing infiltration. The Korean Grocers Association, the Japanese American Citizens League, and the Asian Pacific American Alliance also came out strongly against Measure 9, and it failed in Oregon.

Stephanie Smith: The right wing essentially says that lesbians and gay men of color don't exist. White gay people are complicit since they have not promoted leadership by lesbians of color. They have not stepped aside and looked at their own racism. The movement has merely paid lip service to empowering lesbians or gay men of color, and their tokenism has come back to haunt them.

Evelyn White: I see the problem as a void of leadership in the Black community in general and in the Black clergy in particular. The Black church is our most powerful institution. It has proven that it can and will do right, and it has uplifted many people. Were the clergy to take a strong stand against homophobia, there is no question in my mind that people sitting in the pews every Sunday would change their tune. Right–wing infiltration would be easily nipped in the bud were Black leaders to present a unified front against it. The clergy have only to stand in their pulpits with the Good Book in front of them and say: "I used to feel this way, but I understand things in a different light now." That would be the end of the story.

Third Force: What is the role of lesbian/gay people of color?

Stephanie Smith: We need to lead this one. The right–wing agenda renders us invisible. As the people most profoundly affected by the bile going back and forth, we have the most to lose.

Evelyn White: Speak out about whatever we can, wherever we feel comfortable. Certainly if we're church members we can stop putting money in the collection plate: stop paying ministers' mortgages, putting them in Armani suits, or feeding them chicken.

Scot Nakagawa: To address the broader agenda of the right we must talk about economics. The Religious Right is part of a broader movement. At its inception, economically motivated people like Phyllis Schlafly decided they wanted to create an economy where greed could go unchecked. Trickle–down theory didn't motivate people, so they recruited the fast–growing evangelical Christian movement: Jimmy Swaggart, Pat Robertson, and the other committed activists essential to forming political organizations.

We need to show our communities the real right–wing agenda. We need to change our message from "Hate is not a family value" and communicate about the price of bread. Talk about holding fundamentalists accountable to communities of color. The right wing belongs to a broad political spectrum designed to keep us economically exploited and without hope.

Steve Takemura: We can never underestimate the organizational skills of the Religious Right or their level of commitment. Our own people are potentially that committed. We need to educate people that gay rights are not "special rights"—they're basic civil rights that apply to all people.

Carmen Chavez: In a way, our role is already defined. We play ambassadors to communities of color and educate the white lesbian/gay community. We can become more visible—we can work that!

Many lesbians have a hard time talking about our sexuality. Our own internalized "isms" have not been worked through. We can't ignore lesbians who sleep with men. Bisexuals are often compartmentalized within the movement, which limits us all. There's no room for judgments here. We don't have the luxury of excluding anyone. We may be afraid of how bisexuality affects our constructed definitions of being gay. Change can show us our own demons. The gay community needs to confront this issue.

Erna Pahe: The Navaho have a tradition of honoring two–spirit people. We call them Nahaali. Two–spirit people can hunt, stay at home, grind corn, or butcher sheep. They have a special appreciation of the pain a woman has and the pain a man has. Medicine people have a two–spirit beginning and may take same–sex or opposite–sex mates. Seeing beyond gender enables them to communicate with all of the spirits. Their strength comes from Mother Earth, Grandfather Sky, and all of the animals without distinguishing between male and female: they're all people.

Two–spirit people are teachers. We are all put here to live a certain life. Not everyone has chosen their way. Society has us brainwashed about male and female gender roles, yet gender is only an identifying word that someone has thrown upon us. The two–spirit person brings us to the understanding that we are all people—teaches us how to be human beings again.

Michelle Garcia, based in California, is a contributing editor to *Third Force* magazine, a publication of the Center for Third World Organizing. This article originally appeared in the September/October 1994 issue of *Third Force.* © 1995, Michelle Garcia.

Soundbites Against Homophobia

Articulate Responses to Lies & Rhetoric

Robin Kane

Right–wing opponents to civil rights for gay, lesbian, and bisexual people use similar arguments and rhetoric around the country, whether they're in Prineville, Oregon; Colorado Springs, Colorado; Knoxville, Tennessee; or Anchorage, Alaska. These pages are tools for action. They include responses, ideas, and themes you can use to counter the right's erroneous allegations. Each topic begins with the rhetoric used by the conservative right, followed by some ideas on how to respond.

Rhetoric: Homosexuals are already covered under the Constitution just like the rest of us. What they want are "special rights." We oppose "special rights" for homosexuals.

Response: The right wing rhetoric of *"special rights"* skews the issue. The right to get and keep a job based on merit is not a special right. Equal access to housing is not a special right. Renting a hotel room and being served food in a restaurant are not special rights. The right to have and raise children without the state seizing them is not a special right. The right to walk down a street and not get attacked because of who you are and whom you love is not a special right. Gay and lesbian people want the same rights guaranteed to all American citizens. However, without civil rights laws which specifically ban discrimination based on sexual orientation, gay people can lose their jobs, their homes, and their families, and be refused service at public accommodations simply because they are gay—with no legal recourse. Right–wing zealots who speak of special rights want the very special right to discriminate against those they hate. They want "special righteousness."

Rhetoric: Local ordinances for gay men and lesbians force the rest of us to live against our religious beliefs. We're entitled to our rights, too.

Response: Extending civil rights to one sector of society does not withdraw rights from another. Most civil rights ordinances provide exemptions for religious institutions. In addition, many gay and lesbian members of various religious denominations are organizing within their faith so that religious institutions may become more accepting of the diversity of their following.

Rhetoric: They want to be treated like a minority, like an ethnic minority. The Supreme Court says they're not. And we know they're not because they never rode in the back of the bus and they are not economically deprived. Studies show that gay men have more disposable income than the rest of Americans.

Response: Gay men and lesbians are a numerical minority in American society. Like ethnic minorities, we do face job loss, eviction, non–service at public accommodations, and the loss of our children simply because of who we are. And like other minorities, gay people face harassment, physical assault, and murder based on an assailant's hatred against us as a group. A Department of Justice study reported that "homosexuals are the most frequent victims" of hate crime. "Minority status" affords no benefits to anyone; rather, it provides guidelines to attempt to redress the inequalities that impair the exercise of constitutionally–guaranteed freedoms, including equal protection under the law. Our Constitution says that all people are created equal—that must include gay and lesbian people as well.

Rhetoric: Homosexuals lead an abominable lifestyle. People who care about traditional family values must not encourage the open expression of this sexual depravity.

Response: Discrimination is the abomination, not gay and lesbian people. The family values we uphold are support, love, understanding, and respect between family members. Discrimination and bigotry are not traditional family values.

Rhetoric: You can't let gays be near children; since they can't reproduce, they recruit. And they are all pedophiles.

Response: Statistics show that the vast majority of sexual abuse is committed by men against women, usually within the heterosexual family structure. Pedophiles are criminals who derive illicit pleasure from sexual abuse of children, and whose adult sexual attractions are almost always to members of the opposite sex. One 1992 study from Denver showed that children are 100 times more likely to be molested by a family member than by a gay person. Lies perpetuate stereotypes that are then used to deny gay people our rights. It is wrong to deny us our rights based on these myths.

Rhetoric: *Gay people want to force their lifestyle on us and take away our rights.*

Response: Civil rights laws that include lesbian and gay people do not limit the rights of others. Instead, they extend to gays and lesbians the same rights already enjoyed by most Americans—the right to obtain and keep employment based on ability to do the job; the right to equal access to housing; the right to raise their children; and the right to live free of violence. There is no so–called "gay lifestyle." Gay men and lesbians are members of every social class, religious faith, ethnic group, occupation, and political affiliation. Gay people are not interested in forcing anything on anyone—just the opposite. We demand the freedom to live our lives with the same freedoms and rights that are accorded to all citizens, without fear that our liberty will be usurped by far right bigots and religious intolerance.

Rhetoric: *What this is really leading to are marriage licenses for gay men and lesbians, joint benefits, child adoptions, formalized domestic relationships, and the destruction of the American family. This is wrong.*

Response: Civil rights laws including gays and lesbians do not automatically grant us the right to marry. While the Christian Right perpetuates the stereotype of all gay people as sexually promiscuous individuals, society denies us recognition of our committed unions. Gay people are struggling to gain basic employment benefits for spouses equivalent to our heterosexual co–workers in their committed relationships.

Rhetoric: *What about bisexuals? They sometimes pretend to be normal heterosexual people, but they engage in the same abnormal, unhealthy sexual practices as homosexuals. Bisexuals are getting AIDS from homosexual sex and then spreading it throughout the heterosexual community.*

Response: Bisexual men and women live, work, and organize within the gay and lesbian community and in the larger human rights community. Lesbians, gay men, and bi people are all targets of the same oppression, excused on the basis that we value sexual and affectional relationships with members of the same gender. The US Department of Defense "ban against gays in the military" also includes those acting or identifying as bisexual. Many right–wing initiatives, including Colorado's Amendment 2, target bisexuals along with gay men and lesbians in their petition language and in the effects of their discriminatory legislation. Lesbians, gay men, and bi people work together to oppose these attempts to legislate against our civil rights. AIDS is the cumulative effect of immuno–suppression exacerbated by the presence of a virus (HIV) that critically impairs the ability of the body to keep itself well. Viruses do not target specific people or discriminate on the basis of sexual orientation or identity. The prevention of HIV/AIDS ultimately rests with each individual person's responsibility for her or his own actions, regardless of sexual orientation, class, race, gender, or sexual identity.

Rhetoric: *It's within our First Amendment rights to say what we think of homosexuals.*

Response: Right–wing organizations hide their homophobia behind the First Amendment. While the right wing demands the right to speak out against homosexuality, they are running well–financed campaigns to censor and squelch positive images of gay and lesbian people on television, in schools, and in the arts. The hatred and lies that right–wing organizations spew create a hostile environment for gay and lesbian people. Their rhetoric bolsters the hatred expressed by the bigots who physically attack gay men and lesbians. A national study conducted by the National Gay and Lesbian Task Force (NGLTF) Policy Institute documented 1,898 anti–gay incidents in just five US cities in 1992, a 172 percent increase over the number of incidents in 1990.

Robin Kane is an experienced media specialist who has worked for the National Gay and Lesbian Task Force and other human rights groups. This article previously appeared in the NGLTF publication, *Fight the Right Action Kit.* © 1995, Robin Kane.

Responding to Hate Groups

Ten Points to Remember

Center for Democratic Renewal

• Document the problem and stay informed. Your first step should be to conduct thorough research about hate group activity and bigoted violence in your community. Develop a chronology of incidents drawing on newspaper accounts, victim reports, and other sources. Stay informed about developments by clipping your local newspaper, subscribing to other publications, and networking with other individuals and agencies.

• Speak out and create a moral barrier to hate activity. Communities that ignore the problem of hate group activity and bigoted violence can sometimes create the impression that they don't care. This silence is often interpreted by hate groups as an invitation to step up their activities. Through press conferences, rallies, community meetings, and public hearings, you can create a climate of public opinion that condemns racism and bigotry right from the start.

• Match the solution to the problem. Whatever strategy you use to respond should be tailored to the specific situation you are dealing with; don't rely on rigid, formula–type solutions.

• Build coalitions. Hate violence and bigotry against one targeted group helps to legitimize activities against other groups. If you involve a wide spectrum of people representing diverse constituencies, you will have a better chance of achieving a unified, effective response.

• Assist victims. Providing support and aid to hate violence victims is central to any response strategy. Don't get so busy organizing press conferences and issuing proclamations that you forget to make a housecall and express your personal support.

• Work with constituencies targeted for recruitment. People who join hate groups usually do so out of frustration, fear, and anger; they might even be your neighbors next door. By offering meaningful social, economic, spiritual, and political alternatives you can discourage participation in hate groups by the very people most vulnerable to recruitment.

• Target your own community as well as the hate group. Organizations like the Ku Klux Klan don't create social conflict out of thin air; they have to feed off existing community tensions in order to exist. The enemy of community harmony is not always the hate group itself, but the existing bigotry and division the group can exploit. For these and other reasons it is also essential to conduct anti–bigotry education programs on an ongoing basis, *after* the hate group has left your community.

• Encourage peer–based responses among youth. Young people respond best to leadership that comes from within their peer group. While adults can provide valuable resources and insight, it is essential that youth groups develop and cultivate their own leaders and implement programs of their own design to combat bigotry.

• Remember that hate groups are not a fringe phenomenon and their followers don't always wear white sheets. Although the number of active white supremacists and neo–Nazis probably totals no more than 25,000 in the United States, as many as 500,000 Americans read their literature. This movement is complex and made up of numerous sometimes competing and sometimes cooperating organizations. Hate groups impact the mainstream of society in a variety of ways, including: running candidates for public office; publishing sophisticated propaganda; buying radio time and media outlets; distributing cable television programs; manipulating the media; and building alliances with more respectable conservative groups, including some fundamentalist and evangelical Christian organizations.

- Broaden your agenda. The problem is more than criminal. Hate activity is a political and social problem requiring a range of responses beyond those initiated by police. Citizen advocacy groups, religious agencies, and others should develop a public policy agenda that addresses a wide range of issues, including appropriate legislation, mandatory school curricula, expanded victim services, etc.

The Center for Democratic Renewal in Atlanta, Georgia, is a national organization assisting community–based groups fighting prejudice and hate crimes. This article is drawn from the 1992 CDR handbook *When Hate Groups Come to Town*. © 1995, Center for Democratic Renewal.

Common Sense Security

Sheila O'Donnell

Popular consciousness of environmental issues has seen tremendous growth in the past few years. People organizing or speaking out against environmental degradation in this country and abroad are facing an escalating pattern of harassment. Increasing also is the number of arsons, robberies, burglaries, and attacks on environmental activists, especially on women—who are often on the front lines in isolated rural areas. Investigators have learned of more than 100 cases since 1990. A pattern is emerging in these attacks which is similar to attacks on civil rights, anti–war, and Central America activists in the past.

As our movements have become stronger and more sophisticated, the techniques of the state, corporations, and right–wing groups have also become more sophisticated. We have seen government agents, corporate security and right–wing intelligence networks share information as well as an ideology. For instance, the FBI's COINTELPRO operations targeted dissidents in America in the 1960s and 1970s. Caution and common sense security measures in the face of the concerted efforts to stop us are therefore both prudent and necessary.

Spend a few minutes to assess your work from a security point of view: understand your vulnerabilities; assess your allies and your adversaries as objectively as possible; do not underestimate the opposition. Try to assess your organizational and personal strengths and weaknesses. Do not take chances. Plan for the worst; work and hope for the best.

Here are some specific suggestions for protecting yourself and your projects:

Office

• Never leave the only copy of a document or list behind; take a minute to duplicate an important document and keep the duplicate in a safe place off–site.

• Keep mailing and donor lists and personal phone books out of sight. Always maintain a duplicate at a different location; update it frequently.

• Know your printer if you are about to publish and know your mailing house if you contract for distribution. The loss of camera–ready copy or a change in text could feel like a disaster.

• Back up and store important computer disks off–site. Sensitive data and membership lists should be kept under lock and key. Do not leave sensitive files on the hard disk; use floppies, back them up, and store the disks in secure spots. Use an encryption program to protect your data.

• Know the background of anyone you are trusting to work on any part of a project that is sensitive. Projects have been bungled because an untrustworthy person has purposefully intervened or inadvertently screwed up.

• Don't hire a stranger as a messenger. Your message might not arrive or could arrive after being duplicated for an unintended party.

• Sweeps for electronic surveillance are only effective for the time they are being done, and are only effective as they are being done if you are sure of the person(s) doing the sweep. Sweeps tend to be expensive because one must sweep a large area to be effective. Many experts contend that the most sophisticated federal government and private agency taps cannot be detected.

• Keep a camera handy at all times.

Trash

• What you consider trash could be a real treasure to someone looking for information about you or your projects. Don't throw information out in your trash. Garbology has become a tactic because it is so useful.

• Keep a "Burn file" in a secure place and occasionally burn it or use a shredder. Make sure you shredder creates confetti because strips can easily be reconstructed with a little patience.

Telephone

- Do not list your address with your phone number in the directories. Consider having yourself unlisted.
- If you receive threatening calls on your answering machine, immediately remove and save the tape.
- Never respond to a query over the telephone from an unknown person—lottery tickets, fabulous prizes, jury questionnaires, etc. notwithstanding. Ask for a telephone number and call the party back considerably later or the following day. Check the phone book to see if the phone number they gave you is legitimate. Check it out. Do the same if a reporter calls.
- Never say anything you don't want to hear repeated where there is any possibility of being recorded or overheard. Don't say anything on the phone you don't want to hear in open court.
- Don't talk in code on the telephone. If you are being tapped and the transcript is used against you in court, the coded conversation can be alleged to mean anything by government code "experts."
- Don't gossip about sensitive people or projects on the telephone. All information that can make an outsider "in the know" about you and your projects is valuable and makes everyone vulnerable.
- Keep a pad and pen next to the telephone. Jot down details of threatening or suspicious calls immediately. Note the time, date and keep a file.
- Don't waste time worrying about phone taps or imagining that strange clicks or hums or other noises indicate a phone tap. Many taps are virtually impossible to detect. Trust your instincts. If you think your phone is tapped, act accordingly.

Mail

- Get a mail box through the United States Post Office or a private concern. Be aware that the Post Office will give your street address to inquirers under certain circumstances.
- If you receive a threatening letter, handle it as little as possible. Put both the letter and the envelope in a plastic bag or file folder. Give the original to the police only if they agree to fingerprint it. If not, give them a copy because you may wish to have your own expert examine it.

Automobiles

• Keep your automobile clean so you can see if there is an addition or loss.
• Put no bumper stickers on your car which identify you as an organizer. Make your car look ordinary.
• Put your literature in the trunk or in a closed box.
• Keep your car locked at all times.

Police

• Report any incidents to the local police and ask for protection if you feel it is warranted.
• Report threats or harassment to your local police. Demand that they take a report and protect you if that is necessary. Talk to the press and report the police response as well as the incident(s).
• Report thefts of materials from your office or home to the police; these are criminal acts.

Under Surveillance?

• Brief your membership on known or suspected surveillance. Be scrupulous with documentation. Do not dismiss complaints as paranoia without careful investigation. The opposition can and frequently does have informants join organizations to learn about methods and strategy.
• Discuss incidents with colleagues, family, and membership. Call the press if you have information about surveillance or harassment. Discussion makes the secret dirty work of the intelligence agencies and private spies easier to spot.
• If you wish to have a private conversation, leave your home or office and take a walk or go somewhere very public and notice who can hear you.
• If you know a secret, keep it to yourself. As the World War II poster warned: loose lips sink ships.
• Photograph the person(s) following you or have a friend do so. Use caution. If someone is overtly following you or surveilling you, she or he is trying to frighten you. Openly photographing them makes them uncomfortable. If you are covertly being followed, have a friend covertly photograph them.

- If you are being followed, get the license plate number and state. Try to get a description of the driver and the car as well as passengers. Notice anything different about the car.
- If you are followed or feel threatened, call a friend; don't "tough it out" alone. "They" are trying to frighten you. It is frightening to have someone threatening your freedom.
- Debrief yourself immediately after each incident. Write details down: time, date, occasion, incident, characteristics of the person(s), impressions, anything odd about the situation.
- Keep a "Weirdo" file with detailed notes about unsettling situations and see if a pattern emerges.

Break–Ins

- Check with knowledgeable people in your area about alarm systems, dogs, surveillance cameras, motion sensitive lights, dead bolt locks, and traditional security measures to protect against break–ins.

Visits From the FBI

- Don't talk to the FBI or any government investigator without your attorney present. Get the names and addresses of the agents and tell them you will have your attorney contact them to set up a meeting. If you have an attorney, give her or him the name and phone number. Under any circumstance, get the agents' names and addresses. Information gleaned from a conversation can be used against you and your co–workers. The agents' report of even an innocuous conversation could "put words in your mouth" that you never uttered or your words could be distorted or made up if you don't have your attorney present.
- Call the National Lawyers Guild, American Civil Liberties Union, or other sympathetic legal organizations if you need assistance locating a reliable attorney in your area.
- The FBI rarely sets up interviews with counsel present. Often when the demand is made to have the interview with counsel, the FBI loses overt interest.
- Don't invite agents into your home. Speak with the agents outside. Once inside, they glean information about your perspective and lifestyle.
- Don't let agents threaten you or talk you into having a short, personal conversation without your lawyer. Don't let them intimidate or trick you into talking. If the FBI wants to empanel a

Grand Jury, a private talk with you will not change the strategy of the FBI. Don't try to outwit the FBI; your arrogance could get you or others in serious trouble.

• FBI agents sometimes try to trick you into giving information "to help a friend." Don't fall for it; meet with the agents in the presence of your attorney and then you can help your friend.

• Lying to the FBI is a criminal act. The best way to avoid criminal charges is to say nothing.

• Any information you give the FBI can and will be used against you.

• Write for your government files under the Freedom of Information Act and keep writing to the agencies until they give you all the documents filed under your name.

• Don't let the agents intimidate you. What if they do know where you live or work and what you do? We have a constitutional right to lawful dissent. You are not required to speak with the FBI. They intend to frighten you; don't let them.

• Do not overlook the fact that government agencies sometimes share information within the government and with the private sector, particularly right–wing organizations. This has been documented.

Remember

If you feel you are being surveilled, your phones tapped, or that you are being followed, the best overall advice is to trust your instincts. If you feel something is wrong, trust the feeling. Your instincts are usually right. Most of us recall the times when we "felt something was wrong" or we "knew better but did it anyway."

Talk to colleagues and make yourself as secure as you can. Experts claim that people who resist get away from attackers more often than those who do not. The same logic applies to keeping outsiders out of your business; it is a more subtle form of attack.

Trust your instincts and resist when possible. One of the biggest blocks to resistance is the failure to recognize that we are under attack. None of this advice is intended to frighten but to create an awareness of the problems. A knowledge of the strategies and tactics of your adversaries will strengthen your movement. Cover yourself; it's a tough world out there.

Suggested Readings

• Caignon, Denise and Gail Groves. *Her Wits About Her: Self Defense Success Stories by Women.* New York, 1987.

• Churchill, Ward and Jim Vander Wall. *Agents of Repression: The FBI's Secret Wars Against the Black Panther Party and the American Indian Movement.* Boston: South End Press, 1988.

• Donner, Frank J. *The Age of Surveillance.* New York: Random House, 1981.

• Gelbspan, Ross. *Break–ins, Death Threats and the FBI: The Covert War Against the Central America Movement.* Boston: South End Press, 1991.

• Glick, Brian. *War at Home: Covert Action Against US Activists and What We can Do About It.* Boston: South End Press, 1989.

Uniting to Defend the Four Freedoms

Chip Berlet

We all need to spend some time considering how best to defend liberty and freedom, and what unites us as a nation concerned with democratic values. In doing so, we need to commit to a process that respects civil liberties, *and* civil rights, *and* civil discourse.

The armed militia members claim to defend liberty and freedom. They claim to be the new patriot movement, harkening back to the Minutemen who resisted government tyranny at Concord Bridge and Lexington Green. What happened at Waco to the Branch Davidians, and at Ruby Ridge to the Weaver family, must be condemned, but opposition to excessive force by government agents does not imply we should seek alliances with right–wing populists simply because they criticize the government. Militia zealots conflate real acts of repression and injustice with their fantastic conspiratorial scapegoats. Such movements quickly can swing far to the right with murderous consequences, as those who fought fascism in Europe can explain in horrifying detail.

My Dad wouldn't talk with me about World War II except to say it was brutal and bloody and that he lost many friends. So when he swapped war stories in the basement with his drinking buddies, I would sit in the dark at the top of the stairs and listen.

I learned how his hands and feet had been frostbitten during the Battle of the Bulge, and that one of his Bronze Star citations was for taking out a Nazi machine gun nest. He thought the

Germans were decent people whose big mistake was not standing up to the thugs like the Brownshirts who broke the windows of Jewish-owned stores on *Kristalnacht*. As I remembered this, I watched mountains of broken glass being swept up in Oklahoma City as the death count rose.

News of the bombing reached our family on vacation in coastal Georgia. I had been writing about the historic and social roots of the militia movement and, after visiting a museum preserving a former rice plantation, had talked with my son about how the Ku Klux Klan had formed as a militia during the economic and cultural turmoil following the Civil War. I had little doubt that the blast was somehow linked to the armed militia movement.

Reports of the carnage at the Oklahoma City federal building, the selfless efforts of rescue crews, and the horror of even some militia members, mingled eerily with stories commemorating the 50th anniversary of the end of World War II in Europe and the 20th anniversary of the end of the Vietnam War. I found history lessons connecting these events in an old brass–bound wooden chest, inherited after we buried my Dad at Arlington Cemetery 20 years ago. Inside were brittle photos of a young lieutenant, a dried flower sent to my Mom from "somewhere in Belgium," crumbling newspaper clippings on the fighting near Bastogne, and a leather case filled with war medals.

Like many White Christians in the late 1950s, Dad held stereotyped views about Blacks and Jews. His actions spoke differently, though, and were the durable lesson. When neighbors in Hackensack, New Jersey, told him that our town was not ready for the Little League team he coached—with a Black player, a Jewish player, and a Jewish assistant coach—Dad simply said he had picked the best, and shut the door. He told me he had seen Jews and Blacks die along with everyone else fighting the Nazis; then he pointedly invited the entire team and their families to our yard for a very public picnic. Later, the stones crashing through our windows at night merely hardened his resolve.

In the 1960s we moved up the commuter rail line to Hillsdale, New Jersey. My brother went to military school and played in the marching band. In college he was sports editor of the campus newspaper and joined ROTC. After graduation he shipped out to fight in Vietnam. I went to church–basement coffee houses and marched with the civil rights movement. In college I edited the campus newspaper and joined the anti–war movement. After the killings at Kent State and Jackson State in 1970, I editorialized in favor of a student strike.

The next year, after a commemoration of Kent and Jackson, a professor sent me his Korean war medals as an act of protest against our government's policies. He felt a need to stand up, and his conscience told him that "it is all of us that are guilty—we who sit there and do nothing." We sent the newspaper with a story about the medals to the printers, then I sat up all night trying to unravel conflicting emotions over family expectations, my hope for my brother's safe return from war, career plans, and what my personal moral obligations demanded of me, given my views about peace and social justice. When morning came, I quietly joined other anti–war protestors and engaged in my first act of non–violent civil disobedience at a federal building near Denver.

My Dad was Grand Marshall of Hillsdale's Memorial Day parade. When a tiny peace group in the early 1970s asked to participate, it created a furor. Dad was a lifelong Republican, pro–war, and anti–communist, and his idea of America came right out of a Norman Rockwell painting. He told the town officials that if the peace marchers followed the rules, they were entitled to march. And they did. Mom told me he came home from the debate shaking his head, asking how people could forget those who gave their lives to defend such rights.

Reunited as a family one Thanksgiving, we all toasted my brother's safe return from Vietnam with the crystal wine glasses my father brought back from Germany. It was a mirrored tableau of Rockwell's "Freedom From Want," a painting of a family sharing abundant food. The "Four Freedoms" series appeared as *Saturday Evening Post* covers during World War II; and as corny and steeped in stereotyping as they were, the theme helped unify and rally our nation at a time of crisis. Sure, politicians had other more cynical and pragmatic justifications for the war, but most Americans were willing to fight because they believed in the four freedoms.

Years later, battling cancer, my Dad was determined to don his uniform one last time on Memorial Day. As I helped him dress, I asked him about the war. His only reply was to hand me one of his medals. Inscribed on the back were the words "Freedom from Fear and Want. Freedom of Speech, and Religion." The four freedoms. My Dad fought fascism to defend these freedoms, not just for himself, but for people of different religions and races, people he disagreed with. . .even people he was prejudiced against.

Today, the four freedoms that millions fought to defend are under attack—in part because we forget why people fought World War II, we deny what led to the Holocaust, we fail to live up to the promise of the civil rights movement, and we refuse to heal the wounds of the Vietnam War era.

Freedom of speech needs to be defended because democracy depends on a thoughtful debate to build informed consent. This is impossible when the public conversation—from armed militia members to talk–show hosts to mainstream politicians—is typified by shouting, falsehoods, and scapegoating. The Nazi death camps proved that hateful speech linked to conspiracy myths can lead to violence and murder. The solution is not censorship, but citizenship—people need to stand up and speak out in public against the bigots and bullies. Democracy works. The formula for democracy is straightforward: over time, the majority of people, given enough accurate information, and access to a free and open debate, reach the right decisions to preserve liberty. Thus democracy depends on ensuring freedom of speech.

Freedom from fear is manipulated by those demanding laws that would undermine freedom of speech. The same agencies that spied on the civil rights and anti–war movements are again peddling the false notion that widespread infiltration of social movements is effective in stopping terrorism. Meanwhile, demagogues fan the flames of fear to urge passage of even more authoritarian crime control measures—while doing little to find real societal solutions that would bring freedom from fear to crime–ridden communities.

Freedom of religion is twisted by those seeking to make their private religious views into laws governing the public. But it is also abused by liberal critics who patronize sincere religious belief as ignorance, and litter the landscape with hysterical and divisive direct mail caricaturing all religious conservatives as zealots. Freedom of religion means we must have a serious debate on the issues with our devout neighbors, while condemning the theocrats who claim to speak for God as they pursue secular political goals.

Freedom from want has been shoved aside in a mean–spirited drive to punish the hungry, the poor, the children, the elderly, the disabled, the infirm, the homeless, the disenfranchised.

For many in our country, the four freedoms remain only a dream, but at least in 1945 it was a dream worth fighting for. How many of us today are willing to stop shouting and just talk with each other about how best our nation can defend the four freedoms?

Chip Berlet, senior analyst at Political Research Associates, is co–author with Matthew N. Lyons of *Too Close For Comfort: Right Wing Populism, Scapegoating, and Fascist Potentials in US Political Traditions.* (South End Press, 1996). A shorter version of this essay was circulated to newspapers by the Progressive Media Project. © 1995, Chip Berlet.

Resources

For More Information:

Political Research Associates has more extensive and regularly updated
lists of who to contact, who to challenge, and what to read. These are
available online by computer (see connect information on the next page), or
by mail in print form. To obtain a complete resource list of print materials
by mail, write to:

Political Research Associates (PRA)
120 Beacon Street, 3rd Floor
Somerville, MA 02143
(617) 661–9313

For in–depth coverage of issues and trends on the right, don't forget to
subscribe to PRA's newsletter:

The Public Eye
$29 for four quarterly issues (individual rate)

Write for institutional and low–income rates

Where to Connect

Expanded and updated versions of the material in this resource section
are available online along with numerous other text files.
Please note that PRA does *not* answer e-mail information requests, but posts all
of its electronically–available information online at the sites listed below.
Write PRA for a list of print resources available by mail.

Internet

Web Home Page & Searchable Databases

URL: http://www.publiceye.org/pra/

URL: gopher://gopher.publiceye.org:7021/

Gopher Site & Searchable Databases

gopher.publiceye.org:7021
(gopher to server "publiceye.org" with server port set to "7021")

Electronic Mail Lists for Information Sharing

<rightdocs>   for long study documents concerning the political right.
<rightforum>   for alerts & discussions concerning the political right.

To join the list send e–mail to the computer address: "majordomo@igc.apc.org"
with the single line message: "subscribe rightdocs" or "subscribe rightforum."
If you wish to get off the list send to "majordomo@igc.apc.org" the single line
message "unsubscribe rightdocs" or "unsubscribe rightforum"

Bulletin Board System

For free direct access to the Public Eye BBS, call using computer telecommunications software to (617) 221–5815. No fee or connect charges other than your
normal long–distance billing. 24 hours/day. Settings: 300bps–14,400bps, 8N1.
Co–sponsored with the National Lawyers Guild Civil Liberties Committee.

PRA Conferences on IGC Peacenet

<pra.publiceye>   Back issues of the *Public Eye* magazine.
<pra.bibliography>   Bibliographies & reading lists.
<pra.prodemocracy>   List of groups promoting democracy & diversity.
<pra.reactionary>   List of reactionary, orthodox & traditionalist groups.
<pra.reports>   Reports, monographs, & other lengthy text files.
<pol.right.docs>   Conference echoing <rightdocs> list (see above).
<pol.right.forum>   Conference echoing <rightforum> list (see above).

Democracy Works Home Page

Join PRA and other pro-democracy groups at the Democracy Works home page,
sponsored by the Institute for Alternative Journalism:

URL: http://www.alternet.org/an/demworks.html

Who to Contact

Compiled by
Political Research Associates

Alternative Radio

Alternative Radio
PO Box 551
Boulder, CO 80306

Supplies interviews and other public affairs and documentary programs to over 120 non–commercial radio stations across the US and Canada. A catalog of tapes, including many relevant to challenging the right, is available for $1.

Alternet

Institute for Alternative
Journalism
77 Federal Street
San Francisco, CA 94107
(415) 284–1420

http://www.igc.apc.org/an/alternet.html

Electronic news service and information clearinghouse for editors, journalists, and activists on the myriad aspects of the culture war, particularly attacks on freedom of expression.

Union (ACLU) American Civil Liberties

132 West 43rd Street
New York, NY 10036
(212) 944–9800

Interested in threats to civil liberties posed by aspects of the Religious Right, including school prayer, school vouchers, right to die, equal education and employment opportunity, reproductive freedom, welfare reform. Write for full list of resources.

American Jewish Committee

165 East 56th Street
New York, NY 10022 –2476
(212) 751–4000

Examines the rise of the Religious Right and the far right, especially armed militias. Has excellent short pamphlet on Religious Right: *The Political Activity of the Religious Right: A Critical Analysis*. Many other useful publications.

American Jewish Congress

15 East 84th Street
New York, NY 10028
(212) 879–4500

Coordinated publication of instructive pamphlet: *Religion in the Public Schools: A Joint Statement of Current Law*, endorsed by wide range of religious and secular groups. Many other useful publications.

American Library Association (ALA)

50 East Huron Street
Chicago, IL 60611
(312) 944–6780

Censorship, school curricula, library protests, legal decisions. Coverage frequently involves local campaigns by religious and political right. Newsletter: *Newsletter On Intellectual Freedom*. Bi–monthly, $30.

Americans for Religious Liberty

PO Box 6656
Silver Spring, MD 20916
(301) 598–2447

Several books and pamphlets available. Write for a current list. Newsletter: *Voice of Reason*. Quarterly, $20.

Americans United for Separation of Church & State

1816 Jefferson Place, NW
Washington, DC 20036
(202) 466–3234

Monitors the Religious Right and promotes church–state separation. Opposes public funding of parochial schools. Supports religiously neutral public education. Write for information and resources. Newsletter: *Church and State*. Monthly, $18.

Anti–Defamation League of B'nai B'rith (ADL)

823 United Nations Plaza
New York, NY 10017
(212) 490–2525

Most frequently cited resource on anti–Jewish bigotry. Print and electronic media resources are extensive. Study on the Religious Right is a lengthy, cautious overview. National leadership defends close relationship with government law enforcement agencies.

Applied Research Center

25 Embarcadero Cove
Oakland, CA 94606
(510) 534–1769

General and contract research on issues involving race, racism, and diversity. Newsletter: *Race File*, a collection of topical articles. Bi-monthly, $48.

Catholics for Free Choice

1436 U Street, NW, Suite 301
Washington, DC 20009–3916
(202) 986–6093

Write for a current list of publications in English and Spanish.

Center for Democratic Renewal (CDR)

PO Box 50469
Atlanta, GA 30302
(404) 221–0025

Largest community–based coalition fighting hate group activity. Every civil rights or human relations office should have a copy of *When Hate Groups Come to Town* to provide a ready response to hate–motivated violence or intimidation. Write for resources. Newsletter: *The Monitor*. Quarterly, $35.

Clearinghouse on Environmental Advocacy and Research (CLEAR)

1718 Connecticut Aveenue NW,
Suite 600
Washington, DC 20009
(202) 667–6982

Works to expose corporate agenda of the Wise Use movement. Newsletter: *A Clear View.*

Coalition for Human Dignity

PO Box 40344
Portland, OR 97240
(503) 281–5823

Works to expose the far right and theocratic right in the Pacific Northwest. Provides support to community organizations and monitors national Christian Right organizations and white supremacist activity. Excellent comprehensive study of the far right in the Northwest. Journal: *The Dignity Report*. Monthly, $30.

CovertAction Quarterly

CovertAction Publications
1500 Massachusetts Avenue, NW
   Suite 732
Washington, DC 20005
(202) 331–9763

Back issues with articles on religious and political right available. Previous topics have included "Covert Tactics and Overt Agenda of the New Christian Right," and a special issue on the Religious Right.

Data Center

464 19th Street
Oakland, CA 94612
(510) 835–4692

Research on contract into a variety of topics with special expertise in corporations and current political issues. Large collection of clippings and specialized computer skills for searching electronic databases. Newsletter: *Culture Watch*. Write for complete resource list.

Facing History and Ourselves

16 Hurd Road
Brookline, MA 02146
(617) 232–1595

High school curriculum on the Holocaust, slavery, Armenian genocide, and theories of prejudice and violence.

Fairness and Accuracy in Reporting (FAIR)

130 West 25th Street
New York, NY 10001
(212) 633–6700

A media watchdog group that publishes a bi-monthly newsletter: *Extra!*

Gay Community News (GCN)

29 Stanhope Street
Boston, MA 02116
(617) 262-6969

A politically progressive national newspaper that provides analysis, commentary, and cultural reflections on queer life.

Institute for First Amendment Studies (IFAS)

PO Box 589
Great Barrington, MA 01230
(413) 528-3800

Tracks Religious Right and covers separation of church and state issues. Reliable expertise on Religious Right and Reconstructionism. Newsletter: *Freedom Writer*. Eleven per year, $25.

Montana Human Rights Network

PO Box 9184
Helena, MT 59624
(406) 442–5506

Frontline human rights group in the heart of militia country. Newsletter: *Network News*.

National Campaign for Freedom of Expression (NCFE)

1402 Third Avenue, Room 421
   Seattle, WA 98101
   (206) 340–9301
918 F Street, NW, Room 609
   Washington, DC 20004
   (202) 393-2787

Focuses on art censorship with special attention to attacks by Religious Right. Publishes the *NCFE Bulletin* quarterly.

National Coalition Against Censorship (NCAC)

275 7th Avenue, 20th Floor
New York, NY 10001
(212) 807–6222

Coalition of over 40 participating organizations. Write for long list of topical resource materials. Newsletter: *Censorship News*. 5 issues per year, $30.

National Gay & Lesbian Task Force (NGLTF)

2320 17th Street, NW
Washington, DC 20009
(202) 332–6483

A national gay and lesbian rights organization. Organizes at the regional and national levels and publishes *Fight the Right Action Kit*.

Northwest Coalition Against Malicious Harassment (NWCAMH)

PO Box 16776
Seattle, WA 98116
(206) 233–9136

Coalition of organizations that monitors supremacist groups and activities. A good resource for community activists.

People Against Racist Terror (PART)

PO Box 1990
Burbank, CA 91507
(310) 288–5003

Produces reports with a radical analysis of racism, white supremacy, anti–Jewish and anti–Arab activity, and facism that feature substantial research and an accessible style. Send $1 for a list of resources. Newsletter: *Turning the Tide*. $15 donation.

People for the American Way (PFAW)

2000 M Street, NW
Suite 400
Washington, DC 20036
(202) 467–4999

Has numerous reports on the Religious Right. Write for a current list of resources. Newsletter: *Right–Wing Watch*. 10 issues per year, $15.

Political Research Associates (PRA)

120 Beacon Street, 3rd Floor
Somerville, MA 02143
(617) 661–9313

Research center with extensive archive on right-wing movements ranging from the New Right to white supremacist groups. Publishes numerous information packets and bibliographies. Write for a full list of resources. Newsletter: *The Public Eye*. Quarterly, $29.

Poverty & Race Research Action Council (PRRAC)

1711 Connecticut Avenue, NW
#217
Washington, DC 20009
(202) 387–9887

A networking group that puts serious researchers and advocacy groups together for joint projects of common interest. Publishes *Poverty & Race*.

Progressive Magazine

409 East Main Street
Madison, WI 53003

Publishes monthly, $30.

Project Tocsin

PO Box 163523
Sacramento, CA 95816–3523
916 374–8276

Covers Traditional Values Coalition and other Religious Right groups.

Radio For Peace International

PO Box 20728
Portland, OR 97220
(503) 252-3639

A short-wave radio program covering peace and social justice, but with a weekly media watch radio program discussing right-wing radio programs.

Simon Wiesenthal Center

9760 West Pico
Los Angeles, CA 90035
(310) 553-9036

Extensive collection on the Holocaust and the dynamics of prejudice. Library open by appointment. Write for a complete list of resources.

Southern Poverty Law Center (SPLC)

400 Washington Avenue
Montgomery, AL 36104
(334) 264-0286

Has developed a Teaching Tolerance curriculum. Write for details. National leadership defends close relationship with government law enforcement agencies. Has an excellent and informative newsletter: *Klanwatch Intelligence Report.*

Speak Out!

PO Box 99096
Emeryville, CA 94662
(510) 601-0182
speakout@igc.apc.org

National not-for-profit progressive speakers and artists agency. Includes Action for Democratic Education and School for Art in Politics.

Third Force

Center for Third World Organizing
1218 East 21st Street
Oakland, CA 94606
(510) 533-7583

Third Force magazine aims to help communities of color organize, develop leadership, broaden their bases of information, and build alliances with other communities with the goal of constructing an independent, grassroots, multi-racial movement for justice. Bi-monthly, $22.

University Conversion Project

PO Box 748
Cambridge, MA 02142

Promotes peace activism and investigative journalism on campus. Questions widespread military and right-wing funding on campus. Excellent guide to fighting the right on campus. Newsletter: *Study War No More.* Quarterly, $25.

Western States Center

522 SW Fifth Avenue, Suite 1390
Portland, OR 97204
(503) 228-8866

Covers the right, especially Wise Use, in the western states. Publishes *Western States Center News.*

Z Magazine

116 Saint Botolph Street, #1
Boston, MA 02115
(617) 236-5878
18 Millfield Street
Woods Hole, MA 02543
(508) 548-9063

An independent political magazine of critical thinking on political, cultural, social, and economic life in the US. Publishes monthly, $26.

Who to Challenge

Compiled by the
Institute for First Amendment Studies
This is a list of the most influential theocratic
groups of the hard right.

American Family Association

PO Drawer 2440
107 Parkgate
Tupelo, MS 38803
(601) 844–5036

Founded and led by Rev. Donald Wildmon, originally under the name National Federation for Decency. Wildmon also founded Christian Leaders for Responsible Television (CLeaR–TV), led by Rev. Billy Melvin of the National Association of Evangelicals. There may be few genuinely active chapters. Their last annual conference drew members from fewer than 40 chapters. There are 24 state chapter directors. The AFA employs about 150 people, and had an annual income of about $6 million in 1993.

Chalcedon

PO Box 158
Vallecito, CA 95251
(209) 736–4365

Founded in 1964 as a 501(c)(3) non–profit, tax–exempt group, Chalcedon (cal–SEE–don) is a leading think tank of the Christian Right. In 1991, Chalcedon received $634,264 in contributions, gifts, and grants. The group also received $57,486 in tuition at their Christian day school; $5,533 from journal sales; $3,571 in speaking and writing fees; and $10,092 from sales of tapes and videos.

Some of Chalcedon's books are published by Ross House Books, a separate non–profit, tax–exempt affiliated organization.

Christian Coalition

PO Box 1990
Chesapeake, VA 23327
(800) 325–4746

Founded in 1989, the Christian Coalition has about 1,700 chapters (in all 50 states) and 1.7 million members. Their 1995 budget is $25 million. The coalition operates under a provisional status of a 501(c)(4) organization. They cannot legally endorse or oppose candidates. While they are not required to pay taxes, contributions to the group are not tax–deductible. In 1993, the Christian Coalition had full–time staff in 20 states and claimed 50,000 precinct leaders and 25,000 church liaison leaders.

Since November 1991, the Coalition's annual Road to Victory (RTV) national strategy conferences have drawn delegates from every state. About 800 attended the first RTV; about 1,500 attended in September 1992; and 4,200 attended RTV in September 1995. RTV is followed up with state and local Leadership Schools. These political seminars use a "nuts and bolts manual on how to start a chapter; how to fund raise for your candidate; how to be a candidate; and how to canvass your voters." They also deal with how to handle the media. Over 70 Leadership Schools were scheduled in 1993.

Coalition on Revival

89 Pioneer Way
Mountain View, CA 94041
(408) 253-8852

Founded in January 1984 as a non-profit, tax-exempt 501(c)(3) organization, the Coalition on Revival (COR) mostly works behind the scenes to unite politically active fundamentalists, Pentecostals, and charismatics. COR's annual budget of around $100,000 is small compared to many of the Christian Right organizations. However, its purpose is also different from most of the other groups. COR does not solicit membership from among lay people, operates as a think tank and networking group of ministers and theologians.

Concerned Women for America

370 L'Enfant Promenade SW,
Suite 800
Washington, DC 20024
(800) 458-8797

Founded in 1979 in San Diego, California, as a 501(c)(3) organization, CWA moved to Washington, DC, in 1985. CWA claims 600,000 members (anyone who has donated time or money in any given 18-month period) and over 800 chapters. CWA receives some foundation money (e.g., DeMoss Foundation), but most of its income comes from direct mail solicitations. CWA also makes a profit on conferences. Tax returns indicate a recent conference netted over $220,000. Total CWA budget is about $10 million annually.

Focus on the Family

102 North Cascade
Colorado Springs, CO 80903
(719) 531-3400

Focus on the Family (FOTF) was founded in 1977 as a 501(c)(3) organization. 1992 budget: $78 million.

Employees: almost 1,000 (as of 1993). FOTF publishes eight periodicals; and produces five different radio programs which are broadcast on more than 1,550 stations worldwide, including many in the former Soviet Union. Originally located in California, it moved to Colorado in 1991.

Free Congress Foundation

717 Second Street NE
Washington, DC 20002
(202) 546-3000

Founded in 1978 as a 501(c)(3) organization, FCF evolved out of the Committee for the Survival of a Free Congress. FCF's lobbying arm, Coalitions for America, is 501(c)(4). Generally considered on the secular side of right-wing politics, FCF has close ties with the Religious Right through the coalition activities, staff liaisons, and board of directors. FCF's 1988 budget of $3,340,000 represents an average annual increase of 19 percent over a six year period. 1993 income was estimated at between $6 and $7 million.

Major donors include members of the Coors beer family; the Krieble family of the Loctite Corp.; Nancy DeMoss; Michael and Helen Valerio of Papa Gino's; Howard Ahmanson Jr. of the Fieldstead Foundation; the DeVos Foundation; and Richard and Helen DeVos of the Amway Corp. FCF's National Empowerment Television (NET) has a $2.1 million budget that is expected to double by 1997.

Paul Weyrich is president of NET; former Secretary of Education, William J. Bennett, is chairman; Robert W. Golas is vice-president. Ralph Reed of the Christian Coalition is a director.

National Association of Christian Educators

PO Box 3200
Costa Mesa, CA 92628
(714) 251–9333

Founded in 1983 as a 501(c)(3), non–profit, tax–exempt organization. CEE is a division of NACE. The group claims over 1,250 chapters. With California in the lead, NACE/CEE has chapters in almost every state. NACE/CEE's annual budget is about $700,000. Most of this comes from individual donors; NACE/CEE also receives financial support from the Coors beer family through the Coors Foundation.

Operation Rescue

PO Box 127
Summerville, SC 29484
(407) 259–9557

Founded in Binghampton, New York, in 1987, OR is not incorporated, so IRS records are not available. OR has claimed annual donations of up to $300,000 a year, including an early contribution of $10,000 from the Rev. Jerry Falwell. During 1991's "Summer of Mercy" campaign in Wichita, a reliable source in a local bank counted $150,000 in checks earmarked for OR in one day. OR has no formal affiliates or franchises. Local groups in several states use the name Operation Rescue.

Traditional Values Coalition

100 South Anaheim Boulevard
Suite 350
Anaheim, CA 92805
(714) 520–0300

Founded in 1983, as a 501(c)(4) organization, TVC claims connections to 25,000 evangelical churches, including 6,500 member churches in California. TVC's 1990 budget was about $500,000. Affiliated groups include Traditional Values Lobby (also known as California Educators for Traditional Values), also a 501(c)(4). The American Liberties Institute (doing business as California Coalition for Traditional Values) is a 501(c)(3). California Business for Traditional Values is a 501(c)(6). TVC's newest group is the National Task Force for the Preservation of the Heterosexual Ethic in America.

What to Read

Compiled by
Political Research Associates

Theocratic Right

The Case Against School Vouchers. Doerr, Edd, Albert J. Menendez, and John M. Swomley. (Silver Spring, MD: Americans for Religious Liberty, 1995).

The Coors Connection: How Coors Family Philanthropy Undermines Democratic Pluralism. Bellant, Russ. (Boston, MA: South End Press/Political Research Associates Series, 1991).

The Covert Crusade: The Christian Right and Politics in the West. (Portland, OR: Western States Center and Coalition for Human Dignity, 1993).

Culture Wars: The Struggle to Define America. Hunter, James Davison. (New York: Basic Books, 1991).

God, Land and Politics: The Wise Use and Christian Right Connection in 1992 Oregon Politics. Mazza, Dave. (Portland, OR: Western States Center and Helena, MT: Montana AFL/CIO, 1993).

Heaven on Earth? The Social and Political Agendas of Dominion Theology. Barron, Bruce. (Grand Rapids, MI: Zondervon, 1992).

Jesus Doesn't Live Here Anymore: From Fundamentalist to Freedom Writer. Porteous, Skipp. (Buffalo: Prometheus Books, 1991).

The New Religious Right: Piety, Patriotism and Politics. Capps, Walter H. (Columbia: University of South Carolina Press, 1990).

The Old Christian Right. Ribuffo, Leo P. (Philadelphia: Temple University Press, 1983).

Old Nazis, the New Right and the Republican Party: Domestic Fascist Networks and Their Effect on US Cold War Politics. Bellant, Russ. (Boston, MA: South End Press/Political Research Associates Series, 1991).

"The Political Activity of the Religious Right in the 1990's: A Critical Analysis," Pamphlet. Forman, Rabbi Lori. (New York: American Jewish Committee, 1994).

"Religion in the Public Schools: A Joint Statement of Current Law," Pamphlet. (New York: Joint Committee, 1995). Available by writing "Religion in the Public Schools," 15 East 84th Street, Suite 501, New York, NY 10028.

Roads to Dominion: Right–Wing Movements and Political Power in the United States. Diamond, Sara. (New York: The Guilford Press, 1995).

Rolling Back Civil Rights: The Oregon Citizens' Alliance at Religious War. Gardiner, S. L. (Portland, OR: Coalition for Human Dignity, 1992).

Spiritual Warfare: The Politics of the Christian Right. Diamond, Sara. (Boston, MA: South End Press, 1989).

To the Right: The Transformation of American Conservatism. Himmelstein, Jerome L. (Berkeley: University of California Press, 1990).

Redeeming America: Piety and Politics in the New Christian Right. Liensch, Michael. (Chapel Hill: The University of North Carolina Press, 1993).

Understanding Fundamentalism and Evangelicalism. Marsden, George M. (Grand Rapids, MI: William B. Eerdmans Pub. Co., 1991).

Visions of Reality: What Fundamentalist Schools Teach. Menendez, Albert J. (Buffalo, NY: Prometheus Books, 1993).

Whose American Family? An AJCongress Analysis of the Christian Coalition's "Contract with the American Family." AJCongress Commission on Law and Social Action. (New York: American Jewish Congress, 1995) Available by calling (212) 879–4500.

General Books & Reports

A Scapegoat in the New Wilderness: The Origins and Rise of Anti–Semitism in America. Jaher, Frederick Cople. (Cambridge, MA: Harvard University Press, 1994).

The Activists Almanac: The Concerned Citizen's Guide to the Leading Advocacy Organizations in America. Walls, David. (New York: Fireside/Simon & Schuster, 1993).

The Age of Surveillance. Donner, Frank J. (New York: Random House, 1981).

Agents of Repression: The FBI's Secret Wars Against the Black Panther Party and the American Indian Movement. Churchill, Ward and Jim Vander Wall. (Boston, MA: South End Press, 1988).

America's Original Sin: A Study Guide on White Racism. Sojourners. (Washington, DC: Sojourners Resource Center, 1993).

Architects of Fear: Conspiracy Theories and Paranoia in American Politics. Johnson, George. (Boston: Houghton Mifflin, 1983).

Break-ins, Death Threats and the FBI: The Covert War Against the Central America Movement. Gelbspan, Ross. (Boston, MA: South End Press, 1991).

Challenging the Christian Right: The Activists Handbook. Clarkson, Frederick, and Skipp Porteous. (Great Barrington, MA: Institute for First Amendment Studies, 1993). Available by calling (413) 274–3786.

Chaos or Community?: Seeking Solutions, Not Scapegoats for Bad Economics. Sklar, Holly. (Boston, MA: South End Press, 1995).

COINTELPRO Papers: Documents from the FBI's Secret Wars Against Dissent in the United States. Churchill, Ward and Jim Vander Wall. (Boston, MA: South End Press, 1990).

Debating PC: The Controversy over Political Correctness on College Campuses. Berman, Paul, ed. (New York: Laurel/Dell, 1992).

Eichmann in Jerusalem: A Report on the Banality of Evil. Arendt, Hannah. (New York: Penguin, 1963).

The Emergence of David Duke and the Politics of Race. Rose, Douglas D., ed. (Chapel Hill: University of North Carolina Press, 1992).

FBI Secrets: An Agent's Expose. Swearingen, M. Wesley. (Boston, MA: South End Press, 1995).

Freedom Under Fire: US Civil Liberties in Times of War. Linfield, Michael. (Boston, MA: South End Press, 1991).

Habits of Mind: Struggling Over Values in America's Classrooms. Fine,

Melinda. (San Francisco, CA: Jossey–Bass, 1995).

Patriot Games: Jack McLamb and Citizen Militias. Crawford, Robert, S. L. Gardiner, and Jonathan Mozzochi. (Portland, OR: Coalition for Human Dignity, 1994).

The Populist Persuasion: An American History. Kazin, Michael. (New York: Basic Books, 1995).

Race in North America: Origin and Evolution of a Worldview. Smedley, Audrey. (Boulder, CO: Westview Press, 1993).

To Reclaim a Legacy of Diversity: Analyzing the "Political Correctness" Debates in Higher Education. (New York: National Council for Research on Women, 1993). Available by calling (212) 274–0730.

The War Against the Greens: The "Wise Use" Movement, the New Right, and Anti-Environmental Violence. Helvarg, David. (San Francisco: Sierra Club Books, 1994).

War at Home: Covert Action Against US Activists and What We Can Do About It. Glick, Brian. (Boston, MA: South End Press, 1989).

White Lies / White Power: The Fight Against White Supremacy and Reactionary Violence. Novick, Michael. (Monroe, ME: Common Courage Press, 1995).

Watch on the Right: Conservative Intellectuals in the Reagan Era. Hoeveler, J. David. (Madison: University of Wisconsin Press, 1991).

Reference Shelf

A New Rite: Conservative Catholic Organizations and Their Allies. Askin, Steve. (Washington, DC: Catholics for Free Choice, 1994). Available by calling (202) 986–6093.

Extremism on the Right: A Handbook. Anti Defamation League of B'nai B'rith. (New York: Anti-Defamation League of B'nai B'rith, 1988).

Fight the Right. Gregory, Sarah Crary, and Scot Nakagawa, eds. (Washington, DC: National Gay and Lesbian Task Force, 1993).

Get the Facts on Anyone. 2nd edition. King, Dennis. (New York: Macmillan, 1995).

Guide to Public Policy Experts: 1993–1994. Atwood, Thomas C., ed. (Washington, DC: Heritage Foundation, 1993).

How to Win: A Practical Guide to Defeating the Radical Right in Your Community. Radical Right Task Force. (Washington, DC: Radical Right Task Force, 1994). Available by calling (202) 544–7636.

The Northwest Imperative: Documenting a Decade Of Hate. Crawford, Robert, S. L. Gardiner, Jonathan Mozzochi, and R. L. Taylor. (Portland, OR: Coalition for Human Dignity; and Seattle, WA: Northwest Coalition Against Malicious Harassment, 1994).

The Right Guide. Wilcox, Derk, Joshua Schackman and Penelope Naas. (Ann Arbor, MI: Economics America, 1993).

UCP's Guide to Uncovering the Right on Campus. Cowan, Rich, and Dalya Massachi. (Boston: University Conversion Project, 1994). Available by calling (617) 354–9363.

When Hate Groups Come to Town: A Handbook of Effective Community Responses. Center for Democratic Renewal. (Atlanta, GA: Center for Democratic Renewal, 1992). Available by calling (404) 221–0025.

Index

About Political Research Associates

Founded in 1981, Political Research Associates (PRA) is an independent, nonprofit research center that researches and analyzes the US political right. While we actively collaborate with many other organizations that oppose the right, PRA is uniquein two important ways. First, we monitor the full spectrum of the right, from the right wing in the electoral sphere to paramilitary organizations such as the armed citizens' militias. Second, we are nationally known for our anlaysis of the right in the US and for unfolding events as they occur.

PRA has been tracking authoritarian and anti–democratic movements and trends within the right since 1981. We have detailed information on every facet of these movements—from their ideologies and hidden agendas to their financing, tactics, and links to one another.

We use this depth of knowledge to help expose and challenge the right. We provide support for organizing efforts, especially among immigrants, welfare recipients, people of color, gays and lesbians, and others targeted as scapegoats of right wing attacks. And we broaden public understanding of the dangers posed by the right through media and public education work.

About *The Public Eye*

PRA's quarterly newsletter, *The Public Eye*, represents the resurrection of a venerable newsletter of the 1970s and 1980s, published at various times by the Repression Information Project, Citizens in Defense of Civil Liberties, and the National Lawyers Guild Civil Liberties Committee, among others.

Each issue of *The Public Eye* features one in–depth article on a current right–wing trend or development, a resource list for readers interested in pursuing that topic in greater depth, brief updates on right wing activism, book listings and reviews, and letters to the editors. Recent and upcoming issues focus on the right's anti–immigrant and anti–welfare campaigns, the anti-feminist women's movement, Black conservatives, Holocaust revisionism, Christian reconstructionism, and gay conservatives.

POLITICAL RESEARCH ASSOCIATES

120 Beacon Street, 3rd Floor
Somerville, Massachusetts 02143
ph: 617.661.9313   fax: 617.661.0059